Unbridled Spirits

Women of the English Revolution: 1640–1660

STEVIE DAVIES

D0555858

First published by The Women's Press Ltd, 1998
A member of the Namara Group
34 Great Sutton Street, London EC1V 0LQ

This paperback edition published 1999

British Library Cataloguing-in-Publication Data
A catalogue record for this book is available from the British Library.

ISBN 0 7043 4489 0

Typeset in Garamond by FSH Ltd, London
Printed and bound in Great Britain by Cox & Wyman Ltd, Reading, Berkshire

Stevie Davies, who lives near Manchester, has published widely on the seventeenth century: she is the biographer of Henry Vaughan and the acclaimed author of books on Renaissance feminism, Donne, Shakespeare and Milton in the English Revolution. She holds an honorary appointment as Senior Research Fellow at Roehampton Institute, London, and is a Fellow of the Royal Society of Literature. Her many works of biography and criticism include *Emily Brontë: Heretic* (The Women's Press, 1994).

She is also the author of seven novels, all published by The Women's Press: *Boy Blue* (1987), winner of the Fawcett Society Book Prize in 1989; *Primavera* (1990); *Arms and the Girl* (1992); *Closing the Book* (1994), which was on the long-list for the Booker Prize, and the short-list for the Fawcett Society Book Prize; *Four Dreamers and Emily* (1996); *The Web of Belonging* (1997) and *Impassioned Clay* (1999).

Acclaim for the hardback edition of *Unbridled Spirits*:

'Humane, vibrant and unconventional . . . Davies captures the anarchic energy of the period, the danger, the sense of life on the edge . . . *Unbridled Spirits* is as exciting an account of the Civil War period as we're likely to get.'
Lucasta Miller, *Independent on Sunday*

'Davies has provided a text both immensely useful to the academic and entirely accessible to the absolute beginner. Rendering clear the sense in which religious and political issues were inextricably linked during the English Revolution, she brings alive for a secular age the burning issues of the time, in which women involved themselves in an unprecedented fashion.' Sarah Burton, *Times Higher Education Supplement*

'A remarkable, vivid tapestry of the lives of our foremothers.'
Antonia Fraser, *Sunday Times*

'These women emerge clearly through their extraordinary words, their biblical cadences and puffing subjectivities . . . they record their physical suffering so matter-of-factly that the reader feels the rats crawling up the leg; smells the faeces smeared on the walls; suffers the toothaches, agues, colds, hard beds and brandings that made up these extraordinary lives.'
Janet Todd, *Literary Review*

'Davies pursues biographies with laudable scholarship, to produce richly painted pen-portraits that, far from merely "recalling echoes" from the past, contrive to raise the dead.'
Justin Wintle, *Financial Times*

'A passionate testimony to those women who found a way to express themselves within a culture defined by the 'scold's bridle' . . . This is marvellous popular history, bringing home the impact upon human lives of concepts such as Quakerism and millenarianism.' Anna Beer, *History Today*

'This is a rich and compelling book, the work of a literary critic and distinguished novelist who now proves herself, besides, a fine historian . . . this captivating book about the first radical women deserves a wide audience.'
Anthony Fletcher, *Times Literary Supplement*

'Scholarship and imagination are powerfully matched in this raw and cruel but inspiring story. A tempest of a book not to be missed.' John Carey

'Her narrative drive gives her account of these women's lives an impressive and gripping immediacy . . . This is a human, balanced, yet impassioned description of women in a turbulent period – an admirable supplement to Christopher Hill's own pioneering account. A very useful, unorthodox, scholarly and enjoyable book.' Margaret Drabble

for Frances Hill
with love

*

and for my mother
Monica Davies

CONTENTS

ACKNOWLEDGEMENTS

I am grateful to the Librarian and staff of the Friends House Library, London, for invaluable assistance in exploring the riches of the collection; to the staff of Chethams Library, Manchester, especially Dr Michael Powell and Mr DR Evans, who went to considerable trouble to track down rare books, offered helpful suggestions and assisted me with datings; to the staff of the John Rylands Univerity Library of Manchester Rare Books Collection; to the British Library, for access to the Thomason Collection.

I am grateful to Wendy Ridley, temporary Warden of Swarthmoor Hall, for showing me Swarthmoor and for answering multitudinous questions with patience and skill.

Everyone writing in the field of seventeenth-century radicalism owes a great debt to writerly historians such as Christopher Hill, Keith Thomas, Lawrence Stone, BS Capp, EP Thompson, Brian Manning. Not least, they have recreated for the general reader a sense of vivid actuality of life as it was lived moment-by-moment during the 1640s and 50s. A major aim of this book is to kindle the imagination of readers coming fresh to the seventeenth century but who may have a dismaying sense that the period is inaccessibly difficult.

Hill especially has breathed life into a complex intellectual and political landscape, never forgetting that history is the story of people, not abstractions.

Unfortunately he has tended to equate people with men. The thrilling subject of the women radicals of the Revolution has been opened up by a number of women whose books have been indispensable: I will here mention the work of Antonia Fraser, Dorothy Paula Ludlow, Phyllis Mack, Patricia Higgins, Alice Clark, Bonnelyn Kunze, Hilary Hinds and Frances Hill, whose work on the Salem witch-trials has been an inspiration.

I owe much to Frank Regan for every kind of loving support, from tracing and fetching books to listening without complaint to the ravings of an obsessed companion who seemed to have taken up residence in the seventeenth century; and I must thank my friend Ann Mackay for all her kindness, not least for practical help in ferrying me and my books around. Conversations on the Renaissance with Andrew Howdle over twenty years have fed into the book. I thank Lyndall Gordon for a valuable exchange and sharing of ideas and Patsy Stoneman for all her support. I am grateful to Margaret Argyle, Beth and Cliff Brownhill, Joy Anderson, Penny Cannon, Dorothy Buchanan, Marcelle D'Argy Smith, Penny Glenday, Johnnie Gluzewski, Brian Loughrey, Leon Stoger, Carrie Thomas, Pat Tyrie, John Powell Ward, Barbara Wilson, Joyce Workman and my mother, Monica Davies, for all their encouragement.

And lastly I thank three young radicals, Grace, Emily and Robin, for at least trying to tiptoe past my study door.

A NOTE ON DATES AND SPELLING

Before 1752, the New Year was dated from Lady Day, 25 March, rather than from 1 January: to avoid the confusion produced by double-dating (eg 1648/9 for 1 January – 24 March), I have observed the custom of amending dates to the calendar we now recognise (though without making the yet more confusing 10-day adjustment which the change to the 'New Style' Gregorian calendar necessitated).

I have modernised the spelling in quotations, for the sake of clarity, with the exception of a few specified examples and the titles of books.

Mid-seventeenth-century spelling habits had the pleasant zaniness of an age in which spelling was only just becoming standardised: this has had a negligible effect on the present book, except in the case of people's names. Katharine Chidley is usually cited as 'Katherine' in modern editions: however, this is not how she signed herself, and my usage is governed by hers. In the case of Elizabeth Pool(e), Katharine (Katherine) Evans, Elizabeth Hooton (Hooten), Hester (Esther) Biddle, Sarah Chevers (Cheevers) and others, I have used the most usual form in which (to my knowledge) they are represented.

PRELUDE – TRAVELLING ABROAD TO THE PAST

> Come clowns, and come boys,
>   Come hober-de-hoys,
>   Come females of each degree,
> Stretch your throats, bring in your votes,
> And make good the Anarchy.[1]

St Paul had told them to keep quiet; Luther had insisted they obey
the anatomical imperative of their weighty female hips by sitting
down at home and bearing children; king and Parliament ordered
them to get on with their knitting and dish-washing.[2]

But the revolutionary women of this book were out on the
streets protesting, petitioning, demonstrating, preaching. Some
heckled statesmen, roughed up mayors, tossed stools in church,
bawled abuse at ministers and were whipped, stocked or carted off

to prison. Once locked up, they continued to preach, mock, sing, and write – indefatigably our radical foremothers wrote, though some began as illiterates who had to teach themselves to read. Others settled down to write the history of their times; outline programmes for a better world; issue peremptory advice to the powers-that-be. All learned from radical reading of that incendiary book, the newly affordable pocket Bible – a book which had for centuries been used to mute and subject them. What they read there overcame the feminine timidity indoctrinated from birth, convincing them that their tongues could and must speak out.

Their battles were not ours; their dialect, a rich brogue of militant Christian English, was rooted in Bible soil as in the motherland of common speech. Nor did their demands involve women's rights as we now conceive them. Our secular individualism would have been quite alien to their minds, which belonged to an age when politics and religion were inextricably linked; attacks on bishops were a matter of militant politics and a civil war waged between Parliament and king involved religious upheaval. In this maelstrom, women's revolutionary claims for spiritual equality and a say in church and state affairs did not necessarily imply a refusal of social deference (though they might). *Unbridled Spirits* is a time-travelling book which visits the past as a foreign continent, with its own complex mental terrains: yet in listening to the voices of these women – Katharine Chidley, Mary Cary, Lucy Hutchinson, Anna Trapnel, Katharine Evans, Margaret Fell, Mary Fisher, and many others – there has come a recurrent sense of uncanny closeness, as if, with their audacious, God-driven energy, they were only a breath away.

Of course the extremist women (and they were only ever a few) were soon chased away and their memory buried. Most women continued to eke a subsistence in poverty and illiteracy, bound in to the cycle of toil, child-bearing, child-burial and widowhood: they register in history as silence. Eerily, I was aware of this mass silence as I listened to the few voices that could make themselves heard. This book is about a nearly forgotten generation of exceptions who dared speak out in conditions of female repression, telling God-given and anomalous truths. Prophetesses predicted the crash of king or Cromwell. White-ribboned Peace

Women marched against war. Green-ribboned Leveller women attacked oppressive legislators, lawyers, lords and abusive taxes; they claimed the right as women to petition and be heard as citizens. Fifth Monarchist women prophesied, spied, acted as messengers and agents, attacked the government and proposed political programmes of reform. Separatist women founded or attended dissenting ('gathered') churches and spoke for liberty of conscience. Some fiery spirits wanted all the churches in England demolished. Radical Quakers damned the universities as madhouses for the over-privileged, whose degrees marked them out as certifiable. They vilified the paid priesthood as 'hirelings', selling the free Word of God as if they were prostitutes.

Writing this book, I have winced at the penalties they paid and marvelled at their courage. Quaker women of the 1650s were suspected as witches, thrashed as whores, expressing Christ in proud bare backs that were turned to the lash through the streets of Cambridge or London. Briefly Quaker men and women opened up a mental world where Christ was present in a woman as much as in a man; where all were ministers. Gender distinctions could seem so peripheral that a male Friend, John Perrot, could sign himself 'I am your sister in our spouse, John'.[3]

The anti-female backlash in the period was hysterical, and readers of this book will draw their own analogies with the present 'crisis of family values'. A sense that women were out of hand caused convulsive alarm. Women's escape from the patriarchal family would be the final anarchy: 'Liberty of conscience so called, may in good time improve itself into liberty of estates and liberty of houses and liberty of wives,' warned Thomas Case in 1647.[4] Female outrages were stop-press news during the period of escalating social turmoil, culminating in the 'Ranter' scare of 1650 (discussed in Chapter 1), with its sensational revelations of 'women on top', like this tidbit in *The Ranter's Religion*:

> that Sister among them who can make the beast with two backs the most strenuously, *viz.* entertain most men longest, and oftenest, hath a sufficient canonisation for a Saint triumphant.[5]

If women threw off the yoke of marriage, patriarchy would founder and with it law, sanctity of property, caste. After all, it had happened before. Eve's insubordination in Genesis (a historical event), had entailed hair-raising consequences: the exile of Adam and all his progeny from Eden; animal predatoriness; temperature extremes; the skewing of the universe; the enlargement of Satan's empire. All this horror from one women's momentary lapse. All lost for a mere fruit and a mere female.

Milton's *Paradise Lost* (1667), the greatest literary creation of the epoch, showed marriage as the basis of civilisation and property rights. By married love: 'Relations dear, and all the charities/Of father, son, and brother first were known' (IV 756–7). The tragic (or pathetic) irony of patriarchal marriage and government is fully implicit here. For what is 'civilisation'? – the network of male superiors, 'father, son, and brother'. What holds it together? – the agency of mother, daughter and sister, an inferior glue. The 'higher' is dependent on an underclass, whose unwillingness to perform its allotted function had been obvious from Day Six of the Creation.

Paradise Lost plays out that nightmare of idealised Puritan marriage under seismic stress from women's desire for autonomy. Milton's divorce tracts, published in the early 1640s, proposed a solution: get rid of her. But at least one renegade woman snatched at Milton's solution as a Godsend and turned it round: get rid of *him* (see pp108–110 below).

*

In the 1930s, a farmer's wife named Waspe protesting against tithes set her beehive on the bailiffs. Tithes, against which Quaker men and women resisters had gone to prison in their hundreds, decade after decade, were not finally abolished in rural areas until the mid-twentieth century. Church-and-state, hand-in-glove, milked the poor for wealth and privilege. In 1659, Quaker women petitioned against tithes: 7000 signatures, column upon column of names, some we recognise and some we don't – part of a huge resistance movement which fought an unjust, profane tax. They were fined; imprisoned; fined again. Tithes remained.

Suffragettes in our century bombed churches. Some seventeenth-century women and men (for different reasons) wanted the whole lot razed to the ground, as places desecrated by idol worship. The Anglican church was an arm of patriarchal government, instrument of social control, with its own law courts, wealth and authority. In an iconoclastic age, our 'extremist' fore-mothers were comprehensive in their aims as God-inspired dissenters. If it took the demolition of every church in England, a Puritan like Katharine Chidley would have volunteered to put her hand to the clearance work. Quaker women espoused a plan to melt church bells as a wealth-creation scheme (leaving one in each area as a fire alarm). They denounced swindling, profiteering, oppression of dissidents and the desperate hunger of the poor. The radicalism of their claims should never be underestimated simply because they are not couched in the language of secular democracy. These women were prepared to forfeit freedom, property, health and even life for such causes.

The drive for autonomy was fraught with the complexity and double-bind of acculturated guilts and taboos. The dreaming, preaching women were aware of the mental toll exacted by their female conditioning; the universal scorn and aspersion under which they lived. The psychological cost of speaking out when your entire training induced you to docile silence might be supported by stratagems: lip-service to the status quo 'in respect of the weakness and contemptibleness of the instrument', as Elizabeth Avery described herself in 1647.[6] But admission of feminine feebleness or even vacuity generally functioned as a prudent curtsy to convention. You dipped to duck under the ban. Drastic political repercussions might be evaded by the recourse undertaken by Anna Trapnel, the Fifth Monarchist prophet, who claimed to be in a state of divinely inspired trance while delivering her seditious utterances against Cromwellian tyranny. When she 'woke', she could not remember a word she had said. Her story is a poignant, comic parable of women's manipulation of their straits.

What did they achieve? Nothing material? A statement and no more?

At most they were a minute minority, shunned by a common sense majority as pests and aberrations. Law-abiding, norm-approving persons of all persuasions tended to abominate the women of this book. Mobs went for them, sometimes with sticks, knives or meat-cleavers, calling them whores; constables whipped and locked them in gaol or bridewell (house of correction). When the Restoration of King Charles II came in 1660, most people closed ranks against the disorder of the zealots. 'Zeal' and 'enthusiasm' became dirty words for generations who remembered the tumult of the Revolutionary years. History swept most of that turbulent generation back into the household sphere, and reinstated their immemorial blinkers and gag. Their pamphlets, petitions and broadsheets were doubtless amongst the junk books of yesterday, which found their destiny as linings for trunks, or greasy food-wrappings and toilet paper; Dryden's 'Martyrs of pies, and Relics of the bum'.[7]

*

Scattered copies found their way into antiquarian collections, where they acquired rarity and curiosity value. The pale paper scorched with their burning beliefs and affirmations dimmed in the gloom of little-visited private or public libraries; and scholars sometimes turned the mottled leaves, edged with damp and flecked with decay. Over the centuries a reader would jot in their margins, in ink today sepia with age; a pipe-smoker might drop an ember, branding a carbon-dark hole through a gathering of pages. He too would fall away into the common oblivion.

Yet opening these books, one is arrested with a pang as if the dead got up and spoke forcibly, freshly, from the page, and the library stillness is filled with characterful voices arguing. The leaf, like a freckled face, bears all the signs of time, yet the voices retain their dissident energy. If their immediate quarrel has been consigned to the chest of the quaint and antique, related arguments are still in hot dispute. If there is a sense that we are all informed by the whole of the past (even those parts which seemed to flake away into oblivion), then these women – from Mary Cary to Mary Fisher – being our past, are also part of us. Reading them, we listen in to voices from which our own tongue derives.

*

The women of the English Revolution were rarely otherworldly mystics. They bore witness for a still relevant social programme to place bread in the mouths of paupers, find work for the unemployed, care for the sick and ease the trauma of oppression by rackrenting landlords and greedy churchmen. Such women as Fifth Monarchist Mary Cary stood alongside the underclass, speaking directly to all in 'Parliament and Synod, City and Country'. 'But,' says Mary in *A Word in Season to the Kingdom of England* in 1647,

> though this discourse concerns all, and therefore in general
> I call upon you all to attend unto it; yet in a more peculiar
> manner I shall direct it to ... the heads and rulers of the
> people, and are in places of authority: for you are to act for
> the whole kingdom, and what is done by you is done by
> them ... Oppression of the poor, & suffering the violent
> man to afflict the needy, and the neglect of doing justice in
> their behalf, is not the way to happiness.[8]

Here is a woman who encompasses in her thirty-odd years of life centuries of development. She speaks in a rationally persuasive voice of authority to the highest earthly powers. Dividing her discourse under numbered points, she unfolds a radical programme (including wage ceilings, stamp tax for poor relief, and a post office system) to her readership, which constitutes 'all', men and women, but specifically 'the heads and rulers', males who have had the best education money, caste and privilege could buy, but are ignorant, and need instruction. Mary signed pamphlets, 'M. Cary, A Minister', or 'A Servant of Jesus Christ'.

In practice only a prodigy or a tight-knit group of like minds (she would have said 'remnant') could aspire to such programmatic optimism.

Who was listening to Mary? Few, perhaps.

Even fewer three hundred years later when Marxist historians of the 1960s and 70s made their exciting recovery and analysis of the testament of the Revolution. I was raised on Christopher Hill, and remain inspired by his works. I didn't notice when I first read his brilliant *The World Turned Upside Down* (1972) that he had all but censored out, unread, women of the calibre of Cary, Trapnel and Fell. Women were presented as Ranter sex objects, in a web of witty anecdote. Political issues as they related to women were likewise obscured. Hill describes the Army's *Agreement of the People* of 1647 as 'amended so as to include a substantial extension of the franchise – to all soldiers, and all others except servants and beggars'. '*All* others'? – only if you exclude 50 per cent of the nation. The omission, still distorting some recent male accounts of the Levellers, is pregnant with sad ironies: it suggests a root-system of assumption, buried in the minds of politicians and historians from generation to generation, which still cannot quite take women's claims seriously.

Twenty years later, in *The English Bible and the Seventeenth-Century Revolution* (1993), Hill confesses that Mary Cary was 'one of the most interesting and least studied of the Fifth Monarchists'.[9] It isn't quite an apology. In *Liberty Against the Law* (1996), women are again marginalised. Amends are being made by readers of the stature of Antonia Fraser, Phyllis Mack, Bonnelyn Kunze, Patricia Crawford, Elaine Hobby, in bringing to light our militant foremothers.

'Have we not an equal interest with the men of this nation, in those liberties and securities contained in the Petition of Right, and other good laws of the land?' asked the Leveller women. Their demand echoes down to the now enfranchised female citizens of the twentieth century with painful timeliness.

*

The testaments of the women I study in this book are a story teller's dream, so strong is their vitality and the freshness of their language. After a discursive introduction, *Unbridled Spirits* tends to take the form of personal narrative. I say 'narrative' rather than the diminishing 'anecdote', because I have held close to the accounts of their lives and thoughts given by the women and their contemporaries. They presented their inner world and activities as story, with vivid dialogue, description, asides, images – intensely revealing of the minutiae of women's conflicts, motives, needs, ends. By taking account of what sager historians might dismiss as naïve prattle, I found that an imaginative experience welled up with its own truth to the mental world in which these women lived. The gossipy 'I-said-to-her-and-she-said-to-me' dialogue which is the heart of human tale-telling often takes the delightful form in their tracts of 'I-said-to-God-and-He-said-to-me'. I admit to a sharp appetite for quirk and foible, which I balance by setting the stories in a larger analytic context. Occasionally reported speech in the tracts has been silently converted to direct speech, which, after all, is where it began; and nearly all spelling has been modernised. A guiding principle has been to try to bring to life everything that I could 'see', always uneasily aware of how occluded and partial my vision must be. To offset this, I offer enough raw material here for the reader to form personal (and, it may be, entirely discrepant) impressions and interpretations.

I want to haunt readers with the revolutionary women's stories, recalling echoes of their lives to the page, through using their own words, capturing their gestures, the flair and resource of their actions; the gritty spiritedness of their endurance. They could mime, sneer and scoff as well as their opponents. Sometimes the reader will be disappointed by the fact that the narrative is condemned to meet its unruly women in mid-gesture and leave them suspended in mid-air. Born off the page, they retire to the margin to die. History took little extended notice of mere females, documenting their presence only when they made a spectacular nuisance of themselves or improvised testaments of their own. The record is fragmentary, cryptic, unsatisfying. Sources may be mendacious or bias-riven. But a well-woven fragment may act as a sample, and some of the samples are so vivid that a living eye glistens through the rubble of time and stares straight into ours; a face turns sharply out of shadow.

1

WOMEN OF SPIRIT: AN INTRODUCTION

Women and Revolution

William Harrison in his *Description of England* in 1587 drew scandalised attention to females swaggering round London wearing 'doublets with pendant codpieces on the breast ... galligaskins to bear out their bums ... it hath passed my skill to discern whether they were men or women'. Another Puritan, Philip Stubbes, in his *Anatomie of Abuses*, became heated about 'double dealing ambodexters' and Stephen Gosson deplored the breaking of God's own dress code by tranvestite males, for 'garments are set down for signs distinctive between sex and sex', those breaking this code being 'abhomination to the Lord'.[1] Elizabethan England seemed plagued by women refusing to be women; wittily defying the dress codes, which still had a quality of civil and divine taboo, from an epoque when the sumptuary laws had legislated in detail on what garments might and might not be worn by distinct ranks of people. Clothing was a nuanced language, with strict codes. The social order was expressed in obedience to these codes, and most fundamental was not the attire that distinguished labourer from gentleman but man from woman.

Breeches were self-evidently designed by God for males. Codpieces had dignity and utility, and were not to be dangled as decorations by mannish women from wanton nipples. As to the adoption of 'galligaskins' (wide, floppy breeches) to bolster fast women's backsides, Harrison, trawling for enormities in a picturesque capital, seems fascinated. To wear 'galligaskins' or any form of breeches would, to our way of thinking, have been more modest than women's required wear. For under smock, corset, waistcoat and several layers of under-petticoat no English woman wore knickers. God apparently did not see this draughty arrangement as an 'abhomination'.[2]

During the reign of James I, bullish female cross-dressers were still in evidence. In 1620, the king transmitted a message through the Bishop of London to be disseminated through all London clergy to their congregations:

> to will them to inveigh vehemently against the insolency of our women, and their wearing of broad brimmed hats, pointed doublets, their hair cut short or shorn, and some of them stilettos or poniards ... adding withall that if pulpit admonitions will not reform them he would proceed by another course; the truth is the world is very much out of order.[3]

Just as it was a commonplace that all servants secretly envied their masters, so it was understood that all women (anatomised by current science as inside-out defective males) ludicrously aspired to usurp not just male breeches but the phallic equipment of blades, worn by gentlemen at their sides. Cropped heads and wide-brimmed hats aped the trappings of authority. Female dress should be the dress of deference. The misogynistic James spied open rebellion in male-impersonating fashions.

Anxiety about female insubordination had taken on a shrill quality of alarm by the earlier seventeenth century. The ancient debate on woman ('flyting')[4] found a savagely modern voice in the publication of Joseph Swetnam's bestselling *Arraignment of lewd, idle, froward and inconstant women,* which was reprinted ten times between 1615 and 1634. This was answered brilliantly by a woman, the nineteen-year-old Rachel Speght, in *A Mouzell for Melastomus* ('A Muzzle for the Black Mouth') in 1617,[5] objecting not only to the 'excrement of your raving cogitations' but also to her adversary's vile grammar, 'a mingle-mangle invective against women' (p61). Rachel, the daughter of a London minister, argues from Scripture that if woman is the 'weaker vessel', that is because she is made of crystal not stone (p65); that Eve was fashioned from Adam's side, not head or foot, 'near his heart, to be his equal' (p66). She knows she's young, she says, and lacking in formal education, but she has more learning than Swetnam, and the Black Mouth cannot be allowed to get away with it. Her spirited counter-attack on misogyny foreshadows the independent-minded, assertive women of middle-class origin in the left-wing sects of the Civil War and Interregnum.

The spirited, sexy women with the cropped heads and daggers must have been exceptions: but visible, electrifying exceptions, who created unease in the patriarchal establishment by showing themselves as a symptom – like a red rash or bubo – of a malaise at the core of society. They seemed to stand for a chaos and conflict at the heart of a state travelling for decades toward catastrophe. Of course the sense that women were out of control and unsatisfied with their God-given lot was ancient. 'She rampeth in my face and crieth ... I wol have thy knyfe and thou shalt have my distaf and go spin': Chaucer's *Monk's Tale* gave a zestful picture of the incorrigible female lust to abdicate her function and snatch yours.[6]

Unruly women were taken seriously by being laughed down by the whole community in seventeenth-century England, and local government kept apparatus and employed officials to enact rituals of shame on them. 'Scolding' (causing a nuisance by loud invective), a woman's offence, was a petty crime on the increase in the pre-war years, along with a general sense that women were becoming more rebellious against the divine, natural and moral order.[7] Fears about social dislocation and instability in the patriarchal order often expressed themselves as denunciations of women's unfeminine assertiveness. Between 1560 and 1640, court records suggest intensifying concern about women running out of control, whether by defying or beating their husbands, 'scolding' or brawling with neighbours. In Southampton in 1603 the Court Leet Records show a jury noting ' the manifold number of scolding women that be in this town'; a year later the mayor was still being 'daily troubled with such brawls'. Towns invested wholesale in machinery for dealing with female offenders such as scolds and whores. Southampton, Marlborough, Devizes, Shrewsbury and many other towns bought cucking stools to duck offenders.[8]

Gravesend porters in 1636 were paid piece-work rates by the local authority for bringing the stool, ducking the offender, and putting away the apparatus, according to regulations. Two shillings for ducking Goodwife Campion; eight pence for storing the instrument when the work was done.[9] Ducking was a licensed act of minor violence, no joke to the woman soused, amid mirth, in a filthy horsepond, perhaps in winter. To fun-starved communities, this constituted entertainment. The ritual of ducking was essentially festive: communal shaming scapegoated a trouble-maker and endorsed a social order which oppressed everyone but the elite. And here all males, down to the poorest labourer or tinker, could count themselves elite, in that they were not women. Although she was punished as an aberration, the scold was more exactly an aberrant norm: 'There is but one shrew and every man hath her,' the popular saying went.

Taming the unruly woman was a popular ritual all over Europe: known as the 'charivari', a procession emitting 'rough music', berserk cacophony, would accompany the 'riding' or 'carting' of whore or scold around the locality. Violent, cuckolding or dominant wives and hen-pecked husbands were subjected to a ritual in which a rabble emitting stridor would process to the couple's house, with a man acting the husband riding back-to-front on a horse or donkey, holding a distaff, symbol of female subjection, while the 'wife', played by a female-impersonator, whacked him with a ladle. In the northern counties, this was known as 'riding the stang'; in the western counties, especially Somerset and north Wiltshire, as 'skimmington' or 'skimmity' riding, still a tradition in Hardy's time.[10] Skimmingtons targeted violations of gender and sexual codes, disorder parodying and punishing disorder. A major mode of punishment for the scold was the bridle or brank, which we shall anatomise.

*

Women had always been passionate rioters, taking prominent roles in enclosure and grain riots, and attacking fendrainers. The all-female mob (embellished by males in women's clothes, and assorted youths) was well known in areas where livelihoods were threatened by 'improvements' and the land-greed of courtiers and speculators, or in times of famine. Difficult to quell because of establishment queasiness about the ethics and bad publicity involved in gunning or hacking them down, female mobs rioted when their livelihoods were endangered. At Soham in 1629, several hundred women stoned and assaulted commissioners attempting to survey and partition Cambridgeshire fens, promising to 'tear the Commissioners and whomsoever else had any hand in the business'. The women of Haxey massed to destroy a dyke, returning on three consecutive days to complete their task. A woman with a local reputation as a witch was described as 'the first mover of [the] mutiny' at the Great Level in May 1637: she was committed to prison at Wisbech, suspected of having hexed the undertakers' helpers. And at Holme Fen, 'a great many women and men' rushed into the fen with scythes and pitchforks, to 'let out the guts of anyone that should drive their fens'.[11]

Such outbreaks of female violence were not attempts to turn the world upside down. Heartbreakingly, they represented a last-ditch effort to keep the world right-side-up in the face of privileged vandals and thieves − uprooters of forests, enclosers of common land. Bread riots, and commons and grazing riots were explosions in which women expressed the protest of the whole community, sheltering behind their supposed (and sometimes actual) immunity to prosecution, and attempting to exploit the legal loophole which labelled married women 'covert'; non-existent like children and imbeciles because covered by the husband.[12] Fenland riots were local and conservative, designed solely to preserve local economies based on common rights, providing pasture, fish and game, reeds and fuel, against exploiters: the women who stormed back again and again to oppose developers were defending homes and family, in active partnership with their menfolk, just as they would have done against any other robbers.

Women had also played a clamorous part in anti-clerical

demonstrations. From the women who stoned a Scottish preacher in a London church, tearing his robes and scratching his face, to those who 'unreverently hooted' at the Bishop of London at St Margaret's in Old Fish Street in 1567, mocking his headgear as having a ludicrous likeness both to a Pope's, a devil's and a cuckold's ('Ware horns!'), to Joan Madison's assault on an Essex minister's head in 1595, so that 'she brake the same' and caused 'the blood to run down', women activists pursued, mocked, mimicked and took their scissors to the surplices of ministers with riotous enthusiasm.[13]

Jenny Geddes became a national legend when, on Sunday, 23 July 1637, she expressed Scottish Presbyterian outrage at the imposition of the Anglican Book of Common Prayer by hurling her creepie-stool at the head of the Dean of St Giles Cathedral, bawling (as he intoned the word 'Collect'), 'Deil colic and waame of thee; out, thou false thief. Dost thou say mass at my lug?'[14] Jenny was a poor 'kerb-woman' and 'kail-wife', who sold cabbage and greens at a pavement stall. She was joined by missile-throwing fellow-women, who surged around shouting 'False anti-christian! Beastly belly-God! Crafty fox! Ill-hanged thief! Judas!', and was credited with precipitating the First bishop's War between England and Scotland, which led in turn to the Second Bishop's War, the English Civil War, the abolition of bishops, House of Lords, the monarchy ... so that the flying stool of an outraged Scottish street-pedlar may be said, by an impudent extension of chaos theory, to have struck King Charles I's head from his shoulders. The approximate position from which Jenny hurled the stool was later marked by a commemorative plaque:

> Constant Oral Tradition Affirms
> That near this spot
> A brave Scotchwoman, Janet Geddes
> On the 23rd of July, 1637,
> struck the first blow
> in the great struggle for freedom of conscience
> which
> after a conflict of half a century
> ended
> in the establishment of civil and religious liberty

Professor JS Blackie celebrated her rowdyism in admiring verses:

> King Charles he was a shuffling knave, priest Laud
>   a pedant fool,
> But Jenny was a woman wise, who beat them
>   with a stool.
>
>   ('The Song of Mrs Jenny Geddes')[15]

Few rioting women acquired such celebrity but many got a heady taste for running amok in a hallowed cause.

A scattering of early seventeenth-century women were already preaching and prophesying – taking upon theselves, in other words, an ultimate authority. When caught, they and their listeners would be hauled before a church court and might be required to do public penance at church. Between 1616 and 1625, St Cuthbert's Church, Wells, saw a number of 'penitents' confessing that they had frequented 'Conventicles where a woman preached'. The Bishop of Bath and Wells denounced addled listeners to a bird-brained woman as 'unworthy to be men that could be so weak as to be scholar to a woman'. He reinforced St Paul by reminding all that women '*must learn*' from men. They must not teach. For 'teaching imports a superiority', and women are inferiors. Ears, please, not tongues, he insists.[16]

But what if we learn and learn for fifty years, assiduously taking in your divine learning, the women must have wondered: what then? There should in logic come a time when we could dole out a little of the benefits of the bishop's wisdom to other souls?

Definitely not, the bishop insisted. Silence was the woman's realm. It seemed she was fashioned like a leaky bucket and, the more she was filled, the further she emptied.

The leaky buckets clanked in their pews, dismayed to learn that there was no hope of their learning anything worth teaching: yet go on learning they must. Christ 'did call no she Apostles,' Robert Wilkinson noted in 1607. Luther had compared pulpits containing women with pigsties.[17]

The only place where women might be permitted to hold service was at home, in the husband's absence, where it was in order to instruct servants and children – quietly. No doubt many women who were to become vociferous during the Civil War and

Interregnum periods built up their public speaking skills in this domestic domain.

*

From 1629 to 1640, Charles I ruled without a Parliament. A deeply shy, uncertain and arrogant man, he cleaved to his Roman Catholic French queen, Henrietta Maria, as 'my jewel', whom he only regretted could not be appointed to his Council.[18] Charles' uxorious dependency, in a patriarchy where no woman possessed what we would regard as civil rights, ironically convinced many Parliamentarians that they were living in a matriarchy. 'A woman as soon as she is married is called "covert"...', explained 'T.E.' in *The Law's Resolution of Women's Rights* (1632), 'her new self is her superior, her companion, her master ... All [of them] are understood either married, or to be married, and their desires are subject to their husbands'. Women have no voice in Parliament. They make no laws, they consent to none, they abrogate none.'[19] But here, in a patriarchal state where the king's coronation oath made him father and husband of his people, was a woman perceived as making up laws as she went along.

Milton, whose disastrous marriage landed him with a wife of royalist family, and who wrote in favour of divorce in the 1640s, smarted at the king's folly in surrendering judgement, Samson-like, to a mere female, foreigner, Catholic, apostate Eve in our English garden. After the execution of Charles in 1649, he wrote sneeringly of the king's effeminacy, with a virulent nib, dipped in the well of his own scathed susceptibilities:

> How fit to govern men, undervaluing and aspersing the great Council of his Kingdom, in comparison of one woman. Examples are not far to seek, how great mischief and dishonour hath befallen to nations under the government of effeminate and uxorious magistrates. Who being themselves governed and overswayed at home under a feminine usurpation, cannot but be far short of spirit and authority without doors, to govern a whole nation ... most men suspect she had quite perverted him.[20]

Charles' dependence on his wife committed him to persistently disastrous advice, intrigues and absolutist aspirations. To 'sum all up,' said Milton of the cache of secret letters between the king and queen captured at the Battle of Naseby, they 'showed him governed by a woman'.[21] Automatic contempt for women was habitual for both sides in the Civil War: one plank in the republican argument was that monarchy allowed women, 'that feeble and weaker sex' unmerited power.[22]

For women did not think, rule, advise, debate, except in a few atypical instances: they deferred. They deferred to an all-male establishment: God the Father and Son, male lords and male bishops, male electorate and MPs, all-male universities, preachers, judges, juries, army, patrilinear heirs. Married women had few property rights. Though a widow, as *feme sole*, controlling her own property and entitled by custom to one third of her husband's estate, was in an advantageous position, married women were barred from holding property or freehold land except through their husbands, and from making wills or appointing executors without spousal consent. Despite some exceptions and complexities, common law did not acknowledge the existence of any women not under the protection of a man: father, husband, brother, guardian. In an equivalent way, the 'meaner sort', the 'lower orders' of society, were conceived of as 'covered' by the elite. As Sir Robert Filmer's classic *Patriarcha* put it, 'As father over one family, so the King, as father over many families, extends his care to preserve, feed, clothe, instruct and defend the whole commonwealth.'[23]

But what if the king neglected to preserve, feed, clothe, instruct and defend his people? What if, hiding up the skirts of a foreign female and detested advisers, flaunting his prerogative, his overbearing rule had antagonised whole swathes of society? Economic, religious and political turbulence spasmed into armed conflict. A pamphlet of 1644, *The Parliaments Kalender of Black Saints*, is a rabble-rousing arraignment of the villains of Charles' reign, from the queen to Archbishop Laud:

> For that thou traitorously, and against the Laws of God and Thy Country, didst seek politicly to alter religion, alter the Laws of the Land, alter the Judges ... thou didst instruct his Majesty to impose strange Taxations, and Monopolies, Knighthoods, Ship-money, New Corporation ... thy

wolvish stomach so sharp that tips of ears must be cooked
for thee, Protestants fried, others strangled, and some ...
soused and pickled in the High Commission.[24]

The juicy ears belonged to the three Puritan martyrs, Burton,
Bastwick and Prynne, cut off by order of Star Chamber on 30 June
1637, for publishing attacks on king and bishops, and featured in
many satirical designs as succulent morsels on the fork of 'His
Little Grace'. As Bastwick went to the pillory for mutilation his
wife rushed up and kissed his ears and mouth, with a loving
defiance which brought roars of praise from the crowd. Prynne had
also been branded in the cheeks with the letters 'S' and 'L':
'Seditious Libeller' – who, as his blood flowed and flesh hissed,
roared exultantly, 'Come sear me, sear. Burn me, cut me, I fear
not!'[25] The young John Lilburne, Leveller-to-be, stood white with
shock at the foot of the pillory, while the blood gushed and the
crowd wept and shouted. Three years later the martyrs were to be
welcomed back into revolutionary London in two triumphal
processions, escorted by a hundred coaches, two thousand
horsemen and a jubilant crowd.

In 1640 to 1641, England convulsed as the old order
collapsed. Seething unrest exploded. The Long Parliament
demolished the machinery of absolutism piece by piece, releasing
prisoners of conscience; executing the king's adviser and favourite,
the Earl of Strafford, and, later, Archbishop Laud for treason;
abolishing the brutal courts of Star Chamber and High
Commission and enacting legislation to protect Parliamentary
autonomy.

With the freeing of institutions came a freeing-up of the
mind. Everything came into question. Riots, mass demonstrations
and petitions became staple in London. Thousands of Londoners
surged around Westminster and Whitehall in 1641 demanding
Strafford's and Laud's deaths; they jostled and intimidated
politicians and peers, and threatened to burn the archbishop in his
palace. Armed campaigners stampeded the Court of Requests
crying, 'Down with bishops and Popish lords!' Twelve bishops were
impeached and on 5 February 1642, bishops were excluded from
the House of Lords. The House of Commons considered

impeaching Henrietta Maria for high treason, after which the
queen was believed to have precipitated the king's abortive attempt
to arrest five MPs by invading Parliament with several hundred
soldiers, 'Go, you coward and pull these rogues out by the ears, or
never see my face more.'[26] This action was political suicide.
Enraged crowds demonstrated and a gang of women roughed up
the Lord Mayor, pulling his chain from his neck. The king would
swiftly leave his capital and declare war on Parliament. The rank
hatred of those times is witnessed by the 'letter' delivered to the
Commons on 25 October 1641. The sergeant received it at the
door from the porter and gave it to Mr Pym:

> who opening it there fell down before him out of the letter
> an abominable rag full of filthy bloody atter [pus] ... Mr
> Pym was called in it bribe taker traitor and other
> opprobrious names ... the author of the letter said that he
> had sent him a clout [cloth] drawn through a plague sore
> which he had running upon him hoping that the same
> should kill him by infection ... whereupon the said Clerk's
> assistant having read so far threw down the letter into the
> house and so it was spurned away out of the doors.[27]

An unknown horseman on Fishstreet Hill had given the porter
twelve pence to deliver the pus-filled rag, a message which struck
revulsion into the House.

*

Twenty years later, at the Restoration, as the second Charles rode
to his coronation, the conduits on the streets ran with wine.
Charles' procession passed beneath a series of triumphal arches,
symbolising past breakdown and the new monarchical order. One
arch supported a women dressed as Rebellion in a blood-red robe
crawling with snakes, a gory sword in her hand. Her henchwoman,
Confusion, wore as headpiece a ruined castle and carried broken
sceptres. 'I am Hell's daughter, Satan's eldest child,' announced
Rebellion.[28] The Revolution was gendered female to a culture
which ascribed to woman lawless, destructive powers. 'She' had
turned the world upside down for a period of twenty years.

Women as low in the social scale as fishwives and oyster-
women had been essential to the war effort. In the building of the

massive fortifications encircling the whole capital in spring and summer of 1643, when Londoners were expecting the onslaught of the royalist army, women constituted a substantial part of the thousands who marched parish by parish, trade by trade, indefatigably to dig and carry earth to the great ramparts, nine foot thick and eighteen high, which stretched eighteen miles round the city. On these ramparts stood twenty-four forts built of earth and timber, surrounded by ditches and stakes, mounted with cannon. Samuel Butler recalled the women's efforts in his satire, *Hudibras*, with wholly involuntary admiration:

> Marched rank and file, or drum and ensign,
> T'entrench the city, for defence, in;
> Raised rampiers with their own soft hands,
> And put the enemy to stands;
> From ladies down to oyster-wenches,
> Labour'd like pioneers in trenches,
> Fell to their pick-axes and tools,
> And helped the men to dig like moles?[29]

Wandering tailor William Lithgow watched as day by day Londoners came: tailors with 8000 men (by his loose accounting) one May morning; watermen with 7000 the next; porters, 'and upon that same day, a thousand oyster-wives advanced from Billingsgate through Cheapside, to Crabtree Field, all alone, with drums and flying colours, and in a civil manner' to add their joint strength to the communal effort.[30]

From the Battle of Edgehill in 1642, through Newbury, Marston Moor, Naseby, the 'Second Civil War' in 1648, through sieges, fratricide, death, England was hacked to the bone with iron. In a men's world, it was officially a men's war. Women took no formal part in set-piece carnage, aside from the occasional 'she-soldier' like Jane Ingleby, daughter of a Yorkshire yeoman, said to have been wounded in the king's cavalry charge at Marston Moor; a pregnant 'Mr Clarke' who 'put on Man's Apparel' to soldier beside her husband and was immortalised in the ballad 'The Gallant She-Soldier'; Anne Dymoke who was unmasked in the garrison at Ayr in 1657.[31]

'Great ladies', it is true, were often congratulated on heroic exploits. Aristocratic women on both sides commanded the defence of their absent husband's castles or houses. Lady Elizabeth Dowdall defended her fortified house against Irish 'rebels', by first hanging ten of them, then: 'I sent out my soldiers with grenades,' to fire the rebels' quarters, and 'I skirmished with the enemy twice or thrice a week'. When Sir Richard Stephenson arrived, drums beating, pipes wailing, to demand her surrender, 'I sent him a shot in the head that made him bid the world good-night, and routed the whole army, we shot so hot,' she swaggered.[32] Lady Brilliana Harley famously held Brampton Castle for Parliament and husband in 1643. The Countess of Derby defended Lathom House for the Royalists. The fortress of Lathom had nine towers, walls six feet thick and a wide moat. Impervious to cannon balls crashing into her chamber, the Countess defied her besiegers, swearing to fight to the death rather than surrender.

But tales of great ladies manifesting what was always referred to as 'masculine' spirit belong to a male and dynastic myth of valour. Another form of courage belonged to ordinary women unremembered by history – four hundred nameless 'ordinary sort of women out of every ward' who worked on the defences of Worcester under bombardment; the firewomen and guards of Lyme, whose courage was celebrated in James Strong's heroic poem *Joanereidos* (1645): 'To most 'tis known/The weaker vessels are the stronger grown'. Endurance went unrecorded in non-combatants who lost husband and livelihood, or saw a child's leg or head blown off during a siege. Women saw more horror than glamour in war. Richard Baxter said his wife was traumatised by 'the storming of her mother's house by soldiers, killing, plundering and threatening the rest', to the degree that she suffered from morbid terrors all her life.[33] When everyday existence could require women's utmost fortitude – childbirth without anaesthetic once every year or two, hard labour for subsistence wages – 'gallantry' and even political loyalty might justifiably seem an indulgence. Mothers begged sons not to join up; wives coaxed husbands to desert. A poignant letter is extant, written by only-just-literate Susan Rodway begging her husband (himself probably 'food for powder' in someone else's quarrel) to come home:

I pray you to send me word when youe doo thenke youe
shalt returne. You doe not consider I ame a lone woemane,
I thought you woald never leve me thuse long togeder so I
rest evere praying for your savese returne.[34]

This letter makes me feel that most ordinary women's attitudes to
the Civil War may have taken a Falstaffian rather than a Lovelacian
form on the matter of martial 'honour'. The virile honour
flourished so exquisitely in cavalier Lovelace's 'Going to the Wars':

> Tell me not (sweet) I am unkind,
>   That from the nunnery
> Of thy chaste breast, and quiet mind,
>   To war and arms I fly.
>
> True; a new mistress now I chase,
>   The first foe in the field;
> And with a stronger faith embrace
>   A sword, a horse, a shield.
>
> Yet this inconstancy is such,
>   As you too shall adore;
> I could not love thee (dear) so much,
>   Lov'd I not honour more

is answered by Falstaff's pragmatic meditation:

Can honour set a leg? No. Or an arm? No. Or take away the
grief of a wound? No. Honour hath no skill in surgery then?
No. What is honour? a word. What is that word, honour? Air.
A trim reckoning! Who hath it? he that died o'Wednesday.
Doth he feel it? No. Doth he hear it? No. It is insensible then?
Yea, to the dead ... Therefore I'll none of it.[35]

It was often left to women to set a leg; to take away the grief of a
wound, nursing men blown apart by other men, on the orders of
men in power. Behind the popular 'Clubmen' risings, local armies
which beat out both sides from their areas, must have been
thousands of women in whom abhorrence of carnage, despoliation,
plunder and quarter was the strongest political passion they knew.

*

But the battlefields are not the landscape of this book, which concerns the tumult of the national mind as old sanctions shuddered and cracked under seismic stress. During the 1640s and 1650s, the sacrosanct and time-honoured came into question. A Parliament acting in the name of 'the people' was shocked when 'the people' spilled out on to the streets, in thousands, demanding a voice. The 'inferior sort' bred chaos, and threatened right reason, true religion and the god Property. The Long Parliament was no less patriarchal than the monarchy in wishing to govern according to a law conserving rank and property. But when the woman Rebellion got a voice, women came out into the streets with her, exercising theirs.

Conservative political propaganda derided the female presence in the national debate. In 'The Anarchy, Or the Blessed Reformation Since 1640', a mob of voices invades the public sphere from the nether regions of society:

> Speak Abraham, speak Kester, speak Judith, speak Hester,
>   Speak tag and rag, short coat and long;
> Truth's the spell made us rebel,
>   And murder and plunder, ding-dong.
>   Sure I have the truth, says Numph;
>   Nay, I ha' the truth, says Clemme;
>   Nay, I ha' the truth, says the Reverend Ruth;
>   Nay, I ha' the truth, says Nem.
>   ...
>   Then let's ha' King Charles, says George;
>   Nay, let's have his son, says Hugh;
>   Nay, let's ha' none, says jabbering John;
>   Nay, let's be all kings, says Prue.[36]

The democratic claim to a say-so is sneered at as a blabbermouthed offence to common sense. Numph and Nem, piffling rival know-alls, gabble alongside the woman preacher, 'the Reverend Ruth', and daft Prue who has got hold of the idea that everyone can be an anointed king. Prue parrots the Puritan belief that each Christian believer is an 'anointed son of God', hence each 'son' is a 'king' – and a woman can be a 'son'. The kingship of all believers is argued by Katharine Chidley in her first pamphlet.[37] In the English Revolution, women's assertive emergence into the public world was equated by anxious moderates with that of tradesmen and the lower orders – an inversion of the pyramid of state and family that seemed self-evidently preposterous. Disorder in the patriarchal state seemed matched by disorder in the patriarchal family unit, its foundation.

The censorship of the press had collapsed. A flood of printed matter, newspapers, books, broadsheets, tracts, ballads, flowed off the presses. Between 1640 and 1660, the total number of known publications exceeded the total printed in England during the previous 150 years.[38] Katharine Chidley, radical separatist and later Leveller, was early into print, in 1641. Given mass illiteracy, meagre education and conditions of servitude, women's tracts are, inevitably, a tiny minority of the total. It is all the more remarkable that middle- and lower-ranking women of this period did learn to read, write and even publish. And (partly because printer's rights continued with the widow rather than descending from father to son) thirty-four women in the period 1641 to 1660 were trading as printers and booksellers. Often women writers chose to publish with women. In the 1650s, Quaker literature began to roll off the presses: 82 out of 650 authors were women, writing 220 out of 3853 publications.[39] From the beginning women were avid readers of the public dialogue about society, politics and religion. Londoners were bombarded with propaganda from all sides, pamphlets being run off rapidly, even overnight, in print runs of anything from 500 to 10,000. Blizzards of ballads might be scattered in the streets overnight; flyposters nailed broadsheets to posts, church doors, even the House of Commons; many women disseminated subversive literature, either to earn an extra pittance or as political activists.[40]

In this information revolution, a chaos of competing weekly newspapers sprouted up: costing a penny (the price of a quarter of a pound of beef), they fought out the Civil War on the printed page. In the later 1640s, the Parliamentary *A Perfect Diurnall*, with a circulation of 3000, became the leading newspaper, assembling the rudiments of a staff of reporters, and employing the first newspaper woman, a 'she-intelligencer', according to a hostile pamphlet of

1647.[41] Newspapers shared a common appetite for women's political activities as good copy, generally spiced by scabrous commentary.

Pamphlets, petitions, books, newspapers, ballads were incendiary documents passed from hand to hand, read and explained by the literate to the illiterate. Political consciousness, especially in the capital, soared. Reciprocally, angry panic haunted the writings of the social and religious elite. As the early Puritan alliance crumbled with the winning of the First Civil War (1642 to 1645), yesterday's radicals became today's conservatives: Presbyterian Thomas Edwards spasmed with shock at the throng of grocers and tapsters, weavers and tailors who set up as preachers of God's Truth. There was a panic 'outing' of female preachers. The very title of a tract of 1641, *A Discovery of Six Women Preachers in Middlesex*, was supposed to elicit an intake of shocked breath at the 'petticoat preachers' and 'apron apostles' holding their unruly meetings. It was like an advertisement for witches. For 'When women preach and cobblers pray/The fiends in hell, make holiday,' ran the jingle.[42]

In the 1640s, radical sects broke away from the national church in democratically organised, local 'gathered churches', and new self-governing sects splintered from the splinters: different colours of Baptist, 'strict' or 'general'; Independent ('Congregational'); 'Seeker'; through a fluid spectrum. These groups were a seedbed of radicalism. Their backbone was formed of people of the 'middling' sort and lower ranks, and especially women, who comprised a majority in congregations and were sometimes allowed to speak or preach during their meetings for worship – an idea anathema to the State Church, Presbyterians, and most men. Snarling quarrels broke out amongst the sects. John Rogers took a dim view of his own sex's contempt for women members, writing, 'most men do arrogate a sovereignty to themselves which I see no warrant for ... It is lawful for women to have office in the church'.[43] He recalls that this issue split his Dublin congregation wide open: it was to split the Quakers too.

Rogers is famous amongst feminists for the parlous one-step-to-the-left-another-to-the-right dance which constitutes his excruciated dither on the subject of women's speaking. We might divide his message into two columns:

> To women, I wish you be
> not too forward   and yet not too backward,
>   but hold fast your liberty ...
>   stand fast ... keep your
>   ground ... maintain your
>   right, defend your liberty ...
>
> And yet be cautious too ...
> not too fast, but first, be
> swift to hear, slow to speak
> ... unless occasion requires
> you; your silence may
> sometimes be the best
> advice of your orderly
> liberty ...   and yet ye ought not by
>   your silence betray your
>   liberty, trouble your
>   consciences ...
>
> but I say, be not hasty nor
> too high ... hold your
> liberty a little in suspense ...   but lose it not for the
>   world ...

(*Ohel*, p76)

Rogers is talking tactics, in an age of mass prejudice, where women occupy a double-bound position, whose contradictions they must somehow negotiate through tortuous and, in the end, impossible footwork.

Yet some dissident groups were founded by women. Bunyan's Bedford church was created by a resourceful group of women. In 1650 it consisted of:

> John Grew and wife
> John Elston, elder
> Anthony Harrington and wife
> John Gifford   all grave and ancient
> Sister Coventon   Sister Fenne   Christians[44]
> Sister Bosworth   Sister Norton
> Sister Munnes   Sister Spencer

In 1673 and 1693, it still had twice as many women as men. Katharine Chidley, with her son, settled the Bury church. Dorothy Hazzard, militant protester and religious subversive, exploited her Anglican husband's vicarage as safehouse for dissidents; her initiative founded the famous separatist church in Bristol which came to be known as Broadmead Church. Women and the lower orders dominated Fifth Monarchist congregations, the 'sisters' having a vocal sub-group of their own at firebrand Venner's church.[45]

Luther had said, 'Every man his own priest'; Mary Cary and many other women adapted it to a version of 'every woman her own priest' or, failing that, they'd exercise their own choice of man, roaming the various groups on offer.

Peter Hausted satirised their congregations as a hysterically sobbing halleluia chorus: 'the wall-eyed Sisters in a row'.[46] If females chose to moon on benches lapping up heresies, that was bad enough; but they might also charge the pulpits, or denounce pulpits altogether, for 'four or five hours together, yea whole days', as Daniel Rogers lamented, with awe.[47] And, lax tongue, loose sex: who knew what they were getting up to in the vestry? Mary Bilbrowe, happy in having a bricklayer husband who could build her a homemade pulpit, was believed to have leapt from the same in mid-prayer, to have sex with a 'gentleman at Bloomsbury', the audience tucking in to pork washed down with claret, to wile away the time of her absence.[48]

*

The Civil Wars, in which a quarter of the male population fought, demolished not only families, homes, and the fabric of civic relationships, but also the boundaries of political thought. It was only a step from the idea of spiritual liberty to that of political liberty; and another (if more audacious) leap to that of political equality. Cromwell's New Model Army became a forum for radical political debate, in which officer-class and middle-ranks thrashed out revolutionary ideas.

The Leveller movement which emerged in the mid-1640s was a radical political party whose programme is strikingly modern. Levellers campaigned for a new social contract between the 'people', understood as male heads of households, and their elected representatives, directly accountable in fixed-term Parliaments. They sought far-reaching constitutional, legal and fiscal reform.

The Levellers were to be crushed, as were the communist Diggers, or 'True Levellers', who emerged as a group representing the interests of the poorest of the poor. Their principles were grounded in the belief that the universally available 'Inner Light' of God in humanity abolished all hierarchy and private property. Their notion of 'the people' embraced all males. To their spokesman Gerrard Winstanley, the Millennium was announcing itself in the revolutionary 'rising up of Christ in sons and daughters'. All property, he believed, was theft, and the so-called law of the land a mere defence of stolen goods; for the world is ours only in stewardship, to share and work: 'No man shall have any more land, than he can labour himself'.[49] There need never again be a beggar in England. Paradise might be built here and now: a group of Diggers assembled in April 1649 on St George's Hill, Surrey, to reclaim, plough and plant the common land for the poor. Within a year they were scoured away by local interest groups. Women played no visible part in the Digger movement, but Winstanley, who, like the Quakers, invariably spoke of freedom for 'the sons and daughters', was mindful of their interests, and the ease with which they could be exploited. Women, as this book will show, were Leveller activists, networking to mobilise petitions and vast demonstrations. Their emergence as a group bears genuine comparison with women's role in the French Revolution, and stands out 'in terms of numbers and planning', as well as its commitment to a secular political programme, from the traditional women's riot.[50]

If the emergence of the Levellers and Diggers alarmed the gentry, so too did the upstart sects: politics and religion were a compound issue. As religious anarchy developed and the lower orders felt free to espouse Gods of their own conceiving, or no God at all, the elite feared the breakdown of all hierarchy. In the mid-1640s, Thomas Edwards, sniffing out theological abominations (often 'destructive to the civil laws and peace of kingdoms')[51] was able to reveal heresies so spectacular amongst the lower orders that they could count (he wrote proudly) as the worst 'since the creation of the world', in particular the statement made by 'one John Boggis' of Great Yarmouth, who, at dinner with the informer's master, was asked by his hostess to give thanks before they ate the shoulder of roast veal set before them on the table:

'To whom should I give thanks, to the butcher, or to the bull, or to the cow?' John Boggis cheekily demanded. Shocked at such impiety, the master's wife replied, 'Thanks should be given to God.'

'Where is your God, in Heaven, or in Earth, aloft or below, or doth he sit in the clouds, or where doth he sit with his— ?'

(Blushful Edwards here appends a marginal note to the reader, 'The word is so horrid and obscene, that I forbear to express it.')

The appalled hostess now felt called upon to have the whole matter out with John Boggis. What about the church? she wanted to know, what about the Holy Bible?

John Boggis supplied her with answers quite disgraceful enough for Edwards: he wished, he said, that he had not known as much of the Bible as he actually did, for after all it 'is but only paper' (p162).

God sitting on his arse! The Bible only paper! This showed what happened when the religious authorities took the lid off the beliefs of the lower orders, with their degenerate tendency to tumble into the muck of materialism, and their age-old contempt and envy of their betters.

Whatever next?

Well, confides Edwards, near Whitehall, a woman (a nurse living in Clare Street) was given to buttonholing godly ministers and slighting the Scriptures, 'and denied there was any such thing as sin, or Hell, or the Devil, or temptation, or the Holy Ghost, or Scriptures; she said, all the Hell there was, was the darkness of the night'. Further to this, she claimed that murder, adultery and theft were no sin. To the aghast minister asking what on earth she was, she replied several times, in cryptic mode, 'I am that I am' – an answer tantamount to a claim to be God.

Through Edwards we learn the kinds of things radical and

outrageous women were saying – or which the elite thought they were saying, which might have been the same thing – in revolutionary England. For a woman to speak in public on such matters was in itself matter for indignation.

This woman seems to have been an antinomian, ('to the pure all things are pure'), with 'Ranterish' views. 'Ranter' is a loose label on a bundle of heresies which, emphasising the Inner Light, might dismiss Christian concepts of hell, sin and damnation as superstitions dreamt up to keep the people in awe – endorsing the holiness of tobacco, alcohol, sex; God in an ivy-leaf; myself God; the Bible wastepaper. Hell was when you cried; Heaven when you laughed. Jacob Bauthumley was burned through the tongue for blasphemously writing that, 'God is in all creatures, man and beast, fish and foul, and every green thing ... and hath his being nowhere else but in the creatures.'[52]

Women were thought highly susceptible to 'Ranterism' as to all heresies, because of their weak minds and sex-crazed, deviant wills. Cotton Mather in New England was always on the watch for heresy among 'silly women', who were 'more easily gained by the devil'.[53] It does seem to have been the case that, once women sipped the fizzy water of heresy, they found they liked the taste very much. Long thwarted power-hunger let rip. Blasphemies by defecting women, collected by Baptist deacons sent as sheepdogs to bark backsliders back into the fold, show women defiantly relishing their new-found assertiveness and self-hatched thoughts. Mrs William Austin of Potton, Bedfordshire, denied sin; denied particular grace; denied Scripture; expressed rapture at the thought that the church would excommunicate her; and galloped into a high-spirited denial of Christ, God, Baptists, speaking witheringly of him 'that died upon the Cross at Jerusalem? He is nothing to me; I do not care for him'.[54]

*

Few women, apart from Lady Eleanor Davies and Mary Cary, actively supported the execution of Charles I. Mary Pope and Elizabeth Warren wrote forcefully against it, and Elizabeth Pool, a prophet from Abingdon, was allowed to deliver two messages to the Army Council debating Charles' trial: she was hustled out when the second turned out to be a firm 'No' from God to regicide. As the Lord President of the trial, John Bradshaw, launched into his opening speech, a masked woman in the Gallery shouted him down. To his claim that the trial was conducted 'in the name of the people of England', Lady Anne Fairfax accurately objected, 'Not half, not a quarter of the people of England. Oliver Cromwell is a traitor'.[55] Muskets were levelled at the Lord General's wife, who was rushed from the courtroom. The regicide was a propaganda victory – for the Crown.

During the Commonwealth and Protectorate (1649 to 1660), England lay under military rule, new taxes and severe new laws. Only in the 'Barebones' Parliament of May to September 1653 did the age-old institutions of oppression, the Court of Chancery and tithes, come near demolition. Fifth Monarchists (believers in the imminent military Second Coming of Christ) were feared as likely to initiate violent insurrection, though in fact most were quietly awaiting Christ's coming before taking to arms. Women predominated in Fifth Monarchist sects as in other radical groups, and it was here that the prophet Anna Trapnel came to the public eye and ear. John Thurloe, heading Cromwell's intelligence network, kept a close eye on this voluble woman, who spoke in catatonic trances lasting hours or days at a time. He was also deeply exercised by the Society of Friends, founded by George Fox in 1652 to 1653, vilified as 'Quakers' because of their ecstatic spasming when under the power of the Spirit. Friends, originating in the north of England, came to number about 40,000 by 1660. Their aggressive refusal of social deference, verbal attacks on ministers in the 'steeple-houses', tithe-strikes and the women's apparently anarchic behaviour made them seem a potently subversive force, remote from their later quietist image. Quaker women were granted unprecedented spiritual and apostolic equality with men: their revolutionary journeys and heroic witness, imprisonings and whippings, are recorded in their own writings, broadsheets, tracts and spiritual autobiographies.

Throughout the two decades of revolution, an undertow of popular conservatism and royalism was constant, accompanied by fierce resentment of Puritan abolition of the festivals of Christmas and Easter, harvest home, maypoles, minstrels, plays, football, morris dancing and the Church calendar.[56] Most yearned for peace, stability, allowable pleasures, the Prayer Book, communion in the old-fashioned way. Only about 5 per cent of the population ever belonged to the radical sects. A standing army of 10,000 to 14,000 was loathed by the population, with the burden of free quarter and (in periods when the soldiers were unpaid and starving) of pillage. The Protectorate could sustain itself little longer than Cromwell's life; his son, Richard, was weak and incompetent, and military rule in 1659 brought anarchy. The Restoration of King Charles II was welcomed with genuine relief by the majority whose world had been turned upside down.

Silence and Scolding

In writing this book, I have been painfully aware of the silence of the majority of seventeenth-century women, which accompanies the historian like a mute, spectral companion, of whom little can be recorded save her existence. What were the conditions and mechanisms that gagged and blinkered so many; and how did the loquacious few circumvent them?

Most women inhabited a silent, politically inert hinterland, bound into cycles of child-bearing and child-burying, ignorant of contraception except for prophylaxis. The masses toiled for a bare subsistence, often hungry and ill, in the wage-labourer and small husbandman class (tenants of small plots often scarcely sufficient to feed their families). This peasant world was referred to by derogatory formulae such as 'the rude sort', 'the meaner sort'. Within this order, the women's world constituted an inferior subgroup. Above this class were yeomen (generally defined as freehold farmers worth forty shillings per year), craftsmen and traders – the 'middling sort' from which many of the radical women came, but most were not radical women. Beneath wage-labourers were the homeless poor, of which women constituted about a quarter. Homeless women, often pregnant and deserted, might be hustled from parish to parish by officials whose job it was to ensure that the double burden of mother and child did not fall to their charge. Their babies were born in ditches, barns or doorways. If poor women got work, it reaped starvation wages, on average one penny per day, half that of a male worker. 'The full misery of the labourer's lot was only felt by the women,' writes Alice Clark.[57] Cumbered by starving children, they were immobilised. Such women were entirely voiceless.

Female literacy was the lowest of all social groups. While 15 per cent of labourers and 21 per cent of husbandmen could sign their names, as against 56 per cent of tradesmen and 65 per cent of yeomen, only 11 per cent of women of all classes could sign their names, the standard test of literacy.[58] Signing one's name, however, is no test of fluency in writing. More women could read than write; and literacy was higher in London. Even so, the statistic of 89 per cent illiteracy helps to focus the fact that the women in this book are a fraction of a fraction.

Ignorance and credulity characterised the mass of women: how could it have been otherwise? The superstition and sensationalism rife in popular culture are witnessed in a later 'tabloid'-style news-sheet, *Wonderful News from Bristol* (1676), which tells of how:

> a Hen on the 3rd of July last, brought into the world a Kitling or young Cat, to the unspeakable Admiration of many people present, Both the Hen and Cat being still alive, attested by

Elianor Holder (*Widow*)

Mary ⎤		Thomas Fisher ⎫
Joan ⎬ Holder (*her*		Thomas Holbrook ⎬ (*Neighbours*)
Martha ⎪ *daughters*)		Sarah Holbrook[59] ⎭
Sarah ⎦		

The publisher promises ten guineas to anyone who can discredit this miraculous event, backed up by citations from Plutarch on 'sodomitical or heterogeneous copulations' between species, and also the well-remembered birth of a piglet with a human shape in Bromley, Kent, not seven years back. In the present case, the hen was shooed from under a dresser. One of the girls, peering down at the mewing hen, shrieked, '"What has this fellow done? he has spoiled my hen, see all her guts are coming out"'. But 'behold!' cries the author, what should they see but a live kitten 'hanging forth at the hen's fundament'. The hen reeled up and down in torment, watched by all eight witnesses, kitten half in, half out.

Upon delivering its strange egg, the hen showed no desire to bond but scuttled off, and the cat took over. It will be noticed that six of the eight witnesses to this marvel were women.

The quality of their lives is suggested by Shropshire antiquarian Richard Gough's vivid *The History of Myddle* (1701–6), written by the elderly resident of a parish on the English border with Wales. In Gough's account, anomalous women embraced not God or political causes but drunkenness or sexual promiscuity. The nearest he comes to 'women of spirit' is a bored housewife who, conspiring with other disaffected wives to 'poison their husbands all in one night', killed hers and took off to the wilds of Wales, where she was unforgettably found 'dancing on the top of a hill amongst a company of young people'.[60]

A few self-supporting women are mentioned in *Myddle*, as well as local 'wise women', healers, surgeons and midwives. The quality of life in an age of such medical ignorance and poverty was low. Margaret Davies' rheumatic disability, perhaps osteoporosis, caused decades of slow degeneration, ending in her being 'so bowed together, that her knees lay close to her breast ... About a year-and-a-half past, her two thigh bones broke as she lay in bed, and one of them burst through the skin and stood out about an inch, like a dry hollow stick' (pp150–1). Margaret had to be buried doubled up in her coffin since she could not be straightened without snapping her bones.

If ordinary women's lives were burdened by toil and illness, they also tended to be lived on a local level, within the limits of shire or parish. Although there was considerable mobility in the population as a whole, the capital seemed remote from the local order. Naturally enough, home and family life composed the centre and horizon of perception, even among relatively affluent gentry families. The Royalist Alice Thornton's *Book of Remembrances*'s account of the climactic year 1648 to 1649 places its priorities as follows:

1648

My cousin Edmund Norton married Mr Dudley's daughter and heir of Chopwell, Jane Dudley, 10th February, 1648 at Chopwell.

My cousin Edmund Norton died at York of a pleurisy or stitch in his side, 30th November, 1648.

King Charles I beheaded at Whitehall, London, 30th January, 1648[9].

My cousin Julian Norton died at St Nicholas.

My cousin Julian Norton died at Richmond Green at her father's, 9th April 1649.

My uncle Sir Edward Osborne died at Kiveton of a surfeit of eating melons, being too cold for him.[61]

In the minuscule notebook in which Alice wrote this, her first account of her life experiences, the royal death which shook England is a jotting on a level with family losses; but there are longer records of epoque-making personal events, such as the death of a loved mother in 1659; and the infection of Alice's nipple after her baby Christopher's death, with fever, weakness and 'fear of a gangrene'. These relative perspectives reveal the Third World actualities of existence for a generation to whom the infant mortality rate (15 per cent before the age of one; 10 per cent before ten) and death in childbirth (about 15 per cent) might make existence a perpetual war against its conditions. Only three of Alice's nine pregnancies produced a child who survived for more than a few weeks; and those deliveries could be anguish. The baby she bore in 1657 came feet-foremost and was 'strangled': 'I was upon the rack in bearing my child with such exquisite torment as if each limb were divided from other'.[62] In an age before Caesarian section, medical textbooks offered guidance on how (in the case of an obstructed birth) to dismember a baby in the womb. Other wars might justifiably seem less focal.

The institution of marriage was a means of patriarchal control of women, children and household servants by male heads of households. Yet Puritan marriage in particular was a conflicted institution, the site of seismic stresses, as I shall show. It weakened and strengthened; muted and released women. The famous diary of Ralph Josselin in revolutionary Essex gives us glimpses into the interior world of his wife, Jane. Though she never took autonomous political or religious action, her millennial visions during the 1650s show the extent to which the common consciousness in this age of upheaval was permeated with a sense of apocalyptic meaning. Josselin's support for his wife as *her* helpmate blurred the border between spheres. Nehemiah Wallington's wife, Grace, was a model of severe Puritan rectitude and political commitment, whose pronouncements the London turner quotes with awe. Alongside these marriages, we can place that of Lucy and John Hutchinson, through Lucy's magnificent biography of her husband, the republican and regicide. Her *Life of Colonel Hutchinson* is a vindication of the radical elite by a powerful, and powerfully conflicted, woman who espouses the doctrine of female inferiority behind an invincibly proud persona.

This double-bind burdened outspoken women of every rank and persuasion, who could either throw off their chains with disdain, like the Quaker Margaret Fell, or brag them like a monstrous necklace, like Margaret Cavendish, Marchioness of Newcastle. In her *A True Relation of my Birth, Breeding and Life* (1656), she insisted that she was next to mute in public, only able to express herself with her husband, 'yet then I rather attentively listen to what he says, than impertinently speak'.[63] Yet Cavendish was an exhibitionist, displaying outrageous fashions of her own devising ('I always took delight in a singularity'). Though a published author of drama, poetry, orations, natural philosophy, biology, biography, and fiction, she mouthed her deference to the distaff: 'true it is, spinning with the fingers is more proper to our sex than studying or writing poetry'. Lofty rank screened the marchioness from the prejudice against publishing women as unchaste, offering pages like petticoats to be riffled through by grubby hands in the bookshop. Rank and wealth screened her – but not entirely.

Dorothy Osborne giggled in one of her now famous letters at the thought of the grotesquerie of Cavendish's *Poems and Fancies* (dashed off in three weeks flat) in 1653; her mouth watered to read it, for 'they say tis ten times more extravagant than her dress'. She felt a woman must be 'a little distracted' to venture on such a 'ridiculous' project as 'writing books and in verse too'.[64]

But her tone is complex. There is a certain wistfulness in such a witty stylist as Dorothy Osborne vowing never to demean herself by publishing.

Most of the women of this book had little defence against the cry of 'whore' which smeared women who stepped out of the private sphere into the searchlight of publication.

*

Just as Puritan marriage empowered and disempowered seventeenth-century women, so membership of sects might release and constrain them. Therapy and solidarity were offered by gathered churches and political organisations. Within same-sex subgroups of the sects, the individual gathered courage to speak her own truth within a family of kindred minds: the 'sisterhood'. The heroism of women Quakers, Fifth Monarchists, Levellers, Independents, occurred within a matrix in which social abnorms became the group's givens. But there was a shadow-side to the dissident experience, which reinforced women's female conditioning and might fill them with turmoil and despair.

Conviction of personal worth was contingent upon assurance of salvation. This was often hard-won, and harder to maintain. Susanna Parr was a strong-minded woman who took on the minister and elders of an Independent congregation. In *Susanna's Apology Against the Elders* (1659),[65] she sketches her one-woman battle against the tyranny of church and minister, Mr Stucley. At 'the death of a dear child', she felt 'the flashings of hell-fire in my soul, the wrath of God that lay hard upon me': interpreting the loss of her child as punishment for quitting her original church, she abandoned Stucley and found peace, only to be visited by posses of Independent male bullies, and was (with another woman member, Mary Allein) excommunicated. In Susanna, we see the conflicts engendered by a system whose twin emphases on liberty of individual conscience and the policing of the individual by the group were complicated by a tortuously ambiguous attitude to women members. Stubborn, outspoken, Susanna was a thorn in the elders' flesh. The squabble exploded into a national furore, bringing odium on the group. The defiant Susanna was wounded, not by the loudmouthed Stucley, but by the implications of her child's death.

In the Puritan culture of introspection, where Calvinist notions of election and reprobation were always in the air, psychological sloughs such as Bunyan describes in *Grace Abounding* and *Pilgrim's Progress* often lay over the next hill. The dark side of women's experiences issued in the seventeenth-century equivalents of hypochondria, anorexia, 'clinical depression', suicidal mania, which were recorded in women's spiritual autobiographies and conversion narratives. John Rogers' Independent/Baptist congregation in Dublin in 1650 to 1652 contained many women, whose experiences he gathered. Elizabeth Avery's faith in 'Free-grace' was tested by 'great afflictions':

> and amongst all others, by the loss of my children, God's rod was laid heavily upon me, insomuch, That he struck three of them together; and one child above all, a most sweet child, and one, that I least thought of them all would have died, was very ill ... I went into the garden to wail and moan myself; but soon after my husband came and told me my child was dying: at which I was left in an horror, as if I were in Hell, none could comfort me, none could satisfy me, no Friends, nothing. (pp402–3)[66]

This cry of inconsolable maternal grief is full of desolation, despite the therapy of her faith, which released her, after racking stuggle, from earthly attachments:

> I was content to part with all, and to let all go; then God tried me, and took away another child from me, and I could bear it very well, and was nothing troubled, but rather did rejoice within me to be thus tried ... I continued in this strength (I praise God) pretty long. (pp403–4)

But only 'pretty long': not for ever and finally. The poise of Elizabeth's prose, as she recounts God's removal of yet another child, has the fragility of one treading with delicate care over the unstable landscape of grief. During the Civil Wars, Elizabeth felt strong and focused; afterwards, for lack of a guiding pastor, 'my faith was gone, and hope was gone, and all gone, and flew from me ... yet,' she comforts herself, 'love remained'.

These women's souls were in a familiar Reformation dilemma, in the binary world of a God whose embrace inexplicably gave way to the ice of his absence or the fire of his wrath. Such abandonment was always merited: sin tainted every mortal thought, and only Christ's imputed Grace could wash it away. Women (already indoctrinated in a culture of female guilt and impotence) lay open to crisis and confusion, struggling in a world where truths were verifiable solely by subjective experience – but the self was hopelessly tainted. Calvinist terrors haunted some, like Ruth Emerson, who 'thought I heard how the damned roared in hell, and blasphemed God to his face; – O this! – this cut me to the heart, to think I should be one of those that should blaspheme God' (pp411–2). Life-calamities challenged faith, like the murder of all Mary Tarrant's children by Irish 'rebels' in 1641 and her husband's death.

After these testimonies, Rogers adds his own. It excels all the rest for wild emotionalism. Rushing into barns, stables, privies, 'anywhere', to 'pray, sigh, weep, knocking my breast, curse that ever I was born', seeing devils with rolling, flamy eyes ('like saucers'), he spoke to trees as angels, and shrank from bushes as devils. Suicidal desires shook him. One day, having fasted, he hurled himself on his bed, fell fast asleep and woke up 'so much changed that I was amazed at myself' (pp430–1). Behaviour socially construed 'female' or 'hysterical' happened to be identical to the expression of 'godly' pathology. Rogers was impressed by the quality of his women saints, whose souls he compared with malleable gold as opposed to male 'steel and iron, hard to work upon' (p474).

Desperate women seeking comfort for all-too-human losses found their darkness glowing with compensatory light, which could then be transmitted to others in the form of a kind of sublime psychotherapy. Male experts found them out and advertised them, like James Fisher's anthology of the 'marvellous' utterances of a young epileptic girl of eleven and Henry Jessey's raising of select, attention-seeking adolescent girls to brief celebrity. Jessey's protegée Sarah Wight became the equivalent of a full-time psychotherapist to the troubled who needed counselling. But in adult life she retired to silence and anonymity, save for a single tract, which was published by a male mentor apparently without her co-operation.[67]

*

Outspoken women risked punishment for breaking silence. Witch and scold had risen together as 'alienated outsiders, casualties of a changing social order'.[68] Society exercised on them the machinery of control, in the form of cucking, witchcraft and whore accusations, whipping, bridewell and brank. How did women of the Revolution cope with these threats?

Because the scold's bridle or brank became and has remained a misogynist joke, it is not generally realised how terrible a punishment this could be. I shall describe it in detail, to suggest the courage required by a woman challenging social norms.[69]

The brank was composed of bands of iron, often painted in gay colours, to match the carnival air of the occasion. A protrusion of metal was attached to the inner part of the iron hoop, to receive which the woman had to open her mouth when the bridle was fitted and locked into place. This was the 'bitt', measuring from one to three-and-a-half inches long, which would reach the back of her throat. If she panicked, she would retch or vomit throughout the experience of being 'ridden' around town. The bitt came in several styles, either lying flat or turned down at the end, holding down her tongue, which would be spiked by, for instance, a design such as the bridle held at Stockport,[70] whose gag terminated in a rounded extremity, fitted with nine iron pins with sharp points three on the upper surface, three on the lower, three pointing backwards. This torture implement was only equalled by the witch's bridle at Forfar, in which condemned witches were led to the stake, the bitt being a spur, with three sharp-pointed spikes, to pierce the tongue and the roof of the mouth. Even the least barbarous scold's branks were liable to shatter the teeth as the 'rider' tugged the wearer along. She stood in danger of breaking her jaw, since with every jerk of the lead, the cage on her head twisted. She might be whipped at the same time.

The procession generally headed for the market square, where the victim was tethered and left for a stipulated period, exposed to ritual humiliation such as spitting, stone throwing or urination. Pain, din and shock would traumatise her. Women did not set this experience on record: they were likely to come from the illiterate poor and, in any case, the brank was an efficient instrument of social control. Scolding was next to cursing, and cursing next to witchcraft.

Only one personal account is known to exist of the experience of wearing the bridle, by Dorothy Waugh, a militant Quaker during the revolutionary years. Quakers, for reasons I shall show, were thought of as 'the ultimate scolds', proud to shout down their society, defying the codes of deference which operated in every social transaction. They were immune to humiliation. Dorothy Waugh published in 1656 her testament of her penalty for speaking in Carlisle marketplace the previous year 'against all deceit and ungodly practices'. I found her story the last account in a slim volume of Quaker tracts, *The Lamb's Defence Against Lies*, published in 1656. The pages were brittle and speckled with brown mould, and the type had faded to a vulnerable thinness, even by the standards of seventeenth-century tracts. In this frail hiding-place, Dorothy's powerful testimony flamed into indignant life.

She came last year, she tells her readers, to Carlisle and was arrested by the Mayor's officer for preaching at the market cross. To the Mayor's question as to her place of origin, 'I said "Out of Egypt here thou lodgest"', contrasting his slavery with her freedom.

Wasting no further breath on questioning Dorothy, the irate Mayor called for the scold's bridle and conferred a summary sentence of three hours. Dorothy seems never to have seen such a contraption, which she describes as:

> like a steel cap and my hat being violently plucked off which was pinned to my head, whereby they tare my clothes to put on their bridle as they called it, which was a stone weight of iron ... & three bars of iron to put over my face, and a piece of it was put in my mouth, which was so unreasonable big a thing for that place as cannot be well related, which was locked to my head, and so I stood their time with my hands bound behind me with the stone weight of iron upon my head, and the bitt in my mouth to keep me from speaking; and the Mayor said he would make me an example to all that should evercome in that name.[71]

At seeing her 'so violently abused', the people around wept – further frustrating the mayor, as he watched his scheme backfire. He had not envisaged that a scold's brank, exposing the wearer to public ridicule, could stand as a martyr's crown. He wanted her hooted at and belittled: '"For foolish pity, one may spoil a whole city",' he snarled.

Meanwhile the man at the prison gate expressed his entrepreneurial spirit by charging visitors two pence a go to view the bridled Quaker.

After three hours the 'stone weight of iron' came off but Dorothy was kept in prison. When the mayor returned, he had her locked into the bridle a second time, insulting her with 'very vile and unsavoury words, which are not fit to proceed out of any man's mouth' (presumably 'whore' and its various synonyms). She was then whipped out of the town, to be sent from constable to constable, 'till I came to my own home, whereas they had not anything to lay to my charge', ends Dorothy bitterly.

This ordeal had no effect upon her moral courage save to strengthen her indignation against the godless tyranny which could devise and use so barbarous an instrument. She details the ferocity with which her hat (symbol of her personal dignity) is torn off by the ruffian officials and replaced by the headgear of the 'scold'. She notes its great weight and the obscene size of the metal tongue. Far from shaming her into silence, this experience goads her into denouncing the shame and criminality of her torturers. An aghast perplexity characterises her telling. How can such wicked contrivances be current?

A nineteenth-century antiquarian sketched branks and cucking-gear uncovered in dungeons; together with smirking speculations as to use and fit.[72] It is impossible to avoid pondering the sexual connotations of the infamous 'bitt': no doubt these would customarily have been made specific by fellatic jests from the populace. Sexual sadism was licensed, as in the case of Quaker Margaret Newby and her friend stocked at Evesham, with their legs spread apart. When they asked for a block to sit on, a block was forthcoming: it was shoved between their legs, as a substitute for that something else the mayor knew they wanted 'between their legs'.[73]

In Dorothy Waugh, they had bridled the wrong woman. Derision simply amplified her sense of personal worth and dignity. Christ was so ridiculed: the earthly bridle was a visible version of the heavenly crown. This heroic transcendence, powerful and moving as it is, was not and could never be the experience of the common woman in the village, perhaps a cussed wife or difficult neighbour, who received payment for compulsively belligerent talkativeness in a shattered jaw and a mouth filled with blood and vomit.

This book ponders a shift of consciousness that occurred during the middle years of the century in a minority of women. How could Dorothy Waugh, who began as an illiterate Westmorland serving maid, raise the courage and power to speak out her own singular truth, against a society which punished the anomalous woman so violently?

*

That dissidence was all the more awe-inspiring because women like Dorothy were open to the charge of witchcraft, a felony which King James I in his *Demonologie* had placed above murder.[74] Compared with the Continent, English witch executions were modest in number, a mere thousand citizens being hanged between 1550 and 1685 (the date of the last hanging). Scotland, with a population one fifth the size, burned 4000. It is fashionable – and surely perverse – to claim that witchcraft should not be analysed as a product of misogyny. Around 90 per cent of known witches in England during the seventeenth century were women; of these, 45 per cent were widows or spinsters, chiefly elderly and on the vulnerable margins of poor communities. The majority of accusers were also women, generally of a slightly higher social status. Hence, both witches and witch accusers belonged to a powerless underclass *within* the underclass, turning under stress against its own weakest members, especially those who bore a noisy grudge.

The denial that witchcraft expresses communal misogyny grounds its argument in the fact that witchcraft was not a crime specific to women; 'Men actually made up around 25 per cent of the total of 40,000–50,000 executions' in Europe.[75] But 75 per cent is hardly an insubstantial majority, and is angled to blur the potency of the 90 per cent statistic for England. Witchcraft-charges demonised women and stemmed in part from primitive and pathological male fear of women as the origin of sin and sexual pollution, with immemorial roots in Hebraic and European culture. The closeness of 'scold' to 'witch' expresses the same pathology.

Behind the 'mere thousand' witches convicted and hanged lay a world of failed prosecutions and cases that never reached court; and around these specific cases swirled the swamp of name-calling, grudge, rancour and rumour in which the witch trials floated. In this brew of neighbourly conflict and superstitious scapegoating, it could be dangerous to be old, female, ugly, cussed, mentally ill, highly intelligent or anomalous. Most authorities agreed on the kind of person to look out for. Reginald Scot recognised in his sceptical *Discoverie of Witchcraft* (1584) that witches tended to be culled from the 'old, lame, blear-eyed, pale, foul and full of wrinkles ... lean and deformed, showing melancholy in their faces ... doting, scolds, mad, devilish'.[76] Many hanged women answer such descriptions: the three Bideford witches executed in 1682, for instance, were aged and confused women well placed to agree with the berserk 'confessions' fathered on them by their tormentors.

Temperance Lloyd, Susanna Edwards and Mary Trembles, the first two being widows, the last a spinster, also graphically exemplify the use of that essential forensic implement, 'the pin'. Investigation involved searching the body for protruberances which, when pricked, failed to hurt: the 'witch's mark'. Sceptics like the radical, John Webster, scorned these pseudo-scientific procedures. Poking needles into 'warts and hollow excrescences', he said, was an occupation for madmen. He noted that in his own remembrance 'here in Lancashire':

> diverse both men and women were accused for supposed witchcraft, and were so unChristianly, unwomanly, and inhumanely handled, as to be stripped stark naked, and to be laid upon tables and beds to be searched (nay even in their most privy parts) for these supposed witch-marks ...
>
> That there are diverse nodes, knots, protruberances, warts and excrescences that grow upon the bodies of men and women is sufficiently known to physicians ... Some have them from their mothers' wombs, some not, some fistulous and issue matter, some hollow and indolent, and many other ways ... Now if all these were witch-marks, then few would go free, especially those that are of the poorer sort, and that have the worst diet, and are but nastily kept.[77]

Discovery of the witch's 'teat', with which she had suckled her familiar devil, required the searching of genital organs and breasts for flaps of skin or irregularities by panels of matrons, skilled in detecting demonic signs in the age-slackened folds of the labia minora or the hypertrophied clitoris.[78]

At Bideford, the chief witch-finder, Anne Wakeley, and her panel were able clearly to discern two inch-long teats in Temperance Lloyd's private parts. Such discovery convinced even Temperance of her guilt; she confessed that these had been sucked by a 'black man' in the shape of a magpie.

Dorothy Waugh in the brank came perilously close to the margin between scold and witch. Quaker women ran about, sometimes half-naked, recklessly threatening and cursing the inhabitants of Leeds or Derby, Cambridge or Bristol in the name of God, and quoting biblical curses. They exhibited behaviour suggestive of demonic possession: trembling, quaking, blaring, trances, ululations, wild singings and gibberings. To them, divine delinquency signified God's indwelling presence. Removing items of dress to enact prophetic rituals truanted dangerously from human laws and the gender code: in a woman such display was interpreted as sexual rather than spiritual.[79] They stood on what has rightly been called a 'slippery continuum', at one end of which was the stereotype 'holy woman' but at the other 'the polluted whore or witch'.[80] How could the signs exhibited by a woman in a holy ecstasy be distinguished from those of an hysteric, a bewitched victim of a witch, or a woman who had sold herself to the devil?

They could not, except through pin, interrogation, and close sifting of 'evidence' by a pious judiciary. Frances Hill, in her illuminating account of the Salem witch trials,[81] has shown the establishment's reliance on the testimony of unstable teenage girls, exercising the only power available in a repressed Calvinist society by falling into 'fits' of possession through which they incriminated those they disliked or envied. 'Fits' characterised the mad, the damned, the possessed and the holy. Anne Bodenham, an elderly Wiltshire teacher and 'cunning woman', was a visionary who was executed as a witch in 1653. Her powers were interpreted as those of 'either a witch, or a woman of God'. Her trial took place in deafening uproar, in which, so excited were all parties, at times neither accused nor judge could hear one another speak.[82]

Anna Trapnel felt jittery about being searched as a witch, during her Cornwall expedition: a qualm came over her as she met the witch-trying woman's eye. Accusation would have triggered the downward spiral that ended at best in ignominy and at worst in death. We shall see her queasy stratagems for evading this threat. Mary Fisher and Ann Austin were searched as witches by the New England authorities. Barbara Blaugdone was nearly thrown overboard on her Irish journey on suspicion of raising the storm threatening the ship. George Fox himself, with his legendary charisma and hypnotic eyes, was suspected as a witch, for reasons he considered risible. But Fox himself boasted a genius for witch detection. Most of the witches mentioned in his *Journal* are women.[83] It was during the revolutionary years that the biggest English witch hunt of all time was conducted by yeasty-brained witch detectors Matthew Hopkins and John Stearne in East Anglia from 1645 to 1647: up to 200 witches were hanged, the detectors (whose motives seem to have been an uneasy combination of Puritan zeal with financial gain) using sleep deprivation, 'swimming' and disorientation to extract confessions, bolstered by popular testimony.

Long ago, Reginald Scot had perceived that the 'chief fault' of witches 'is that they are scolds'.[84] The cucking stool at Honiton was shown to a foreign visitor in 1760 as a museum piece which had once been used to punish witches. None of these sanctions could deter the magnificent scolds and shrews whose lives I have tried to capture in this book.

*

Their scolding still resonates today because they were able to scold in print, often in defiance of their own menfolk. 'Your printing of a book, beyond the custom of your sex,' spat Elizabeth Avery's bilious brother in 1650, 'doth rankly smell, but the exaltation of your self in the way of your opinions, is above all.'[85]

The Friends House Library in London has a box of vituperation exquisitely entitled 'The Bugg Box'. When you open this box, an explosion of invective flies out between the Quaker, Anne Docwra, and her ex- and anti-Quaker cousin, Francis Bugg.

Daughter of Royalist Judge, Sir William Waldegrave, she

tolerated no high-handedness, and when Fox came up with his plan for separate women's meetings, got straight on the stagecoach for London to upbraid him with her customary shrill bale. Writing in the 1680s and 90s, she looked back to 'the lash of the late times' and exhorted Friends to remain true to the revolutionary truths for which they had paid so dearly, especially the spiritual equality of men and women.[86]

Her exchange of abuse with Bugg in 1699 has all the relished acrimony of family feud. Bugg in *Jezebel Withstood, And her Daughter Anne Docwra, publickly Reproved* (9 April), complains she's a liar and a slanderer; he'll flatten her and then flounce off, to 'leave the old woman with her incoherent fables'. Railing against Anne as a Jesuitical prevaricator, he has to stop himself in mid-rant, 'else I shall exceed my half sheet, which I am willing to wind up this old woman in'.

He will tell 'this venomous woman', he splutters, that he is 'a man of as good name, fame and estate, as any Docwra I yet ever knew ... every way HER superior ... liar'.[87]

Anne has attacked him with *An Apostate-Conscience Exposed*, 'By an Ancient Woman, and Lover of the Truth'. She laments the appearance in print of a quarrelsome Suffolk Bugg; defends the Quakers as law-abiding (when they approve of the laws) and labels this detractor, this mere Bugg, 'a shatter-headed man', fit for the madhouse.[88]

He has had the effrontery to call her a 'She-Prelate'. 'She-Lawyer' perhaps. For she proudly attests that her father, the eminent judge, took away her girlish books and introduced her to the joys of reading 'the great Statute Book that lay upon the Parlour window', saying it was just 'as proper for a woman as a man to understand the laws, because they must live under them as well as men'. 'F. Bugg', knows perfectly well that during the persecution, her legal knowledge helped dissenters to argue their cases.

Bugg to the Quakers: 'turn this She-Goat out'.

Docwra to Bugg: 'of a shattered conscience, and shattered head'.[89]

Bugg of Docwra: 'I thought I had done, when I showed in *Jezebel Withstood* how this woman wheels about ... [but] with the dog turns and licks up her own vomit, which she spewed forth many years ago ... Quakers ... confident liars, abuseful forgers, Jesuits'.[90]

Close the Bugg Box, and a subdued murmuring is left thrumming under the lid: the seething quarrel of sect with sect, man with woman, patriarchy with dissident. A new conformist age sought to moderate or mute the dissidents of the second and third generation, but there would always be assertive, mutinous souls who would not forget; who refused the blinkering bonnet and the saintly servitude of the long counter-revolution, when, as Anne Docwra rued, the word 'enthusiasm' would be disowned. Don't be frightened, she exhorted her readers: 'this strange word *Enthusiasm*, is from a Greek word, and signifies in English, *inspiration*'.[91]

The women of this book represent the people Dryden satirised:

> A numerous host of dreaming saints succeed,
> Of the true old enthusiastic breed.[92]

The daughters and granddaughters of these enthusiasts would be the 'Female Inspirados' of the eighteenth-century 'Women's Meetings', 'perked up in their Pulpit Galleries', as their opponents continued to growl.

2
THE WRITING ON THE WALL
LADY ELEANOR DAVIES

Lady Eleanor Davies, daughter of the Earl of Castlehaven, is the forerunner of the prophetic women of the English Revolution. The anagrammatical, anti-grammatical prophetess predicted the deaths of Strafford, Laud and Charles I, as well as a host of lesser fry; undertook spectacular direct action against Church and State; published copiously and was committed to Bedlam, the Fleet, the Gatehouse and the Tower. 'Abominable stinking great simnel face excrement,' gnashed Christopher Brooke, one of the many who got on Eleanor's wrong side, 'a notable sluttish ornament of Bedlam'.[1] High-strung, autocratic, resentful of all patriarchal authority, Eleanor was a deviant who faced out her enemies with aristocratic fury.

The focal event of Eleanor's career occurred at Englefield, the Berkshire estate of her first husband, poet and lawyer Sir John Davies, on 28 July 1625. Eleanor was now in middle age, with a local reputation as a witch. Early one morning, under the Gallery at Englefield, she distinctly heard the prophet Daniel telling her, in the timbre of a trumpet, 'There is nineteen years and a half to the Day of Judgment and you as the meek Virgin.'[2]

The meek Virgin spent the next nineteen and a half years, from 1625 to 1644, as a hectically busy personal secretary to the Most High, admonishing the Antichrist and his minions. Her pen screeched across the page in pamphlet after pamphlet; her jagged handwriting scores the margins and frontispieces of her personal copies of her works, livid and ugly, defying and denying the profane government in the name of God, Daniel and Eleanor. The title page of her pamphlet, *Given to the Elector* (1633) carries an illustration of a woman's right hand, holding a quill. It issues from a gap in the wall, upon which it has written 'Mene peres': quoting from the 'writing on the wall' which the Babylonian tyrant, Belchazzar, received in the Book of Daniel, when, with wives, concubines, priests and a thousand high-born guests he was carousing from the sacred gold and silver vessels plundered from the temple of Jerusalem. Legs turning to jelly, he called for Daniel to interpret. Daniel, refusing a fee, answered as follows:

MENE: God hath numbered thy kingdom, and finished it.
TEKEL: Thou art weighed in the balances, and art found wanting.
PERES: Thy kingdom is divided, and given to the Medes and the Persians. (Daniel 5:26–8)

The tyrant died that night, his kingdom vanquished by Darius the Mede. Reformation painters loved this scene: Rembrandt's Belchazzar, a well-fed oriental, turns from the cluttered table to gape like a boor at the evolving writing, reminding us of the dramatic importance of the Daniel story as a reading of history. Lady Eleanor's learned contemporaries studied the Book of Daniel in conjunction with the Book of Revelation, basing complex computations of the manner and date of the Last Days upon the symbolism of their prophetic visions. Study of prophetic history was the ultimate discipline, a branch both of theology and science.[3] The Bible was a template for the study of history, unlocked by visionary master-keys. Recalling this reminds us of the vast cosmic ambition in Eleanor's claim to be a second Daniel, interpreter to her age, casting judgement on history.

A female Daniel? The notion was outrageous, and Lady Eleanor defensively assumed the veil of 'meek Virgin'. In her own maiden name she divined the anagram. ELEANOR AUDELIE: REVEALE O DANIEL. The wrist of the writing hand in the picture is imprinted with the word 'Reveale'. She offered her prophetic warning with a kind of frenzied beneficence, bringing to bear on a modern English Babylon (BELCHAZAR: BE-CHARLES) a message derided not only by Archbishop Laud who, at her first trial, burned her books before her face, but by both husbands.

When Sir John burned the papers she had given to the Archbishop of Canterbury in 1625, advising against the toleration of Queen Henrietta Maria's religion, she predicted her husband's death within three years: JOHN DAVES. JOVES HAND.[4] (At times it seemed expedient to juggle the letters slightly.) The meek Virgin went into immediate mourning and waited. At dinner on 4 December 1626, she burst into a flood of foreknowing tears. Three days later, 7 December, Sir John was dead.

Her second husband, Sir Archibald Douglas, also burned her prophecies. Eleanor, between bale and sorrow, predicted his downfall within three months. On 1 June 1631, Douglas 'was strooken bereft of his senses', while taking communion in St Martin's Church. She crowed that his power of speech deserted him, and that he made 'a noise like a brute creature': 'doubtless his heart changed into a beast's too, for so [he] would put his head into a dish of broth of lettuce or herbs and drink oil and vinegar, and sometimes beer altogether, insatiable that way'.[5] Her description of Sir Archibald's lettuce-lust owes much to her close scholarly reading of the Book of Daniel, for King Nebuchadnezzar fell from potentate to beast on all fours. 'Thy dwelling shall be with the beasts of the field,' Daniel told the scoffing potentate, 'they shall make thee to eat grass as oxen' (ie like oxen) (Daniel 4:32) – all of which comes to pass in the next verse and the 'same hour'. Like Daniel's, Lady Eleanor's predictions tended to come true with alarming rapidity. Courtiers melted away out of her line of advance, for she often named their death dates; and had alarmed many by accurately dooming the hated Duke of Buckingham.

*

Lady Eleanor was brought to trial by the Court of High Commission in 1633 for illegal publication of her books. In so doing, the revelatory lady perceived that the authorities damned themselves. She was charged with interpreting scriptures, 'which much unbeseemed her sex'; being a fake prophetess; and illegally printing books in Holland, and dispersing them in England. Laud, having been served with a handwritten sheet, 'to give him a taste or warning of his judgement at hand' (Daniel's 'writing on the wall'), was unimpressed with his branding as Belchazzar, and made a pyre of her books – to Eleanor an act worse than child-murder and rape, as she vehemently stated.

Suave court official, Sir John Lambe, had discerned, he informed the court, an anagram of his own in the remarkable lady's name. Would the court care to hear it? DAME ELEANOR DAVIES: NEVER SOE MAD A LADIE. Pantomiming her own style of delivery, he presented her with her own personal copy of the anagram to study at her leisure, to the convulsed mirth of the court.[6]

Fined £3000 (never paid), ordered to do penance at St Paul's Cross (refused) and confined to the Gatehouse Prison (protesting), Eleanor retorted every step of the way, decreeing a death sentence on Laud, and scrawling across her manuscript copy of the transcript of the trial, 'The gates of hell shall not prevail against her'.

The meek Virgin was visited by a vastly reassuring angel while in the Gatehouse: he not only consoled her with the promise that London would burn down but took his ease upon her bed, and on leaving, wafted an amber glove, so that an 'odoriferous scent' hung on the air, perfuming the malodorous room.[7] Angels, martyrdoms, revilings: all confirmed her high calling, even as she smarted from insults and witticisms aimed at one sublimely innocent of a sense of humour. After release in 1635, she exercised a preference for staying at inns called 'The Angel'.

In midsummer 1636, Lady Eleanor descended on Lichfield, where the cathedral was being beautified with gorgeous Laudian trimmings: swathes of arras were hung behind the altar, which was moved to the east; communion rails were erected and a bishop's seat built. Eleanor scrutinised these idolatrous anathemas. At

Michaelmas she moved from The Angel to lodge in the Cathedral Close with a clerk's wife, Susan Walker. Eleanor seems (for the only time in her life) to have enjoyed the solidarity of a tightly knit radical underground group of women, in whose company she discussed spiritual matters and hatched militant projects. On the given sign (presumably from God via Daniel to Eleanor) the group moved in on the cathedral. First they violated the status codes by occupying the seats reserved in the choir for gentlewomen; graduating to those beside the bishop's throne reserved for the posteriors of the wives of bishops, deans and canons.

No reaction.

Eleanor sent an astringent letter of protest to the bishop.

No answer.

Eleanor arose and again entered the cathedral. Applauded by Daniel, angelic hosts, Susan Walker and Marie Noble, the meek Virgin ascended to the bishop's throne, upon which she plonked herself down with all conceivable relish, and loudly declared herself to be Primate and Metropolitan. The group had brought along oblations, in the form of a kettle filled with hot tar and wheat paste, which Lady Eleanor in an original ceremony poured over the new altar hangings; abominable cloths she later denounced as coarse, woollen and purple.[8]

The nether region of a woman on a consecrated male chair was in itself a polluted and polluting affront to the holy bottoms of the ordained. Eleanor intended this affront. Her action was a complex symbolic violation by mirror reversal of an institution which had affronted God and the godly by pride, idol worship and oppression. It is possible that Eleanor had been briefed by an angelic messenger in a dream. In any case, she was only emulating the exhibitionism of the Old Testament prophets, with their bizarre parodies of corrupt societies, by profaning the profane. A generation later, the Quaker women would follow in her footsteps.

Let us pause to consider the nature of Lady Eleanor's insult to the bishop. The medieval image of woman as 'a temple built over a sewer' still held. When Lady Eleanor sat her female behind on that holy seat she placed there a contaminant – menstrual blood. Pliny had defined it as a 'fatal poison', corrupting and decomposing urine, depriving seeds of their fecundity, destroying insects, blasting garden flowers and grasses, causing fruits to fall from branches, dulling razors etc.[9]

If it is objected that Pliny had written this centuries ago, the reply is that male seventeenth-century 'science' believed that the more classical the opinion, the more settled its authority.

If it is objected that Lady Eleanor had probably reached the age of the menopause, and could hence offer no threat to episcopal purity, we must answer by pointing out that this made matters even worse. Post-menopausal women still collected the noxious blood in their wombs but could not shed it, so that it collected in a 'lump, & they are by that means so infectious, that they infect men with their breath.'[10]

Lady Eleanor knew exactly what she was doing when she assumed her position as Primate and Metropolitan. She knew that the bishop would have severe qualms about sitting there again. Consecrated water might have to be used to suit the throne to the rump of the Ordained.

The common women stood by Lady Eleanor: Susan refused outright to eject her from her house even when required to do so by the Chancellor of the Diocese. But Eleanor never mentioned these lowborn companions again.

This time she was condemned as a lunatic and sent to Bedlam, the asylum for the insane. This cannot have been unexpected. Women prophets ran a high risk of being judged mad, witches, or frauds; and the very enormity of a woman proclaiming her headship of the church, in conjunction with her determined bull-charging of authority and the derangements of her written (and perhaps spoken) style, must have suggested madness. There was also the problem of what to do with an unruly aristocrat. Besides, she had soiled the seat of highest cleanliness. Laud wrote to King Charles requesting that Eleanor 'may be so restrained, as she may have no more power to commit such horrible profanations'.[11]

More quarrelling in Bedlam. The steward, a noted drunk, complains that she keeps trying to escape.

Lady Eleanor protests about the foul manners and beastly practices of the steward.

A special room is built for Lady Eleanor, to muffle the high-caste, high-nuisance guest in this inferno of misery, in which the wails of pitifully chained sufferers torture her like the spirits of the blaspheming damned: 'the grave exchanged for Hell', she says of quitting the Gatehouse for Bedlam.[12]

Nothing quenches her: new insights dawn, even in this pit. The archbishop has condemned her because he is mad, she sees that clearly, pondering the name of her prison – BETHLAM: LAMBETH. The angry anagram says it all.[13]

The previous year, Charles and Henrietta Maria, taking an afternoon off to visit Bedlam, amused themselves by coming to 'see the mad folks', and were reportedly 'madly entertained'. By the time Eleanor is released, via the Tower, in September 1640, the writing on the wall stands out luminously for Charles and the queen whom Eleanor denounces as his Delilah in *Samsons Legacie* (1643). The tide has turned, and, staying at the Angel, Kensington, strapped for cash, alternately exulting in freedom and vindication and tingling with bitterness at her wrongs, Eleanor is able to watch her prophecies come true one by one: Strafford's execution, followed by the joy of the loathed Laud's decapitation in 1645. This is a timely coincidence, as Eleanor's confidence has been wavering. When Daniel confided that the world would end in nineteen and a half years, she took his arithmetic at its face-value: hence, 1644 and 1645 see a surge of fifteen published tracts. In spring of 1645, she writes to her daughter Lucy her regret that she has not been able to visit for so long: the End of the World has kept her urgently busy. She would have come 'had not this been the long expected time come of seeing the end of such a troublesome world'.[14]

1645 comes and goes. Eleanor slows down, to take stock. Minor annoyances buzz around her in the form of debts she high-handedly brushes off, which land her in prison, and a quarrel with Gerrard Winstanley the Digger, who demands pay for men who have worked on her estate. Lady Eleanor pecks him with her angry beak in the barn at Pirton: does he not know she is the 'prophetess Melchisedecke', Queen of Peace?

Winstanley, concerned with the food in men's mouths, has no interest in the abstruser aspects of prophetic computation. 'What's the reason men call upon you for money, which you truly owe them,' he demands, 'and you either put them off by long delays, or else make them spend ten times more to it in suits of law, whereas you have estate sufficient that you might pay all?'[15]

Across Winstanley's irritating letter, the meek Virgin scrawls, 'Hee is mistakne', and leaves it at that.

All things (apart from money matters) are working together to validate Lady Eleanor's prophecies. Her head is kept in a constant state of fermentation. The king's execution in 1649; Cromwell's victory at the Battle of Worcester in 1651. New anagrams are begotten in the ferment, notably CROMWELL: HOWL ROME. And look at his initials: surely the O is like an eye? the C like a horn? Like lambs' eyes and horns? Like the sun and the moon? Her pen scratches its inspirations as she decodes the arcane meanings that glint through our darkly hieroglyphic alphabet from the Other World.

She died in July 1652, aged 62, to be buried by her loyal, long-suffering daughter, Lucy, who honoured her mother with a magnificent epitaph, including tributes to her humility (a quality uncourted by the meek Virgin), her learned, lofty mind and her 'pleasing affability, singular modest: In a woman's body a man's spirit ... Nay she was full of God'.[16]

*

Demonic, deranged, or too brilliant a mind, linguistically challenging? To make an assessment, we need to remember that Lady Eleanor's hieroglyphic theory of language was only an extreme form of a venerable Christian tradition of language as a code for God's hidden reality. Language fell with Eve and Adam, but the fall had left vestiges of original meaning. Abstruse eccentricity was at home in this decoders' world. Add to this the fact that a prophet would be expected to speak a different dialect from the non-prophesying masses.

Studying the microfilm of Eleanor's tracts, one's head swings with vertigo. For she did not conceive herself bound to grammatical rules. Her grammar is at once haughty and distraught, a stunning scramble of ideas which relate by an interior dynamic.

If I were to represent it on this page, I would want to present it as a mindprint of electrical discharges, chain-reacting along arbitrary links of words. This mindstorm evolves its own kind of logic, after which the trained, if giddy, reader of Lady Eleanor learns to stumble. In *Samsons Legacie*, she attacks King Charles' dependence on his Catholic queen by linking his history with that of Samson and his two disastrous wives. Lady Eleanor subscribes to a patriarchal account of history (blaming perverse government on the influence of a *femme fatale* on male laxness), but favours Protestant queens, like 'old Samuel, godly Queen Elizabeth' (p8) who, like Eleanor, transcends gender. She begins by telling Parliament that, if they do not seize the hour, on their own heads be it. Blame themselves, not Lady Eleanor, who has a recipe for bringing 'Him again to Himself, I mean the king; after absent so long from his Parliament', ie, she will reconcile the king's 'two bodies', his own person and his Parliament.

> Her before, named his *Heifer*, and *this* woman she of the *Philistines* breed too, both of them one in effect: or two witnesses as it were: Herewithall bidden to take heed all, of Close-under-hand-dealers: For the *holy Ghost* is not without a double, or two-fold meaning in these thirty shirts wrapped up. (p4)

Her before? Heifers? Thirty shirts? It is Eleanor's method to shoot in and out of the Bible, traversing two thousand years in a second, on a perpetual two-way journey that is no sooner travelling hither than it is on its way back thither. The Old Testament Samson took not just one but two non-Jewish wives, the 'woman of Timna' and Delilah. The Jews could have seen disaster coming. Likewise, Charles engaged himself in a notable farce to the Spanish Infanta, another Catholic, before he married the French Catholic. Eleanor had no time to squander on spelling it out for the reader, but this is the gist.

And, for God's sake, why should a busy prophet be clearer about it than she is? For after all, 'these [writings] not for disputation-sake; but made for dispatch, not so wide and full of stuff as others are acknowledged. If it sit close, 'tis as becoming Joseph in making himself known to his brethren, in haste told them, I am Joseph' (*Samsons Legacie*, p6). In other words, these are not argumentative or weightily studious works but whirlwind jottings and memoranda, taken down on the run from galloping Inspiration to target a concise warning on history hurtling to Doomsday: never mind verbs or word order. Sort it out yourself. Impatient 'etceteras' flick neurotic tails from paragraph-ends, while the prophet crabwise scuttles from strange puns to stranger anagrams.

Occasionally Eleanor flings a scrap of hope to the reeling reader: a promise of clarity she might (and might not) fulfil: 'And to be somewhat ... plainer herein'. Charles lost the chance for 'rooting that slip out, *blind Heresy Her* Majesty's *darling*' (p7). Yet again the electrical discharge sparks: 'MAGORMISSABIB' may the queen's army be called. 'But to return ...' (pp16–17).

Return to what? Endlessly Eleanor is recalled to her own most traumatic memories: the odious little archbishop on the never-to-be-forgotten day of her books' crucifixion, simpering as he brings the candle flame toward her precious work: 'the word of God, in the month October 23. was burned, suffered martyrdom by a candle, *from his own hand*, at the High Commission board sacrificed'; at which time two armies were striving for victory in the fields near 'where the Heavenly voice was heard first at Englefield House' (pp8–19). Again and again she told the stories of her prophetic call at Englefield to take a central part in world history; and her degradation at the pudgy hands of Laud. In the end, hers is a personal story of self-assertion against the gender order, church and state, in the name (as she without false modesty signs herself) of 'the Blessed LADIE, In her day of Lent etc'.

*

Precursor to the prophesying women of the Revolution, Lady Eleanor Davies outdid every radical popular hero for manic drive and martyrdom. But unlike Prynne, Bastwick, Burton and Lilburne, she was never a popular hero. She was too odd an angel. Her pride was not magnanimity; her singularity never brought under its wing a people's cause. She was elect above the elect – her very name proved it: EL-EANOR: EL-ECT: EL-IAS (the prophet). A disturber of the peace, with megalomaniac compensation fantasies, she had nothing to offer the parched or needy soul, whether of spiritual refreshment like Margaret Fell or civil justice like Katharine Chidley. She challenged patriarchy by vesting truth and knowledge in a matriarchal consciousness, and confounding the word order by a not-quite anarchic unruliness.

3

PEACE WOMEN & SEA-GREEN LEVELLERS
ELIZABETH LILBURNE, MARY OVERTON
& KATHARINE CHIDLEY

'Away with these women, we were best to have a parliament of Women!' snarled the Duke of Richmond, waylaid as he struggled to enter the House of Lords on 31 January 1642, by a throng of several hundred petitioning women.[1] He was carrying his ducal staff, and perhaps ill-advisedly used it as an oar to scull his way through the crush, for some of the desperate women clutched this symbol of privilege, demanding an answer to the petition they had delivered the day before. They were hungry; the economy had nose-dived into depression, and mobs of the 'rabble' were daily clamouring for relief at the House of Lords ('popish Lords' whose lack of co-operation they blamed for their present catastrophe). What the women needed was bread for their children, who they threatened to plant on the Lords to mother. What they got was the scoff of the king's cousin, and the wagging of his ensign of office in their faces.

The women wrenched at the staff; the affronted Duke yanked it back, and the staff stuck in mid-air between the two grappling parties, then cracked. The Duke, voted a dangerous malignant by the Commons,[2] was pitched deeper into farcical indignity by a pack of females, with absolute desperation in their faces. He was forced to send for another staff.

Lord Savage was more conciliatory and mindful of his accoutrements. He offered blandishments and delivered the petition to the Lords,

> and upon reading, and some debate thereof, they gave order that twelve of the petitioners should be called into the House of Lords, to declare their grievances, which was done accordingly.

The women must have looked round in wonder at the august interior of this centre of male and aristocratic power, its walls invisibly quaking under the shock of incipient civil war.

On Tuesday, 1 February, women surged around the Commons, who were informed of the presence of:

> great multitudes of women at the Houses, pressing to present a Petition to the Parliament; and their language is, that where there is One Woman now here, there would be five hundred tomorrow; and that it was as good for them to die here, as at home.

Sergeant-Major Skippon, commander of the City Militia, was asked to do his best to 'pacify the multitude, and send them home in quietness'. He was to explain that the gentlemen had weighty matters under consideration, and would take care of everything in due course.[3]

4 February: more women, with a petition against bishops. Mrs Anne Stagg, 'a gentlewoman and brewer's wife', led a deputation said to consist of others 'of like rank and quality'. These women were warmly welcomed. Substantial citizens' wives, they brought precisely the message Parliament wanted to hear. Pym, Strode and Penington, the cream of the Commons, sallied out to thank and commend them, assuring them that the petition 'is come in a seasonable time'. All smiles and friendliness.[4]

So far, the women's petitions had been amiably received, apart from the fracas over the Duke's staff. But all that was to change.

*

8 August 1643. Shoals of Peace Women wearing white ribbons in their hats and pinned to their breasts mobbed Westminster. With uproar, crying, 'Peace! Peace!', they demanded an end to the civil conflict ruining livelihoods and killing their husbands. At one point they charged the entrance to the House and, crowding up the staircase, blocked it, creating pandemonium; soldiers beat them back with the flat of their swords. 'Yesterday in the afternoon,' reported the newspaper *Certaine Informations*, with the English press's legendary spirit of objectivity:

> two or three hundred oyster wives, and other dirty and tattered sluts, took upon them the impudency to come to the honourable House of Commons, and cried for Peace and Propositions, and they so filled the stairs that no man could pass up or down, whereupon a man upon the top of the stairs drew his sword and with the flat side struck some of them upon the heads, which so affrighted them that they presently made way and ran down.[5]

Only one paper, *The Parliamentary Scout*, reported the demonstration without snorts of scorn. The Peace Women retreated, promising speedy return.

Next day, 9 August, they were back, in fuller force, wearing white silk ribbons claimed to have been provided by one or both of two great ladies resident in Westminster and Southwark respectively: for how could females of their class have afforded to buy a piece of silk for political statement? The Peace Women were observed by scoffing male hacks to be mostly 'whores, bawds, oyster-women, kitchenstuff women, beggar women, and the very scum of the suburbs, besides abundance of Irish women'.[6] These dregs of society had taken upon themselves to invade the sanctum of government, to make known their rage against the powers that be. But such women had no political existence – even a minus quantity of existence, being 'covered' by voteless males.

Legally speaking then, this loudmouthed horde did not exist. But the noise went on; the voiceless gave voice to their sense of wrong. Headcounts of these nobodies varied from five hundred to six thousand, according to the political affiliation or imagination of the person doing the counting. They were alleged to pounce on figures of authority, roughing them up. Yesterday Sir Simonds d'Ewes, MP and diarist had heard them threatening to do violence to those in Parliament who were enemies to peace; though other observers said they protested peacefully, with babes-in-arms.

Today they beat up the Trained Bands' sentinels at the Old Palace yard, and swarmed in. Women arrived by water, clashing with another batch of sentinels, whom they eluded by landing 'a little higher ... upon the West side of the yard:

> and then all of them cried out mainly, we will have Peace
> presently and our King, and this was their constant cry to
> all the Peers as they came to their House.

Cries were heard not only for Peace, but keening for 'their slain and imprisoned husbands'.[7] Even if these women were being exploited by Royalists, as the war party claimed, their feelings and interests were deeply engaged on the side of peace. Many women begged their sons and husbands to go underground rather than fight for either side. Jonathan Priestley, child of a West Riding clothier, vividly remembered his mother accompanying his brother Samuel a quarter of a mile along his way to join up with Fairfax's Army, and 'besought him with tears not to go'. Samuel saw no option. '"Mother," saith he, "Pray be content; if I stay at home I can follow no employment, but be forced to hide myself in one hole or another ... I had rather venture my life ... in a good cause."'[8]

The Peace Women derided the soothing oil which a bland spokesman discharged on their stormy waters. They turned nasty (it is said) and assaulted MPs and officials going about their business, ripping the cloak and band of a particularly short-haired Minister, crying out 'A Roundhead!' Beating the outer door of Parliament, they attempted to rush it in powerful surges, clamouring for leaders Pym and Strode and select roundheads to be sent out and be ducked in the Thames: a punishment for scolds.

For two hours they womaned the door at the head of the upper steps, having flung the sentinels down. No MP could get in or out. The Trained Bands fired blanks at them, at which they

scoffed, 'Nothing but powder!' and flung a hail of brickbats, to a
united yell of 'Give us these traitors that are against Peace, that we
may tear them in pieces, give us Pym!'

In the end, Waller's Horse charged ('Waller's Dogs!' the cry
went up),[9] and though they claimed to use only the flat of the
sword, women's faces and hands unavoidably ended up bleeding,
and one woman's nose was chopped off. She is reported to have
died thereafter and another young woman was shot. Everyone else
ran away; a few of the more ferocious, and those suspected of being
men in women's clothing, being removed to Bridewell, amongst
them 'a most deformed Medusa, or Hecuba, with an old rusty
blade by her side'.[10] It was thought prudent to tie the hands of this
aged person as she was marched off to custody.

Her comrades had promised to return the following day with
guns and swords, and to demolish all the defensive fortifications
around London. This was no empty threat, as women built some
of them in the first place.

*

On 9 August, Sir Thomas Knyvett, a little man in a big quandary,
implicated in the Royalist Lowestoft rising and trapped in London
struggling in the mesh of threatened sequestration, is an eyewitness
to the Peace Women's exploits and the militia's heroic deeds. His
pen, as he transmits the day's events to his wife, Katherine, quivers
with the stress and distress of the historical moment. He is at his
wits' end as to what to advise concerning Katherine's coming up to
London. On Monday night, following a day of blaring anti-Peace
demonstrations in which louts crammed every adjacent passage-
way, the Commons voted down the Lords' six proposals for Peace.

> Tuesday morn a multitude of women came & made an
> outcry for Peace. Some verbal satisfaction they had, & no
> hurt done that day. This day they came again in a far greater
> number, & fell to be more unruly, wch occasioned a sadder
> spectacle, diverse men & women being slain by the trained
> guard. Such a combustion hath been today, & likely to be
> worse, that, as well as I love thee, I cannot wish thee here
> yet. I rather wish myself with thee, or in some other place
> out of this town.[11]

Knyvett ends by dating his distraught letter 'this unhappy Wednesday'. In reading, we have the sense of history experienced in the moment; a moment which is eternally volatile and out of control. For the next morning, Thursday 10 August, everything seems amazingly calm. Hypertensive emergency has given way to the tranquillised detachment of anecdote:

> Sweet
> Heart, every day alters our minds here ... This day all is calm and the great storm over, wch we hope now will continue. There was much mischief done by the horse & foot soldiers, diverse killed dead. One remarkable passage – A man that keeps a shop by the hall door that sells Spectacles had a daughter served a sempstress in the hall. This man, being heard to say, but a little before, that he had rather see the streets run with blood than that we should now have Peace, soon after, one told him there was a pretty young wench shot dead in the churchyard. 'No matter,' quoth this wretch, 'if a hundred of them were served so,' and, going to see this joyful spectacle, found it his own daughter. You may be bold to report this, for 'tis very true. Now my thoughts are settled, I wish thee here with all my heart.[12]

Knyvett, who is himself of the Peace Party, wanting nothing more than to be at home with Katherine and his daughters 'Buss and Muss', eating cheese and ham and keeping the mutinous tenantry in their place, crows over the Nemesis reaped by the militant optician. But the Puritan Sir Simonds d'Ewes praises the spectacle-maker as 'a religious honest man', whose daughter had been targeted by a 'profane fellow' with a grudge,[13] and notes that the bereaved father could 'never to this day procure justice to be done upon the malefactor'. The trooper, sent to the Gatehouse, has claimed that his pistol went off by mistake. One thing is clear: the servant girl was not a Peace Woman. Like so many of the civilian casualties of war, she got in the way. Her young life, so vital one day, so shocking in its sudden extinction, is by the following morning the stuff of tales written up by Puritan diarists or posted home by exiled husbands, in a world of lightning turbulence which longs to earth itself in tittle-tattle. A world, moreover, of pamphlets and broadsides advertising themselves as 'A True Relation', 'A True Account', in a teeming culture of hearsay, rumour mongering, slander, bent facts, delusion and false witness. '*You may be bold to report this, for 'tis very true*', Knyvett assures Katherine, acknowledging the tallness of the tale in a culture where everything has come into question.

*

No one was cowed by petticoat mutiny, the mood being one of amused exasperation, save insofar as the demonstrations were viewed as symptomatic of a breakdown in order and the machinations of Royalists and the Peace Party in Parliament. The newspaper, *The Parliamentary Scout*, in August 1643 pointed out: 'Thus we see, to permit absurdities, is the way to encourage them; tumults are dangerous, swords in women's hands do desperate things; this is begotten in the distractions of the Civil Wars.' The venture of women into public life was seen as self-evidently ridiculous, token of the tendency of the revolutionary world to turn everything upside down. Mockery of the women, labelling them sluts, down-and-outs and Irish, however, defused one threat only to kindle another: fear of the vast class of paupers scraping a living, crumbs away from destitution, a constant threat to 'law and order' and property. Women were at the bottom of this surging mass of near-destitution.

When the Peace Women were slandered as 'Whores, bawds, oyster-women, kitchenstuff women, beggar women ... scum of the suburbs ... Irish women', the slanderers were biting hands that had fed them. For Billingsgate fishwives and oyster-women had been mobilised for some time. With the breakdown of English institutions in the throes of the Civil War, the whole of London had been on the streets, shouting slogans. All classes and both genders were politicised:

> The oyster-women locked their fish up
> And trudged away to cry 'No Bishop'.[14]

The problem for Parliament during the 1640s was shrewdly discerned by Charles I, in his reply to Parliament's Nineteen Propositions of June 1642, pointing out that the politicised mass of 'have-nots' would recognise their enemy not just in the Crown, but in all the 'haves': they would 'set up for themselves, call parity and independence liberty ... destroy all rights and properties, all distinctions of families and merit'.[15] The Peace Women's assault derived its focus and attack from energies the Revolution liberated. Yet the Peace Women used this new consciousness to express an essentially counter-revolutionary view: uncommitted to either side (though possibly exploited by Royalist sympathisers in London and the Peace Party in Parliament), they were driven not by ideology but by pragmatic hatred of war.

*

September 1646. Women were back. Members of Parliament and civil servants squinting out of windows registered their presence with irritation. They found the corridors and stairs blocked; as well as the door of the Chamber. An order was issued to the guards to clear them out. The principal women differed both in class and cause from the Peace Women. Fishwives were less evident. Led by Elizabeth Lilburne, wife of the imprisoned Leveller leader, they comprised 'some scores of gentlewomen her friends' and 'follow the House day by day, with importunate widows' crying for unpaid pensions and arrears.[16] The war widows riled Bulstrode Whitelock with their 'rude and impetuous' behaviour, as they screamed at MPs shouldering through the crowds, ' "Pay us our money, we are ready to starve", and seeming ready to tear their clothes from their backs'.[17] Whereas the Peace Women were assumed to be a front for Royalists, the demonstrations inaugurated in 1646 represented the womenfolk of the radical left-wing which Parliament found at least as odious.

The waves of women who petitioned Parliament in the late 1640s were led by 'gentlewomen' or women of 'middling' rank. The viragos wore green ribbons rather than white; attached to black ones when they followed the procession at the funeral of the executed Leveller Army leader, Robert Lockier, on 29 April 1649: 'the bonny Besses in the sea-green dresses'.[18] This funeral was one of the greatest political demonstrations of the Revolution. Staggering numbers shoaled through the city, members of the New Model Army distinguished by red ribbons on their left arms, signifying solidarity to death. The women's green and black ribbons at once maintained and mourned a cause virtually lost with Cromwell's and Ireton's expert manipulation of the Army's radicalism and liquidation of some of its leaders.

Women again stood out vividly amongst the reputedly 10,000 strong crowd which petitioned Parliament in August 1648 to release Lilburne from prison or give him a fair trial. In April and May 1649 they presented a 'humble' petition denouncing military rule and arbitrary power, the decay of trade, soaring cost of living, starvation, unemployment, tithes, excise, monopolies, free quarter. They demanded the release of the four Leveller leaders: John Lilburne, William Walwyn, Thomas Prince and Richard Overton. The petition of 23 to 25 April was allegedly signed by 10,000 women and delivered by 500. A hostile reporter spotted fishwives out in force: 'the meek-hearted congregation of oyster-wives, the civil-suited sisterhood of oranges and lemons, and likewise the mealy-mouthed muttonmongers'. Blankly, sleekly, the Government turned down the petition. The Sergeant at Arms was despatched to remind the women that politics was a mystery beyond the compass of the female brain. Let them return without more ado to their kitchens, there to wash dishes and attend to 'your own business ... your housewifery'. We have none left to wash, retorted the women. The Government reminded them that it had already replied (negatively) to their husbands' petition. It was surely obvious that no civilised, breeches-wearing, short-haired government was accountable to persons flouncing around in petticoats.

Accounts vary as to how and when the women dispersed. Some say they confronted the soldiers, and that a woman who grabbed Oliver Cromwell by the cloak and refused to let go, subjected him to a vigorous political lecture. Others say the women departed quietly.[19]

*

Who were the Leveller women and what was their motivation? Though they mobilised a large-scale political organisation comparable with that of the Quaker women, a network able to respond in emergency with lightning rapidity, little is known of them individually. Only Katharine Chidley and Elizabeth Lilburne remain really visible, together with the wives of the other Leveller leaders: Mary Overton, Mary Prince and Mrs Walwyn. Of these, Katharine Chidley as the spokesperson of the Independent movement (separatists emphasising the supremacy of individual conscience) gives a clue to the structure of the sophisticated organisation operated by the Leveller women. The organisation had access to the web of Congregationalist cells, a system of militantly radical contacts extending throughout the capital and southern shires, each cell having loose affiliates which could be called upon for signatures and support. The women's petition for the release of the four Leveller leaders was promoted at several Independent meetings on Sunday 22 April, all women being advised to 'deliver in their subscriptions to the women which will be appointed in every ward and division to receive the same'.[20] This networking relied not only upon the existence of an underground administration of local women who could be called into action at any time but upon access to the means of clandestine printing. Richard Overton, Thomas Prince and William Larner were all radical printers who published illegal pamphlets, distributed by Levellers, especially women, whose gender offered a certain camouflage. Leveller texts were busily run off the presses, passed from hand to hand, inflammatory broadsheets posted on walls and tracts bundled into safe houses: a kindling for the mind, incendiary to the state. When Leveller printers were jailed, their wives continued to print and distribute.

*

How women came to espouse the Leveller cause with such passion and commitment we cannot know for certain, although (as their petitions show) many of their concerns were obviously 'women's issues'. The soaring cost of living and the scarcity of basic foods in London hit poorer women hard; high taxation, the breakdown of trade, unemployment and arrest for debt amongst the ruined were of desperate daily concern to women. In September 1647, the Essex minister, Ralph Josselin, records in his diary: 'things are at that rate as never was in our days, wheat 8/-, malt: 4/-, beef 3d., butter 6. ob. [halfpenny], cheese 4d, candle 4d, candle 7d, currants 9d, sugar 18d, and every other thing soever dear.'[21] In the capital, the collapse of the economy under the strain of years of war and chaos, and new taxations, was more dire. 'The Mournful Cries of many thousand Poore tradesmen, who are ready to famish through decay of Trade' in January 1648, articulates urban desperation:

> Oh that the cravings of our stomachs could be heard by the Parliament and City! Oh that the tears of our poor famishing babes were bottled! Oh that their tender mothers' cries for bread to feed them were engraven in brass ...
>
> O you Members of Parliament and rich men in the City, that are at ease, and drink wine in bowls, and stretch yourselves on beds of down, you that grind our faces and flay off our skins ... Is there none to pity? ...
>
> O Parliament men, and soldiers! Necessity dissolves all Laws and Government, and Hunger will break through stone Walls; Tender Mothers will sooner devour you, then the fruit of their own womb.[22]

This inflammatory pamphlet was probably compiled by Leveller tradesmen of Wapping and Southwark. It emphasises economic hardship as it bears upon the carers of households, making militants out of those who trusted in Parliament to amend their grievances. The Leveller women's petitions emphasise the misery of debtors' wives and children; the horror of watching children starve; the gross inequity of the law as it affected the poor: 'Our houses being worse than prisons to us, and our lives worse than death' (5 May 1649).[23] In the Levellers, women could see a group of people prepared to speak to their needs and those of the community.

For some it was a matter of personal devotion. Both men and women responded to the charisma and courage of John Lilburne: Katherine Hadley, an elderly spinster, cared for him in the Fleet Prison after his flogging all the way from the Fleet to Westminster on 18 April 1638, an ordeal of five hundred lashes of a three-thonged corded whip upon his bare back, which left his shoulders 'swelled almost as big as a penny loaf with the bruises of the knotted cords', as Mary Dorman testified.'[24] Katherine Hadley devoted herself to the shackled Lilburne and his cause, hectoring the authorities, smuggling out manuscripts and distributing his clandestine pamphlets amongst apprentices holidaying at Moorfields at Whitsun, 1639. She was immediately arrested, but the pamphlets had the effect of sending the apprentices to riot round Lambeth Palace. Imprisoned amongst prostitutes in the filth and squalor of Poultney Counter and then Bridewell, Katherine protested vehemently; at her release a year and a half later, Lilburne squeezed a few pounds compensation out of the Lord Mayor. Mary Dorman was vocal and defiant in testifying for Lilburne, bearing witness to his public whipping, and berating the judge amid the 'furious hurly-burly' of his 1653 trial. A woman got up in the pulpit of Somerset House and preached on his behalf; and Elizabeth Lilburne placed her body between his and the soldiers' muskets when he was taken to the Tower in 1648.

In Elizabeth Lilburne we see the stresses involved in being the female partner of a driven, turbulent idealist, adversarial, incapable of compromise, facing prison with manic fortitude and requiring support from a family he kept at full stretch. The indefatigable Elizabeth petitioned at the bar of the House of Commons, heavily pregnant, during his Oxford captivity by the Royalists, saving his life; she set up house with him in Newgate Gaol in 1645, this time the prisoner of Parliament, charged with slandering the Speaker. Again she was pregnant, only to have all her baby-linen filched from her house by the Stationers' agents rummaging out seditious books (and anything else they could find) in her chest at home. The crowds' champion, Lilburne was daring, reckless and magnificently pugnacious in defence of 'this sick, swooning, bleeding, and dying nation'.[25] Dragging along in his wake was a family of little Lilburnes, also often sick, swooning, bleeding, dying, whose welfare was not guaranteed by their warm-hearted father's sublime self-immolations: 'the miseries of the widow and fatherless', compassionated in *England's Birth-right Justified*, the earliest manifesto of the Leveller party, were experienced by Elizabeth and her children long before she was literally widowed in 1657.

In 1647 Elizabeth was arrested for disseminating Lilburne's propaganda and was brought, with him, before the Committee of Examinations. As the Committee constantly interrupted her husband's flamboyant diatribe, querying the right of the assembly to act as a court, she gave vent to an outburst of rage:

I told thee often enough long since, that thou would serve
the Parliament, and venture thy life so long for them, till
they would hang thee for thy pains, and give thee Tyburn
[the gallows] for thy recompense, and I told thee besides,
thou shouldst in conclusion find them a company of injust,
and unrighteous Judges, that more sought themselves, and
their own ends, than the public good of the kingdom, or
any of those that faithfully adventured their lives therefore.[26]

Lilburne, all milky-mild irony, requested the Chairman 'to pass by
what in the bitterness of her heart being a woman she had said' –
that is, what they both thought. The moment is enlightening not
only in colouring the character of Elizabeth Lilburne with a vivid
dye of defiance, but in showing how women could flauntingly
capitalise in public upon their supposed weakness of control and
intellect. As Lilburne whimsically confides in his fellow males, she's
only a woman; she can't help scolding. Elizabeth was discharged on
the grounds that she was misbehaving under her husband's
instructions: 'covert', and therefore not responsible for her own
acts.

Petitioning, marching, agitating, producing and dispersing
subversive books, bearing two of her children in prison (one in
Newgate, the other in the Tower, himself christened 'Tower'),
Elizabeth's struggles took an immense toll. She had to watch two
sons die of smallpox. Lilburne's triumphant acquittal of high
treason in 1649 was followed by exile, during which Elizabeth
miscarried. Driven to selling or pawning her household goods, she
angrily refused to sanction any further heroics. Her letters were, he
complained, 'filled with womanish passion and anger'. In 1653 he
wrote to Cromwell blaming him for breaking her spirit, for 'some
of her late childish actions' have 'in some measure, produced an
alienation of affection in me to her'. He spoke of her as one 'whom
I *formerly* loved as my own life'. When Elizabeth disagreed with
Lilburne, she was acting 'womanishly'; when she acted in his cause,
she was a woman 'of a masculine spirit'. Recklessly he returned to
England, to face a new trial – another acquittal – new
imprisonments, during which she pleaded with Cromwell to
release his 'impatient spirit, wearied out with long and sore

afflictions',[27] promising to be answerable for his quietness. He died a Quaker in 1657, in Elizabeth's arms, leaving her to beg a pension from Cromwell. In a life of toil and storm, the personal was sacrificed to the public.

Leveller women endured dawn raids by soldiers, the rifling of households, seizure of their husbands, and (because of their own political activism), imprisonment and separation from their children. They might be left at home penniless, sick, with the family business to run, not knowing whether their husbands would live or die. These experiences constituted an unnerving political education in what can happen in a 'free' country to those stepping out of line. The violence they experienced fed their unintimidated assaults upon the doors of Parliament.

*

On 11 August 1646, soldiers with swords and muskets smashed their way into the house of Richard and Mary Overton, on the order of the House of Lords, removing Richard to the Prerogative Bar of the Lords and thence to Newgate. In a second raid, soldiers ransacked the home, plundered Mary's goods and removed the source of the family's livelihood (a printing press), requiring Mary, together with Richard's brother, Thomas, to testify before the Lords. Since the Levellers regarded the House of Lords as an illegal institution of arbitrary power, forced on the English nation at the Norman Conquest, Mary refused to go. She was committed to Maiden Lane prison, carrying her six-month-old unweaned baby: 'we, our husbands, brethren, friends and servants, contrary to all Law ... are kept and mewed up in your starving, stinking, murthering prison-houses', while scores of Royalist delinquents are pardoned and rehabilitated, complains her petition.[28] If Richard wrote Mary's petition for her, as has been suggested, it was inspired by her heroic resistance to armed violence and sexual harassment, wrenched from her three elder children, pregnant, with an unweaned baby in her arms. The baby was to die.

From Maiden Lane Mary was ordered to be removed to Bridewell, but as Overton comments in his grimly comic account, *The Commoner's Complaint,* the officers encountered problems in removing so powerful an adversary. She tells the Marshall 'in plain downright terms' that she will not obey, since she does not recognise the legality of the House of Lords.

> The Turkey-cock Marshall ... bristled his feathers and
> looked as big and as bug as a Lord and in the height and
> scorn of derision (just as if he had been Speaker to the
> House of Peers ...) out he belched his fury and told her, that
> *if she would not go, then she should be carried in a Porter's*
> *Basket, or else dragged at a Cart's Arse.*[29]

No, she replies mildly to this civilised persuasive, she will not go:

> out he struts in his Arbitrary Fury, as if he would have
> forthwith levied whole Armies, and Droves of Porters, and
> Carmen, to advance the poor little harmless innocent
> woman and her tender Babe to Bridewell. (pp7–8)

The Marshall, rattled, barges in and out again, shooing away her
friends, and returns with two porters, who quail from this
distasteful duty. They rapidly quit, saying this is work for gaolers
not porters.

Off marches the Marshall to raise new forces, returning with
the carter, who likewise backs off.

Finally the official, baffled by the fundamental decency of the
common man, collects a gang of gaolers, servants 'or hangmen
Deputies, and therewith resolved to storm her'. Sidling up to the
door, he smooths his tongue to woo Mary into coming quietly; but
Mary refuses:

> Whereupon he caused his men to break open the door, and
> entering her chamber, struts toward her like a crow in a
> gutter, and with his valiant looks of mettle assails her and
> her babe, and by violence attempt[s] to pluck the tender
> babe out of her arms, but she forcibly defended it, and kept
> it in despite of his manhood. (p19)

The underlings manhandle Mary downstairs into the street, the
baby screaming as they half-drag, half-carry her on two cudgels,
bawling 'strumpet' and 'whore', to ruin her sexual credit if and
when she gets out of prison (p20). The abuse of Mary is the
propaganda-centre of Overton's tract: the State is seen as violating
the traditional sanctity of the mother–baby bond. Her physical

fragility is stressed, to reinforce her defiance. The tract documents the courage of a woman handicapped by a middle-class seventeenth-century wife's human burdens and responsibilities, in defying the state machine. As a mother, she is presented as ordinary and typical; as a Leveller, extraordinary and inspiring. Mary Overton's experience is central to Overton's message because it shows what *could* happen to any commoner in England; and too frequently did.

At four o'clock in the morning of 28 March 1649, in orchestrated raids, a couple of hundred armed men surrounded the households of Lilburne, Prince, Overton and Walwyn. Lilburne's wife and children were terrified as he was removed to the Council of State, where, after interrogation, he put his ear to the door and eavesdropped on Cromwell ('I am sure of it') thumping his fist on the table and saying 'I tell you Sir, you have no other way to deal with these men, but to break them in pieces', and (thumping again), 'if you do not break them, they will break you'.[30]

The Leveller women were intimately involved in resistance to this campaign to break their party. Thomas Prince's account gives a strong sense of a private domestic interior, going through its regular routines, invaded by armed soldiers. Mary Prince is up in the early hours with a sick child, when she hears aggressive knocking:

'Who is there?'

'Is Mr Prince within?'

'Yes.'

'I would speak with him concerning some butter and cheese for Ireland.'

'My husband is not stirring.'

'We must speak with him, it is not for his hurt.' After this bizarre dialogue, Mary rushes into her husband's room crying, 'Husband, what have you done, here is a troop of horse and many soldiers at the door for you?'[31]

Her house is systematically turned upside down by soldiers who poke about in the cistern and the oven, rummaging in beds, asking 'who lay in this bed? and who in that bed ... and turned and tossed the bed clothes'. Colonel Axtel, with pistol and muskets, arrests Prince for high treason. Mary's shock gives way to outrage:

Is this the men my husband hath stood for, and adventured his life, as he hath done, and trusted the Parliament in their necessities, above six years past, with above £1,000 and is yet unpaid? I am sure my husband is above £2,000 the worse in his estate, for assisting them. (p50)

Mary's preoccupation with money in this emergency highlights the Levellers' raw sense of betrayal by men in whose cause they freely staked life and economic means. This grievance was shared not only by women like Mary Prince, whose family had a thousand or two to give, but by impoverished men and women who had contributed what little they had to Parliament. As one of the April 1649 Women's Petitions complains: 'time hath been when you would readily have given us the reading Petitions, but that was when we had money, plates, rings and bodkins to give you. You think we have none now.'[32] To fund Parliament's army in the Civil War, maidservants and sempstresses had given brooches and earrings, pins and rings to voluntary collections in town and country: only to find, when Parliament had won the war, the door slammed in the face of their needs.

The men's accounts emphasise the victimisation of the Leveller women, who are depicted as dependent housewives and mothers, tough and resistant but essentially quietist. Womenfolk are seen as the traditional 'helpmeets', valiantly shouldering a joint burden: patterns of the Puritan partnership-ethic set forth in conduct books like Daniel Rogers' *Matrimonial Honour* (1650), man's nearly-but-not-quite equal, anatomised out by God from Adam's side to create 'an equal siding, or sitting close to the side ... a true fellow in the yoke ... equal peers'.[33] But just as the Puritan marriage ideal is riven with contradictions (near-equality of twinned souls in tension with male supremacy), so the Leveller women occupy a position of conflicted stress, for they are obedient partners, yes, but to those labelled *rebels*; they are 'helpmeets' who forsake their subdued, private realm for the public domain. In taking to the streets to obtain the release of their 'yokefellows', they find themselves aggressively defining themselves as petitioners in their own right, speaking on behalf of the people of England. Further to complicate this double-bind, they are impelled by the liberationist strand of left-wing Protestantism, with its insistence on the right of every soul to count for one. The militant petitions which continue to be taken to Parliament and Protector until 1653 speak of a powerful sense of collective identity as women; a mass solidarity new in English history of women asserting their right to be heard in the public forum. If Parliament will be satisfied with nothing less than the Leveller leaders' blood, demand the women, 'drink also, and be glutted with our blood, and let us all fall together: Take the blood of one more, and take all; slay one, and slay all'.[34]

*

27 October 1651. The Leveller women delivered a new petition: *The Women's Petition ... to Cromwell.* The king had been dead for over two years, since which time injustice and oppression had not only continued, but the 'impious, oppressive, dilatory, and most chargeable practice of the law' had become itself an instrument of tyranny.[35] Redress was demanded for the poor, the ruined, debtors; for arbitrary arrest and imprisonment. The women pleaded a full programme of Leveller claims. Back they came in 1653, again demanding Lilburne's release. They declared themselves incensed by the trappings of luxury in which the Protectoral court strutted about, parading its fashion-conscious, Frenchified lifestyle, with scarlet outfits, etiquette and sumptuous menus, upon the ruin of the common people.[36] Women were putting themselves forward as representatives of the people.

This had the virtue of furnishing light relief to the newspapers, scouring around for uncontroversial copy that would reinforce solidarity in factious times. The usual jokes were reprinted in the newspapers: put on breeches if you wish to be taken seriously; get back to washing the dishes 'and meddle with the wheel and distaff', 'we shall have things brought to a fine pass, if women come to teach the Parliament how to make laws'.[37]

The irked, jaded answer to the present Petition came back, to the effect that the government had better things to do than take notice of female hot air: 'the House could not take cognisance of their petition, they being women, and many of them wives, so that the Law took no notice of them.' They were reminded that married women had no voice; they did not exist.

'We are not all wives,' some bright sparks might have retorted, as they did in 1653, nipping through the loophole that accorded some autonomy to single women and widows.[38]

*

'What's become of all my brave viragos, the ladies-errant of the seagreen order?' enquired a newspaper. 'Why do you not again muster up your petticoats and white aprons, and like ... bold Amazons advance your banners once more in the palace yard and spit defiance in the teeth of authority; tell the Parliament that it is liberty they fought for, liberty you come for?'[39] Like the Suffragette processions of the early twentieth century, with singing women in white dresses and sashes and banners in their colours of green, purple and white, the Leveller women offered a splash of carnivalesque colour to the political scene. Perhaps the man in the street missed them when they ceased their activities. Henry Neville made money reviving the vintage joke about a parliament of females, in a series of obscene pamphlets in the late 1640s, on the theme of *The Parliament of Ladies*, in which the married ladies of the honourable Brothel enact laws calling upon men to copulate with their 'fellowfeeler' twice a day; gynaecologists are employed by the House to deliver their bastards, and a hermaphroditic 'Madam with a Dildo' breaks in to become their biggest member.[40] The aristocratic 'Ladies Rampant' are still at it in 1650, spreading clap and receiving named Grandees and Presbyterians in at both entrances. The second of the 1647 pamphlets reflects the mass petitions of the radical women:

> The next day, the house being met, a Petition was delivered, entitled the humble Petition of many thousands of citizens' wives, in and about the City of London, the substance of which was, that whereas diverse weak persons were crept into places, beyond their ability ... they therefore desired that men of able parts, and greater abilities, might be put in their rooms.[41]

The lucrativeness of these drivelling squibs demonstrates the inability of the average male to see campaigning females as anything more than walking genitalia.

It is against the background of this prejudice that we must

measure the Leveller women's stoical audacity. The Suffragettes were to have it no more easily. But unlike the Suffragettes, the Leveller women were not primarily seeking an equal stake in the political establishment. They were a complex phenomenon, generated by the stresses of a turbulent epoch, and as much an ancient phenomenon as they seem a genuinely modern one. From early times, women had acted as petitioners and intercessors in societies they did not control: their role here is traditional. Knyvett, writing home to Katherine in May 1644, requested that she come to London to plead before the Committee of Examination, 'for women solicitors are observed to have better audience than masculine malignants'.[42] During the English Revolution, women took a public role and assumed a public voice in part because the men who 'covered' for them were in prison, battle, or exile. They appeared as representatives of their invisible menfolk. Had their menfolk materialised, they would hypothetically have disappeared. The authorities' out-of-hand dismissal of their petitions as being those of mere females made it pragmatically necessary to formulate an argument for women's right of petition.

By the mid-seventeenth century, women had a venerable tradition of participation in food, fen and enclosure riots (see pp14–15 above). The Isle of Axholme, a centre of resistance against fen drainage and enclosure, was receptive to Levellers and a stronghold of nonconformity. But the Leveller women in London were not a mob like the fen rioters. They represented themselves as a branch of a political party, with its own programme, organised to speak its own truth and stand in solidarity with the disempowered.

*

Can the Leveller women in a meaningful sense be thought of as feminists? Is it anything more than anachronistic wishful thinking to claim them as partners in the drive for women's equality?

They themselves were casting about for a tradition to justify the emergence of women in public life. In the Bible they could draw attention to various bloody-minded or fair-minded exceptions to the rule of female subjection: Deborah the warrior-judge of Israel, Jael, Abigail, Esther. In English history, they pointed to the heroic example of the Anglo-Saxon women defenders of Britain against Romans and Vikings. The trouble with

women's appeal to and argument from precedent is that it yields a
ragbag of female anomalies, culled from the gaps in the patrilinear
system. If Boadicea was a national heroine, icon of resistance to
imperial tyranny, she was also an exception, whose lustre was
engendered by royal status and in any case open to doubt. Milton
(a revolutionary with close links to radicals, Levellers and
Quakers),[43] condemns Queen Boadicea in his *History of Britain* as
a maniac, her reign indicative of a perverted state of society: 'the
rankest note of barbarism, as if in Britain Woemen were Men, and
Men Woemen ... right barbarians'. He spits upon her warrior
exploits as 'the wild hurry of a distracted Woeman, with as mad a
crew at her heels'.[44] A female in power over men was a sign of
depravity or degeneracy in the body politic. Milton
characteristically spelled 'woman' 'Woeman', in a period of
unstable spelling which allowed a choice of 'weoman', 'weman',
'woeman' and (more normally) 'woman'. The Leveller women were
faced with a tradition which equated them with scolds, gossips,
shrews, emitting a noise construed as meaningless and mindless.

The fragile broadsheets of the women's petitions are amongst
the most moving of all the surviving printed material. It is difficult
not to feel, opening the great red covers in which these brittle one-
page statements are preserved, rustling the silky tissue-paper aside,
the forceful freshness of their voices. A broadsheet has a handled
quality, leaving a sense of its being passed round from hand to
living hand, with novelty value now grown paradoxically venerable.
How many eyes read these women's intense assertions and pleas as
carefully as they composed them or we study them? To pore over
their broadsheets in the library is like receiving a message so belated
that it has arrived 340 years late.

To add insult to injury, many have questioned or denied
whether women wrote these petitions at all. They squint sidelong
at the women as probably puppets of their menfolk, skilled at
shopping lists perhaps, but inept at political writing.[45] I should like
to have heard Katharine Chidley's trenchant answer to *that*; she
who thrashed the misogynist Thomas Edwards with her books
single-handed, the iconoclast who used her son as secretary.
Katharine was seen at the head of a Leveller protest on 29 July
1653 to Parliament, handing in a petition:

> On Wednesday there came to the Parliament about twelve
> women, with a petition in the behalf of John Lilburne, it
> was subscribed by above 6000 of that sex, the chief of these
> twelve women was wife to one Chidley a prime Leveller,
> they boldly knocked at the door.[46]

The woman in question would certainly be Chidley's notorious mother rather than his wife, who is not known to have been politically involved.[47] It is inconceivable to anyone familiar with Katharine's scorchingly aggressive writings that she would have tolerated male interference with her petition-penning. This was the Leveller women's second petition to Parliament during the month of July 1653 – the 'Barebones' or 'Nominated' Parliament, which had replaced the dismissed Rump with a band of 'saints', containing sixty 'radicals' as against eighty-four 'moderates'.[48] These radicals, however, were not Levellers but Fifth Monarchists who shared with them certain political aims. Now, if ever, the door was ajar for a programme of reforming legislation. At 'Barebones'' first meeting on 4 July, Cromwell (over whom the saints were swooning as 'our Moses', 'the great Deliverer'),[49] spoke emotionally of this Parliament as the 'door to usher in the things that God has promised': 'We know who they are that shall war with the Lamb against his enemies.[50] Katharine Chidley and Elizabeth Lilburne, too shrewd to share these ecstasies, may have harboured legitimate hopes that Barebones would enact genuine reforms.

On 15 July the radicals put forward a motion for the abolition of tithes; on 27 July, the probable day of the Leveller women's second petition, a motion for freedom of preaching was narrowly defeated. In August a bill would be drawn up for the abolition of the hated Court of Chancery, and a motion carried to overhaul the legal system. Those who could foment such changes could surely free a Lilburne? But the women were right to leaven hope with serious doubt. By November, Fifth Monarchists were denouncing Cromwell and his manipulation of a bag of bare bones as 'the man of sin, the old dragon'.[51] December saw Cromwell seize power, driving the godly remnant from the House of Commons.

The women's first petition was a tact-free warning to 'Barebones' to avoid the 'ready proneness to the spilling of blood' of its predecessor, warped by delusions and worldliness, which was the 'main cause that God forsook them'. The earlier Parliament were scandalous hypocrites, 'deaf to Petitioners and Prisoners'. But Barebones was complicit in a miscarriage of justice so gross that, the petitioners remark with irony, 'even women perceive the evil of it'. The petition was rejected.

The second petition, *The humble Representation of divers afflicted Women-Petitioners*, presented by the twelve women led by Katharine Chidley, begins by expressing the women's sadness 'to see our undoubted Right of Petitioning withheld from us, having attended several days at your House-door', for 'it is the known duty of Parliaments to receive Petitions: and it is ours and the Nation's undoubted right to petition, although an Act of Parliament were made against it'.[52] That is, Parliament is bound by the common law, which limits its powers and asserts its obligations. The women present themselves as 6000 Esthers arisen in modern England to enact the intercessive role of the biblical Esther:

> Truly we cannot but judge the said Act against Mr Lilburne to be of no less concernment to ourselves and the whole nation, than unto Mr Lilburne, since what is done or intended against him (being against common right, and in the face thereof) may be done unto every particular person in the nation.
>
> Your Honours may be pleased to call to mind that never-to-be-forgotten deliverance obtained by the good women of England against the usurping Danes then in this nation. You may likewise consider the readiness and willingness of the good women of this nation, who did think neither their lives, nor their husbands' and servants' lives and estates to be too dear a price for the gaining of yours and the nation's ancient rights and liberties out of the hands of encroachers and oppressors.
>
> And therefore we hope, that, upon second thoughts, your Honours will not slight the persons of your humble Petitioners, nor withhold from us our undoubted right of petitioning, since God is ever willing and ready to receive the petitions of all, making no difference of persons.

Here we see women formulating for themselves *as a class* a rough and ready concept of petitionary rights based on democratic status as 'persons' in common with every other citizen of England who has earned rights by services to the state. A notion of what we would now call 'women's history' emerges,[53] with examples from Jewish and British history. But their primary aim is the release of John Lilburne, not women's rights, which Leveller women are forced to defend by Parliament's contumacious rejection of their voices as those of non-persons.

At this distance, one can see that this petition was never likely to appeal to the godly Barebones militants, who, if they borrowed the idea of the 'Norman Yoke' from the Levellers, were centuries apart in temperament. Despite drawing support from the lowest ranks of society, they were essentially anti-democratic, believing in a thousand year rule by a new elite of 'the saints', hand-picked by the Almighty. Fundamentalists whose programme included the introduction of the punitive Mosaic code of laws, they suspected the Levellers as atheists.[54]

*

Examining the Leveller women's petitions of the 1640s and 50s, we are fitfully struck by the powerful tone in which a theory of gender equality is argued. The equality of all souls under Christ is its lynchpin: 'Christ has purchased us at as dear a rate as he hath done men.' From this it follows that 'the happiness of women as well as men' is essential to the full expression of religion. Women's participation in the sufferings and struggles of the Commonwealth is put forward as qualification to state political views and share in the making of decisions. Crucially, the women claim rights as citizens: 'we have an equal share and interest with men in the Commonwealth' (April 1649). The petition of May 1649, perhaps written by Katharine Chidley, though sometimes attributed to Elizabeth Lilburne, is especially powerful in its claim to the autonomous right of women to a political voice and action:

> since we are assured of our creation in the image of God, and of an interest in Christ equal unto men, as also of a proportionable share in the freedoms of this commonwealth, we cannot but wonder and grieve that we

should appear so despicable in your eyes as to be thought unworthy to petition or represent our grievances to this honourable House. Have we not an equal interest with the men of this nation, in those liberties and securities contained in the *Petition of Right*, and other the good laws of the land? Are any of our lives, limbs, liberties, or goods to be taken from us more than from men, but by due process of law and conviction of twelve sworn men of the neighbourhood? And can you imagine us to be so sottish or stupid, as not to perceive, or not to be sensible when daily those strong defences of our peace and welfare are broken underfoot by force and arbitrary power?

Would you have us keep at home in our houses, when men of such faithfulness and integrity as the four prisoners, our friends, in the Tower, are fetched out of their beds and forced from their houses by soldiers, to the affrighting and undoing of themselves, their wives, children, and families? Are not our husbands, our selves, our children and families, by the same rule as liable to the like unjust cruelties as they? ...

And are we Christians, and shall we sit still and keep at home, while such men as have borne continual testimony against the injustice of all times and unrighteousness of men, be picked out and be delivered up to the slaughter? ...

No, far be it from us. Let it be accounted folly, presumption, madness, or whatsoever in us, whilst we have life and breath we will never leave them nor forsake them, nor ever cease to importune you ...

For we are no whit satisfied with the answer you gave unto our husbands and friends.[55]

This is strong language by the most modern standards. Claims brought forward by Victorian feminists two centuries later would be couched in far less threatening terms. The voice is angry, scathed and scathing. It is the testimony of a mass of women, whose political experience has been gained at great personal cost, in a period of violence and upheaval. Their sacrifices, war work, services, apparently count for nothing; and now they are expected to exercise tame endurance of oppression by the very people they helped advance to power. The women's argument is based on an appeal to civil, natural and divine law, which they claim the government has violated and to whose protection they claim an equal right with men. They have been prey to acts of institutionalised terror. The women claim that the laws exist to protect their rights and interests as well as those of men.

The word 'equal' recurs insistently, alongside 'the same' ('interest in Christ *equal* unto men', '*equal* interest', 'by *the same* rule ... *the like* unjust cruelties' [my italics]), in a political discourse which abstains from recognising the unenfranchised and voiceless condition of women under the law. They point to the crimes of the regime as an imperative to them to speak out: 'Shall the blood of war be shed in time of peace? ... And are we Christians, and shall we sit still and keep at home' when the spokesmen for justice have been incarcerated for bearing witness? Their repetition of the phrase 'keep at home' suggests gall at being bundled back into their ransacked domestic sphere. The author (or authors?) hits a note of urgent defiance which satirically echoes the stridor commonly attributed to the 'scold': 'No ... we will never cease to importune you'.

Is there a note of despair in the voice? Does the voice, for all its assertiveness, admit the probability, almost the inevitability of failure? The 'scolding' accents pick up a tone men claimed to know intimately: the nagging, hectoring insubordination of the 'shrew', mouthing her perennial discontent. If wives were reported by their spouses to be all tongue, the gist of the tongue's message was that it would never be quiet. 'No,' said the Leveller women, 'Let it be accounted folly, presumption, madness or whatsoever in us, whilst we have life and breath, we will never cease to importune you.' It is as if they conceded in advance that their pleas would not be heard because they were spoken by women. From this derived the simmering rage of their petition: it was the anger of a foreknown, because eternal, defeat. Women would not be listened to because their speaking would be accounted 'folly', whatever they said. Their appearance in the political arena would be condemned as 'presumption' – the sin for which Lucifer and Eve fell. Their petition would be dismissed as the ravings of 'madness', whatever it said: the female pathology being considered prone to lunacy. Nevertheless, the women would speak. They would never cease to speak. If nothing else, their speech would gall and goad.

*

At the 'Putney Debates' of October and November 1647, the Council of the New Model Army debated the kind of commonwealth they desired to bring into being. Cromwell and the grandees were faced with the demands of Levellers who had made the army a centre of revolutionary dialogue. The debates were recorded in shorthand, so we can overhear those voices exactly as they spoke. They were arguing about the relationship between property rights and privilege, the Levellers asserting the right of 'all inhabitants that have not lost their birthright' to have 'an equal voice in elections' (Mr Petty); the democratic right, therefore, of each person who was not a criminal, insane, or in servitude to speak and be heard. Henry Ireton argued with scarcely repressed choler for the rights of the propertied as essential to order and government. It was at Putney that Colonel Rainborough made his unforgettable speech on behalf of the rights of 'the poorest he that is in England':

> For really I think that the poorest he that is in England hath a life to live, as the greatest he; and therefore truly, sir, I think it's clear that every man that is to live under a government ought first by his own consent to put himself under that government; and I do think that the poorest man in England is not at all bound in a strict sense to that government that he hath not had a voice to put himself under.[56]

When Ireton angrily countered, Rainborough demanded to know 'what we have fought for' (p61). These twin messages echoed and re-echoed: what have we fought for? – democratic rights for all, without account of property.

Leveller demands were understood by all present as the demand for universal suffrage; indeed, modern editors and commentators still freely gloss them in these terms. In listening in to this dramatic exchange of modern-sounding views, aired centuries ahead of its time, it is easy to forget that the eloquently pleaded Leveller case extended to far less than half the population of England.

The 'poorest he' was not the 'poorest she'.

The word 'person' denoted 'every male person' or possibly 'every male householder'. All persons should count for one; but only males counted as persons, a bizarrely Orwellian notion for the modern woman voter but obvious common sense to the seventeenth-century participants in the debate. Few, if any, would have entertained the notion of advocating women's suffrage. Everyone present in this men's world of fighting men still warm from the battlefield assumed that 'woman' was covered by 'man'. It would have been as laughable to introduce the 'poorest she' into the dispute as to extend debate to a discussion of animal rights. Lilburne in *The Freeman's Freedom Vindicated* (1646) included women in his ideology of government by consent 'of every particular individual, man and woman ... by nature all equal and alike in power, dignity, authority and majesty'.[57] But he seems to have assumed that women would delegate their right of choice to husband or male guardian: nowhere in the Revolution do we find an assertion of women's equal political rights. It is against this background that we should read the audacity of the Leveller women's petitions, which transgressed into an area which both sides regarded as the territory of the absurd.

Ironically, although the Leveller women used the men's ideology as the ground on which to mount a brief and limited campaign which included women's rights, it was Ireton's conservative position which, if extended to women, could have widened the political powers of at least a segment of women. Women in considerable numbers owned property, including widows and single women. But, by another irony, this class of women was being stripped of political rights previously enjoyed. The seventeenth century, which seems to embody a spirit of liberation, actually witnessed a clamp-down on vestigial rights some women had once held by default, and exercised in an age when property was the primary qualification for authority. From this perspective, we can see the period as the tail-end of an era for women rather than a libertarian dawn, even a false dawn. Just as women had lost business parity with the decline of the specialised craft guilds, where in medieval times married businesswomen had often enjoyed full status in their own right, so their vestigial rights both to vote at local and national elections and serve as local officials were drawing to an end.[58]

In some areas of the country their rights took longer to die: the West Country is a notable instance. In Devon, Kilmington had twelve women churchwardens between 1556 and 1606; the St Budeaux parish rolls show women serving in this capacity, and the electoral list of Killhampton, Cornwall, shows four women householders registered for service in 1616. More importantly, women appeared on national electoral registers as substantial freeholders who could claim to vote at national elections. Hence, some women had for centuries legitimately enjoyed a Parliamentary voice – counting as 'persons' since voting rights were grounded in a system built to consolidate the 'permanent fixed interest' of the country in property. In the medieval period, abbesses had named Parliamentary representatives; under Elizabeth I, two female borough owners had returned Members of Parliament. In the reign of James I, judges in at least three cases ruled that a '*feme sole*' who was a freeholder, could vote. In 1628, Sir Henry Slingsby attempted to manipulate the votes of widowed burgage holders in Knares-borough.[59]

But the tide turned in 1640, and the manner of its turning clarified the extent to which the female presence in the electorate had been an anomaly. The holes in the system were sealed. At the October elections in the borough of Eye in Suffolk, several widows appeared, were 'sworn', and duly cast their votes. After outraged protests, these votes were discounted. Sir Simonds d'Ewes expressed the general revulsion, 'conceiving it a matter very unworthy of any gentleman, and most dishonourable in such an election, to make use of [women's] voices, though they might in law have been allowed'.[60] The phrase, 'unworthy of any gentleman' exquisitely articulates the dependence of the hierarchical values of gentry elitism on the exclusion of large classes, considered as contaminants to a well-regulated system. 'Gentlemen' of both sides would be equally mortified at votes cast by non-gentlemen, whether riff-raff or females. Common law, the law of the nobles, overtook the law of locality and custom, sanctioned by public opinion which had not wholly excluded women.

In 1644, the jurist Sir Edward Coke's authoritative *Institutes* were published, disqualifying from suffrage all males who were minors (under twenty-one), 'all that have no freehold ... and all women having freehold or no freehold'. Women were effaced from the electorate in one stroke of the pen.[61] The epoch of Revolution whose watchwords were 'rights' and 'liberties' saw the disenfranchisement of women. A woman born in 1645 would belong to the first generation in which every single member of her sex was shorn of all political rights.

4

A NOTE ON 7000 INCENDIARY HANDMAIDS
THE QUAKER WOMEN'S PETITION OF 1659

Petitioning implies at least a fiction of respect and expresses the hope that those in power will set abuses to rights when these are brought to notice. Petitioning is 'humble'. It requires a certain form of words; a form evolved over centuries of negotiation between rulers and ruled.

Moving from the Leveller women's petitions to that of the Quaker women against tithes, delivered to Parliament in 1659, *These several Papers*,[1] is to move from a mindset which observed venerable forms of procedure, because it wished to reclaim the notional long-lost justice they represented, to a mentality which scorned all postures of human deference, all forms of words. It is to move from trammelled but incensed wives to incendiary women confident of their equal spiritual status with men.

The Quakers waste no time in ducking and curtsying to the rogues in Parliament, nor in disputes concerning law, custom, the

Norman Yoke, or women's right to petition. Citizens of another world, exponents of a higher law, each one a minister in her own right, the Quaker women's petition storms Parliament with an address of unveiled contempt. The petition was prepared for the press by Mary Forster. A modern reader is moved, turning the seventy-page document, at the names unrolling down sheet after sheet, some familiar and well known, others now forgotten, all riding three columns abreast – 7000 names in all (though it must be said that, as in all mass petitions, a few signed twice). The ranks of names are arranged area by area, just as they were gathered in by nationwide local Meetings, the earliest being those of Margaret Fell and her seven daughters. Districts add spontaneous statements of their own. Leafing through, the sense of the communal energy and solidarity of these women, mobilised up and down the nation, is explosive.

How biddable the language of the Leveller women appears beside that of the Quakers, though they were at one on this issue, which was potentially the most revolutionary of the Interregnum.[2] These women are embattled tithe strikers, tempered steel in the fire of persecution, announcing themselves as the voice of their Friends 'that hath been prisoned till death, in nasty holes and corners' (p3). They do not ask, beg or plead but categorically demand that Parliament 'throw down the power of the Papists in these nations, that set up tithes' and rid themselves of those 'filthy beasts', the paid ministers. Whereas the Leveller women commonly referred to their menfolk as 'our husbands' or 'friends' (which could then carry familial meaning), the Quaker women speak an egalitarian biblical language of 'our brethren'. They launch the main body of their petition with a statement of their singular power and millennial destiny as women: 'We who are of the Seed of the Woman, which bruiseth the Serpent's head, to which the Promise was, Christ Jesus in the Male and in the Female ... do bear our Testimony' (p7).

Our eyes rove the pages mesmerised: names ... more names ... Elizabeth Kitchin, Anne Wilson ... northern mountains and moorlands, Northumberland, Cumberland ... Cheshire adds a disdainful message remarking that Christ did not send his disciples out 'with a bag' to plunder the storehouse of the poor, but sent them 'without a bag, and said, Freely ye have received, freely give' (p20).

More names, more counties ... Yorkshire, Durham, Northampton-shire, Nottingham, Lincolnshire, East Anglia. Parliament is treated to a harangue objecting to the inane palaver of having to petition a profane bunch of cynics who ought to do justice as a matter of course; shouldn't have to be asked; shouldn't need to be thanked:

> Now friends, you being first chosen by the nation as a Parliament for to do the nation the right, and to take off the nation's oppressions; are not you to search out the oppression? and are not people to lay their oppressions before you, without petitioning you to do them justice? and is not petitioning often for exalting such that will not do justice without flattering petitions, and then have but thanks, and seldom the thing done?
>
> ... the cry hath been, It hath not been a petition, it hath not been an address, because it hath not been in the world's method and form ... when the thing is made known unto you in the simplicity and innocency, without flattering petitions and addresses, you ought to do them justice, (for that end are you of the nation chosen) if the grievance to you be made known. (p33)

Not 'Sirs' but 'friends', Parliament is called to account and told to get on with the business for which it is employed as a public servant. God will smash them if they fail to take notice.

The voice takes on southern dialects ... Berkshire, Hampshire, Wiltshire ... memorandum concerning the Beast, false prophets, Antichrist ... Somerset, Oxford, 'a remnant of the Lord's handmaids in Buckinghamshire', Warwickshire, Gloucestershire, which slams in the question 'How do you who are the heads of the nation expect we should pay your taxes, when you suffer the priests to take away our goods, that do no work for us?' (p51).

London emits five crisp demands, followed by a statement of betrayal that those who have stood for Parliament in and since the Civil Wars 'have suffered more by these plundering priests, than by the plundering Cavaliers' (p54). Demands for the abolition of colleges training ministers: sell up all church and royal lands and properties ... more names from Wales and Herefordshire, with the prediction that God will 'remove you as unfit for his use', together with a call to sell all church lands and colleges, pay off the impropriators[3] and set up schools in their place ... melt down all church bells except one per village for use as a fire warning ... religious toleration ... feed the poor with confiscated lands, for 'there need never have been this lamentable cry for bread and clothes among the poor of the nation' ... religious toleration for all ... stop whipping God-fearing travellers (ie Quaker prophets and ministers) as vagrants ... money-grubbing ministers extracting ten or twenty shillings for a sermon over the dead, sprinkling babies, churching women are superstitious fakes, 'just like the Heathen as they make their Pow-wows' (p66) ... Dorsetshire, Hertfordshire ... more names, more taunts, more threats.

We shall meet some of these women individually whom now we see through a glass darkly as a unanimous throng of militants, many voices speaking as one, published in 'London. For Mary Westwood. 1659'.

5

MASTER EDWARDS' GANGRENE
THOMAS EDWARDS, KATHARINE CHIDLEY & MRS ATTAWAY

Rumours of new subversive sects, dividing to spawn a fresh generation of heresies, multiplied daily in the 1640s. The Presbyterian establishment which was replacing the Anglican episcopacy could hardly keep up with them and evinced a fascination for the new heresies less forensic than it was pathological. For the cleric Master Thomas Edwards, the national outbreak of heresy was a gangrene in the modern church, a gangrene efflorescing and putrefying into forms unimaginable seven years ago before this mortification set in. His tract, *Gangraena*, went through three parts in 1646, for he found himself breathlessly updating it as new abominations came to his notice. The first part appeared in February, the second in May and the third late in December, each ebullition being met with a volley of tolerationist retorts, which only ripened the gangrene.

At or near the centre of Edwards' disclosures was the obscene eruption of women preachers, like pus from a wound. *Gangraena*[1] is a deeply interesting and vivid document which, despite the flagrant bias of the author, conveys the authentic drama of an age in which unheard-of licence was taken by the lowest of the low in the name of God. It gives the sense of being hot off the press: Edwards has a network of ministers spying out abominations all round the country, beetling home from radical meetings to report to Edwards in letters detailing novel horrors. *Gangraena* is a tissue of anecdotes, denouncing the 'whirligig spirits' of the the times and their apostate beliefs. Indeed, Mr Edwards has detected a total of 176 such heresies, which he methodically lists; and we have the feeling that, so faithfully did he keep his nose to the ground to sniff out errors, he would have discovered (had he lived) a further 176 by the following year. The heresies range from the denial of hell and sin to the belief that all creatures, including every animal and bird that has ever lived, will be resurrected on Judgement Day; denial of the Scriptures, church, sacraments, baptism and the sabbath; to the widespread belief that any man can preach the Gospel as well as another. This is Number 123. Number 124 is even more heinous:

> 124. That 'tis lawful for women to preach, and why should they not, having gifts as well as men? and some of them do actually preach, having a great resort to them.[2]

As if this were not enough, five heresies later, Edwards has detected a belief amongst ten or eleven women in one area that it is unlawful for women to hear a *man* preach, whether publicly or privately.

Community of goods and women; legitimacy of divorce, pacifism, vegetarianism ... the list goes on, until Edwards has exhausted his 176 heresies. Even then he comes up with a few extras, including the shameful belief that a wife is free to milk her husband's capital, against the husband's consent, to subsidise the church of her choice. The sanctity of the wallet is violated at the very heart of holy matrimony. Whatever next? Well, there is more. Edwards has heard, he confides,

> There have been many blaspheming speeches, in a way of derision of the Holy Ghost ... asking what kind of bird it

was? whether – but I dare not speak it. (p38)

This is an obvious temptation to the reader to speculate: duck? booby? parakeet?

Did Edwards make it all up, or does his delicious list of abominations reflect the genuine state of the sects in England during the mid-1640s? We need to ask this question and to place him in a context of heresiographers because the details on preaching women which, in relish and fascination, he supplies, are so full and detailed. Obviously, it was part of the stock in trade of conservative propaganda to vilify the sexual mores of the radical sects, accusing them of promiscuity and calling their womenfolk 'whores' and Jezebels. Hence the author of *A discovery of 29 Sects in London* (1641) conventionally reports The Family of Love as believing that 'a man may gain salvation by showing himself loving, especially to his neighbour's wife'. But the extent to which heresy hunters tended to become carried away on flights of indignation is shown by the way this thoroughly ignorant pamphleteer, having run out of authentic heresies before he has reached his twenty-nine, starts making them up as he goes along, finding Londoners who are worshippers of the King of Macedon ('Macedonians'), Heathens, Panonians, Saturnians, Junonians, Bacchanalian boozers and 'The Brotherhood', namely 'whoring rogues' who call one another brother and sister.[3] This tabloid mentality is seen even in the works of Presbyterian divines like Robert Baillie, whose *Anabaptism*,[4] published the year after *Gangraena*, was scare-mongering hearsay of hearsay.

Everyone was fascinated by the goings-on in Münster in the previous century, where for several months the Anabaptists under their 'King' John of Leyden, a former tailor, won control of the city, proclaiming it the New Jerusalem, instituting a programme of polygamy, a savage Old Testament legal code, the abolition of private property and the inversion of the social order. Münster was a warning case of the political and sexual anarchy sure to prevail when the lower orders and their crackpot theories of the end of the world gained control of a state: Baillie shows how acts of compassion were outlawed, so that one of the leaders' wives, manifesting pity for the starving people, had her head struck off in the marketplace, whereupon the rest of his wives 'did sing a psalm to God for this so excellent an act of Justice, the King himself led all the 14 in a dance through the streets of the town' (pp10–11). Nudity and incest were also licensed, the only sexual law being that sleeping with one's own husband was illegal. Daily expecting the New Jerusalem and Christ's Second Coming, one of their women in Switzerland (Baillie reports) 'gave herself out for the Queen of the world and Messias for all women, sending out her twelve she-Apostles for their conversion to their way' (p11).

The message of Baillie's tract is not subtle: watch out, England. Münster yesterday, London tomorrow.

He goes on to report the antics of modern separatists, haunting them with echoes of Münster, and focusing on one of Thomas Edwards' chief bugbears, the preacher Mrs Attaway:

> many more of their women do venture to preach ... *Attaway* the mistress of all the She-preachers in *Coleman Street* was a disciple in Lamb's congregation, and made Antipaedo-baptism oftentimes a part of her public exercises: the other feminine Preachers in *Kent, Norfolk*, and the rest of the Shires had their breeding, as I take it, in the same or the like school. (p53)

'Antipaedobaptism' is the belief in adult baptism by total immersion ('dipping'), practised in rivers on converts, and in the minds of the establishment associated with sexual 'filthiness'. This was claimed by Daniel Featley in his entertainingly vituperative *The Dippers Dipt* (1645) as a form of water-pollution ('they defile our Rivers with their impure washings').[5] He enthralled his respectable readership with a juicy account of how the Baptists 'strip themselves stark naked, not only when they flock in great multitudes, men and women, together to their *Jordans* to be dipped, but also upon other occasions, when the season permits', a nudism which they defend on the grounds that '*the truth is naked*' (p167). This flavoursome pamphlet does not tie in women's sexual licence with their public speaking; neither does Ephraim Pagitt's *Heresiography* (1645), which repeats the charge of Baptist promiscuity and tells a tale or two of adulteries, and how, when Mr Studley, the 'Chief Prophet' of Mr Johnson's Brownist

(Independent) congregation was discovered hiding behind a basket in lewd Judith Holder's house, he upped and, rising to his full height, in a holy manner declared that as an elder of the church it was his duty to keep an eye on proceedings in the bedrooms of the more buxom souls.[6]

It was for Edwards to articulate a three-way connection between women's preaching, sexual looseness and the threat from the lower orders: damning each by association with the other. His account of the adult baptism of females snoops into the nocturnal wickedness, at once murderous and erotic, of the dipping 'saints':

> they have baptised many weakly ancient women naked in rivers in winter, whereupon some have sickened and died; they have baptised young maids Citizens' daughters, about one and two o'clock in the morning, tempting them out of their fathers' houses at midnight, to be baptised, and parents being asleep and knowing nothing. (p67)

The passage is crammed with lubricious fantasy. According to the gangrene-discoverer, the fanatics seek out, strip and expose to the icy waters, aged women, with what possible end but to swell the population of hell with deluded hypothermics? They make trysts with the nubile daughters of godly, snoring burghers, seducing them out to bare their all in a river-orgy 'about one and two' in the morning. What citizen can sleep secure in his bed at night, knowing that his aged mother or virgin daughter may be lured out to her death, or worse?

Is Dr Edwards sincere? Yes, of course. He is profoundly concerned for the innocent citizens of London, who are being robbed of their females by designing agents of Satan. Girls are gullible. One man had five daughters, all of whom were converted by an illiterate preacher. As he dipped the five maidens, he assessed them, rump and pap, and chose the best-endowed to marry, without her parents' consent. Another young woman, desiring to be baptised, stripped off and stood cowering on the river bank, covering her private parts with both hands in an agony of shyness, while the Dipper prayed. Morally indignant at this shameful embarrassment, the Dipper remonstrated. What Jesus wanted her to do, he said, was not to hold her hands down but to lift them high, high with her heart in Jesus' name, up towards heaven (like this, he urged her, do it like this). This being too much for the blushful girl, she scuttled off and was seen no more.

The Independent, John Goodwin, replied to *Gangraena* in a witty and urbane tract which questions the sanity of the man, wondering why someone self-licensed to fabricate heresies 'should stay his pen at so small a number as 180; and did not advance to ... ten thousand times ten thousand and a thousand thousands'. He admits he has only read a quarter of the work, but this happens to include the tale of the shrinking nude woman, 'a story which makes the tale of *Gargantua* and *Don Quixote* with his windmills to look like Gospels in comparison of it'.[7]

Fiction or truth? In the 'dipping' stories, women appear as the silly victims of exploitative males, half-quack, half-fanatic, wholly Satanic. But the burden of *Gangraena*'s obsession with gender casts women amongst the exploiters and rebels against order. For once dipped, a maiden becomes a monster. Mr Edwards is deeply fascinated by these monsters, but he is also terrified of them, and articulates a communal gentry fear of the subversion of order by the rabble. The rabble and the women are one. They are the forces of chaos, ignorance and envy, rushing up into the pulpit, overwhelming the church with their desecrating garrulity. Featley had protested, pinching his nose against the fumes, about the great unwashed who set up as self-elected priests, turning stables into temples, stalls into choirs, shopboards into communion tables, tubs into pulpits, aprons into linen ephods, and 'mechanicals of the lowest rank to Priests of the high places'. He railed against 'the prating housewife ... the old dotard ... the wrangling sophister', and wondered how come the doors, posts, and walls failed to sweat off the fliers advertising that '*On such a day such a Brewer's Clerk Exerciseth, Such a Taylor expoundeth, Such a Waterman Teacheth*'.[9] The class basis of the church hierarchy, with its monopoly of education, authority and especially the publicly spoken word, is focused in the scorn for 'sublime coachmen, and illuminated tradesmen' which spits and groans from their writings.

John Vicars, in *The Schismatic Sifted* (1646), dedicated fulsomely to the Mayor of London, takes Thomas Edwards' part as he parallels the speaking of women with the lower classes:

Is it a miracle or a wonder ... to see young saucy boys (in comparison) bold botching tailors, and other most audacious illiterate mechanics, to run rudely and rashly (and unsent for too) out of their shops into a pulpit; to see bold impudent housewives, without all womanly modesty, to take upon them (in the natural volubility of their tongues & quick wits, or strong memories only) to prate (not preach or prophesy) after a narrative or discoursing manner, an hour or more, and that most directly contrary to the Apostle's inhibition; but where, I say, is their *extraordinary speech poured out upon them ... in gifts of miraculous healing the sick and sore*, and such like? where, I say, are any of these in our old or young tradesmen, or bold Beatrices of the female sex?[10]

The bite and bale of the anti-Independent tracts come from the religious elite's perception of lower-class and female preachers as intrinsically ridiculous. How can people not see, they wonder, how absurd it is for a 'bold botching tailor', addled in all but the knack of sewing garments and frequently not much good at that, to set up as teacher and preacher? The fellow can't even read. He doesn't know Latin. Has no acquaintance with the difference between substance and essence or the abstruser points of the Trinity. Tailors are bred for tailoring. What they do is what they are. Likewise, housewives are designed by God and bred by man for housewifery. The fact that they never stop talking because of a defect which seems built into their tongues, courtesy of Eve, does not equip them for public speaking. They claim 'inspiration': but their yatter is merely a public ventilation of the windy fits common to gasbags. In putting themselves forward in public, they are seen as 'impudent', 'immodest' and 'bold', all terms which link them with sluts.

It is not so much that these females delude themselves into thinking that they can preach, for such delusion is only to be expected of the hen-brain. What shocks the clerics in the *Gangraena* controversy is that anyone actually listens to them:

Among all the confusion and disorder in Church-matters both of opinions and practices, and particulars of all sort; of

mechanics taking upon them preaching and baptism, as smiths, tailors, shoemakers, pedlars, weavers &c, there are also some women preachers in our time, who keep constant lectures, preaching weekly to many men and women. In Lincolnshire, in Holland and those parts, there is a woman preacher who preaches, (it's certain) and 'tis reported also she baptiseth, but that's not so certain. In the Isle of Ely (that island of errors and sectaries) is a woman preacher also.
(*Gangraena*, I & II, p84)

Edwards has to scribble furiously to keep up with new outbreaks of gangrene in the shires: but he maintains his concern for forensic scrupulosity of reporting the spread of disease – distinguishing between what he thinks he knows for sure (the Lincolnshire woman's preaching) and frank rumour (the woman's baptising of converts). And despite Edwards' bitter hostility to women and the sects, he seems to have avoided making stories up lock, stock and barrel. What need to invent when the world had turned upside down? – a freak show on which Edwards could glut his appetite for shock, where a woman in Lincolnshire, one in the Isle of Ely and another in Hertfordshire took it upon themselves to expound God's Holy Writ to devout congregations. The woman of Ely is verifiable from other sources: she was the Antinomian Anne Hutchinson's role-model, 'a Woman of 1000 hardly any like to her', as she told the disgusted Puritan minister, Hugh Peters.[11] If Anne had learned the rebellious intellectuality of the style with which she parried her judges at her New England trial for heresy in 1637 from the 'apostle of Ely', that woman must have been formidable indeed.

And, had Edwards been making it all up as he went along, surely he would have come up with more women, behaving more diabolically? There is something stuffily honourable in Edwards' refusal to go further than he felt warranted, to satisfy his craving for abominations. One real monster, however, might make up for the paucity of specimens. London provided Edwards with an inflammation in the form of Mrs Attaway, seller of lace in Cheapside, resident in Bell Alley in Coleman Street (a centre of radical religion), and holder of religious meetings every Tuesday at four o'clock.

Without Edwards' bilious account of Mrs Attaway, she would certainly have perished with her sisters in the historical memory. Through Edwards, she lives in the record; and though he views her through bile-green lenses, if we can wipe away the livid discoloration, we are left with an intriguing scene of a seventeenth-century woman about her business of preaching to a large congregation, some of whom were devotees, but many of whom had come along for an outing, to mock and heckle, or to oppose outright the 'she-preacher's' right to speak.

*

One of Master Edwards' snoopers (an unnamed 'godly Minister') has infiltrated the flock awaiting the arrival of the women ministers. Whether he takes surreptitious notes or relies upon his memory of the scandalous proceedings is not clear. At any rate, he supplies Edwards with a detailed report. The meeting proceeds in a ritualised manner, which the author expects his reader to recognise with shock as modelled on a godly meeting: a female burlesque of the solemn parade of male authority which happened every time the minister appeared before his congregation, or the father of a godly household reinforced patriarchal authority by presiding over twice-daily family prayers.[12] The modern reader needs to be alert to the political nature of all worship in the seventeenth century to register the height and depth of Edwards' shock. Every action and detail of furniture carries meaning in terms of the power structure of the assembly.

Mrs Attaway and two fellow women process into the meeting room from an inner chamber, carrying Bibles. They arrange themselves around three sides of a table: 'the lace-maker' (a term constantly repeated, with a wince) placing herself 'at the upper end', indicating her primacy. Her colleague, a gentlewoman, 'the Major's wife', sits near to her, and the third woman, dressed 'in her hoods, necklace of pearl, watch by her side, and all apparel suitable' (like a parody priest, perhaps?) stands opposite to the Major's wife. Now a pantomime unfolds in which all three women decline to speak. Mrs Attaway invites the well-dressed woman to lead off, 'extolling her gifts and great abilities'. But she refuses. She is not fit to do it, she bashfully exclaims, she couldn't possibly, and she begins to lavish praise on Mrs Attaway and to beg her to open the meeting. But the lace-woman is having none of it. She insists it's nothing but excess of Christian humility and modesty on her colleague's part. Vehemently denying it, the woman again inventories the spiritual gifts of the lace-woman (pp84–5).

But no: Mrs Attaway is still resolute. She pleads bodily infirmity and, turning to the listeners, who might well be shifting and yawning by this time, wonders if anyone has 'a word of exhortation' to share with the company. Embarrassing silence reigns.

To Edwards and his informant, the non-proceedings display a farcicality bizarre to the point of berserk. To us, perhaps the quivering indecision which afflicts the women as they confront their congregation may suggest their vulnerability as women in the face of a society which requires them to be silent in the public sphere, and labels them whores (as Edwards will crowingly do in the course of the pamphlet) if they speak out of turn or make exhibitions of themselves. The authority they assume is an equivocal blessing, entailing a psychological burden of distress. Nervously, they try to hide behind one another; and, as a last resort, appeal to the crowd to bail them out.

Alternatively, Mrs Attaway and her co-ministers may be subtly manoeuvring to obtain immunity to the charge of brazenness, by showing through mutual deference a properly feminine dislike of the whole business of public speaking. They are curtsying to convention as a preliminary to transgressing it. For the next minute, the lace-woman has taken the floor and is presenting her credentials for speaking, by quoting the Scriptural promise from Joel 2:28–9 that, in the latter days, 'God would pour out his Spirit upon the handmaidens, and they should prophesy'. She launches into a half-hour prayer, followed by a three-quarter-hour explication of the text, 'If ye love me, keep my Commandments'. Evidently the pangs of nerves, if such they were, have passed away, as Mrs Attaway confidently proceeds according to the normal pattern of male Independent preaching. When she asks for objections, no one ventures any. Mrs Attaway sits down.

Now the woman with the hoods, pearls and watch takes the floor, explaining that she is not feeling very well, but that she will take up her 'sister's' theme. Off she goes but in so low a voice that people cannot hear (or affect not to be able to hear), and there is a cry of 'Speak out!'. She raises her voice, only to be greeted by a second cry of 'Speak out!', 'so that upon this the Gentlewoman was disturbed and confounded in her discourse', which becomes more and more garbled and distracted, 'speaking nonsense all along'. More catcalls; more gibberish. Hectoring and heckling from the floor, until the poor woman keels over into her chair, defeated (pp85–6).

But Mrs Attaway is not so easily vanquished. Springing to her feet, she wrathfully frowns upon the rude audience and begins an extempore prayer to close the meeting, avenging her colleague by bringing to the Almighty's attention the existence of wicked persons 'who despised his Ambassadors and Ministers that he had sent into the world to reconcile the world'.

'Ambassadors? Ministers? you, Ambassadors?' parrot jeering members of the company.

At this the dauntless lace-woman 'prayed expressly that God would send some visible judgment from heaven upon them; and upon those words some of the company spake aloud, praying God to stop her mouth, and so she was forced to give over' in the bawling, braying, laughing, and tumult that erupted. During this 'inexpressible' confusion, Mr Edwards' hyperventilating informant, fearing lest the candles be extinguished and folk fall to murdering one another under cover of the darkness, slips away, his prejudices thoroughly confirmed (p86).

The following Tuesday, as Edwards learns from a resident of Bell Alley, who estimates (imaginatively) that a thousand people come to hear the women, the three women hold their meeting at the Old Bailey. On 30 December, a minister sees them at it again, noting sourly 'a great deal of lightness' amongst the audience (p87); and at 3 p.m. on Thursday, 8 January, one 'Mrs Atomy', whom Edwards takes to be one of the Bell Alley trio (but surely a misnomer for 'Mrs Attaway' herself?), preaches to fifty people, male and female, delivering 'many dangerous and false doctrines', including the beliefs that it is not consonant with the nature of a loving God to damn any of his creation eternally; that God the Father and Son have abdicated, giving over the kingdom to the Spirit, which is poured out upon all creatures; that in a 'general Restoration', all human beings will be reconciled and saved. These heresies were standard tenets amongst the extreme left-wing sects. It is interesting to see a woman preacher presenting to her hearers a God of universal compassion, who will save you even against your will; and removing that great safeguard against mutinous behaviour, hellfire.

Mrs Atomy observes the custom amongst the free-thinking churches of asking for objections, and gets them. A woman stands up demanding to know what 'warrant' she has to preach in that manner? Hastily, as if this were a familiar challenge, Mrs Atomy interrupts before the woman can complete her objection, saying she knows just what she means, she should only preach to those 'under Baptism', and in any case, she speeds on, she is not precisely *preaching*, she is 'exercising her gifts', an obligation to the Spirit who inspires her rather than an impertinent advancing of her own merits. But the sister is not satisfied and carries on probing. A verbal tussle ensues, in which Mrs Atomy is driven back on Scripture, to pelt her adversary with texts which direct elder women to teach the younger. And this, she demurely states, is how it all started, by addressing members of her own sex,

> but when she considered the glory of God was manifested in babes and sucklings, and that she was desired by some to admit all that pleased to come, she could not deny to impart those things the Spirit had communicated to her: but still her Sister insisted upon her former objection, & said she ought not to preach to the world. (p88)

At this a third woman joins the squabble, turning upon Mrs Atomy's challenger to say 'that Truth sought no corners, why should she say so?'

Now a man stands up and demands to know what Mrs Atomy means by 'those who are under Baptism' anyhow? and a colossal argy-bargy breaks out about legal and illegal baptism.

*

But let us pause here while they wrestle over Simon Magus, Ananias and other biblical touchstones – as incomprehensible to the secular twentieth-century mind as they are crucial to the seventeenth century – to consider the tendency of the discussion so far. When Mrs Atomy's challenger arose in the form of that hot-under-the-collar woman at present confronting her, it was not to take issue with her revolutionary message concerning the non-existence of hell, the salvation of all creatures, etc, which one would think matter for long and deep debate. No: these topics are simply ignored. They are not at issue, at least in Edwards' version. The dispute begins and ends in the question of the speaker's right to speak. And if the four disputants are now at it hammer and tongs about baptism, that is not because it is being considered as a subject in itself but solely as it affects the woman's right to speak.

This illustrates the major problem for women ministers of the period: their inaudibility. When they spoke, their words and arguments were not listened to. Only the fact that they were speaking at all was registered, and became the subject of irate dispute.

What was a woman preacher to do in these depressing circumstances? One answer was: pray. No one can quarrel with a prayer, at least while it is going on; and one can get in a few sharp jabs to the opposition under its cover. Mrs Atomy now prays, beseeching God to discover the iniquity in the hearts of those present who do not 'acknowledge his weak ones' who speak God's Truth. She also (rather optimistically, perhaps) thanks God that there has been no riot this time.

But the baptism issue seems to have beaten even the intrepid Mrs Atomy. Acknowledging that she is 'not very fit to argue these questions', she abdicates the Table, totters back and retreats to the fireside, 'and then another Sister said, You have heard what was delivered, and may rest satisfied' (p88).

How jubilant Mr Edwards is at this direct hit. We seem to see him lay aside his quill and smirk to himself in a less than angelic manner, rubbing his hands. She's down. Theology (he did rather well at Queen's College, Cambridge, where he became University Preacher) will always floor a woman – or a holy draper, or a pious butcher. In his fantasy, Mrs Attaway, or Atomy, or whatever she calls herself, grovels before his mighty pen.

And now he comes to think of it, he has been informed this very week 'by a Minister who came out of Kent', that at Brasted where John Saltmarsh (another inveterate enemy) is minister, there is yet another woman preacher, '(one at least if not more) in which company besides preaching, 'tis reported ... that they break Bread [ie dispense communion] also, and every one in their order' (p89).

When John Saltmarsh came to read this, and the rest of *Gangraena*, he was livid. What a waste of paper, what a waste of time, he snarled, between groans, in the addendum to his pamphlet, *Groanes for Liberty*, in which he answered the gangrenist in March of the same year. There's no such woman preacher in Brasted, the groaner states; and her non-existence is the measure of the grand fantasist, Mr Edwards.[13] He keeps it short, for 'I had said more to ye, had ye printed more Reason, and less Reviling, and something more than Stories and Winter Tales' (p32). Not so Jeremiah Burroughes, another of the aspersed. In July Burroughes brought to the press his *Vindication of Mr Burroughes, Against Mr EDWARDS his foul Aspersions*. He saw in Edwards a moral equivalent of a physical disease in which the patient 'cast[s] up the excrementitious filthiness at the mouth', the product of an 'exulcerate mind'. Mr Burroughes, boiling with indignation, saw Edwards' work as a great vomit which sullied all in its path, and lamented the power of calumny to stick. How do you answer a tissue of attention-seeking falsehoods, he wondered, for human beings are so made that they have a yen to lick up slander of their neighbours, the viler the better?[14]

Poor Mrs Attaway: she never answered back. For by the time the second part of *Gangraena* had gone to press, she had not only been heard to mull over the idea of divorce with approval but put theory into action by eloping with a lewd lover. Two gentlemen of the Inns of Court, given Edwards' seal of approval as 'civil and well disposed men'[15] had told him about their chat with Mrs Attaway, whose preaching they went along to hear 'out of novelty'. Mentioning Mr Milton's notorious *Doctrine and Discipline of Divorce* (1643), she asked their opinion of the book, 'for she had an unsanctified husband' whom she could do without; she would definitely look into the work. And, adds Edwards, grinning from ear to ear, she has been as good as her word, for she has run away with another woman's husband, this *saint* of yours, Mr Goodwin and Mr Saltmarsh, this 'wretched woman'.

In a combustible world exploding at every corner with

ironies, few are more tremendous than Mrs Attaway citing John Milton on divorce. For although Milton describes carnal relations in a bad marriage as 'two carcasses chained unnaturally together; or, as it may happen, a living soul bound to a dead corpse',[16] he argues overwhelmingly for the *male* right to divorce a morally and spiritually degenerate female: 'if the woman be naturally so of disposition, as will not help to remove, but help to increase that same God-forbidden loneliness', the mismating will lead to suicidal despair, brothels and adulteries. Created as a helpmeet for her husband, woman is inferior and secondary. In *Tetrachordon* (1644) he does admit that even a woman, matched with a godless sot, is 'being herself the redeemed of Christ ... not still bound to be the vassall of him, who is the bondslave of Satan'.[17] Such women will always be the rarest of the rare, exceptions that prove the rule. They would hardly include a vulgar, loudmouthed Mrs Attaway, lace-maker of Cheapside, whom Milton would have classed amongst pollutants. But Milton helped open the bag out of which the revolutionary cat charged.

To change our metaphor: just as the wise old saying has it that 'Erasmus laid the egg that Luther hatched' (meaning that the Catholic Erasmus' attempt to reform the Roman Church from within generated the Protestant revolution he deplored), so we might call Mrs Attaway Milton's chick.

In a stop-press Appendix,[18] breathlessly exulting at his victory, the gangrenist is able to report that his suspicions have been only too richly vindicated. 'Mistress Attaway the Lacewoman', having been interrogated by the Committee of Examination for her preaching, has bolted with her follower and paramour, William Jenney. This scandal happened just a fortnight ago, and it is known that the lascivious hypocrites have fled overseas.

Worse, William Jenney has left his wife pregnant at home, with other children, utterly distraught.

Worse still, Mrs Attaway has deserted her husband, an army man.

Just as shocking: she has abandoned her own children, leaving them 'exposed to the world at six and seven', removing all her goods of any value.

Yet more heinous: Mrs Attaway, claiming to have been tipped

off by a local prophet, has milked her congregation of a prodigious amount of money, on the pretext that the end of the world is nearer than had been thought, and that she and an elect group must go to Jerusalem to repair it. She had £10 from one young girl for this pious purpose.

Better still: Mr Edwards has got hold of a pair of incriminating personal letters by the lovebirds, which he will forthwith print. The first is a nasty dismissal by Jenney of his wife, dated 15 February. The second is a love letter by Mrs Attaway:

> Dearest Friend and wellbeloved in the Lord, I am unspeakably sorry in respect of thy sufferings, I being the object that occasioned it, how shall I ever be able to answer it, I need such love, I shall desire to dedicate my spirit to the Lord, to seek him in thy behalf, that he would be pleased to set thee at liberty [from his wife] ... when *Jehosophat* knew not what to do, he looked to the Lord, let us look to him ... not questioning but we shall be delivered [Edwards interpolates sardonically: 'Now they are run away together they are delivered'] in the mean season I shall give up my heart and affections to thee in the Lord, and whatsoever I have or am in him who is our head, thou shalt command it ... I shall rest in the possession of thy love. (p115)

So excited has Mr Edwards become by his scandalous discovery that it seems to have infected the printer, for the pagination goes wildly astray here. What a gift to the heretic-detector. The charlatans decamp, leaving behind them destruction and odium. And the message to be gleaned by the discerning reader from the episode? – 'the world may see what these women preachers are, thus to write to another woman's husband and now go away together' (p115).

*

Were there more trenchant reasons to fuel Dr Edwards' misogynist rants, over and above the acculturated scorn of women which was his inheritance? Say the word 'Katharine Chidley' to the gangrenist, and he turned pale. It is a curious fact that he prefers in the earlier parts of *Gangraena* the ripe pickings of rotten female fruit, Mrs Attaway, over a skirmish with the dreadful Katharine.

For Katharine Chidley, the first of the great female controversialists of the revolutionary era had singled out Master Edwards, several years before, as her special adversary.

When John Lanseter, a Bury St Edmunds shopkeeper and member of the local gathered church founded by Katharine Chidley, was brought the text of the second part of *Gangraena*, in which he was called a pedlar who had opened (instead of his pack) the Book of Ezra to a meeting, he felt the onset of the same inflammation as tended to afflict all Edwards' victims. His pamphlet, *Lanseter's Lance,* FOR *Edwardses Gangrene: or A ripping up, and laying open some rotten, putrified, corrupt, stinking matter*, is one of the choicest contributions to the gangrene controversy. Lanseter is furious at being called a 'pedlar', scum or dregs. Yes, he went to the meeting but he didn't say the things Edwards accuses him of. Yes, he said a lot (all of it pious and humble), but not that. The only way to sort this out, he feels, is to go and have it out in person with Edwards. On 29 June, he turns up on Mr Edwards' doorstep, with *Gangraena*, Part II, in his hand, and some friends as witnesses. In *Lanseter's Lance* he relates the conversation verbatim.

'Sir, do you know me?' asks Lanseter.

'No, I do not know you.'

'Sir, my name is Lanseter, and I come from Bury, and you have mentioned me in your book.'

'I have so,' admits Edwards, his stomach no doubt churning.

'Sir, do you know that those things are truths which you have written here of me?'

Edwards squirms: 'They are none of mine, but the relation of others.'

'That's all one, seeing you are the divulger thereof, and this book is yours: Sir, what if these things be proved false: how then?'

'It will not lie upon me, but upon those from whom I had the relation.'[19]

Lanseter wants to know who they are: Edwards, flustered, temporises, promises to write to his informers, but can't at this moment lay hand on the letters. He will look round later, he murmurs. Lanseter insists he can prove that the information is false.

Then Edwards has his brainwave: perhaps, he hazards, it's another Lanseter, not you at all.

There's no other Lanseter in Bury. None whatsoever.

Another brainwave: 'Lanseter' may not be the real Lanseter but an impostor. The gangrenist has had impostors at his door before.

Lanseter insists on being Lanseter, *the* Lanseter who lives in Bury, 'and I am the man, and there is no other of that name'.

'How shall I know that?' asks Edwards cunningly.

One of Lanseter's witnesses vouches for his identity and character; and Lanseter demands to know why he's being called a pedlar when he's served his master, a mercer, for eleven and a half years and has a shop in Bury? What's all this about packs and preaching on Ezra? The chorus vociferously agrees.

And even if he had called the Ministers of the Church of England names, says Lanseter (even though he didn't) what would have been wrong with that?

Now Edwards feels on stronger, because theological, ground, among unlettered yokels; he launches into a statement of the wickedness of attacking the ordained Ministers of God. A bitter battle of tongues ensues, in which Lanseter and his men asperse Edwards' church as Roman Catholic. Finally Edwards refuses to say another word, whereupon Lanseter concludes, immortally: 'Neither have you spelled my name right; for it should not be Lansister but Lanseter', a grievance which has evidently been festering (pA4^v).

Off flounce the visitors, back to Bury, having received no pledge from Edwards to vindicate the non-pedlar if Edwards' tale is proved wrong. When a deputation returns on 27 July, Mr Edwards' loins are girded. He will not talk to them, he snarls; he knows their way of lying, they may be gone, he will not have anything to do with them, etcetera etcetera until they are out of earshot (pBl').

All goes quiet in his study as Edwards recovers from this brush with Bury bumpkins.

Then Lanseter hurls his lance. Edwards is confronted on the first page with the memory of the dreadful name, Katharine Chidley: in large, aggressively swirling type, eighteen lines to the page, with an illuminated 'W' initiating the word 'When', Lanseter brings the gangrenist face to face with his Nemesis:

When Mr Thomas Edwards his book against Independency
and Toleration, came forth, about four years ago, O what
boasting there was then among the Prelatical party, and
Temporizers, as if the day had been their own! But when the
woman came and strook the nail of Independency into the
head of his Sisera, with the Hammer of God's holy word;
then their sport was spoiled and quashed, the effects whereof
appeareth: for since that time he could never set anything but
Gangraena, or such like stuff (as his *Antipologia* before it,
which the same party answered and presented as a new-years
gift, that he might break off his old sins, etc.). (pA1)

Edwards had been notably abstinent in mentioning Katharine
Chidley in the first part of *Gangraena*, deigning only to repeat a
tale of how, last August, when she came to Stepney, where she had
poached a few souls, she ranted against the Independent, Mr
Greenhill, for preaching in the old Anglican churches, which she
regarded as centres of idol worship, consecrated to idolatry 'under
the names of saints and angels'. They ought to be pulled down, and
certainly not prayed in. Well if you come to that, Edwards has
Greenhill retort to the church-demolitionist, the whole of England
has been set apart to St George, Scotland to St Andrew and so on,
so by her reasoning the whole country has been desecrated and left
polluted for prayer. The story ends with the jaded Mr Greenhill
sloping off, plagued to death by Katharine's 'talkative and
clamorous' refusal to accept her put-down (*Gangraena* I,
pp79–80).

The retort about England and St George attributed to
Greenhill is an old chestnut which could not have floored a
disputant as sharp and experienced as Katharine Chidley. The story
is patently a wish-fulfilment fantasy by the humiliated Edwards,
who conceives a fictional come-uppance for the woman who has
bankrupted his own credit. For what Greenhill is alleged to have
done to Katharine, Katharine has in fact done to Edwards. Mrs
Chidley (says Lanseter) was the Jael whose pamphlets drove a nail
so deeply into the skull of the unholy Edwards that the wounds
have suppurated ever since, rendering him impotent to utter
anything but gangrenous matter. The indignity of being worsted

by a mere woman was evidently an affront Edwards keenly felt. And yet Lanseter does not emphasise humiliation at the hands of a woman: for him, Katharine Chidley is a powerful ally and zealous campaigner, mentioned with respect as having effectively struck dumb the champion of an opposition as vociferous as it was smug. Lanseter knew her as a formidable representative of the Duppa-Chidley gathered church in London, with its lay pastorate, who had come out to settle the daughter church.

*

Katharine Chidley's two tracts against Edwards predate anything so far discussed in relation to Edwards. Her *Justification of the Independent Churches* takes us back to 1641, when London was in a ferment of excitement, Parliament besieged by petitions, demonstrations, mass preachings, cavalcades: the time when nonconformists, persecuted for so many years, came bursting out of the underground. Katharine was a Shrewsbury woman, the mother of seven surviving children, of whom the eldest, Samuel, became her secretary, as well as the treasurer of the Leveller party, a close friend from early days of John Lilburne. She was a woman of immense, focused energy, an activist from the tradesman classes, who spoke on behalf of the poor and dispossessed. In Shrewsbury, rife with radical sectarianism, she was in frequent trouble with the minister of Saint Chad's, Peter Studley, for non-attendance at compulsory services. No doubt she was one of those whose obduracy the much-crossed Studley lamented in his pamphlet of 1633, *The Looking-Glass of Schism*, a 'sect of men and women' causing him insufferable 'vexation and trouble of mind' with whom he had wrestled for thirteen years without being able to straighten out their 'wandering fancies' or enforce their conformity. Katharine and her husband are recorded as being presented to the Ecclesiastical Court for absenteeism, and Katharine is one of seven women reported for refusal to be 'churched' after childbirth (see pp117–18 below). Afterwards she seems to have complied, with gritted teeth, for Studley withdrew the charge.[20]

In her 1645 retort to Edwards, *A New-Yeares-Gift ... to Mr Thomas Edwards; That he may break off his old sins, in the old year*, Katharine implies that her family was bullied out of Shrewsbury by the church authorities, (which must have been in 1629, shortly after the birth of her fourth son):

> Both I, and my faithful yokefellow have jointly tasted of the
> pressures of the Hierarchy above these 20 years, and the
> Bishops-Priests have driven us out of our place of abode 16
> years ago: and we (amongst the rest of the people of God,) are
> now prosecuted afresh by Mr Edwards, and such as he [as]
> the movers of sedition, and disturbers of the kingdoms.[21]

Evidently her fight with Studley in Shrewsbury trained her for the
combat with Edwards in London, where she and her family fled,
although she claimed that Edwards' works were so 'frothy' that they
answered themselves before they were written. She seems to have
been personally familiar with his magniloquent style of pulpit
oratory, which she describes in her *New-Yeares-Gift* as being that of
'a brave warrior' who can fight well up there 'where you are sure
none shall come near you' (p1).

The Chidleys were tailors, and Katharine was to manage the
business, care for the children, evangelise, write and lead political
demonstrations with the boundless energy that characterised all her
dealings. In 1651, she would supply the soldiers in Ireland with
4000 pairs of stockings and in 1652 with another thousand. How
Edwards' Christian patience must have been tried at the thought of
being taken on in single combat by a female seller of stockings. Part
of the qualification for being a gentleman was that you did nothing
useful to earn your keep.

Katharine was a fighter, and entirely lacking in false humility.
She went for Edwards in her *Justification* like a dog to a rat, with a
perfunctory bob of the head to her lack of scholarship and
supposed womanly 'weakness', suggesting that, should the reader
find fault with her unsystematic answers, he should patiently think
it through and amend for himself where necessary. This rationality,
utterly foreign to Edwards and most university men, is sustained
throughout the document. Because she was God-fearing,
Katharine was fearless. Convinced of her state of Grace, a member
of a classless elite, she spoke with confidence. One feels from the
aggressive toughness of Katharine's address how belonging to a
'separated', 'gathered' and 'particular' church empowered women,

as members of an elect minority, who were required to develop the power to argue and assert opinions. Katharine was an opinionated woman of this new generation, self-schooled to answer back boldly in public. She probably had little formal schooling, beyond the tuition in elementary reading and writing skills taught in a 'dame school'. By contrast, Edwards had benefited from the most formidable education his country could offer. But Katharine claimed in her *Justification* that her training was incomparably superior: the teachings of Oxford and Cambridge, as radical sects were never tired of repeating, boiled down to gilded rubbish. Katharine proudly claimed that she has been 'trained up in the School of Christ' (p7). Who could speak against her?

How did Katharine know she was right? Through her calling. God called; she answered – it was as simple as that. The Bible's truth is described as 'plain' (p2). She speaks for the duty of separation from the national Church by 'all the Lord's people, that are made Kings and Priests to God' and therefore 'have a free voice' in electing ministers (p5). Gathered congregations are subject to no king but Christ (p11), and have the power to elect ministers. To Edwards' charge that dissenting men and women are so boldly assertive that they draw many to them, she answers with a pithy and acidic aphorism that sheep that have found good pasture commonly beckon their fellow sheep to join them, 'But Hogs will not do so', being jealous of their swill (p24). To The Great Hog's apprehension that liberty is seductive to 'mean persons, and such as have been kept under', she ripostes:

> that they that have been kept under, have been kept under
> by the tyranny of the Men of Sin; This you confess to be
> especially the poor, upon whom those Taskmasters have laid
> the greatest burthens. Therefore for them to affect liberty is
> no wonder. (p24)

Although Katharine denies any tendency to disturb the peace or create disorder, she is overwhelmingly on the side of those who 'have been kept under'. In this respect, she is also better taught than her antagonist: she lives in the same world as the oppressed. She sees the pauperism and hunger of the common people, and she knows who to blame. The reader of Edwards' and Katharine's tracts is struck by the gulf of knowledge that lies between the two. Edwards knows nothing but scorn and fear for the mass of the underclass; Katharine lives in the same world with those who have been 'kept under', breaks bread with them and shares their sufferings.

Her attack on the established church helps a modern reader to understand why the clergy was so hated, as beneficiaries of an institution which was not only an instrument of law and government but a means of taxation, whose priests raked in profits from the poor. The Canon Law is evil, she says, being run by evil men on a market system. The most vivid passages come when she details priestly extortion. Priests:

> oppress the people, by their cruel forcing of them to pay so much as they demand ... they will force poor people even to pawn their clothes for I am able to prove that they do demand of poor people before they can have a child (that is but fourteen, or fifteen years of age) buried in one of the out-Church-yards of the great Parishes (which land is the free gift of the dead, for the help of the poor) ... it will cost the poorest parent seven or eight shillings.

The congregations are taxed at every stage of their lives, from birth (you're charged to be baptised, and baptism is compulsory), through marriage (the priest needs paying for the ceremony), to death (you pay for the funeral service and a patch of consecrated ground). Try not to give birth, for you'll be taxed for suffering the indignity of being 'churched'.

'Churching': here we can feel the indignant smart in Katharine's voice. She speaks for generations of women who had suffered the public humiliation of being ritually cleansed from the 'impurity' of childbirth. This ritual derived from the Book of Leviticus, where the Hebrew purification laws had declared a woman to be impure for forty days after the delivery of a son and eighty after a daughter: a woman had to come to the church, making sure not to touch any consecrated object. Her head was to be covered by a veil, sometimes stipulated by churchmen as a white shift or a veil hanging right down the back. She had to kneel at the Communion rails and sit in a special pew, bench or stool, rather than on the pews where unpolluted bottoms might repose. As she knelt at the rails, the priest would utter a set incantation, at which Katharine sneers in her *Justification*:

> before the mother dare go abroad, she must have their blessing, that the Sun shall not smite her by day, nor the Moon by night, for which blessing of theirs, they must have an offering, and the like they require for all the children that be born into the world, though there live not one of six to be men and women. (p57)

Women of all classes abhorred this mumbo-jumbo as a spell or relic of Roman Catholicism, thinly disguised under a veneer of Protestant acceptability when the 1552 Prayer Book changed the title from the medieval 'Purification of Women' to 'Thanksgiving of Women'. They resented the idea that their bodies were polluted and pollutant; the veil was a particular insult, since women found guilty of illicit sex were paraded in church wearing a sheet or veil. Indignation was compounded by disgust that until they had been 'churched' they were not allowed to take Communion (perhaps their lips would soil the cup?) and, if they refused to be churched (and to pay the fee for churching), they would be excommunicated. Thus, not only had they to go through the mortal danger of childbirth, which might happen every year for twenty-five years; not only might their babies die; not only must they pay the priest a so-called 'offering' but they were threatened with damnation if they resisted this expensive stigma.

Joan Whitup turned up for 'churching' in Essex wearing her hat. No veil. She stomped to her own pew and sat her unsanctified behind on it, to the horror of the episcopate. Nobody but whores wore veils, Joan bitterly said, and it was a whore that first dreamed the whole charade up. Was Joan accusing the Church of being the Whore of Babylon? She was. Can we wonder, given this level of rage, that radical Protestant women had taken their scissors to vicars' surplices? Dorothy Hazzard, the Dissenting wife of an Anglican Bristol minister, set up a safehouse for women wishing to avoid churching. They could stay at the parsonage during their 'lying-in', thus avoiding the ceremonies by residing in her liberal husband's jurisdiction.[22]

The church for Katharine Chidley maintained the 'locusts of Egypt', a costly plague, fining poor men for working on Sundays, living in tax-free, rent-free houses, eating out all round the parish; raking it in by licensing midwives and teachers. At the end of her tract, Katharine invites Edwards to a six-a-side debate: she will choose five colleagues and he may come with an equal number of Presbyterians (bring more if you like) and a live debate will 'save you a labour for publishing your large Tractates'. However, she wickedly adds, if you win, it will be no victory, 'for I am a poor worm, and unmeet to deal with you' (p80). Poor Edwards could not win against a woman so agile, unscrupulous in turning her disadvantages into unassailable vantage-points. Brag he might in his next fusillade, *Antapologia*, that women, being naturally weak in the head, tended to gravitate to the sects, 'not able to examine grounds and reasons';[23] but he was seriously daunted and discomfited. He had somehow attracted an adversary who was here, there and everywhere, stirring up trouble, threatening to knock down churches with her demolitionist son whose *Thunder from the Throne of God against the Temples of Idols* (1653) was to be suppressed by Order of Parliament. Samuel, truly a mother's boy, spoke with intense pride of how God had used Katharine to 'totally rout all the forces of Mr Edwards, that great Champion for the Church of England, as may appear by her works extant in print'; she'd done, he felt, more in a few months than others in a lifetime to tear down the establishment.[24]

Samuel was for smashing those 'old Chiming chimneys of the drunken Whore of Babylon' as he called the church bell-towers, 'not a stone of them remain upon another'.[25] You feel that this man who did not care how haywire his contemporaries thought him and gabbled his thoughts down on to the page as his incensed conscience insisted, itched to undertake the clearance work with his own two hands. Likewise Katharine: 'forward in this good work of pulling down of the Idols' Temples'.[26]

Movingly, he carried on her concern for the desperate position of the poor: in *A Cry Against A Crying Sin* (1656) he wrote against the death penalty for small-time thieves, publishing the pamphlet in blood-red ink. He has been called 'gentle Samuel':[27] I do not read him or his pugnacious Leveller mother as gentle people. The Chidley collaboration brought back the passion into compassion; the angry action into love of fellow beings. All Milton's prose works stacked in a tower two foot tall would not yield a tithe of the human empathy that fires Samuel's *Cry Against A Crying Sin*, which blasts the judiciary of his day for hanging people for theft of property worth over one shilling ('grand larceny') or burglary. Although juries committed 'pious perjury' to save criminals from the gallows, and the literate could save themselves by 'benefit of clergy' (ability to read a biblical 'neck-verse'), pilferers were still hanged under a punitive legal code that offset low detection rates with severe deterrent sentencing.[28]

Never-say-die Samuel reports how he pestered the mayor and Common Council, the Court of Oyer and Terminer, Newgate, the Old Bailey, the Army Council, inveighing against the hanging of the poor for theft. 'To take away their lives is A SIN, A CRYING SIN; yea ... it's a NATIONAL SIN', which God would avenge (p14). People have a right to eat. Hunger confers the right to steal. The true child of his mother, Samuel refused to give up. He urged the reader of his blood-red pamphlet to direct action.

A complex character, with the Puritan business acumen wheeler-dealing with property, he was good but not good enough with figures. As Commonwealth Registrar of Debentures, Samuel amassed property by speculating in the sale of Crown lands, only to lose it all. He experimented with newspaper publication, lobbied, petitioned, protested, was arrested, schemed, through to the end of the 1660s, when he drops away from our sight in the Hearth Tax return as being in prison and in arrears. He had been seen as an ass, his mother as a hyena, collaboratively affronting the ears of contemporaries for over twenty years with truths they did not want to know.

*

When in 1646 Lanseter brought the detested name of Chidley to the gangrenist's attention, a rosy flush mottled his terminally ill features. Winter was coming on, and he had not long to live. Maddocks and Pinnell, in their *Gangraenachrestum, or, A Plaister to Allay the tumor* had noticed in September that he was looking seedy, so that 'you read his sickness in his forehead'.[29] But Edwards' fury still had enough spleen in it to generate Part III of *Gangraena* in December, and scratch down a livid pen-portrait of Katharine Chidley:

> an old Brownist, and her son a young Brownist ... who not content with spreading their poison in and about London go down into the country to gather people to them, and among other places have been this Summer at Bury in Suffolk, to set up and gather a church there ... about seven persons .... Gaffer Lanseter of Bury (for so he was unless he hath commenced Master by preaching) ... was a great man with Katherine Chidley and her son, and is left Preacher to that company ... and I have great reason to think by the Epistle to the Reader that Katherine Chidley and her son made that book called *Lanseters Lance*, because Katherine Chidley and her son's Books (for the mother and son made them together, one inditing and the other writing) are highly magnified, and the brazen-faced audacious old woman resembled unto Jael.[30]

Certainly Edwards is wrong to assume that the Chidleys wrote his tract for 'Gaffer' Lanseter. His class-bound assumption that the 'pedlar' couldn't write is just as off-beam as his notion that Katharine would have taken the trouble to puff herself in ghosting Lanseter's book. She was a professional polemicist who could never have conjured up Lanseter's vivid narrative of his visit to the gangrenist. She had better things to do. 'Brazen-faced' she was: a qualification for her work. 'Audacious' she would have been proud to admit herself. 'Old woman' she might be: but, like those aged Quakers, Elizabeth Hooton and Joan Brooksop defying authority in England, Barbados and New England, Katharine gave the phrase 'old woman' a new and challenging bite.

Edwards had a few more nuggets, he said, concerning Lanseter, Chidley and their fellow anarchists, which were too savoury to be squashed into a postscript: expect them in the Fourth Part. Sadly (especially in view of the fact that Lanseter was to fall to the bottle and 'heinous and beastly sins' which would get him thrown out of the Bury church in 1654)[31] there was no time. After penning a dry-as-dust treatise, *The Casting Down of the Last ... Hold of Satan*, to keep his hand in theologically, Edwards left

England for Holland in June 1647, and died in August. And with him died the cornucopia of vicious gossip which has given us these precious images of the radical mother dictating while her secretarial son inscribes her words.

6

THE SPIRIT OF THERAPY IN AN EMPTY NOTHING
CREATURE

SARAH WIGHT & HENRY JESSEY

'Miss A':	I must be damned.
Miss Sarah Wight:	I am damned already, from all eternity to all eternity: it's nothing to do, but it's done already.
'Miss A':	I was a great Professor, but I was but an hypocrite, and an hypocrite's hopes shall perish.
Sarah:	I have been an hypocrite, a revolter, a backslider.
'Miss A':	I know it shall be well with you.
Sarah:	As well as it was with Judas, who repented, and hanged himself: which I must do, before I shall be free from these torments.
'Miss A':	[upon departing]: I think I shall perish before I see you again.[1]

Two young gentlewomen sit together politely vying for the

lugubrious laurels which would go to the more spectacularly damned. Accompanying them is Henry Jessey, renowned Baptist minister and eminent busybody, scratching notes with his quill as to the details of their dolorous wrestle. Each girl seeks to checkmate the other. Miss A's first move is to announce her damnation.

Sarah, somewhat over fifteen and a half years old, replies with a stratagem derived from the Calvinist belief in reprobation, to the effect that her damnation dates from before the creation of the world.

Piqued by this claim to longevity, Miss A counters by recalling that her claim to odium rests on her earlier unctuous vaunting of herself as a Puritan high-achiever. She repeats the word 'hypocrite' with relish.

Sarah has been a hypocrite too. And worse.

Miss A resorts to a head-on charge, denying Sarah's claim to fame altogether: 'I know it shall be well with you.'

What a thing to say! In such a conversation, it counts as a snarling breach of etiquette.

Sarah retorts with grandiose irony. Oh yes, *very* well: as well as the greatest traitor that ever lived, Judas, whose exemplary suicide she hankers to emulate. No common sinner she.

Time passes before Miss A can summon an adequate response. As she rises to leave, and the polite formula about looking foward to meeting again comes to mind, she is struck by a brainwave. Off she blusters to perish in perdition, and never see Sarah again, thus proving her point.

Only she doesn't perish. Jessey notes that she is still alive. So is Sarah, but Sarah has changed her tune dramatically, and is now practising as a 'saved' (if blind, deaf, starved and bed-ridden) counsellor for souls who, like her erstwhile self, believe themselves damned. Her practice is thriving; she dispenses therapy and information to people 'of quality' and eminent ministers, as well as her fellow girls, and even, as Jessey writes his stop-press preface to *The Exceeding Riches of Grace ... In An Empty Nothing Creature* – after all of seventy-five days without food and sixty-five without drinking on two consecutive days – is beginning 'first to EAT, and to ARISE, June 11, 1647. Then (on Midsummer day) to WALK' (ppF,131).

Jessey accurately notes that cured despairers can make the best therapists, despite being (of themselves) 'empty nothing' females. Enraptured, the naïve minister sits studiously on, in the theatre of Sarah's bedroom, through nights and days taking down revelatory utterances, while something very canny in Sarah's subconscious mind giggles up her sad sleeve. How did all this come about?

*

Sarah's mother Mary lived in Lawrence Poultney, London, a highly respectable woman (Jessey makes it clear we are not dealing with riffraff but gentlefolk whose testimony can be trusted).[2] Mary had connections in Shrewsbury, and the maidservant called in to help the distraught mother cope with her ever-raving daughter (and will herself testify to the household's miracles) came with good references: being known to 'Mr Cradock of Wales' – surely Walter Cradock, radical lecturer at Allhallows the Great in Thames Street, who had left this same year to become an itinerant preacher in Wales.[3] We are among the fiery nonconformist left-wing, with their flock of strenuous women members.

We are also in a far more ancient, pre-Reformation tradition of 'Holy Maids', like Elizabeth of Leominster, Anne Wentworth of Ipswich and (most memorably) Elizabeth Barton, 'the Holy Maid of Kent', a marian prophetess whose raptures, convulsions, ventriloquistic 'belly-voices' and miraculous *inedia* (survival on no or little food apart from the Eucharist), oracles and faith-healings made her chapel a site of popular pilgrimage in the early sixteenth century. But Elizabeth was political dynamite. In the last of three warnings, the young nun burst into Henry VIII's presence at Canterbury, to tell him that, if he married Anne Boleyn, 'he should die a villain's death'.[4] Elizabeth was hanged and beheaded for high treason, with male confederates, in 1534.

Sarah's drama had no traumatic political reverberations. Hers was the story of a marginalised adolescent writing her own name in that margin; finding a way through personal trauma in meaningful work as a therapist.

*

Mary Wight, Sarah's widowed mother, was an old protegée of Jessey's, who herself had experienced religious turmoil; and Sarah's story really begins with the bout of despair by which 'about ten or eleven years ago' (around 1636), Mary came to Jessey's notice as a soul-sufferer in the grip of Calvinist 'sad despair', which had been going on 'for some years together' (pK). During these throes, Mary had been so incapacitated that her little daughter was turned over to 'her godly Grandmother, Mrs Wright [Wight?] of Daintree', where she imbibed, from about the age of five or six to nine, wholesome principles.

Religious trauma therefore ran in Sarah's maternal family – and her father, like those of many women preachers and prophets, was dead. If her mother's trauma had lasted 'several years together' when she met Jessey, it means that the little girl (who was then about five or six) had never known a mother who was otherwise than in a state of what we would now class as clinical depression. Then she had experienced abandonment by a parent legitimately relieved of all maternal responsibilities. From her childhood, Sarah is described as being 'of a tender heart, and oft afflicted in Spirit'; but these symptoms did not become overwhelming until the age of puberty, 'about twelve years old'. By this time, she must have bottled a great volume of hurt rage against a mother who had held the spiritual limelight. This anger was inturned as violent self-loathing, generated as a hysterical bid for attention which, sensational and well-aimed as it was, represented a common response to intolerable pressure by many Puritan women – and not a few men.

Spasms of guilt erupted in trembling fits 'in her hands and body'. Trivial misdemeanours were magnified within her by a pervasive culture of self-abasement and introspection into a weltering inner drama of heaven and hell.

Where is your hood? asked Sarah's mother one day, when Sarah came in hoodless. To which she 'suddenly answered, *My grandmother hath it*'. Overwhelmed with guilt at this shocking lie (for she knew she'd carelessly lost it), the tremblings came on, and Sarah embarked upon her great horror of being '"shut out of Heaven, and must be damn'd, damn'd, damn'd"'.

Now began Sarah's mother's penance. The house must have rung with the cry of 'damn'd' day and night. Sarah often 'attempted wickedly to destroy herself: as by drowning, strangling, stabbing, seeking to beat out her eye and brains: wretchedly bruising and wounding herself' (p7). This self-mutilation opened the door to a stream of ministers, exceedingly eminent in Independent and separatist circles, from Thomas Goodwin to John Simpson, the cream of the London gathered churches. Ministers travelled to Sarah from Shrewsbury to bestow their counsel. And Jessey reproduces a vast list of genteel lay people who visited, comforted, prayed, and restrained the tormented girl.

Sarah got worse and worse. A month before her crisis and turning-point, she headed for the Thames to throw herself in, but, changing her mind, went to a pious lecture instead.

Being beside herself gave Sarah the chance to say the taboo thoughts which her culture censored. She would say 'there was no God, no Devil, no Heaven, no Hell, but what she felt within her' – Ranterish and Antinomian heresies which must have brought her mother out in cold sweats. By denying God, Sarah would have achieved a complex gratification: she could shock her elders, unleash repressed aggression, and 'prove' (if there was a God) that she was damned.

Mother and daughter wrestled in Electral power struggle.

Sarah took hold of a cup. '"As sure as this cup shall break, there is no Hell,"' she raved; and hurled it histrionically to the far side of the room, where it failed to smash.

Mother did not neglect the opportunity to soothe her daughter with the lesson from divine Providence: '"Lo here Child, it is not broke."' No doubt she was hoping Sarah would not repeat the experiment.

Sarah swiped it up and furiously tried again. And again. Flung it at the edge of the door. The cup rolled peacefully to rest. Maddened, Sarah threw it a couple more times, until she managed to chip it. But no more than the merest 'nip', Jessey insists. (The cup became her favourite after her conversion, but a careless waterbearer having accidentally smashed it, the keepsake no longer survives, Jessey earnestly chronicles in his endless bid for scrupulous authenticity (pp11–12).)

On careered Sarah in her headlong charge to perdition. She developed a fondness for quoting the curses out of Job and Jeremiah.

Her 'tender and good' mother, notwithstanding harassment by a daughter chanting '"Let the day perish wherein I was born ... Why died I not from the womb?"' (Job 3:3,11), kept watch night and day. Eventually, worn out by sleep starvation, on Tuesday, 6 April she called in the services of the maid vouched for by Mr Cradock of Wales.

As delivery approached, Sarah's condition paradoxically worsened. She began to blaspheme horribly.

Alarm must have been mingled with relief amongst the watchers round that tempestuous bed when Sarah lapsed into a trance lasting from Tuesday till Saturday, during which period she drank only two to three cups of water. Sarah's victory over Satan, mother, appetite and the constraints of her role as an 'empty nothing' female was about to begin.

*

At midnight on Saturday, 10 April 1647, Sarah 'began to experience the first experience of comforts', reports Jessey. Unusually, this took the physical form of being 'struck blind and deaf: her eyes being fast closed up, wrapped up together' (p14). But if eyes and ears were sealed, resisting the tyranny of the outside world, her mouth was open and her tongue volubly active. She would not take in, but she was free to give out. Sarah now began to preach from her bed, exclaiming her elation that Christ came to save '"the meanest"', and '"To me, the chiefest of sinners"' (p16).

St Paul, greatest of Apostles, was the original 'chiefest of sinners'. This staple manoeuvre by 'meaner' and female pretenders to divine inspiration was seized by Sarah Wight with gusto. Here was the ticket of Christian paradox which immunised the holder from the muting effects of earthly handicap (being female, base-born, poor, uneducated, sinful). Proclaim yourself a grovelling worm and take centre-stage. Indeed, this passport did more. Being nothing and nobody was the best and quickest way up – the Almighty could locate himself more entirely in an empty house:

> But God [said Paul] hath chosen the foolish things of the world to confound the wise; and God hath chosen the weak things of the world 'to confound the things which are mighty. (I Cor 1:27)

Preaching away, deaf and blind, for the better part of a fortnight, Sarah makes up for all the lectures and sermons that have bored her helpless ears; the rebukes and constraints; the biddable silence she has held ever since she learned to speak. On and on she talks – and the thralls round the bed listen.

During this reversal of roles, Sarah renegotiates her relationship with her mother, so as to claim a larger portion of power and intimacy on her own terms. Mother has had a nervous breakdown; Sarah's breakdown transcends Mother's by cracking her apart to reveal an inner glory. Mother is rebuked by her holy daughter as a chattery nuisance when she coos at her to take a little sustenance, 'laying her hand upon hers, (for she heard nothing which was said unto her)' Sarah flicks her off in vexation, snapping '"Why do you hinder my Communion with God?"' and is righteously indignant for some time afterwards (p18). Obediently, mother backs off.

The night of 13 April brings an epic battle to Sarah's bedroom. She starts convulsively and cries out, '"The Devil fights with me, as he did with Michael and his Angels. Do you see him? Do you see him?"' and she flaps the hell-hordes away with the back of her hand. Everybody stares at the air she is heroically walloping. '"But the Angel shall prevail,"' shouts the jubilant girl, and then, '"He is come, he is come, he is come"'. A cosmic and apocalyptic war wages over the super-important soul of the 'empty nothing' creature. Valiant as Michael the warrior-archangel who purged Heaven of Lucifer, she is also befriended by this Angel, harbinger of Christ, of whom she repeats nine or ten times to her audience ('speaking somewhat louder'), '"Love him, love him, etc."' Parched by these efforts, Sarah now requests water, improving the occasion by phrasing it thus: '"Give me a little water, good people; Christ hath given you water freely"' (p20).

More cups of water; more pious counsel; further reflections on being '"a poor empty, disconsolate, sinful, vain, contemptible worm ... Yet hath Jesus Christ loved me."' Two days' pause, from Tuesday till Thursday, 15 April and she is off again, calling for Mother.

Mother speeds to the bed, and tenderly placing Sarah's hand on her neck, is recognised by Sarah by a scar there. Sarah bursts into tears on Mary's bosom and, stroking her face, says, '"I know you, Mother, and I love you with another love, than I loved you before."' She wonders if someone will wash her eyes, so that she can look at her mother. But this proves ineffective. Then Mrs Dupper their neighbour (and possibly wife or relative of John Duppa,[5] the ferocious separatist to whose church Katharine Chidley belonged) has the practical idea of prising apart Sarah's eyelids with her fingertips, 'and she saw, and knew her Mother and then immediately her EARS were opened', records the scribe (p25).

However, directly Mrs Dupper lets go, Sarah's eyelids close again. She (or God) is not yet ready to forfeit the privileges of holy blindness. But from now on, Sarah's sight and hearing keep coming and going, according to her need to pursue transactions with the outside world.

Sarah gives audience to her brother, whom she is able to see after an eye-bath. Things go well until she recalls that her brother, possibly a half-brother, has always been more filial-minded than herself. '"You never murmured so much against God, and against my Mother, as I have done. Ah, ah, ah," (fighting and weeping). "But I speak the rather ... that none should despair, because I have found mercy"' (p30). Resurgent pangs of sibling-rivalry (perhaps Sarah felt that the boy-child was preferred, and, yet worse, justly preferred) are staunched when Sarah remembers her new profession, founded on her previous wormhood.

*

Sarah's therapeutic techniques are closely modelled on her pre-conversion 'I'm-more-damned-than-you' disputes with her peers. But now they are benign and emollient. On 24 April, a deeply damned young woman visits to discuss her case:

> *Maid:* None can be in a worse condition than I; full of fears.
>
> *Sarah:* Of late my case was so, that if I had been all day burning in a fire, they could not have been in a worse condition.
>
> *Maid:* I was in ... extremities.
>
> *Sarah:* So it was with me ... (pp47–8)

Sarah's celebrity swells. Persons of quality flock. Saints, including

Jessey, wrestle verbally to get food, cordial, drink into the wasting maiden. The girl who called on 24 April returns for further sessions, and soon other afflicted women seek spiritual cures. The burden they overwhelmingly bring to Sarah is female guilt. And Sarah learns fast how to help them out of the sink of self-loathing in which they wallow. They shudderingly confide thoughts to her which they would never have admitted to anyone else: and they are able to do this because she is a woman who has been there. Nothing they confess shocks the once-damned counsellor.

A woman confides in Sarah (and her indefatigable amanuensis) that she has '"cursed thoughts of God continually"'. When her husband died, she thought, '"what is become of his soul? and what would become of me that had made him worse by my perverse words to him, when he was faulty"'. The hereafter becomes in these women's imaginative landscapes a dimension of double horror, in which a wife who has betrayed her marital vow of obedience by rowing with her husband (when *he* was 'faulty') may have clinched not only her damnation but his. The guilt which is a common phase of bereavement is magnified for this widow, so that she wakes one morning to a bedroom choked with smoke:

> and suddenly a fire went in at my mouth, and went down
> hot into my belly, and there it went flutter, flutter: Then ...
> I suddenly flew out of my bed, into the midst of the room;
> and a voice said within me to my heart, *Thou art damn'd,*
> *damn'd.* I felt the smell of Brimstone. (p77)

She did not sleep for six or seven weeks after this experience, which mimes demonic and sexual possession (the hell-flame enters her 'belly' through her mouth, whence the 'sin' issued), and the quickening of pregnancy ('flutter, flutter').

Sarah's response is to offer a personal mirror ('"I was as desperate as ever any"') together with reassurance ('"He'll show mercy"'). When the widow replies, '"But not to me, I cannot believe it",' Sarah again puts up the mirror of identification: '"You cannot believe it. I could not believe it, that he died for me"' (p79). To each negative, she replies by saying that she knows *exactly* what the sufferer means, and she too will come to experience release. The widow is difficult to convince.

Lady Ranelagh (the Puritan intellectual, friend of Milton) arrives, and Mrs Fiennes '(wife to Lord Say's eldest son)', snobbish Jessey gloats, plus Mrs Brice – a trio of distinguished saint-spotters who cross-question Sarah on her recovery. Sarah, having her wits about her, passes the test.

Sarah's counselling work becomes shrewd and practical:

Maid: I would fain be out of this life.
Sarah: Would you be sooner in Hell? is not that worse?
Maid: I would be sitting alone, and musing, and not work, because I have no hope.
Sarah: When you work not, have you no thoughts?
Maid: Yes, thoughts of sin and misery.
Sarah: Then 'tis better for you to be employed in business.

(p109)

Here Sarah initiates a dialectic which, tackling the illogic of the religious depressive's suicidal mindset (why do you want to be dead when hell has unnerved you in the first place?), moves on to give a sharp jolt to the inertia of depression, which perpetuates the symptoms. Her approach asks the patient to query whether she really wants to be cured.

3 May: a physician, Dr Coxe, subjects Sarah to tough sceptical questioning as to how she knows it is 'no delusion' (p114). Sarah passes creditably. Only women come for healing; men to assess the phenomenon.

When a depressed Moorish girl comes, Jessey cannot make out what she is saying and has to guess from Sarah's answers. A black girl in a white society, and presumably a slave, she has to be assured of the 'whiteness' of her soul, a formula which could only have perpetuated her double alienation – from society and from herself.[6]

Sarah, having forgotten what it feels like to be hungry and thirsty, is revolted by the smell of tasty food (p32). But on the seventy-sixth day, there is a turning-point: she agrees to try a little delicious broiled fish. The fish slips down nicely, and 'with joy in the Lord', Sarah 'did eat of it heartily before them'. In no time at all, she is calling for her clothes and is on her feet. Miracles, insists

Jessey, have *not* ceased. Witness Sarah's further progress toward normality on 25 June, when she 'opened her head and combed it': for twenty-four weeks now, she has been unable to bear the scraping of comb-teeth on a sensitive scalp (pp42–3). Sarah's head must have been quite a nasty nest by this time.

Soon she was sitting veiled in a godly meeting and on 30 June appeared at Mr Simpson's sermon at Allhallows the Great: Anna Trapnel's Simpson. Perhaps Anna was sitting in the same meeting when the trance-prodigy appeared, for Trapnel was another of Simpson's protegées. Anna's trances (which, if my calculations are correct, pre-date Sarah's (see p162 and note 8 on p310 below) had hair-raising political content: Sarah's constituted no radical anathema to the authorities, who probably kept a quiet eye on the hundreds of visitors tramping in and out of the house at Lawrence Poultney. After the fast-day sermons, Sarah found another two young counsellees, in deep despair, and on 1 July, another woman became her patient.

Her stamina, now she was fully conscious, was unequal to this excitement. Sarah's breakdown cured itself; purging her sense of atrophy in genuinely meaningful work. Sarah retired to Highgate to recoup strength. In the 1652 edition of his immensely popular book, Jessey sent a 'Christian friend' off to look up Sarah in her retreat. We are given a glimpse of the twenty-year-old woman looking rather feeble, sitting with a Bible open where she had been reading. Six years later, a last glimpse is offered, this time of a mature, thoughtful woman, in *A Wonderful Pleasant and Profitable Letter ... to a Friend* (1656),[7] published without her consent, perhaps by Robert Bragg, Independent rector of Allhallows the Great. The letter tells of her sadness at the death of a beloved half-brother, an ordained minister, probably from suicide: could this be the brother whose superiority brought her out in mortified shrieks as she lay in her dramatic bed ('"Ah! ah! ah!"') a decade before? Here she says that his death, which she has endured through faith and love, was far more testing than any childish affliction. The family melancholia, passed from mother to both children, seems to have found in Sarah a passage through mysticism and transient celebrity to a sombre and continent wisdom with which she could bear to live.

Meanwhile, Jessey, trawling London for wonders, found two young (and insufferable) girls, who had evidently been programmed from an early age to spout pious axioms. Mary Warner, aged six, sobbed at the thought that her fine clothes would send her to hell. At eight, in response to bonfires and the drinking of healths in London, little Mary inveighed against wicked joy and wondered if the offenders would be stuck dead by morning. Henry Jessey had a peculiar horror of 'the Odious Sin of Drinking of Healths' and wrote ferociously against it, in an apocalyptic tract, *The Lord's Loud Call to England* (1660), in which he evidenced recent earthquakes and plagues of toads and flies as signs of God's Wrath on bibulous Restoration England, where, as Pepys recorded, folk were 'drinking of the King's health upon their knees in the streets, which methinks is a little too much'. Jessey's Mary died at the age of ten, handing round pious advice to her elders and betters. Jessey was not the only girl-collector. Eleven-year-old Martha Hatfield's name was made by James Fisher in *The Wise Virgin* in 1653.[8]

These youngsters existed at the conjunction of two traditions: *sancta simplicitas*, the 'holy maid' of Catholic England, and the 'holy death', exemplified by the deathbed utterances of Jane Ratcliffe, Mary Simpson and Joan Drake. What distinguished Sarah Wight was her genius for survival, together with a message which seemed to call upon London radicals to unify rather than splinter into schism. Most female celebrities were dying candles, on the numinous threshold between earth and eternity. Their light could be registered only in the flare of its expiry.

A Nottinghamshire sixteen-year-old, a husbandman's daughter, died in 1641 but returned to life shortly before her funeral, announcing that God had sent her back for five days with a message. She denounced vanity and the Roman Whore, and predicted the final wars, dying punctually.[9] Adolescent Elizabeth Furly, dying of smallpox in Colchester, took advantage of her new-found, if brief, authority to vent her sibling-wrath upon her naughty brothers, going particularly for the wayward James: '"Mind what I say, O dear Brother, the Fire of Hell never goes out, no, never, is not that a long day?"' All she said was recorded in shorthand, including a vision of a lovely little boy with '"a crown upon his head, and he picked at my nose; But when I spoke to him in the name of the Lord, his crown fell from off his head, and almost all his hair, and so he vanished away"'.[10] This poignant rambling of Elizabeth's crumbling mind was interpreted by her father as a vision of the Holy Spirit – a Spirit who might look to a secular eye all too baldly mortal.

An explosive girl in Revolutionary England could call upon these traditions to unleash rebellious energies with impunity, through cunning – and unconscious – manipulation of the terms of female subordination. Sarah Wight mirrors to us both the parlous state of spiritual despair that grasped Puritans, especially women, and the way in which they could address it. From their low estate as 'empty nothing creatures' they could not realistically hope to escape. But, like that of the Belgian prophet, Antonia Bourignon, this empty state might offer an 'admirable vacuity' for God to fill.[11] The visitors who crowded into Sarah's bedroom shared the presence not of a mat-headed hysteric but of a fiery ecstatic dispensing sanctity at whose ardour they could toast their own less radiant spirits.

7

WOMEN COUNSELLORS FOR MEN OF BLOOD
ELIZABETH POOL, MARY POPE, ELIZABETH WARREN, MARY CARY

What gave Mary Pope, a salter's widow, the right to think she could lay down the law to the lawgivers?

How did sempstress Elizabeth Pool come to muscle in on the deliberations of the Army Council as they wrestled with the problem of bringing the king to account?

Who did the Suffolk schoolmistress Elizabeth Warren think she was to declare the doctrine of the divine right of kings in *A Warning-Piece from Heaven*?

These women came forward in the latter years of the 1640s, in person and in print, with the express purpose of changing the course of history. Was this forwardness obedience or disobedience? A double-bound question, now that all issues of allegiance and law had come into doubt, so that 'obedience' was a word in binary strife within itself. To whom should one be obedient? – the wronging king or the usurping government? Who should teach the upstart governors: why not a salter's widow, a needlewoman or a Suffolk schoolmistress? If the body politic had turned head-over-heels, so that the so-called representatives of the 'people' were standing as judges over their king (who could not in law be judged, because he had no equals), what logic could bind politically passionate women to their proper sphere? To intervene decisively in political affairs became, as far as they could see, an unprecedented duty.

The trial and execution of King Charles I in January 1649 marked a turning-point in English history. It was in no sense a popular move. The Army Council grabbed at any way to persuade the people of the king's guilt and his destroyers' integrity. It was a time of image-mongering and image-breaking. Milton on behalf of the regicidal regime smeared the image of the dead king, which glowed with new lucidity through the murky aftermath of his execution. In *Eikonoklastes*[1] (meaning 'The Breaking of the Image'), Milton cast odium on a tyrant 'dipped from head to foot and stained over with the blood of thousands that were his faithful subjects', cloaking this 'horrid purple-robe of innocent blood that sat so close about him' with the 'glorious purple' robe of royalty. In this 'gory pickle', Charles Stuart had wrapped himself in royal immunity to deny his guilt. *Eikonoklastes* makes brutal reading. Its scoffing tone to a dead man is a measure of the threat posed by a butchered king (who had inconveniently died supremely well) to a shaky new regime. To Royalists, the killing of a king was a heinous crime against God: parricide and even deicide.[2]

The Army Council had winced as it powered inexorably toward the trial and inevitable death sentence. These were complex men: warrior-politicians, ruthless and canny; but also rueful and impassioned Christians with a hunger for divine sanction no less genuine for its expediency.

*

A curious intervention shows how far the military regime was prepared to open its ear to (and to manipulate) persons claiming to bear divine messages – even women, who might previously have been considered deviants, witches or lunatics. On 29 December 1648, the Army Council debating the trial of King Charles paused to listen to a young prophetess from Abingdon named Elizabeth Pool.

Elizabeth seems to have been a defecting member of William Kiffin's Baptist Church, who joined the congregation of John Pendarves, later a focus of Fifth Monarchist activity. She was described by parties of various persuasions as 'virgin', 'girl', 'woman' or 'monstrous witch full of all deceitful craft'.[3] Royalists sneered that she was a puppet who had been lodged for the night at Whitehall and coached by Cromwell. That is unlikely, to judge from her rambling lucubrations. If Cromwell had decided to programme a prophetess, he would surely have selected a more adept learner of scripts.

The prophetess was ushered in with courtesy to declare an urgent message. The iron men took careful note of Elizabeth's counsel. She told them that she had been '(by the pleasure of the most High) made sensible of the distresses of this Land, and also a sympathiser with you in your labours'.[4]

The great men nodded gravely. This modest countrywoman, despite her undeniable tendency to witter, might strengthen the warrior-statesmen's claim to divine sanction; and be seen to strengthen it.

Elizabeth, having read the Army's revolutionary statement, the *Remonstrance*, had, she explained, gone into a sympathetic decline with England's ills. The 'pangs of a travailing woman were upon me, and the pangs of death oft-times panging me, being a member of her body, of whose decaying state I was made purely sensible'. All this panging was perfectly in keeping with a prophetess's necessary birth-throes: the politicians continued to attend carefully. Elizabeth used her feminine role (mother of a vision) to endorse her unfeminine assertiveness as a citizen of England, a 'member of her [England's] body'.

Her vision was as follows: 'a woman crooked, weak, sick, & imperfect in body' signifying 'the weak and imperfect state of the Kingdom' is to be cured by 'A man who is a member of the Army ... as I by the gift of faith on me should direct him' (*A Vision*, p1) 'The divine will,' she went on authoritatively, 'calls me to believe, and you to act', through prayer, humility and indifference to worldly ends. The Council read this allegory as a divine sanction to proceed with the trial. The prophetess, who showed a tendency to bumble when pressed for more specific messages, was cordially thanked, and away she went.

But back she came again, on 5 January. On this occasion, the Moguls were less receptive. Events had moved on. The Army-controlled House of Commons ('the Rump') had passed the Ordinance to try the king on the charge of treason, for seeking to 'subvert the ancient and fundamental laws and liberties of this nation ... [and levying] a cruel war in the land',[5] overruling the objections of the Lords (all twelve of them). The Council was prepared to listen to the prophetess again, provided she said what they needed to hear.

Elizabeth failed to stick to the expected script. She handed over a paper urging clemency toward the king. After much fuzzy discourse, she was asked point blank 'whether she spoke for or against' bringing Charles Stuart to trial. The Abingdon sage was alarmingly clear about this, and there can be little doubt that she was speaking for the vast majority of the English people when she counselled: 'Bring him to his trial, that he may be convicted in his conscience, but touch not his person' (p13). He must not be executed. His life was sacred, full of error though he might be as a ruler. Sent out of the room by the Council, she was recalled, grilled, admitted she did not really know what she was talking about, and dismissed.

Elizabeth could not leave it there. She refused to be tossed aside by these warrior-statesmen, with their desperate agenda. She published three tracts after this rejection, opening the Army's can of worms to public view and promising God's wrath upon the king's executioners: 'I have seen your carcasses slain upon the ground'.[6]

Elizabeth's counsel was characterised by a curious argument from the gender code, which sheds light on the impossible double-bind in which all revolutionaries found themselves. Her mind was fixated on the relation between husband and wife in marriage as the measure of all power bondings. However, during the Revolution, marriage too was problematic. She brought to the messy openness of politics a solution just as messily open to interpretation.

In his coronation oath, Charles I had pledged himself to his country not only as *pater patriae* ('father of the nation') but as *sponsus regni* ('husband of the realm'). But each soul (including the king's) was also *sponsa Christi* (bride of Christ, gendered feminine). These were not just symbolic terms, as people often assume, but legal and binding on both parties.[7] Therefore, when Elizabeth first went to the Army Council and reminded them that 'the King is your father and husband, which you were and are to obey in the Lord, and in no other way', she was recalling the Army Council to its female subjection. Those great men were a corporate wife of the sovereign: but their wifely duty to the king depended on *his* wifely duty to God, his breaking of which released them from total obedience. The spiritually petticoated grandees found all this marriage guidance highly acceptable on the first occasion: indeed, as Colonel Rich phrased it, an 'unexpected Providence'.

Here was a weaker vessel (woman) instructing a stronger vessel (the Army) that, though it (the Army) was a weaker vessel in relation to the stronger vessel (king as *sponsus regni*), he had himself become a weaker vessel through infidelity to the Almighty (God as Bridegroom), thus releasing the initially weaker vessel (the Army) from its conjugal obligation, to exercise a corrective function to the Body Politic. All this was authorised by weak Elizabeth who had become a vessel of the Almighty.

If this makes your head spin, it should. The Chain of Being which had seemed so fixed, had become destabilised in a world of vertiginous dualities, so that each element was volatile in relation to all others. It doesn't make sense, in a world which didn't make sense. For when Elizabeth returned, she brought with her a different marital theory. Now she informed the Army it was *feme covert*, with no existence or rights of its own:

> You never heard that a wife might put away her husband, as he is the head of her body, but for the Lord's sake suffereth his terror to her flesh, though she be free in the spirit of the Lord.[8]

> you owe him all that you have and are, and although he would not be your father and husband ... yet know that you are for the Lord's sake to honour his person. For he is the father and husband of your bodies.[9]

When the Army Council was accused, in this mere female's *Alarums*, of having murdered its husband, it was understandably irked. Having not only divorced a king, but abolished matrimonial monarchy altogether, it did not take kindly to being accused of being a 'strumpet'. Through his friend William Kiffin's manipulation of the Baptist network, Cromwell seems to have brought his heel down hard on the annoying prophetess by spreading scandal about her sexual reputation.

Elizabeth, used to standing at the centre of vicious controversy, was not very crushable. All the Cromwellian 'glorious glittering images of state policies, religious ordinances, orders, faiths, lights, knowledges ... drawn over [with] beautiful pretences' could not conceal the 'worldly dark part' in the king's executioners, she wrote in her last tract. Corrupt motives were the filth beneath the gilt.

She had really believed that she could alter the course of history. Or rather, God speaking through her mouth could do so. By the end of 1649 she knew better.

*

The Army's desperate agenda brought King Charles to the scaffold erected outside Whitehall on 30 January 1649. Seven years had gone by since he had fled the palace. He walked now through the Banqueting Hall beneath the overarching irony of the great Rubens ceiling depicting the triumph of reason and justice over rebellion and falsehood, which had towered over the masques and ceremonials of his heyday. The windows had long been boarded up, and the darkened Hall was falling into dilapidation. It was the greatest, perhaps the only, coup of a baffled, devious monarch. The poet Andrew Marvell (himself a Parliamentarian, enmeshed in historical complexity) recalled the dignity of the ending played out by the 'royal actor' on that 'tragic scaffold':

> While round the armed bands
> Did clap their bloody hands.
> *He* nothing common did or mean
> Upon that memorable scene,
> But with his keener eye
> The axe's edge did try ...

> But bowed his comely head
> Down as upon a bed.[10]

The head was sliced from the body in one clean blow. A lad of seventeen, wedged far back in the crowd who saw the axe fall, remembered 'such a groan as I never heard before, and desire I may never hear again'.[11] The military regime would never have any propaganda to match the conclusiveness of Charles' keen-eyed ending.

*

Few women wrote in support of the regicide. Those who felt called upon to intervene were concerned to save the king's life and restore him to the throne. Mary Pope, widow of an affluent London salter, had her attacks on the Army Council (*Behold, here is a Word* and *Heare, heare, heare a Word*) printed by the woman printer, Mrs Edwards, in January 1649, and arranged for them to be distributed to Parliament.

Mary's pamphlets are intellectually sharper than Elizabeth's ramblings. From 1640, she was an invalid, having borne ten children. Bodily infirmity afforded leisure for mental enquiry, striving to make hour-by-hour sense of the 'strange workings' of God in England. A Londoner observing events with a caustic eye from her house at St Paul's, she was a propertied businesswoman, as well as a moderate Puritan who remained within the national church and found the separatist radicals odious. It was Mary's nature to take practical steps to head off crisis. Now she had to do something to ameliorate the state of the nation. Her *Treatise of Magistracy* (1647),[12] was dictated to her younger son. Her thoughts on a subject abstruse enough to tax a Cicero flew ahead of her like the wind, and at first, in 1644, she found her speed of composition so supernatural that it could only come from the Holy Spirit. Vexed by anxiety lest people call it 'non-sense' (Mary was self-educated), she suggested that readers blame God: it was all out of the Bible.

Fundamentally, the *Treatise* can be seen as an attempt to clear up a catastrophic mess. She seems to have felt (what inexperienced women pardonably often believed) that if someone, with the help of God, could come up with an answer, the gentlemen at

Westminster would be relieved to implement it.

In 1646 Mary's husband died. With the new autonomy of a widow and merchant, Mary went into action. In January 1647, she wrote to Parliament, explaining to them the problems of the realm.

No answer. Mary waited: every morning she must have awoken in hope that today those men of conscience would call her divinely inspired brain-power into action to resolve the problems of state with which they were having notably small success. In April she wrote again, a more urgent and prophetic letter, enclosing the manuscript of the *Treatise*, asking for it to be checked through for flaws by a committee of 'godly men, two of them ministers' before being printed. Earnest about doing things properly, Mary showed a touching faith in Parliament's equally conscientious wish for Truth.

No response. Deeply exercised, Mary took the first step into dissident action by printing her text at her own expense, without licence: it cost her £50.

Parliament woke up and denounced her venture as an 'abuse in printing'. The person she had hired to present copies at the doors of Parliament was banged up in Newgate, and Mary's work referred to the Committee for Printing Unlicensed Pamphlets.

Mary smarted. She was only trying to help. The book she regarded as her soul's child had been criminalised. She wilted under the 'frowns and strange speeches of those who were my familiar friends'.[13] However, with the new national emergency, her courage was roused. Had Parliament paid proper attention to the *Treatise* at the time, 'our troubles had long ago been at an end, and Parliament and Army both had obeyed God and retained their honour' – but, no, the Army had instead 'nonparliamented Parliament, and they intend to nonking the King, and unlaw the laws'.[14] This jab at 'Pride's Purge' was a shrewd hit at the constitutional weakness of the military dictatorship. Mary pointed out that since Parliament's seizure of power, oppression had worsened: 'men's backs or rather estates have been broken in pieces'. The country, like a 'preposterous' headless body, lurched from one catastrophe to another.[15]

Mary, stationed at her City window, had viewed the whole charade: the surging crowds at Westminster in 1641 and 1642, lightning panics running through them, whipped up out of nothing but 'rumours ... multitudes ... multitudes ... rumours and distractions'. Off they'd all bolt, thinking the king was coming to sack the City. And all bolt back again, with swords and shrieks. She is acute in her bystander's analysis of the crucial role of mutual fear in the dynamic of civil conflict. She had noticed (perhaps within her own household?) that 'disobedience to parents and masters increased in abundant manner' with the breakdown of law and order.

As the Army marched nearer to London prior to the *coup d'état*, she divined the meaning of the louring weather showing God's just displeasure:

> the Heavens all about the city gathered blackness, and presently there was such a mighty storm of hail, thunder and rain; and all of it in and about the City, and four miles off there was none, but very clear weather: But this thunder of hail did hold forth that height of God's displeasure against the Army's disobedience of Parliament. (*Behold*, p12)

That Saturday the Army's march into the City had brought complete mayhem: she recalls people running out of their houses in the suburbs all night as the forces of violence (whose soldiers would have to be fed and quartered by the panicked citizens) gate-crashed the power centre. Mary spoke for the merchant classes in her insistence that only peace and stability could guarantee livelihoods.

Through her eyes we see the painful economic upheaval. By night she heard what by day she saw: greed rampant in the City, as carriers' carts clattered right through Saturday night into Sunday, when godly folk were trying to sleep. She was aware of the growth of a new breed of man – profiteers raking in profits from bureaucracy, while businesses foundered, crops rotted, livestock and estates were gobbled up by twisters. She recalled 'whole cart-loads' of starving and maimed soldiers, with 'their stomachs overgone for want of meat, that they could take little of anything, though never so good or bad'.

Standing in the window, she wondered what had became of all that plate, rings and money freely given to the war effort by loyal citizens at the beginning of the war? Her mercantile middle-class mind focused on the economic catastrophe the Army had entailed on the mass of the people: squander and plunder.

Mary believed in the necessity of curbing the king and his 'wicked counsellors', but not by bloodshed. (She enjoyed the luxury of exemption from the problem that had foxed Parliament of how to seal a compromise with a man who genuinely believed he was above the law, and refused to be bound by his own word.) She reserved her tartest phrases for the Army: 'you have moulded the Parliament to your Model,' she sneered.[16] The Remonstrance which brought on Elizabeth Pool's ecstatic vision made Mary sick: 'your monstrous Remonstrance'. In *Heare, heare*, she spoke with disgust to the 'vermin Locusts' who had usurped power: 'you intend to murder your King, and who else is not revealed' (p27).

Elizabeth Warren, a Suffolk schoolteacher, upheld divine right and rejected the trial of a king by the Commons as illegal.[17] She believed in the conservative status quo but embraced the illogic of the times by quitting her rightful place as a woman to preach that females should return to that rightful place.

Elizabeth Pool, Mary Pope and Elizabeth Warren were surely expressing the views of the moderate silent majority, aghast at government by sword and the judicial murder of a king. They read the signs as pointing not to the imminent coming of King Jesus at the head of the New Model Army but to a godforsaken here-and-now, a war-ravaged nation in poverty, social chaos, galloping inflation and the ruin of trade.

*

Mary Cary, Fifth Monarchist prophet, supported the regicide and argued in favour of the right of violence on the part of the justified against the unjustified. When the Army marched into the City on that hailstorming Saturday, her heart soared.

Hers was one of the most penetrating analytic minds of her generation, male or female. Yet either she or her publisher thought it prudent to cajole three eminent male guarantors into vouching for the quality of her work by prefixing commendations to the 1651 text of *The Little Horns Doom and Downfall*. And what embarrassing reading they make, for Cary's intellectual gifts beggar their condescension. Hugh Peters, the regicidal Puritan minister, comes first. He commends himself with exceptional unctuousness as a 'worthless ... worm', unfit to write or judge books, 'yet owing respect to this Author, I could not deny a word'. The worthless worm enumerates three points of praise, beginning by commending Cary for teaching 'her sex that there are more ways than one to avoid idleness (the devil's cushion) ... They that will not use the distaff, may improve a pen.' Secondly, the worm can reassure us that we shall 'neither see naked breasts, black patches, nor long trains' in this woman's work but 'a holy, modest, and painful spirit'. Thirdly, there is plenty of impressive Scriptural interpretation, 'so well, that you might easily think she ploughed with another's Heifer', ie, you'd hardly believe this a woman's work at all.[18]

All Peters' approval is silver-lined contempt. Henry Jessey, who succeeds the worthless worm, shows a prudential spirit by maintaining that it's worth publishing such prophecies as *The Little Horn* just in case they turn out to be true, for 'it were best to know the worst before it overtake us unaware'. Thirdly, Feake the Fifth Monarchist chimes in by lunging at worldly men who sneer at 'a company of illiterate men, and silly women, [who] pretend to any skill in dark prophecies' (pa4).

I have called Cary 'rational', 'analytic'. How is this reconcilable with her apocalyptic cast of thought, her dating of the End of the World from the Book of Daniel in *A New and More Exact Mappe?*:

Now if the year 0366
there be added 1335
it makes up just . . . . .1701[19]

Counting from Daniel, writing in or around the second year of the Emperor Julian (c. 168 BC), she dates the Last Day to 1701: 'I am persuaded that day will be ... the full and complete deliverance of the Church'. Most readers smile at what we see as the naïveté of Mary's computation. 1701 came and went, and the world went on turning. What then do we say to Sir Isaac Newton's intensive study of Daniel and Revelation to deduce the date of the End of the World?[20] Or Milton's millennarianism, or Cromwell's? Thomas Beverley predicted the end of the world for 1697 but, finding himself still alive in 1698, wrote a book to prove that it *had* ended, unobtrusively. Apocalyptic studies were a theological science made orthodox by heavyweight minds like Joseph Mede, whose *Clavis Apocalyptica* (1627) Mary had studied with the other definitive textbooks. For Mary as for Cromwell and the militants in the 'Barebones' Parliament, whose policies she tried to influence, the Bible was the key to revolutionary history.[21] Mary was doing no less than elaborate a complete social programme for the period leading up to and including the thousand-year kingdom of Christ. The death of Charles I (which she supported) was a sign of the Last Days.

And if she were wrong? If all her prophecies backfired on her?

Mary could live with that: 'I do not pretend to be any more exempted from uncertainty, than any other ... I shall not press any to believe these things ... unless they do hear the voice of Christ and his speech setting them home upon them.' At the same time, she warned her readers not to take the risk of dismissing her thoughts because they seemed weird.[22] Everyone should join in good time.

Her paradisal world had much to offer to the underclass and to women, though at the cost of creating a new elite of 'saints', in which female saints would be just as filled with the Spirit as men and a university education would bring no extra privileges. Women and men would, she was sure, become steadily more filled with shining knowledge, unity, strength. Women, heretofore so shy in public, would share in the power to prophesy. Mary's vision is magnanimous, upbeat, and never grudging. Five years would see a difference, 'but ten years hence much more than now; and twenty years hence far exceeding that ... For these are not ordinary times'.[23] Touchingly, she wrote of a world in which the afflictions commonplace for women in that age of high infant mortality would be no more. Her version of Isaiah's Golden Age promised that:

> No infant of days shall die; none shall die when they are young; all shall come to a good old age. They shall not be afflicted for the loss of their children; for they shall live till they are an hundred years old. (*A ... Mappe*, p289)

The animal kingdom would cease to be predatory; and no person would be homeless, hungry or unemployed. Mary's was a paradise founded on the Puritan work ethic: she could not imagine lolling idle in a cavalier indulgence. Her scheme was planned as a detailed utopia, in which she weighed up issues like vegetarianism, a question seriously pondered by nonconformists. An extremist like Roger Crab (the original 'mad hatter') was a vegetarian turned vegan, whose diet of bran broth and turnip leaves was augmented by treats of parsnips in his latter years. Mary Cary judged the question by analysing what constituted reasonable behaviour in the given universe: 'I see no reason to conclude, that man's making use of the creatures in a reasonable and moderate manner, is ... bondage and corruption.' Animals cannot suffer violent death in the same way as humans do, 'for they fear it not' (pp313–14). She founded her programme in rational argument, convinced that the divine will was accessible to reason as well as faith.

Mary's *Twelve Proposals* of 1653 map out a comprehensive programme of reforms for the politicians at Westminster, including abolition of tithes; liberty of conscience; reform of universities; poor relief; establishment of a Post Office to generate revenue to support the poor, with a stamp tax; equal justice for poor and rich; a wage limit on government employees, and a violent coup by the godly should the ungodly resist this revolution.[24] We are amazed to recall that the author of this political system, rivalling Hugh Peters' *A Good Work For A Good Magistrate* of 1651, had no vote, no higher education, no right to occupy a government position. Unlike Peters, she had never visited the Netherlands or the New World to glean ideas for her ideal commonwealth. She was disqualified but, through her inversion of worldly values, was able to surrender her disqualification as a passport. The last should be first.

We know almost nothing about Mary Cary as a person. By the 1650s she was 'M. Rande' but still publishing under her original name, for clarity's sake. If she wrote on behalf of a small elite, 'the saints', she opened her arms to as many fellows as she could attract in to that fellowship. Her self-esteem was high. Her claim to be 'a very weak and unworthy instrument', no more than a pencil or pen in God's hand,[25] is wrongly interpreted by modern readers as a sign of female anxiety at her breaking of the gender code. Hugh Peters' wormhood is far more grovellingly humble.

Mary goes on to quote the Apostle Paul, the most powerful voice of the early church, 'I am not sufficient to think a good thought, but my sufficiency is of God', an identification that has little to do with feminine humility and everything to do with Apostolic pride ('To the Reader', np).

She ends by demanding that Parliament crack on with 'the work' (p315). In *The Little Horns Doom*, Mary had appealed to them as the saints who had smashed the power of the Little Horn, Charles. She spares neither pity nor animosity for the king: as he reaped, so he sowed. Eulogising Members of Parliament and Justices as uniquely 'precious and gracious', she seems to sit back from her work and read it over, adding this sensible amendment: 'But let me not be understood, as though I hereby assented, that every individual person, that hath been, or is in Parliament, is a Saint' (p36).

For that would strain the credulity of a saint.

8

ANNA TRAPNEL'S JOURNEY TO CORNWALL
ANNA TRAPNEL, FIFTH MONARCHY, & A WITCH-TRYING WOMAN WITH HER GREAT PIN

> Oh it is for thy sake, and for thy servant's sake, that thy
> Servant is made a voice, a sound, it is a voice within a voice,
> another's voice, even thy voice through her ... [1]

Anna Trapnel, the singing prophetess of the Fifth Monarchists,
was a marvel, a threat to public order or a joke, depending on your
political persuasion. By 1654, everyone had heard of the fantastic
magnitude of her voice-box. A prophet who specialised in falling
into catatonic trances at God's direction, she would sing and
prophesy for hours at a time: for three, four, eight, ten, twelve hour
stints, going on through whole days and nights, for weeks together.
During periods of inspiration, Anna was, or claimed and seemed to
be, unconscious. When she came to, she'd shake her head in
amazement when told of her marathon performances, and read

with interest the transcripts of her versified revelations, taken by amanuenses stationed at her bedside. While conscious, Anna did not seem to be able to make a rhyme to save her life. Yet in divine sleep, she metricated effortlessly as other women knit. She prophesied the apocalyptic downfall of the proud clergy and the collapse of worldly power; the imminent coming of a military Christ at the head of an army to wrench dominion from the corrupt human powers (by 1654, Oliver Cromwell and the Protectoral regime); and the thousand-year rule of the saints.

Many listened carefully to Anna's utterances and worked to decode the messages which God had confided to her rapturous mind and broadcast through her passive agency. Others, as Anna noted with rue and bitterness in her account of her Cornish expedition, *Anna Trapnel's Report and Plea*, thought her touched in the head, or worse: 'England's rulers and clergy do judge the Lord's handmaid to be mad, and under the administration of evil angels, and a witch, and many other evil terms they raise up to make me odious, and abhorred'.[2] Anna, despite her galled sense of injustice and the more complex feelings of exposure and nervous susceptibility that make her such a fascinating figure, coped with that. Had not the prophets of old suffered repudiation and scorn, she wanted to know? What about her namesake, Hannah, the mother of Samuel in the Old Testament: when the old priest, Eli, caught her praying with her lips moving, he called her drunk, but had to eat his words when God vindicated Hannah with the gift of a sacred post-menopausal son and the power of sacred poetry.

Anyhow, said Anna, it's not my voice but God's – and you wouldn't want to laugh at that, would you? She accepted that as a woman she was 'a poor inferior' but so the Apostle Paul described himself, and you don't go around sniggering at him, do you? Like Hannah, Anna was a woman inspired, transcendent and triumphant; like Paul, she was the kindled human soul, alive with divine power. Anna hid in the female skirts of the one and behind the other's male robe of authority. Her wonderfully interesting face, peeping through between the two, looks out at us through the pages of her writings, full of naïveté and calculation, a splendour of self-belief and evasion tactics. She is a defiant but sensitive resister, at once funny, impressive, crafty and beguiling. Perhaps most of all she is brave. To stand as a laughing-stock can seem as excoriating as a public whipping. Anna's sublime innocence of a sense of humour perhaps helped her to withstand public scorn. In emergency she could duck out of embarrassing situations by falling into a trance and commencing a singing bout of devastating loudness and longevity.

In January 1654 Anna received an invitation from a Captain Langden to go to visit him in Cornwall. Anna operated in London, a member of the dynamic John Simpson's Baptist community which met at Allhallows the Great in Thames Street, near the centre of government power at Whitehall. In the bosom of her sect, she was at once coddled and reverenced, and her flamboyant gifts were cherished and affirmed by the community. She was protected from the hostile outside world by this closely knit group of devout believers. Solidarity cushioned blows to the ego dealt by norms outside the group. Here she was surrounded by a coccooning family, not uncritical of one another's leadings and behaviour (what family is?), but fundamentally nourishing to the sense of self in one so deviant. Throughout Anna's writings, we feel the deep importance of this 'family' group at home, especially the 'sisters' of the group, on whose nurture she relied. As a single, independent woman, without the bondings and bondage which tied daughters and wives into the fixities of domestic routine, Anna had been able to choose for herself to put down roots amongst congenial spirits. A free woman, she was also surrounded by surrogate kin. The thought of leaving the group to venture into Cornwall put Anna in a flutter.

That flutter reminds us of how far it was from London to Cornwall in those days: a week's journey by water and road, at a time when roads were muddy and the most streamlined form of travel rough and slow, over pitted roads, into genuinely foreign parts, where local custom, dialect and laws would be alien. Anna's westward journey presented itself to her apprehensive inner eye as an epic movement into the unknown, from whose excitements she would gratefully be delivered.

When it was first mooted that she might 'do good to poor souls, with the variety of [your] experience', she instinctively drew back from the prospect: 'There's a far journey indeed!' she reports herself as objecting. 'Do you think I would leave all my friends to go so far from them?' (*Report and Plea*, p1).

Whether these wincings away from her journeyings and self-exhibitions are what Anna really felt, or rather felt she ought to feel as a 'a sober holy woman' with a proper bashfulness is not clear. I incline to interpret the constant emphasis on flinching from her destiny as part of a complex, highly strung character, which at once rushed out to declare itself and shrank in palpitating alarm from the traumas of the visionary's path. However, God as usual decided the matter. Anna's style fluctuates delightfully between the sonorous incantation of biblical texts and a style of friendly chat in which God pushes her on her way and reassures her of his presence: '"Then don't fear to go to Cornwall, though it be a long journey,"' saith the Lord, '"for I will go with thee"' (p1).

Still Anna hangs back. 'Why should I go so far, and among strangers?' she wants to know, and enters into a long confabulation with her Maker, which ends in 'my reasoning gainsaying spirit [falling] flat before the Lord', a prostration pleasantly in keeping with her inclination to recumbent prophecy.

The wayfarer's decision did not at first go down well with her congregation, especially her closest 'sister', who was severely put out. Anna's nervously imaginative temperament pictured the journey stage by stage, as though living it in advance: 'I beheld high rocky-hills, and variety of places and towns, and how I should be as I rode in the coach, much melody I should have' (pp2–3). This 'vision', girding her up for the road, reminded her of St Paul's journey to Macedonia. Cornwall indeed was Anna's Macedonia. She seemed to be standing on imaginative tiptoe, craning for light on the path ahead, nervous and indecisive. A flurry of short journeys preceded her departure, including a trip to Windsor Castle to visit two fellow spirits imprisoned there for their political dissent: 'the Lord's two ambassadors ... Mr Simpson and Mr Feak, who were filled with the Spirit abundant'. As Anna looked about their stone-cold lodgings she must have tested her calling against the possibility of her own incarceration in some such place of detention. But the buoyant spirit of the two revolutionaries also reminded her of the Christian paradox that turns disgrace to triumph; exalts the sufferer into the martyr. She too might share that unnerving exaltation.

After returning to her friends' house in Hillingdon, she went to stay for two nights with other friends six miles away. Nervous agitation deepened. As she walked out into the fields, she tried to tune up, only to discover that her voice had grown unaccountably hoarse. Was this a sign? A shadow passed over Anna's mind. What if she should lose her voice, and never find it again? Horror at the thought of a voiceless life came over Anna, as she stood there in the field with her mouth open, croaking dismally. She feared:

> that I should be hoarse while I lived, like as a woman of the Congregation was, with whom I walk; so should I be, not able to speak but hoarsely, 'And go not thy journey,' said Satan.

Anna must have cleared the Satanic frog from her throat with a good cough, for she is soon back in conversation with her Lord; all the stronger and more loquacious for her tussle with phlegm. For 'it's a lovely life, the life of faith,' she can assure her reader, blithely. Next day she awakens to the morning chorus under the eaves, feeling refreshed and ready for anything, 'And hearing the birds chirrup in the morning early, about my chamber-window' (p4) is inspired with a sense of God's care not only for his feathered songbirds, the sparrows, but also for his human songsters. The nervousness abates.

Soon Anna is in fine fettle and full voice, singing lustily. Back at Hillingdon, she warbles with abandon for most of the first night. Sunday sees her at church, where the minister's discourse induces a rhapsodic frame of mind. She walks out into a 'curious garden, where I saw the pleasant trees, and plants, and walks, and fish-ponds, and hearing the birds pleasant notes,' a sense of the harmonious Presence of God creates a mystical ecstasy, 'that I began to sing forth his praises, and continued while it was so late in the evening, that my friends that walked with me thought it convenient to lead me into the house' (p5). The entire family gathers round to hear her melodious message, delivered con brio, without intermission until midnight; not just any ignorant family either but a very learned and judicious set of people, who would not be fooled by charlatans. She then reflects that the reader might frown at her sanctimonious bragging, which she humbly denies ('Herein I don't boast, but in the rich free love of God'). While prophesying, Anna has neither sense of time nor control over what she is saying. At a certain point she becomes so drained that she collapses, and has to be put to bed, still singing. That night two of her friends share her bed, one at either side, but she does not sleep, and neither (one suspects) do they. People acting as Anna's hosts bargained for a daunting quota of sleep deprivation. She prays straight through to morning light, and is in no state to eat the following day, though people bring all sorts of dainties to tempt her appetite. Starvation, along with insomnia, seems to have induced a vertiginous light-mindedness peculiarly accommodating to the Holy Spirit. Perhaps it also served the dual purpose of impressing her hosts with Anna's superhuman powers whilst ensuring constant attention. Womenfolk would be continually bustling round Anna's bed, with food, comfort and loving fuss.

But during the final week before departure, Anna's spirits take a further downward spiral. She finds herself beset by temptations, the most dramatic of which occurs to her as she is going upstairs.

Why not hurl herself down the stairs and break a leg or an arm? She can hardly be expected to set out on a Cornish odyssey with a broken bone.

Anna resists. Not only would she be ashamed of such a childish ruse, detectable by the caustic eye of God if not by her fellow believers, but perhaps it also occurs to her that she'd rather encounter Cornwall than self-mutilation. After she has got out of her commitment, she will be stuck with a broken leg and no glory.

Then it occurs to Anna that someone will intervene to prevent her journey, and that everyone will mock her aspirations. Perhaps the thought of public ridicule is the hardest thing of all for Anna to endure. She has been laughed at before and will be again. She is the easiest target in London, having espoused a profession that leads, not to dignified humiliation but to the mortifying status of public joke. In claiming to be the passive vessel of God (a traditional female role, sanctioned by Scripture), she protected herself at a time when women's public speaking was a trespass; but opened herself to the charges of being thought, if not mad, dotty, and if not a witch, a clown. She keeps expecting an urgent message to halt her preparation. None comes. Anna carries on packing, with a sinking heart.

On the last Sunday, Anna visits Allhallows to take leave of her community. 'And I that day saw great shinings' (p6). Ten female friends stay up all night in vigil, praying with her for divine guidance. With bleary eyes but peaceful heart, Anna passes by water from Southwark to Whitehall stairs, where she lands and goes to an inn. Here she takes a coach. Many people come to see her off. Amongst them is a member of Oliver Cromwell's Council who stares and darkly states that, had he known in time that she was off to Cornwall to make mischief, he would have got an Order to keep her in London.

The writer's chest puffs out, as it is inclined to do, at this perverse accolade. How many women would the Government of England bother to try to detain from spreading subversive political messages in the provinces? Anna has power and status beyond her gender. Charged with important messages from God, so secret that even Anna does not know what they are – and will not know, even when expounding them, until they are related back to her – Anna Trapnel's coach moves off toward Cornwall.

*

Or did she know perfectly well? How far was her catatonia a form of political camouflage? Was Anna plotting, on behalf of the imprisoned Fifth Monarchist leadership, the downfall of the Protectorate?

Before we continue to accompany Anna on her Cornish journey, let us pause to consider why the Government kept tabs on this warbling woman and seemed to regard her as a threat to state security; why spies reported her movements? She sounds so innocent. Fifth Monarchist pamphlets frequently represented their groups as being guileless as sucking babes. Take the meeting at Abingdon two years later, which was broken up by troopers: the innocent reader of *The Complaining Testimony of some ... of Sions Children* may well receive the impression that this cluster of devout folk, gathering for the funeral of Pastor John Pendarves, and intent only on 'quickenings ... melting & brokenness of heart',[3] was set upon out of the blue and for no reason (p3) by uncouth soldiers. These were led by Commander Barker who, enraged at being asked for his warrant, rode 'furiously about the Inn-yard, striking several of our friends violently with his cane' (p3). Worse was to follow for these innocent lambs. As they attempted to assemble at the marketplace for pious prayer, soldiers attacked with their swords, so that they 'cut diverse, one of our hats being slashed in three or four places' (p3). The gentle souls pondered their sliced hats in dismay. In the mêlée, a saintly old man was struck repeatedly and many men and women were dragged around and ridden down; five prisoners were marched off to Windsor Castle. It is quite untrue, the authors add, that one of their venerable elders challenged a soldier to fight him on Salisbury Plain, and that 'we had thirty thousand men more to come to us' (p4). Peace-loving mourners as they were, how could anyone imagine they meant harm to anyone?

One of the signatories of the pamphlet strikes us as familiar: it is Captain Langden, who had come to view Anna in her trance at Whitehall in January, the very man Anna was on her way to visit in 1654. This was the same incendiary Francis Langden who sat as MP for Cornwall in the 1653 'Barebones' Parliament, along with John Bawden (with whom Anna would also rendezvous). Langden was one of twelve extreme radical members whose base was the Blackfriars godly constituency of Feake and Simpson, those two nice men Anna visited in Windsor Castle before she set out – wild revolutionaries Cromwell needed to silence, particularly after they announced their prophetic vision of his imminent fall, dating it to within six months. But prison could not muffle the Fifth Monarchist voice: Feake urged his congregation to prepare to 'make a standing Army for the King of Saints' when in the near future Christ would return to call them up for active military service;[4] Simpson wrote likewise to Anna's Allhallows group.

What message did Feake and Simpson entrust to Anna, to take down to Cornwall? Who knows? Anna surely had something up her sleeve, put there by Simpson and Feake.

Later in his imprisonment, in 1655, the hyperactive Feake was to charge the castle pulpit, just before morning service, thence to blast divine vengeance against the apostate Cromwell. Wrestled down and sealed in his cell, with sentinels posted at the door, he discharged his godly message by the only route remaining to him, preaching at the top of his terrific voice through his cell window.

The governor was not having that. He ordered up a squad of soldiers, to beat their drums to drown him out. But Feake (supplemented as he grew hoarser by the vocal efforts of his colleague Rogers) could outbawl the drummers. In his own words:

> As soon as the drum had done then I began to sound out my trumpet, and trumpeted out the Gospel aloud; he [the Governor] beat up his drum a second and third time, and still I went on, then he strictly required me to have done. I told him, I would not. He said he had order to silence me from the Lord Protector. I told him, I had order from My Lord to go on; and my Lord's Highness is above his lord's highness.[5]

That afternoon, Rogers prepared to concuss the ears of all comers with a new blast of preaching from his window. The governor, having had no luck with Plan A, tried Plan B. He sent up a sergeant and soldiers to beat Rogers up. Plan B tended to prove a mistake with those soliciting not only trouble but martyrdom: Rogers met every blow with an ecstatic cry of, 'Strike on, for thus did the soldiers deal with Christ, my master!'[6] The belief that the world was literally about to end had a tonic effect on godly confidence. The Lord might even catch the sergeant with his diabolical boot raised in mid-kick. Christ was coming in military glory, at any moment, with swords, pikes, muskets, cannon and an armoury beggaring all imagination, said Feake, Rogers, Simpson, Langden, Bawden ... and Anna.

And Abingdon? This was the site of a national Fifth Monarchist rally, with delegates from London, East Anglia, Hull and Cornwall, in which the saints put the question, 'Whether God's people must be a bloody people (in an active sense)' to which there was a resounding Aye. As the Army smashed up the meeting on the third day, the saints roared, 'Lord appear, now or never for confounding of these, thine and our enemies', while their womenfolk bawled, 'Hold on, ye Sons of Sion!' The Latter Days were nigh; a bloodbath imminent. Thurloe, spider at the centre of Cromwell's espionage web, was sure he'd nipped a full-scale uprising in the bud.

The Fifth Monarchist programme included not only the co-operation of the saints in the final war under King Christ but a full programme of social reform to create conditions for their thousand-year reign. This included the abolition of tithes and the purging of clergy; reform of the law, universities and schools, taxation and a wholesale clean-up of personal morality; the outlawing of swearing, drinking and fornication. Anna's radical friends in the 'Barebones' Parliament, we remember, made a serious and nearly successful attempt to abolish tithes, the Court of Chancery and religious persecution, as well as a complete overhaul of the law. But they were outmanoeuvred and achieved, in the end, nothing at all. The House dissolved itself on 12 December by a mass creeping-in of the 'moderates' at 7 a.m., while the saints were off praying, to surrender the Parliament's powers to Cromwell.

It was in the bitter wake of 'Barebones' that Anna first turned up in the documentary record: she was giving moral support to the fiery Welsh saint, Vavasor Powell, during his examination for treason at Whitehall. Her congregation prefaced her pamphlet, *The Cry of a Stone*, with a brief account of Anna's Whitehall epic. On 7 January, a miscellany of allies assembled in solidarity with Powell at Whitehall, including:

> a maid, Mrs Anna Trapnel by name, who waiting in a little room near the Council, where was a fire, for Mr Powell's coming forth, then with a purpose to return home: She was beyond and besides in her intentions, having much trouble in her heart, and being seized upon by the Lord: She was carried forth in a spirit of prayer and singing, from noon till night, and went down into Mr Roberts' lodging, who keeps the ordinary at Whitehall; and finding her natural strength going from her, she took her bed at eleven o'clock in the night, where she lay from that day ... to the nineteenth day of the same month: in all twelve days together; The first five days neither eating nor drinking anything, more or less. (p1)

Anna fuelled her diet with frugal fare, just enough to keep her voice lubricated and her mind light: once in twenty-four hours, her colleagues solemnly report, she either took a morsel of toast dipped in small beer, sucking out the beer, or merely swilled out her mouth with beer, 'lying in bed with her eyes shut, her hands fixed, seldom seen to move' and expatiating in that time at least once a day 'sometimes two, three, four and five hours together', night and day rolled into one in her bouts of rapture. For eleven days and twelve nights she continued this public performance, so prostrate that she had to be carried to a chair by the fire, when her bed was made. Nobody thought to take notes until Day Five; then a scribe positioned himself with straining ears to take down her messages (not always easy, amid the tumult of coming and going, with Anna's extemporisations swelling and ebbing in volume). And then, on the twelfth day, it was finished. The visionary arose blithe as a lark from bed, stepping out unaided back to Hackney and Mark Lane. Anna Trapnel had made her name.

'I am Anna Trapnel,' she begins her testament in *The Cry of a Stone*, 'the daughter of William Trapnel, shipwright, who lived in Stepney Parish.' Godly parents cultivated a godlier daughter; but her father died while Anna was a little girl, and her mother nine years before Anna began to prophesy – a traumatic loss. But in that loss was contained a special promise and compensation: the certainty of being a special person. Her mother's deathbed words, repeated thrice, had been: 'Lord! Double thy spirit upon my child' (p3).

In *A Legacy for Saints*, written from Bridewell after Cornwall, Anna articulates the conundrum faced by those who feel special. If they are not God's hand-picked elect, they are double-damned. Who's to tell? Her conversion narrative shows Anna's bipolar Puritan pendulum-swing between the sense of being outsider and insider; beatific and damned; God's lamb and Satan's goat. Teenagerly hysterics were magnified into soul-shattering horrors by fear of the Calvinist Law, in which (if she failed to weep in a sermon, or worse, missed one), 'I was damned, one set apart for destruction'.[7]

Suicidal desires swept her, the Devil awakening her in the night with directions as to where to stab herself and which knife to use (pp2–3). God struck her dumb or knocked her asleep while trying to pray.

At the same time, Anna was arrogant and irritable, detesting folk who believed in free Grace, bursting out of the room with mad looks if anyone so much as mentioned it, so that her mother chided, and Anna flounced. Godly people would keep mentioning free Grace: they wanted her to have her helping. But free Grace would bring Anna down off her sensationally capricious high horse. The flashes of hellfire, and the thought of God's thunderous Law, made her inner cosmos a spectacular firework apocalypse, which she was entirely unprepared to surrender. Anyway, Anna wanted to be a special sinner, with nothing in common with the *hoi polloi*: who wants to be on a level with foul-mouthed drunks? she thought. 'Oh what a knotty piece was I for the great Jehovah to work upon!' (p6). Ultimately, the still small voice reassured her, saying, '"Christ is thine, and thou art his"', a voice so real that she'd turn round in the street when she heard it, thinking she was being followed. And there was lovely Mr Simpson's preaching, bathing her in 'joy unspeakable' and the sight of 'Angelical creatures' shining upon her inner eye. She passed virtually a whole year – 1642 – in a state of unparoxysmic bliss.

Then, one Tuesday, Anna's aunt came up to her room with the news of her mother's death. Her mourning mind conjured more devils, so that she feared to go to bed in case devils should tear her in bits. But Christ ravished her from this extreme to its polar opposite. Now she was the victim of violent rapture, waltzing around in a state of speechless transfiguration, her wild eyes giving people a terrible turn when they bumped into her. Tears of joy poured from her eyes. Her aged aunt affirmed she'd lived over sixty years and never seen anything like it: 'she wept to see me so, her heart much affected' (p12). Buzzing with the Saviour, Anna could not help but talk, talk, talk about her ravishing experiences, her sole topic of conversation. She was in her element. Yet in another way, Anna was courting and expressing distress. She notes that she could brave anything, even nicknames, sniggers and rude comments. What she really needed was her mother. But 'great was his care for me, no tender mother like to Jesus' (p13). The feminised Christ mothers his/her female prophet.

More visitations from Angels, who perfume her room. Stormy seas again. Anna is tossed around by theological obsessions. Dumbness. In June 1646, Anna takes to her bed and there undergoes throes of fever – pain – prostration – misery. She becomes helpless and her friends think she's dying. Floods of holy speech astonish them, and now Anna (with pangs of gratification) gets God's go-ahead to exercise her sanctified tongue to rebuke her friends' faults. One sweating night, she bargains deliriously with God, who promises to raise her on the third day.

Burning. Nauseous. Throat sore.

Able to drink nothing but small beer, cherry juice and currant conserve, she moves into further symptoms, in extreme pain 'as if my bones had been pulled asunder ... torture ... sick fits ... breath cold within me' (p29). Now she is in a seizure of trembling. Something is coming to birth in Anna. The body, clay home of the divine spirit, is being racked – and not for nothing. The Voice is being gestated.

Gratifying arrival of ministers at the sickbed: Mr Greenhill, whom she is desperate to detain, and does ... quinsy, sweats ... Anna raving in jubilation ... Mr Simpson ... cherries brought in to tempt her appetite are dwelt on by her sublimer eye as 'the blood of my Saviour' (p38) ... Captain Harris ... a perpetual audience ... trance, the final conflict, and then 'I found strength immediately, and I could walk about the room without fainting.' Anna was up till midnight, praising God whilst spooning in broth.

*

These were the formative religious and emotional experiences that fostered the Voice. She must have been voluble indeed: but also a canny listener, who knew how to direct her messages so that they would arrest the attention of Simpson and Feake, men organising politically for the End of the World. In *The Cry of a Stone*, Anna gives us samples of her successful prophecies. Suddenly we are in the men's world, at the political centre of events in strife-torn London: she takes up where *Legacy for Saints* would leave off, at the life-crux of her illness and focuses in on the content of her visions. Now we see a different Anna, who will emerge at Whitehall as a politically astute stuntwoman, no noisy quietist like copycatting Sarah Wight,[8] but a critic of the slide toward Cromwellian dictatorship, her passive 'prediction' a front for the attempt to change minds and events.

*

In July to August of 1647, the Army assembles outside the City, ready to march in and occupy the centre of power. Suddenly, Anna sees by inward revelation that this is Christ's Army; these the Latter Days. What's going on? she asks her maid at her lodgings in Aldgate. The maid is incredulous at Anna's ignorance of current affairs. Doesn't Anna know there's a national emergency, we've to shut up our shops, and nobody knows what will happen?

I do, thinks Anna, with an inward smile.

Looking out of the window, Anna spots a flag at one end of the road.

See that flag? says God: 'that flag of defiance is with the Army, the King of Salem is on their side, he marcheth before them, he is the Captain of their Salvation' (*Cry of a Stone*, p4).

See that hill? 'At the other end of the street, I looking saw a hill (it was Black-heath)'. The hill has always been there of course, but Anna has never accorded it particular attention. Now she is informed that hills will fall down and become valleys as God's Army advances. Anna, under orders to get out and mingle with the crowds, listens to their ignorant speculations and the inward smile deepens.

Reading between the lines, there is little doubt that Anna expects the End of the World this week.

Well, this year, at any rate. Time passes, and Anna has more military visions. She sees in trance the Army marching very quietly, 'coming in Southwark-way', reassuring her that little or no blood will be shed; 'this was some weeks before their coming in' (p5). That is, Anna claims to have known that the Army would enter the City through the opened gates of the rebel borough of Southwark, as it did at 2 a.m. on 6 August, to put down counter-revolution and mob-rule at Westminster.[9] Cromwell would ride in at the head of his regiment, his New Model Army of 18,000 men wearing sprigs of victorious laurel in their hats.

Nine days into a strenuous fast, Anna begins to see Big Horns and Little Horns, the violent visions of the Last Wars of Revelation. Anna has joined the ranks of the serious prophets: Ezekiel, Daniel, John of Patmos. As she edges towards the centre of the political stage, she is beginning to recognise one central figure (himself a millennarian) as the focus of God's political stratagem: Cromwell, whom she calls 'Gideon', his people's deliverer, the man she foresaw would 'ruinate' the Scots at the Battle of Dunbar in 1650.

Anna's vision of Dunbar during a fortnight's stint of fasting is spectacular, principally because she is there on the battlefield, experiencing the furious advance of the Scots army under a great canopy of light, which suddenly skids across the sky to 'our Army' under Gideon/Cromwell, which smashes the enemy. At first, like Cromwell himself ('God hath a people here fearing his name, though deceived'),[10] Anna was queasy about the thought of going to war against a previous ally 'judging many that were godly in those parts, might be cut off ignorantly' (p5). In other words, Cromwell might be mistakenly butchering fellow saints intended for service in the Fifth Monarchy. However, God settles her mind about this. Her account of the Dunbar vision highlights those misty symbols which could be interpreted with hindsight as referring to aspects of the battle hardly foreseeable by mere common sense – such as the Scots' strategic blunder in abdicating their impregnable position on Doon Hill, thereby forfeiting the benefit of their numerical advantage over the English (23,000 to 11,000 fatigued troops). Six weeks before Dunbar:

> I saw myself in the fields, and beheld our Army, and their General, and hearing this voice, saying, Behold Gideon and the happy ones with him ... and then I saw them in a very ill posture for war, and much dismayed, looking with pale countenances, as if affrighted. (p6)

At this point, the Scots assert their overconfidence, as they would do on the field, by moving their troops down to form a colossal arc around the English position – and serenely going to sleep. Cromwell would advance his forces in moonlit silence, to spring a pre-dawn ambush under the war-cry: 'The Lord of Hosts!' Anna's vision shows the Scots coming on:

> the light of the sky being over their heads ... and they thinking that our Army was running away, they marched up with very great fury against them, and suddenly as our Army turned ... the light of the sky being drawn from the Scots to our Army, they were encouraged, and immediately I saw the Scots fall down before them, and a marvellous voice of praise I heard in our Army: then was I taken weak

in my outward man ... as soon as this vision was over I
broke forth into the singing of their deliverance in Scotland.
(pp6–7)

Important persons' wives are agog, listening round Anna's bed, as
she predicts the battle-to-come: beetling home, they tell their
husbands and Mr Ash, the minister, who is highly impressed when
he comes to hear for himself. Anna's political credit soars, when, as
Bulstrode Whitelock put it, 'The Scots were driven like turkeys by
the English soldiers'[11] in Cromwell's greatest victory.

Next, on 5 November 1652, Anna enters nautical mode. She
foresees in graphic detail the English victory over the Dutch: 'ships
burning, bones and flesh sticking upon the sides of the ships, and
sails battered' (p7). It is appropriate to this maritime theme that
the hospitality of the widow Smith, glazier, with whom she is
staying for this course of visions, expresses itself through seafood
sustenance: Anna proudly records eating only two broiled herrings
during the period of seventeen days. And was visited by sea
captains.

February 1653: nervous reaction sets in. Satan pays a
prolonged visit, tickling her with unbearable yens to blaspheme:
Anna clamps her mouth shut and keeps the foul language in. Until
late April, Satan grapples violently. Godly folk have to watch
nightly at her bedside as Anna's drama enters a phase of turmoil,
involving urges to commit suicide by throwing herself into a well,
accompanied by insidious Antinomian fantasies – people will take
her suicide for murder, and God will accept her into heaven
anyway, as being one of the elect. She has to be collected by
superhumanly patient friends from ditches, where she takes to
lying, and often smuggles knives into bed, which spirits snatch
from her hand in the nick of time. Terror-riddled, tied in knots of
spiritual paradox, Anna rides the storm, to prophesy at Hillingdon
the 'calling in of the Jews', the Last Wars, and (four days before the
event) Cromwell's manic dissolution of the Rump Parliament, 'not
knowing anything of that nature was intended' (p10). Anna is back
on course.

But her 'Gideon' is beginning to shows his true colours. She
foresees his dissolution of the 'Barebones' Parliament in the form

of a gunpowder attack by 'Colonels and Chiefs of the Army' on a white tower containing saints. But the gunpowder won't light. In another vision, diseased oaks smash down upon lovely green shrubs: but a delightful tree (Jesus) raises up the shrubs.

Two nights before Cromwell declares himself Protector, Anna has multiple visions, in the apocalyptic third of which an ambitious ox with a face 'perfectly like unto Oliver Cromwell's' is acclaimed as supreme and fawned upon by lesser bulls, whereupon: 'he ran at me, and as he was near with his horn to my breast, an arm and an hand clasped me round, a Voice said, I will be thy safety' (p13). Ox-Cromwell's horn gores many of Anna's fellow saints, and drives them indoors, but the clouds open, the oxen are scattered, their horns broken and they tumble into graves. In this vision, Anna is again personally present at the centre of the political theatre, engaged against Cromwell and playing the role of the 'woman crowned with the sun, and the moon under her feet' of Revelation (12:1).

This takes us to Whitehall, where Anna's upward spiral brings her into full public view. *The Cry of a Stone* is a transcript of proceedings for each day, in which we detect the apparently catatonic babbler co-ordinating and stage-managing her event, according to a routine in which ecstatic bursts of prose commentary are interspersed with the recital of execrable impromptu verses. Anna as a rhymster may seem to us a joke: but to her contemporaries (even relatively sophisticated people) her sustained bouts of poetry appeared some guarantee of authenticity – like those of her predecessor, Jane Hawkins, a St Ives pedlar who preached in verse three days and nights to multitudes against the Anglican bishops. Where Jane had been discredited, Anna strove with all the manipulative force of her character for respectable celebrity. A letter by an unnamed contemporary, of 21 December 1654, assesses her as a riddling mix of the canny and the uncanny:

> As for ... Anna Trapnel, it is, (to be plain) to me a very strange dispensation, yet I am persuaded she hath communion with God in it, but under what sense [?] to rank it, I am at some stand ... If she did continue in it but for one or two days, I should be apt to think she might do

it when she would ... but for two things. First, she is so stiffened in her body that were she not warm, one would think her dead. Secondly; Because (she saith) she cannot make a verse when she is herself. But it is strange to me she should continue for eight days, as she did now, and I ascertained (from those I believe as if I saw it myself) that she ate nothing all that time, no, nor drunk, save once in twenty-four hours a little (and but very little) small beer.[12]

The writer is sceptical as to whether anything Anna says in trance exceeds what he knows she already knows. But he regards her powers of recuperation as so staggering that nothing earthly could explain them. Hearing her promise to attend a certain meeting next morning, 'which I doubted, seeing how she lay, and had lain', he goes along to see, only to be crept up on by the prophetess, who takes his hand. Watched like a hawk for signs of clandestine nibbling, to account for her upright chirpiness, Anna can be seen to ingest nothing but a modicum of small beer. No, she is not weak, she assures him, and as they bowl along in Lady Role's coach to Lambeth for the rest of the day, she chats serenely about her foodless joys. Anna has by now been taken up by the radical aristocracy. But all this is post-Whitehall and -Cornwall.

*

The content of Anna's Whitehall utterances was political dynamite, and shows her ideological centrality to the movement. She addressed over the fortnight the whole spectrum of the governing classes, from Protector and Army to merchants and religious elite. Singing to the Army, Anna poetically advised them to get on the winning side fast: the one with an arsenal:

> Their Armour shall most lovely look,
> In those thou dost appear,
> Thou art their Colonel indeed,
> Every troop for to cheer.

She added that profane commanding officers would be forced to grovel at the mercy-seat and surrender what 'thou stol'st/From the Commonweal-poor' (pp25, 26). And Cromwell would be stripped of his corrupt title of 'Protector'.

Next day she addressed herself to businessmen, in verses which solemnly wished them good trade and plenty of candied ginger and preserved nutmeg made by 'those Indians/That are so fill of Arts' but pointing out that there are spiritual and eternal ginger and nutmeg, without 'mouldy skins', which do not lose their taste.

Several days into her Whitehall stint, the inn seethed with visitors, some of whom may have been audibly expressing scepticism; for Anna launched into an acknowledgment of how she was a nothing, but God was 'all in nothing-Creatures'. Was she peeping between her eyelids? Was she being poked and prodded by witnesses testing her anatomy for signs of the divine rigor mortis? For she indignantly exclaimed: 'That a poor Creature should subsist without sustenance, what a gazing is there at this poor thing, while you forget the glory that's in it, go to the Marrow, what matters it for the bone' (p38).

Megalomaniac dreams soared, mingled with the tangy smoke of vengeance:

> Oh, I will make you Potentates ...
> And you shall see devouring fire
> Upon your enemies,
> But I will be a light to you
> And up you shall straight rise.

('Having uttered forth this Song,' writes the scribe, '(as she did all the rest) with melodious voice, she proceeded to prayer without any intermission'). Never far from the flood of Anna's thoughts was the knowledge that she had made herself a freak show; that people mocked her gift, as a mere woman's, or worse – madwoman? witch? whore? quack? She wove into the message statements of self-abnegation, in her own defence. She was not Anna, but a Voice: 'a sound, it is a voice within a voice, another's voice, even thy voice through her' (p42). She might have stopped at home away from all this sniggering, but had consented to be called forth to lie on public display, a mere mouth, her vocal cords on permanent loan to her ventriloquial Creator.

As the days passed, her divine warnings became more violently political. The universities and churches were for the pit;

'surplices and tippets' for the scissors (p50). Cromwell ought to be 'ashamed of his great pomp and revenue, whiles the poor are ready to starve, and art thou providing great Palaces? Oh this was not thy Gideon of old ... tell him, Lord, thou art come down to have a controversy with him' (p50). She attacked Cromwell's ambition to rule in his own right and promised divine retaliation. Anna scolded him with zealous relish: 'Oh do not rage, do not thou fume!/When thou art plainly dealt with ...' (p54). It was as if she had him in her mental sights, just within cuffing range.

On her last day, 17 January, she came right to the point. The powers-that-be had made a God of their belly. Presuming upon providential military victories, the government had lapsed into self-seeking evil: 'if ye keep not chronicles, others do' (p65). A 'Lord Protector' is just a politically correct word for 'king'; his sycophants are 'courtiers', full of 'the same superfluity and vanity' as the Stuarts. A sad day for England. To Cromwell, she said:

> thou shalt no more be called Valiant, because thou canst not be contented with the name of thy righteous ones ... As to the name General ... where is thy Victory, thy Righteousness, thy Zeal, thy Love, thy Conquest now? ... hadst thou not better to have died in the field, to have fallen in the tent, than to come into this great Palace which the Lord will rent from thee? (p68)

For in April Cromwell had removed his family bag and baggage into Whitehall, which Lady Cromwell had partially redecorated according to her taste, assuming a royal style of living which included everything from samples of the late king's art collections to a red velvet chamber pot for the Protector's personal use, value fiften shillings.[13] Protector, Council of State, upstart dynasties of rich robbers were all publicly damned by the daughter of the Poplar shipbuilder, flat out on the bed of the inn at Whitehall, as near to the inner sanctum of power as a woman was likely to reach. Seditious songs fanfared their way along the line of informants to Thurloe's office; Cromwell perhaps turned in his chair for a moment, with a raised eyebrow, an unquiet jest, to hear what the singing sibyl had come up with that day.

*

Shortly after this, Anna's carriage shuddered and rattled along the road to Cornwall, a six-day journey in which the travellers alighted each night at inns. On the first day she rode quietly; the second she spent in discussion with her companions; on the third she sang and prayed all the way to Salisbury, where the Judge who had ridden with them disembarked, ears ringing. Anna spent the whole night contemplating Judgement Day, which her Cornish errand secretly advanced; sang all Day Four; the same on Day Five, which she devoted to ditties concerning 'the creation-excellencies, as trees, grass, and several plants, and corn as I went by' (p8). Not the least touching and human of Anna's qualities is this naïve responsiveness to nature. Ignoring the towns they passed through, she was impervious to the coach's jolting on the uneven roads.

At Exeter, a stronghold of Fifth Monarchism and sectarian activity, she lodged with Mrs Winter, one of many widows in the radical sects to use the personal and financial freedom of widowhood to provide for itinerant preachers and assemblies. Hearing a sermon at Exeter Castle, Anna bumped into some London friends and imparted news of the joyful sufferings of Feake and Simpson at Windsor. But what are you doing so far from home, among strangers, the friends queried. They regarded Anna with bemused respect, wondering 'what the Lord would do with me; and so did many' (*Report and Plea*, p9).

Next day, in buoyant form, she sang rampantly of God's intention to smash the 'tottering, shaking' priesthood.

Anna progressed by stages to Tregasow, home of Fifth Monarchist ex-MP, Captain Langden. The Cornish scenery aroused her mystical appreciation of things rocky and mountainous, Dartmoor impressing her with its severe splendour as a wilderness of biblical meaning. Reading her description of her thoughts, we feel an essential timidity in this far-flung, brittle pilgrim, venturing into unknown territory:

> and my thoughts were much upon the Rocks I passed by in
> my journey, and the dangerous rocky places I rode over.
> And whereas I used to be very fearful, when I rode on
> smooth ground, now I feared not, but was very cheerfully
> carried on, beholding my Rock, Christ, through those

> emblems of Rocks: and I sat as in a chair upon the high
> steep hills, without any wearisomeness at all. (p10)

For seventeenth-century Christians, the English countryside might fade into the landscape of ancient Israel, a biblical terrain, imprinted with the hieroglyphs of God. On the same earth as Anna, the feet of Abraham, Moses and Jacob had walked. Highly wrought and nervous, she comforted herself by recalling that real rocks which spell danger to travellers are signs of God's love and support. He is her Rock. Her carriage skimmed the hilltops, in a panorama of divine expectation.

Anna's rocks seem tame compared with those haunted by the bumptious, insecure Welsh ecstatic, 'Arise' (Rees) Evans. Arise, a rival Royalist prophet who foretold the regicide (but no one would listen) and claimed Charles II as the 'day-star to bring the Jews to Jesus' (but no one wanted to know), published his life story, *A Voice from Heaven* and *Echo to the Voice from Heaven*, in 1652: wherein he revealed his wonderful childhood experience on Bwlych Ryw Credire, in Merioneth:

> being come to the top, where the dark clouds about me by
> the wind was driven swiftly, I being fearful in that place
> elevated by prayer the more: and through the fervour of my
> prayer, and vehemency of the winds and clouds I was lifted
> above the earth and carried up a space in the clouds as I
> went on my way.[14]

Anna never claims to have flown. But Arise arose. The Welshman also saw the inside of a gaol, which he sought indefatigably, achieving a hilarious notoriety. Arise's problem was not dissimilar to Anna's: people tended to bend double with laughter when he prophesied. In 1653, cruising the London streets, Arise bumped into an illiterate and previously mute woman prophet, Elinor Channel, who had abandoned husband, children and impoverished home in Surrey to deliver a God-given message to Cromwell concerning fiscal and international policy. Arise published this as *A Message of God (by a Dumb Woman) To His Highness the Lord Protector* (with berserk Royalist augmentations of his own). Arise's comparison of his protegée with Anna Trapnel shows the fame

Anna's prophecies had achieved in Protectoral England:

> And though it be but short, yet you shall find more truth
> and substance in it, than in all Hana Trampnel's songs and
> sayings, whom some account the Diana of the English, Acts
> 19:34, as may appear by this that was written for her.[15]

Anna was doing her best to avoid Elinor's rough fate – Bridewell
and jeering crowds. A bourgeoise, proud to pay her taxes, Anna
manifested a wincing objection to being classed with riffraff
(though she wanted to see them fairly dealt with). Touchingly,
Anna was not of the stuff of which heroes and martyrs are made.
She went on her journey, not as heroic Quakers Katharine Evans
and Mary Fisher would do, but with butterflies acknowledged to
be fluttering wildly in her stomach.

*

Arriving at Captain Langden's house, Anna is unnerved at the
sourness of the greeting accorded her by his acquaintance. She
takes refuge in the garden, where God cushions her welcome by
comparing her rather favourably with Abraham and counselling
her to take suffering in 'a strange country' in an Abraham-like
manner (p11). Fired up, soon Anna is roving the county, making
contacts with local militants like Bawden and Allen in Truro,
testifying and preaching. While local hostility mounts, especially
amongst ministers and judges, rumours circulate that warrants are
out for her arrest. Hearing these rumours, Anna worries about a
forthcoming trial:

> I that day found my timorous, fearful nature work against
> me, what I should do and say against the Magistrate having
> never been before any in that kind, to be abused by them.
> (p19)

There is no reason to doubt the sincerity of this stage-fright. Anna
will have to answer up for herself in the public arena, without the
comfort of a divine swoon. The swaddling of adulation and
support of the Allhallows sisterhood is lacking, and Anna shivers as
she senses the antagonism of the community. But warbles on. The
law arrives in the form of the Constable. His hand shaking (so
Anna is afterwards told), he wrenches at her catatonic form. The

Justices follow, with their minions, making:

> a great tumult ... in the house, and some came upstairs,
> crying *A witch, a witch*; making a great stir on the stairs; and
> a poor honest man rebuking such that said so, he was
> tumbled downstairs and beaten too, by one of the Justices'
> followers ... And they threatened much, but the Lord over-
> ruled them: they caused my eye-lids to be pulled up, for they
> said, *I held them fast, because I would deceive the people* ... One
> of the Justices pinched me by the nose, and caused my
> pillow to be pulled from under my head, and kept pulling
> me and calling me; but I heard none of all this stir and
> bustle. (p21)

Uproar swells. The caustic justices sneer at her so-called trance,
saying she'll pretty soon wake up if they take the whip to her.
When Anna awakens, hours later, she sits up in bed, yawns and
stretches, and innocently enquires of her hostess whether she has
been alone all day, for '"I have had a sweet day."' Her hostess is
astonished at the question: did Anna not hear the justices making
that unholy din in the bedroom around her, bawling in her ear,
pinching, shooting out the pillow from under her head, raising her
eyelids, poking at her? '"No,"' says Anna, wonderingly. She has to
be told the tale of the mayhem of which she has been divinely
unconscious.

But in the triumphalist tone of Anna's narrative is embedded
a sharp flake of fear, for:

> that witch-trier woman of that town, some would fain have
> had come with her great pin which she used to thrust into
> witches to try them, but the Lord God whom I trust
> delivered me from their malice.

The use of the pin would have confounded the logic of Anna's
position; and neatly demonstrates the quandary of female ecstatics,
since the opposites of divine inspiration and demonic possession
manifested themselves identically. Anna's trance, blocking out the
sensory world, was uneasily open to reverse interpretation; for had
the witch detector dug her 'great pin' in Anna's flesh and Anna
failed to jump, she could have been accused of a pact with the

Devil (see pp45–7 above). Who can doubt that, had Anna been subjected to the witch test, some telltale mole or patch of rough skin would have been located?

Anna Trapnel in 1654 counted herself providentially sheltered in escaping the trial by pin that could be the first step to the gallows. She also practised jittery self-help. After her sessions-trial, Anna noted with fainting relief the remark of curious bystanders: '"Sure this woman is no witch, for she speaks many good words, which the witches could not."' She may have been uneasily aware that one of the hostile JPs, Tregagle, had sat at the witchcraft trial of the visionary Anne Jefferies two years previously. Anna's tongue was on trial: whereas before she had just let go and allowed herself to say whatever came into her head, now she had to guard her tongue, cite salient and plentiful passages of Scripture, chapter and verse, and assert her cause. As she moved off to her trial, folk flocked around her, and lads made rude faces and ruder noises. Mocked and derided, Anna held her head high, walking on pins but in the footsteps of her Saviour.

Anna's celebrity was mirrored in the crowded Truro Sessions House, which was gratifyingly packed from wall to wall. The accused and her party were ushered to a table round which sat court officials; above them loomed the justices, leaning over a rail. At their elbow sat one of the clergymen who initiated the indictment. He and the witch-trying woman shot Anna bilious looks, which she (heart beating high) returned, plucking up 'courage to look my accusers in the face, which was no carnal boldness, though they called it so'. This brings out the complex double-bind of Anna's situation as a vocal woman dissident, questioning the 'natural' and 'divine' law of female silence.

She is damned for speaking.

She will now be double-damned if she doesn't speak, for, as she breathlessly reminds herself, public interrogation tended to discover witches, by rendering them mute – an infallible sign, not of nerves, but of guilt (p25).

She is damned for looking her accuser in the face (sign of an impudent whore).

She will be damned if she looks down (sign of guilty conscience).

The JPs bind her over till the next assizes, Langden and Bawden standing surety. Before her is ranged the Cornish gentry elite in the persons of Justices Lobb, Selye, Launce and Tregagle, all of whom are or will be Members of Parliament. They stand for everything Anna despises and expects Christ to destroy at his imminent arrival. Beside her are the two radical ex-MPs for the area, Langden and Bawden, recently toppled, hated and feared by the establishment clergy and gentry. The trial is political; and the justices have come equipped with a copy of Anna's book, *The Cry of a Stone*, seditious passages of which they read to her and ask her to acknowledge. Anna prudently hedges. If the government at Whitehall didn't object to her public prophecies, what right has a provincial court to object? The judges whisper. Getting nowhere, they lay aside the incriminating book.

What is Anna doing in Cornwall anyway, they want to know?

A. T.: I answered I came as others did that were minded to go into the country.

Lobb: But why did you come into this country?

A. T.: Why might not I come here, as well as into another country?

Lobb: But you have no lands, nor livings, nor acquaintance to come to in this country.

A. T: What though I had not? I am a single person, and why may I not be with my friends anywhere?

Lobb: I understand you are not married.

A. T.: Then having no hindrance, why may not I go where I please, if the Lord so will?

An unattached woman on the move is seen as a threat to public order. The justices' instinct is to place her in the criminalised category of 'vagrants', 'masterless' trouble-makers: a 'masterless' (ie unmarried) woman on an independent journey is a lawless element, and probably a whore.[16] Anna's defence is that she is legitimately her own master, and wonders what law she is supposed to be breaking? This the judges cannot yet answer with conviction. Two years later, Parliament would revive the Elizabethan Act against rogues, vagabonds and sturdy beggars, to cover precisely this problem, classing beggars with itinerant preachers, especially 'the Quakers, who greatly increase, and pester and endanger the Commonwealth'[17] (see Chapter 10).

This charge of 'vagabond' sticks in Anna's throat, for powerful reasons of class pride. One of the most powerful and direct passages Anna ever wrote comes at the end of the *Report and Plea*, when Anna asserts her rights as a free citizen, and the state's obligations:

> Again, you call me vagabond; but how will you make that good? ... I lived with my mother till she died, which was about twenty years, then I kept house with the means my mother left me, and paid taxes toward the maintaining of the Army then in the field; and this I did not grudgingly, but freely and willingly; I sold my plate and rings, and gave my money to the public life; you did not call me vagabond then ... [I] fared hard, that so I might minister to the relief of the nation ... Oh Army, and Rulers, that then would not have defamed me ... you have taxes from me still; and am I a vagabond for this? (p50)

Anna's angry *you did not call me vagabond then* argues the rights of a tax-payer, who happens to be a single woman. She maintains her citizenship as a tax-payer who has (like the Leveller women, see pp77, 144) made substantial voluntary contributions to the Parliamentary war effort. The argument about freedom of movement at her trial involves an implicit denial by the authorities that any woman should act autonomously.

Anna sets out her trial in terms of the set-piece drama of Reformation martyrology, which played such a central propaganda role in testimonies from Anne Askew to George Fox, Margaret Fell, John Bunyan. These accused men and women acknowledged only one Master, Christ, who himself was convicted by rigged trial. The drama of the public trial staged the triumph of the elect over the elite. But Anna's account tends invincibly toward the mock-heroic. She represents her judges as a hectic rabble, all gabbling at once, so that she itches to compare them with 'women, all speakers and no hearers' – a witticism one is tempted to suspect came to mind well after the event.

Justice Lobb comes to the point: '"You prophesy against Truro."'

Anna admits that she prays against the sins of the inhabitants of Truro, '"Are you angry for that?"'

Lobb insists that Anna's opposition to authority is seditious and her trances counterfeit, which she is alleged to have admitted to two women who will now testify. But as one woman has collapsed in a swoon and the other has bolted from the court house, this plan is aborted (p27).

As the case draws toward its close, Anna upstages everyone by reminding the justices that another Trial is in the offing, where the JPs won't be swanking on high behind a privileged rail, but sweating down here amongst the defendants. The Judgement Day might be set for next week, at which time the justices will be hard put to account for their behaviour today. 'Said Tregagle, "Take you no care for us"', an amused rejoinder, off-the-cuff, that has all the quality of authenticity. As Anna quits the scene of her first conscious public performance, it appears that the crowd has warmed to her. No one who speaks so well can possibly be a witch, they are sure.

Ten days later, Anna is in an emotional, weepy state, but trying not to upset the kind Langdens; she gets up from the table and reads her Bible, before taking a recuperative walk in the garden, where Captain Langden joins her to learn that she has had a brainwave: she has decided to rechristen Cornwall 'Cornhell'.

*

Arrested, Anna is removed by stages to London. At Fowey, she looks up to see a great crowd of people 'sitting on a high wall, right over where I sat'. She gapes; they gawp. Anna does not lose the opportunity to address a few holy words to them, 'and when I went away, they gave a great shout' (p28).

At Looe she speaks to a blind man about the Light.

At Plymouth, lodged in prison, in high but complex spirits, Anna assures her friends that she has actually achieved a promotion. Prison, she assures them, is infinitely better than that worse pit of depression. She prays and sings all night, while the maid indefatigably sponges away floods of tears Anna does not know she's weeping.

In four days and five nights, Anna only snacks on small beer, cider and a mite of toast.

She is on the ship. But a storm drives it back into Dartmouth, whose inhabitants, casting around for meteorological causes, come up with the obvious: the wild woman must have 'bewitched the winds'. But Anna is able to prove God's special favour through her immunity to sea-sickness. While all and sundry are prostrated by vomiting, the stomach of Anna is in a state of grace. She feels chirpy and sings in her cabin, 'and the sea-men were much affected' (p34). It is true that she hurts her leg against the ship-side; that the wound infects, and that the cabin is sickeningly hot, but these count as trials of mettle. Brought staggering up on deck, she registers with horror that her companions are captured pirates. Nevertheless, Anna forgives her persecutors. And the pirates are entirely courteous.

At Portsmouth, where they land, a food problem sets in. Ensign Baker's wife, with whom she is lodged, considers her a 'frenzy-headed creature' and gives her nothing to eat for three days. But Anna tunes up there night and day, disabusing Mrs Baker.

They are on the coach to London, feeling distinctly battered. But Anna has been given a present of 'partridge eggs of the largest kind' from Guernsey. Anna coddles the precious eggs. The coach breaks down twice and once hair-raisingly turns over: when the bundle is opened, the eggs are discovered to be smashed.

From Fox Hall to Westminster they proceed by water. Anna is still absorbed in the fate of the partridge eggs. Light breaks: she can see now that Christ's gift to her of his jewel, Christ, is infrangible, 'nor like eggs that are subject to rot or break before they come to be large partridges' (p38).

Anna reaches her destination: Bridewell. It is now that the full shock of what she has dared to embrace strikes and overwhelms her. The stink nearly knocks her backwards. An open sewer runs beneath her window and rats scutter on the floor of her room. Anna retches, and can't stop retching, 'these scents entered much into my nice stomach'. Her friends hold their noses and are appalled at the 'hard, flock bed' appointed for the nauseated, exhausted prisoner. In this scene of filth, the squeamish, middle-class woman is beset with temptations. And her record is so faithful that we are moved by

Anna's willingness to bare her unheroic human weakness. For as she gets ready for bed in this hellhole, Anna is tempted by Satan, 'who said, to be so forward for God, see what thou hast got by it'. Anna will be a 'by-word and a laughing stock' as long as she lives, and everyone will point at her, saying, 'there goes a Bridewell bird' (pp39–40).

Cheered though she is by Christ's words of concerned love, she is appalled by the matron. The matron is a gorgon. She bolts her in. Shivering in the unkind bed, heaving with nausea, Anna is helmeted by headache; tosses and turns; yet as daylight greys the window, she flings back the bedclothes and her fellow prisoners will have heard a dawn chorus of tremulous halleluiahs.

The vinegar matron, besieged by Anna's friends, concedes a change of bed and a strewing of herbs to cover the stench. Anna's temperature soars. She cannot drag herself up to appear in court. matron threatens to bring in 'an old man, that called up the harlots and thieves, every morning betimes to beat hemp, he was to flap them up to work' (p42). *He* will shift the malingering Anna, snarls the matron. Behind Anna's text opens up for a moment the hellish landscape of an age's misery: the criminalised, whipped, diseased underclass of seventeenth-century London. In court, Anna complains of her conditions, her sickness.

Friends and family could often share your prison cell in this period. Anna bears witness to the tender support of her friend, Ursula Adman, who 'kept me company seven weeks of my being there: she was a friend born for the day of adversity' (p44)[18] The burden is eased by Ursula's voluntary sharing. As the two women sit in festering filth, rats run about the room. They are amazed at their size, 'like dogs and cats' as they scrabble around.

The Protectoral government comes to feel that its detention of the singing prophetess has backfired. She has taken to writing inflammatory epistles from prison, as if she were St Paul himself. The 'Lord's prisoner at Plymouth Fort' has addressed herself in heroic vein to 'the Lord's Prisoners at Windsor Castle', the seditious Feake and Simpson, with whom she could now compare stigmas on equal terms, advising them to 'continue to the end ... Jesus like, bearing his stamp' (*A Legacy*, p60). 'Oh friends, it's a very high honour to suffer for well-doing,' she reminds them, puffing out her chest (p58), and then, ashamed of her boasting, soliciting their prayers that 'I may not be proud of sufferings' (p60). In Bridewell, she becomes a magnet for visitors: the rats are doing her cause an advertising favour. When the order for Anna's liberty arrives, the authorities refuse to vindicate her. She returns a defiant answer: 'go tell your Masters, though they will not see me they shall be sure to hear from me' (p48).

In an uncertain world, this at least seems definite.

9

THREE PURITAN MARRIAGES
RALPH & JANE JOSSELIN, NEHEMIAH & GRACE WALLINGTON,
LUCY & JOHN HUTCHINSON

Ralph Josselin's private diary is one of the classic documents of the seventeenth century. A moderate left-wing Puritan, Josselin was a clergyman in the Essex parish of Earl's Colne, acting as chaplain to the Parliamentary army, who somehow managed to hold on to his ministry after the Restoration; he was farmer, student of history, millennarian, husband, father, householder and friend, as well as a devoted scribbler, whose quill searched his soul on the page and jotted day-to-day events, domestic and national, with fascinating vividness. Josselin's diary[1] helps us to conjure the experience of living through the century of revolution, at somewhere near the political margin.

And moving through the hinterland of his diary are Puritan women – sisters, wife, daughters, servants, friends – who never demonstrated, preached or travelled. Yet these too are women of the English Revolution. Here we glimpse the turn of a private face, and catch muffled voices.

In 1616, parental joy at the birth of an heir may have been too frankly manifested, for one of Ralph's earliest memories concerns a vicious attack by his second sister who expressed her feeling for him 'by knives being stabbed in the forehead ... a wild child but now I hope God hath tamed and sanctified her spirit' (p1). Above the boy in age, but below him in the hierarchy, the sister from hell took revenge before godly domestication subdued her spirit. Later, economic privation turned his sisters into Ralph's grateful or mortified pensioners, and one was taken on as a family servant (p14).

Anxiety is a key theme of the diary from first to last page. Dangers from fire, water, falls from horses and sibling attack are compounded by sixty-seven years of obsession with plague, civil war, drought, floods, poor yields, childbirth, insect bites, horse kicks, sins. Long catalogues of near-miss accidents are scored against other families' illnesses and afflictions within a providential accounting-system. The whole landscape of the Puritan mind seems laid out in Josselin's busy calculations of economic and spiritual profit and loss.[2]

The death of a child or a tumble in the mud did not just happen to happen. Providence disposed. But God's code often seemed baffling and Josselin, trawling for messages, examined himself for explanatory failings and strove for amendment. He cannot but congratulate himself when lightning strikes elsewhere. Miraculous rescues by spiritual powers abound. Little Mary comes a cropper from the parlour window 'with her face against the bench and had no hurt God be praised a strange providence' (p17). In September 1644 his dear friend Mary Church, in slinging a basin of water from the door, finds she has hurled herself out with the water and takes a crashing fall, but without damage to her person, 'oh how do God's angels keep us in many dangers. We began this day to put the county in a posture of defence' (p19). Large apprehensions are mirrored in trivial neuroses and the diary spasms with a nervous tic of harm close, alongside, avoided. Life is an eternally tenuous Passover.

Yet God invariably embeds in calamity some gracious lesson.

For instance, September sees the Almighty allowing a bee to sting Ralph's nose:

> I presently plucked out the sting and laid on honey, so that my face swelled not, thus divine providence reaches to the lowest things. Let not sin oh Lord that dreadful sting be able to poison me. (5 September 1644)

The following day, he can report with relief that a child in the town was 'burnt almost to death, and mine safe oh mercy and goodness to be adored'.

All too human, Josselin meanly huddles in to his brood. He cannot afford empathy. Ailments groan and sweat through the pages: sore tongue, swelling on the groin, conjunctivitis, colds, agues, fits, rickets, worms, toothache, painful gums; plague and smallpox breathe on the windowpane, and a suppurating navel nags at him for years. Perhaps nothing in the diary admits us more deeply into the consciousness of the age than this eternal vigil through untreatable infection and injury.[3]

Josselin's diary is the story of a partnership which weathered forty-three years, a riven pattern of Puritanism's ideals and conflicts. Ralph married Jane Constable in October 1640, when he was twenty-three and she nearly twenty years old. Ten live children were born in twenty-one years, of whom five predeceased their parents, though only one died in infancy. Five miscarriages are recorded. If you read Josselin's diary alongside a marriage manual like Daniel Rogers' *Matrimonial Honour*,[4] published in 1650, while the Josselins were rearing their brood, you are struck by their enlightened sympathy to the woman's position. Josselin tries to practise what Rogers preaches. Marriage is viewed as a union of not-quite (but almost) equals, with gender-specific roles and spheres, ideally based on mutual attraction, religious consent and respect.

Puritanism was a double-bound system which expanded and contracted the gap of inequality; and these opposing ideologies could both be present in one book (Rogers) or in one life (Josselin), in a state of fluctuating contradiction. Rogers repeats the patriarchal doctrine of female inferiority and subordination, but the 'yokefellow' ideal of 'draw[ing] mutually and equally in one yoke' tends to equalise the relationship, and in practice his manual places greater onus on the male to be forbearing than on the woman to buckle under. The wife's duty of subjection is only reached in Chapter 13. In the volume I read in the John Rylands Library, Manchester, some early reader's irritable pen had scribbled beside Rogers' acknowledgement that it's about time he came to the wife's duties and left off hammering the husband. The jagged line in aged browned ink ends in a blot, as if to say, 'At last'.

Rogers demands that the husband be sensitive and exercise his imagination. In emphasising man's affinity with woman, he seeks empathy with 'another self', who has drawn the short straw in life:

> she hath done that for thy sake, which thou wouldst not have done for her: for she hath not only equalled thee in forsaking her father and mother, and family, that she might be one flesh with thee, but she hath forgone her name, and put all her state and livelihood into thine hand. (p160)

Marriage is an unequal contract, in which the wife forfeits more than her mate, and effectively puts herself at his mercy, suffering the pain of pregnancy, childbirth and nursing. Frailer physically, she carries a disproportionately heavy load: 'Consider oh man ... the drudgery of thy wife' (p161), in a role no man is qualified to fill. The life she has to lead, says Rogers, would drive any man mad in days:

> what man were able to endure that clamour, annoyance, and clutter which she goes through without complaints among poor nurslings, clothing, feeding, dressing and undressing, picking and cleansing them; what is it save the instinct of love which enableth her hereto? ... If God were not in her spirit, she would cast it off ten times, ere she would go through stitch with it, as she doth. (p161)

Rogers is a realist who recognises marriage as a breeding ground of strife, in which compromise is essential. He outlaws male bellowing and wife-beating (legally open to a husband, up to a certain point) as despicable. Marriage must be worked at.

He insists that the male reader grasp the concept that women suffer because of men; and that they are due any compensation that can be devised for their unequal share of stress:

> She is always in grief, & that for thee, & by thy means; what day, week, month is she free through the year, breeding, bearing, watching her babes, both sick that they may be well ... If she lose a child by the hand of God, or by casualty, her tender heart takes more thought for it in a day, than thy manly spirit can in a month: the sorrow of all lies upon her: she had need to be eased of all that is easeable, because she cannot be eased of the rest ... Get her asleep if thou can, but awake her not, till she please. (pp244–5)

The last sentence's practical tenderness resonates movingly for readers of Josselin's diary. His concern for Jane's exhaustion is only matched by his awareness of all she means to him. When preaching on the theme of the biblical Rachel dying in childbirth, 'such a passion surprised me that I could not well speak, the Lord in mercy preserve my dearer than Rachel' (17 October 1647). Rogers even suggests that a wife be given every chance of enjoyment and respite-leave. 'Remember how oft, her faithful biding at home, hath enlarged thee to travel abroad' (p248). Mothers are exhorted to breast-feed: prudent advice since breast-feeding provided some contraceptive protection. None of Jane Josselin's babies was conceived until she had weaned the last, at anything from a year to nineteen months old.

*

When Jane bears their first baby, Mary, Josselin records their mutual relief over a safe delivery and her success in breast-feeding. But:

> my wife's breasts were sore which was a grievance and sad cut to her but with use of means in some distance of time they healed up: this Spring times grew fearful in the rising of the year about Midsummer we began to raise private arms ...
>
> Edgehill battle being fought ... I was told the news as I was going down the churchyard to sermon ...
>
> One spring now my wife weaned her daughter and began to breed again. (pp12–13)

The story weaves in and out of the domestic world of pregnancy and childcare, and the raising of armies, reminding us of the continuum of ordinary life in a period of cataclysm. Around the breeding pair, people pillage Roman Catholic houses; the king enlists troops; indoors, there is murmurous intimacy and child-bearing, mastitis and private woes and joys. Though the male diarist is free to inhabit both private and public worlds, he identifies strongly with interior space. Childhood illnesses are watched over by both parents with anxious eyes. Next year, there is a little girl; then another boy, and with each pregnancy a rhythmic return of Jane's morning sickness and justified fear: 'my dear wife under great fears she shall not do well of this child: ill in her head and back, one night ill as if she should have died, the Lord ... give her comforts. and lengthen her days' (30 October 1647).

Perhaps a modern reader is surprised at the apparent modernity of Ralph's attitude to fathering. At his baby Ralph's death, he records that 'we gave him breast milk at last, and little else' (20 February 1648). That '*we*' expresses the practical and emotional involvement of a father in sustaining his family. A year later – the month of the regicide – a second baby Ralph seems mortally ill 'and his mother sickly and toiling with him' (27 January).

Early March, 1650: the baby 'rested very ill three nights, but the fourth night God heard our prayer and refreshed his wearied mother'. March sees colds, conjunctivitis, viruses, toothache, colic, and the continued sickness of the baby, whom they decide to wean. In May, everyone is ill again and their treasured daughter, Mary, is evidently on her deathbed. Opposing the stereotype of fatherly indifference to girl-children, Ralph is exceptionally close to his daughters. On 24 May:

> my dear Mary voided six worms more this day. I went to bed at night, but was raised up, with the dolour of my wife, that Mary was dying, she was very near death ... 'Oh mother,' saith she, 'if you could but pull out something handsomely here,' (and lays her hand on her stomach) 'I should be well'.

Mary dies three days later at the age of eight years and 45 days, 'our first fruits', which he tries to persuade himself he freely relinquishes to God.

They never linger to bury their dead: corpses putrefy and are healthier underground. Next day the child is buried beneath the church floor, Margaret Harlakanden and Mabel Elliston laying the light burden in the grave: 'I kissed her lips last,' says Ralph, 'and carefully laid up that body.'

Within the week the second baby Ralph and Josselin's close friend, Mary Church, die, and are buried together. He preaches the funeral sermon, shaken to the core. Josselin's friendship with Mary Church, a gentlewoman of forty, was a non-sexual bond between a man and a single woman, which went deep. 'When Mrs Mary died, my heart trembled, and was perplexed in the dealings of the Lord so sadly with us' (4 June 1650). Thinking of his daughter 'I am sometimes ready to be overwhelmed' (p207).

In August Jane is pregnant again; the exhausted parents' nerves grate as their nights are broken by the surviving children's 'sudden cryings out in the forepart of the night, my heart is out of frame because of my unquietness'. A week later, he has decided upon the cause of the children's nocturnal shriekings: worms.

How Jane copes with the stress of this year in which the family staggers from one vile malady to another, losing two children, sleepless, haggard and fraught, the diary does not record – except in a crossed-out niggle against Jane for her irritability (p218). Mighty events have shaken the nation: but even if Jane Josselin had felt the call to participate in the theatre of history, how could she have freed herself from the formidable burden of mothering a seventeenth-century family? The day-to-day stress of her experience focuses the huge personal cost involved in the Quaker women's quitting of family and children for prison or shipboard; why many women prophets and preachers were single or widowed. We grasp more vividly Elinor Channel's husband's aghast prohibition on her mission to Cromwell. A refrain in Josselin's diary is to the effect, 'What would I do without my wife?' Waves of gratitude for 'the care of a tender mother' (9 December 1660) break year after year in the pages of the diary, and when the care of the household falls upon him, Ralph is bemused by the load under which he staggers (24 January 1658).

*

The 1650s, throughout which the Josselin couple (now into their thirties) is breeding, initiate a new phase of life for both partners. The Commonwealth shudders and from its throes a Lord Protector is delivered. The fatally wounded Leveller movement spasms its defiance. Quakers spread down from the north of England, across to Holland, America, the West Indies – and even to the backwater of Gaines Colne, just on the Josselin doorstep. Resonances are felt by the minister of Earl's Colne, not merely in his public vocation as minister but within his home; in his very bed.

Josselin queasily notes in his congregation 'unreverent' persons, impudently 'sitting with their hats on when the psalm is singing' (23 June 1650), signs of a new age where codes of deference have broken down, and man will no longer doff his hat even to God. Before long the first Quakers (to the moderate Josselin sinister delinquents) appear and multiply in the area, buzzing during church services, defying clergy and magistrates. Each Sunday the wincing Josselin expects to be the victim of their heckling.

Worry increases but a secret compensatory agency springs up in the Josselin household, through which it can express its terrors as hopes. Millennial consciousness arises: the end of the world is with us. The whole Josselin household starts dreaming.

*

Millennial fervour[5] was not confined to way-out Fifth Monarchists like Feake, Trapnel and Cary, with whom the Josselins would have disdained association. Such expectation transiently became a norm of consciousness amongst moderates, both men, women and children.

In November 1650, Ralph has his first political dream. Waking in the tester bed beside Jane, giddy thoughts arise that, if the Last Days are indeed with the Chosen Nation, he and Jane, together with their brood, may number among the lucky remnant who never die; further that he may be a chosen prophet divulging and thus helping to shape the pattern of the Last Events.

To a man of Josselin's pathologically anxious temperament, this line of thought offers catharsis on a magnificent scale. Chaos and upheaval turn into signs of imminent glory and deliverance.

The worse things are, the better. The inscrutable welter of history becomes a meaningful code, and even the line of disreputables sitting on the front pew with their rude hats on may be accounted a sign that God is coming (to pull their hats off).

Throughout November and December, Ralph cogitates, aroused, kindled, and searches his dreams each morning for messages concerning the Prince of Orange and the Scots.

One Monday five-year-old Jane gallops in to her parents' bedroom with a message from the Almighty. She has dreamed that Jesus Christ came up into her daddy's pulpit:

> and there he stayed a while, and then he came down, and came into bed to her. She said to him, why dost thou come to me; and he answered her to sleep a little with thee, and he laid down and slept, and again she dreamed that Jesus Christ told her that he should come and reign upon the earth ten thousand years. (2 March 1651)

Childish, filial and millennarian details mingle in little Jane's dream: the wondering, pondering eyes of the whole household are upon her as she tells it, and perhaps for the first time in her life she finds herself the centre of serious attention. Jane's dream tells of a tender and intimately human Jesus, to whom she need not ascend, for he 'came down', to share her bedspace. The Protestant one-to-one relationship with the Deity is transposed in the child's dreaming mind into the closeness of parent with child, whispering apocalyptic confidences under the quilt ('he should come and reign upon the earth ten thousand years'). Her father finds it worth transcribing as a testimony of these Latter Days, and God's favour to the Josselins: and it stands beside sheaves of witness from the mouths of 'babes and sucklings' in this period. However, it is a sign of the spiritual democracy in the Josselin household that Jane did not have to be dying for her father to take her utterances seriously (see pp134–5 above).

*

As the Josselins' millennial awareness grows, smallpox ravages the area. Awaiting the Second Coming and the collection of donations for the conversion of the Indians of New England fails to prevent Ralph from getting edgy with his wife and regretting it:

> I am sure I should be more patient, and counsellable than I am, oh that I could look on my wife not as under weakness but as an heir of the same grace of life, and live with her as such, the Lord help me. (7 November 1652; p289)

Diary-writing gains the husband perspective, to see that marital conflicts are triggered not by his wife's inferiority but by his demeaning of her spiritual equality. Besides, how wretched for Christ to arrive in the glory of his Second Coming, to find Ralph and Jane wrangling.

Winter 1654 brings a new flock of apocalyptic dreams. Night by night, while Ralph has flown up into a sumptuous dreamscape in which he is eyeball to eyeball with the Pope, Jane on the other side of the bed achieves her own afflatus: she dreams that the Josselins are on familiar terms with the Lord Protector (22 November). The following night, Ralph's imagination tends skywards, as he dreams up 'ships and boats loaden in the heavens and a great man on a fierce horse prancing'. But now his wife is in her stride and awakens on the morning of 26 November to report a dream more sensational and cosmic than anything Ralph has yet managed:

> she saw three lights in the sky above Abbots fields which were North by West, and South a body as the Sun or Moon, the lights blazed and filled the sky with light often, and then the body in the South answered it with flames ascending terrible; when the lights ceased there arose three smokes like pillars out of the earth and ascended. She thought of Revelation 19:3: afterwards the lights with a whirlwind and noise filled the whole heaven with sparks, as if it would have burnt all. (pp324–5)

The dream unfurls in symbolism of flowers efflorescing from a root, and Jane awakens in a lather of exaltation, having seen the Last Things. Ralph's entry shows Jane using her own Bible knowledge to interpret the vision for herself: Revelation 19:3 concerns the final destruction of the Whore of Babylon. No doubt this is just a sample of Jane's vivid dream-life. A couple of days later, Ralph nips out to buy Wharton's Almanac, to corroborate the messages God is beaming into the Josselin family psyche. Household excitement rises until everyone is dreaming, even little Tom, who saw Jesus Christ get up into Daddy's pulpit to give him a big hug.

By 25 January 1655 Ralph has persuaded himself that he foresaw Cromwell's dissolution of Parliament. Pyrotechnic phantasms continue to singe the heads of the fervid dreamers as January turns into February: angels are sighted, smoke and fire in the north. Cavalier and Fifth Monarchy risings are daily expected (13 February), to precipitate the final bonfire. Avidly, the diarist scrutinises the news-sheets. Meanwhile, the activities of local Quakers bring Ralph out in goosepimples.

Jane thinks she has a prolapsed womb but it turns out to be 'only' piles.

A strange and portentous snake, as thick as a man's calf, is seen in Taine, at Taller's barn.

Armies are seen in the sky fighting cosmic battles on Tuesday night, 17 August, 'the watch saw it and heard the noise of their muskets'. Ralph resolves to look into it and ascertain the facts. Come to think of it, he saw a very strange orange colour in the sky on (he thinks it may have been) Tuesday.

20 August: between 3 and 4 a.m., a remarkable cross is seen by zealous sky-watchers.

Quakers catcall him: 'Woe to the false prophet.' At White Colne, a man called Brett lambasts Ralph's cuffs as a sign of ungodly pride.

In October fireballs tear through his sleep, and a cryptic black cloud in the shape of a stag bearing a rider. Triplets are born in the parish (January 1657).

The triplets all die.

1657 has come and gone but brought no millennium.

The crestfallen household's dreams peter out. At the Protector's death in 1658, Josselin notes offhandedly: 'Cromwell died. People not much minding it' (1 September), and a frightening 'boil or pile in my fundament' earns far more space: 'on the Lord I roll myself to show me mercy therein, it is black but nothing issueth'. Diary intimacy shows us Ralph squinting to view his anus in the mirror, or soliciting his wife to examine it. As 1658 drags into the chaos of 1659, millennarian ardour wanes to nothing. One day, to Ralph's alarm, a 'Quaker wench came boisterously into the church up almost to the desk' (21 August 1659) but, making no disturbance, leaves quietly. By the Restoration, Josselin is forced to the disillusioned concession that history is a mess which must be a punishment for national sin.

*

In 1664 Jane's last live baby was born, a daughter Rebekah. Jane's life was dominated by morning sickness, birth-terrors, breast-feeding, childcare. To us it is a silent life, voiced only by her husband. Although she seldom appears quite well, Jane must have been tough and resilient: in an age of high maternal mortality, she and a good percentage of her children survived childbirth. Jane was fortunate in giving birth traditionally, surrounded by close female friends, and aided by a trusted female midwife. Only in one labour, a stop-start affair in which the midwife was called, sent away and recalled, was Jane critical of the midwife because the labour was so sharp. This was the birth of the second Mary in January 1658:

> I called up the midwife, and nurse, got fires and all ready, and then her labour came on so strongly that the child was born only two or three women more got in to her ... the child was dead when born, I bless God who recovered it to life. (p415)

We are given a strong sense of the female support group who surrounded one another's deliveries, succouring the mother and receiving her child into an embrace of the whole community.

Ralph's diary is modestly silent about the sexual side of the Josselin union. In the marriages of serious Puritan souls such as the Josselins, sexuality was a taboo topic even in the privacy of a diary, though Ralph often murmurs of cryptically wayward thoughts, presumably libidinal. Daniel Rogers in *Matrimonial Honour* had urged each partner's duty of making love whenever the other so desired but added (confusingly perhaps) that married couples must observe a sober minimum of couplings, so as to avoid degenerating into brutish appetite. Unwilling to offer a rule such as Plato's of once a week or three times a month, Rogers left it with the partners to keep within bounds (pp176–7).

Yet for all this inhibition, Jane's sexual experience is more likely than not to have been fulfilling. The female orgasm was acknowledged, and believed to have a function in conception. Benign consequences flowed from abysmal science, for, though women were anatomised as defective males, with outside-in genitalia, popular textbooks like Nicholas Culpeper's *Practice of Physic* saw female sexual satisfaction as vital to health and wellbeing.[6] Disparaging the new forceps-toting 'men-midwives' elbowing women out of the midwifery profession, Culpeper – and later Jane Sharp and Elizabeth Cellier – attacked male doctors' profiteering intrusion into obstetrics.[7] He diagnosed a major disease of women as 'Womb-Fury', which we would call sexual frustration: 'the patient ... madly seeks after carnal copulation', which he treats as a medical rather than a moral complaint. If all remedies fail (including leeches, mercury pessaries, lotion of water-lily and nightshade 'between the water-gate and the dung-gate', and other horrors), 'some advise that the genital parts be by a cunning midwife so handled and rubbed, as to cause an evacuation of the over-abounding sperm' (ie the supposed female 'sperm').[8] The author of *Aristotles Master-piece* (1684) reassured men that 'there is no vast difference between the members of the two sexes', 'for the use and action of the clitoris in woman is like that of the penis or yard in men, that is, erection'.[9] Hence, retrogressive humoral medicine came up with a progressive attitude: sexual pleasure benefits women.

Nor was Puritan eroticism necessarily 'puritanical'. This is a myth. Milton was not the only Puritan to see passion and pleasure, rightly tempered, as vital to virtue.[10] The greatest Puritan epic of the age, his *Paradise Lost* (1667), was a love poem, in which the frank and tender exchange of erotic love is experienced as the highest earthly joy; the nudity of Paradise as the shame-free vesture of integrity, without need of 'those troublesome disguises which we wear':

> Then was not guilty shame, dishonest shame,
> Sin-bred, how have ye troubled all mankind
> With shows instead, mere shows of seeming pure ...
> So passed they naked on. (IV 313–17, 319)

But Milton's Eve, receiving Adam's advances with 'sweet reluctant amorous delay', allures by a sexy teasing familiar in the fallen world; and the great misogynist structures his drama of Puritan marriage on tensions and contradictions. But if the inequality of the partners in *Paradise Lost* mirrors an unbalanced ideal ('He for God only, she for God in him', IV 299), the poem is also a tragic lovesong, which lays bare the nerve of male need and dependency:[11]

> with thee
> Certain my resolution is to die;
> How can I live without thee, how forgo
> Thy sweet converse and love so dearly joined,
> To live again in these wild woods forlorn?
> Should God create another Eve, and I
> Another rib afford, yet loss of thee
> Would never from my heart. (IX 906-13)

Adam's sin is to cleave to Eve and nature against the patriarchal God and his own hierarchical superiority: into this majestic poem are built the punitive cross-stresses of Puritan marriage.

Milton, like Josselin, valued male chastity as much as female, in a culture of double standards.[12] Most of Josselin's neighbours (as far as he could see) lived chaste enough lives, though scandals were always popular. Josselin records Edward Stevens' arrest on a charge of buggering a mare in a stable at Cogshall (20 July 1662), and one morning discovers an abandoned child in his barn (3 April 1676).

Under the stresses of the Interregnum and their child-bearing years, Ralph's picture is of a fruitful marriage whose trivial rifts were soon healed. The partners did not relish even a few days' separation. But in the early 1670s he begins to complain of Jane's shortcomings: rancour, neglect, shrewishness. Their grown-up children are causing endless trouble. Suffering a chronic injury to his thigh, Ralph remarks pointedly that Lady Honywood rather than his wife 'was my nurse and physician' (27 November 1672). He lectures the diary on his own exemplary patience, bearing 'my infirmities about me, but my wife taxes me for great impatience'. He laments her 'provoking carelessness' and 'impatience too much, that bears nothing but expects I must bear all'.

Four years later there is a crisis in which his wife abdicates her wifely duties altogether, withdrawing not only sympathy but labour: 'at night my wife on some discontent which I know not would not assist me in dressing my poor leg, Mary did' (16 November 1676). Fretful at his growing inability to impose his will on his relations, peeved and querulous, he brandishes the angrily inflamed leg as a martyr's weapon. He moans, 'in the morning my wife had a strange fit, poor heart her passions master her' (1677), 'my wife afflicts me' (1681), 'a forward wife', 'my life very unquiet, especially from my wife' (1682), 'A bitter morning from my wife' (1683). As an economic and child-rearing unit, the Josselin work is done; frugality, toil and shrewd accounting have brought prosperity, and perhaps there seemed to the middle-aged Jane little left worth striving for.

*

The diaries of Nehemiah Wallington reveal, rather more than Josselin's, the extent to which ordinary Puritan women identified themselves with political and religious issues of the day. The Wallingtons, of a lower social caste than the Josselins, were an urban family living at the centre of the Revolution.

No wife, stated clergyman William Gouge in his treatise, *Of Domestical Duties* (1622) should give way to the temptation to call her husband by nicknames such as 'sweet, sweeting, sweetheart, love, joy, dear', let alone 'duck, chick, pigsnie'.[13] Grace Wallington, wife of Nehemiah, a London Puritan artisan and compulsive scribbler, would never have dreamed of addressing her yokefellow as 'pigsnie'. Grace reminds us of the rigour and stoicism of God-fearing women of this period. Nehemiah, a Calvinist turner prone to nervous breakdown, had, like most serious Puritan husbands, read Gouge and commenced his marriage with a New Year's resolution to exercise his prerogative as 'head and governor' of his wife'.[14] In practice, Grace supported Nehemiah through a decade of child-bearing, at the end of which only one girl survived. London, overcrowded and sewage-polluted, was a rats' paradise and a deathtrap for babies. In the plague year 1625, Nehemiah recorded that 'threescore children died out of one alley'. Each of his babies was a source of anguish to Nehemiah, who never learned to temper his love to the transience of children. His account of the last day of health of his firstborn, Elizabeth, is so intimate that we can almost hear and see her prattling in the kitchen, strutting around pretending to be father, and snuggling down in bed between her parents. She is just short of three:

> And about eight o'clock at night [my] wife was in the kitchen washing of dishes, my daughter being merry went unto her mother and said unto her, 'what do you here, my wife?' And at night when we were abed, says she to me, 'father, I go abroad tomorrow and buy you a plum pie.' These were the last words that I did hear my sweet child speak, for the pangs of death seized upon her on the Sabbath morning. (p87)

Clearly this little girl lived in an unauthoritarian household which delighted in her games of let's-pretend, however anarchic; where father- and mother-love was blissfully tactile in the warm shared bed necessitated by shortage of space; where she could drop asleep blessing her father not with pious prayer but with generous offers of plum pie. Nehemiah simply broke down under the shock of Elizabeth's loss. Grace gravely looked on. Then she said:

> Husband, I am persuaded you offend God in grieving for this child so much. Do but consider what a deal of grief and care we are rid of, and what a deal of trouble and sorrow she is gone out of, and what abundance of joy she is gone into. And do but consider, it is your daughter's wedding day and will you grieve to see your daughter go home to her husband Christ Jesus, where she shall never want, but have the fulness of joy forevermore?

Nehemiah gazed at Grace, numb and nonplussed: 'Do you not grieve for this child?' he stammered.

'No, truly, husband, if you will believe me, I do as freely give it again unto God, as I did receive it of him' (pp87–8).

Orthodox doctrine decreed that God gave parents merely temporary custody, putting *His* children 'out to nurse', as Grace reminded Nehemiah during his grief for the loss of his son, John, six months later ('Mame, John fall down, op-a-day ...' wailed the two-year-old through his dying night, p89). But doctrine is one thing; lived reality another. Nehemiah stared bemused at Grace's magisterial otherworldliness. He quailed before that impersonal rigour, an apotheosis of credal passion, which was her survival mechanism. Perhaps Nehemiah made this detachment easier by his own pitiful weakness, carrying a joint grief.

In Grace Wallington we see not absence of response but a kinesis of energy from affliction to impassioned discipline. Her speeches have the ceremonious and exalted character of the textbook Puritan wife ('Husband, I am persuaded'), whose power to rise to her role paradoxically enables her to transcend woman's role as 'weaker vessel'. The only time Nehemiah records her breaking down was when Parliament lost Bristol in 1643.

*

From the marriage of John and Lucy Hutchinson issued another great personal testament of the seventeenth century; Lucy's powerful vindication of her Puritan and Parliamentary husband, *Memoirs of the Life of Colonel Hutchinson* (1671). Lucy Hutchinson, born in the Tower of London in 1620, was of an age with Josselin, and married at around the same time, in 1638. A republican of increasingly radical Independent sympathies, John Hutchinson was governor of Nottingham Castle during the Civil War, and a signatory to the death warrant of Charles I. Disillusion with Cromwell's autocratic rule caused him to retire from active life in the 1650s. He narrowly escaped execution as a regicide after the Restoration, in part because of Lucy's resourceful intercession, but was arrested in 1663 on suspicion of implication in the Northern Plot against Charles II, to die in prison the following year.

While Josselin lived at the provincial margins of the revolutionary world, minor gentry revering noble patrons, Hutchinson belonged to an elite nearer the axis of political events. A portrait survives of Hutchinson with his eldest son: the father is donning armour, with the son acting as armourer, holding his warrior-father's helmet. Two pairs of mirroring steel-grey eyes stare out over anxiously unsmiling mouths; two thin, fastidious faces, tendering elegant fingers. The portrait presents a dynastic ideal of sternly virile Puritan virtue which Lucy Hutchinson's account of her husband also seeks to transmit, offering no sop to fashion in the form of tasselled collar strings, silk sash or gilded laces, such as add decorative interest to other martial portraits.[15] But it also corroborates her comments on her husband's luxuriant hair, in gentlemanly contempt of the 'roundheaded' school of hairdressing affected by Puritan zealots, 'close round their heads, with so many little peaks as was something ridiculous to behold'.[16] John Hutchinson boasts 'a very fine thickset head of hair, kept it clean and handsome without any affectation, so that it was a great ornament to him', despite the scoffs of the 'godly' who deplored unsanctified hairdos. He also wears a fashionable pencil-thin moustache. Milton was later to quote a statutory length when measuring Adam's manly locks: 'not beneath his shoulders broad'.[17]

The cavalier hairstyle for men involved soft waves and ringlets to the breast, caught into love-locks with bows of ribbon and some-times padded out by false pieces and later replaced by a periwig.[18] That males should have turned hairstyles into matter of violent dispute is not a trivial point: minute distinctions of external dress and style had specific hierarchical, religious and gender codes – meanings which were under stress and constantly challenged. Samson shorn by Delilah[19] was a motif obsessional to an age that worried about male vulnerability and female usurpation. In one's hair was virtue and vigour. Milton sneered equally at the tonsured pates of Rome and at the curled wigs of the court, perhaps all the more sharply because he himself had experienced a conflict of masculinity. As sharp-eyed Aubrey noted in his *Brief Lives*, 'He was scarce so tall as I am. he had light brown hair, his complexion very/exceeding fair. oval face. his eye a dark grey ... when a Cambridge scholar [he was so fair that they called him the Lady of Christs Coll:]'[20] This description bears some affinity to Walker's portrait of Hutchinson: under the sombre armour, the mien suggests artistic delicacy, refinement, and well-groomed curls fine as baby-hair, which softly cascade well below the Puritan shoulder-length rule.

Lucy's Colonel Hutchinson is an heroic compound of Reformation Man, soldier of God, soul of honour; 'Roman' republican, all civic virtue and ancient descent; Renaissance Man, distinguished by magnanimity, studiousness and love of music and the arts. He played the viol and enjoyed designing gardens, with groves, fruit trees, 'opening springs and making fish-ponds' (p19).[21] The eyes of this paragon, said Lucy, were lustrous, magnetically delighting all around him. The formal warrior-portrait shows eyes bleak as lead-shot. But the eyes Lucy saw closing in the squalid disgrace of a Restoration prison, for all the Christian dignity of his ending, branded her with a sense of outrageous injustice. Her writing of his life was a mode of resurrection. Paradoxically, we read the *Memoirs* as the testament of Lucy just as much as for her account of John.

Proud, confident, incisive, Lucy's pen expresses her mastery of the subject matter not of a personal life (the memoir is not intimate) but of the grand sweep of history. There is nothing conventionally 'feminine' in Lucy's style, which is a mode of masculine and educated rhetoric, charged with a peculiarly Puritan aloofness and despatch. Aggressively confrontational, Lucy's narrative of her husband's holding of Nottingham Castle against Royalist siege, as its governor, thrills its reader by combined attack and authenticity.[22] She displays effortless understanding of military strategy as well as taking her reader into the heart of the besieged castle and town, rife with internal squabbles, strife between town and castle, godly principle and petty ambition. Gripping action is mediated through a mind whose superbly Miltonic disdain expresses itself through high-minded scorn of low persons, showing not only religious contempt for past enemies (Plumtre, the 'horrible atheist' with his 'intolerable pride, that he brooked no superiors', p96) but high gentry contempt for the yuppies of the age:

> Chadwick ... at first a boy that scraped trenchers in the house of one of the poorest justices in the country ... it is almost incredible that one of his mean education and poverty should arrive to such things as he reached ... a libidinous goat ... glavering and false. (p97)

Whilst Lucy's favourite vocabulary is a lexicon of contumely, wreaking vengeance on Hutchinson's enemies, there is also a suaveness of address, a cultivated intellectualism assuming command of the subject, which declares her authority as a judge of political history. Standing hypothetically distanced from the story, in which she appears in the third person, as the 'Governor's', or 'Colonel's wife', Lucy places the narrative within an analysis of English history from the Reformation to the Civil Wars: this is the only way in which 'he, whose actions I am tracing' can be assessed (p75). 'He' and 'I' are powerful actors, he in history, she as historian. The Hutchinsons' Nottingham and the Josselins' Colne might be built on different planets. Nothing so personal as a boil on the anus, a tiff or folly, will be allowed to show here. The realm of public obituary is rarefied and formal.

Yet the hauteur of this Puritan expositor of history is only matched by her claim to monumental diffidence; a self-abnegation so baroque as to aspire to an artform. Jane Josselin, we know, talked back. Lucy adored. Yet today Jane the bourgeois wife is silent in her shroud, entombed with the husband whose bad leg she ultimately declined to dress; and Lucy is a defiant voice on the page, a verbal crack-shot in an age which equated mastery of the word with the eloquent sword. Lucy represents in the course of her book the whole mystery of Puritan marriage as a site of upheaval and contradiction. Balancing upon the stilts of this duality,[23] Lucy walked tall by belittling herself and created from the abyss of widowhood a high place from which to survey history.

Recalling her husband's tender love, the author is pitched into awareness of present loss. That loss is of self. Her self has died. All that was valuable in her character was the reflex of John. They were indeed one person, one flesh, one spirit: a compound of God-in-John and John-in-Lucy. These are conventional sentiments, but when we look at the way Lucy Hutchinson articulates them, their passionate expression lifts them off the page into poetry:

> And thus indeed he soon made her more equal to him than he found her, for she was a very faithful mirror, reflecting truly, though but dimly, his own glories upon him, so long as he was present; but she, that was nothing before his inspection gave her a fair figure, when he was removed, was only filled with a dark mist, and never could again take in any delightful object, nor return any shining representation. The greatest excellency she had was the power of apprehending and the virtue of loving his. So, as his

shadow, she waited on him everywhere, till he was taken
into that region of light which admits of none, and then she
vanished into nothing. (pp51–2)

The technical term for a widow (not a widower) was a 'relict', 'the
left behind', articulating the continuity of the dynastic union at the
point where it has parted company with itself. Lucy dwells not on
her emptiness but her experience of anomie, non-being, in the
wake of the life that gave hers meaning. But how can we help but
notice that this is a sheer lie? The hand holding this pen does not
belong to a person who has 'vanished into nothing'. Few have ever
spoken more elegantly of being nothing, more brilliantly of being
darkened, or more powerfully of impotence, save perhaps the poet
John Donne in his elegy, 'A Nocturnall upon S. Lucies day': love
'ruined me, and I am re-begot/Of absence, darkness, death, things
which are not.'[24] Nor has the author of this book lost her mirroring
power (the governing symbolism of the passage) in ability to
'return any shining representation'. The book itself is a shining
representation. The vanishing 'shadow' reconstitutes itself in every
word.

Such powerful writings defy or subvert the patriarchal norms
they claim to confirm. Lucy's testament reminds us of the
compound nature of women's status in the seventeenth century. 'I
remain,' she claims, 'an airy phantasm walking about his sepulchre'
(p337). Yet the impression we take from the book is of drive and
purpose: an intelligent mind unswervingly engaged with political
and religious issues, a radical writing against the Restoration where
her beliefs and cause are anathema. The *Memoirs* constitute an act
of resistance.

*

A manuscript fragment of autobiography has survived alongside
the memoir, in which we see how anomalous was the child Lucy,
at once bound into the feminine norms and driving beyond them
from her earliest days. Her father, Sir Allen Apsley, was Lieutenant
of the Tower of London in the time of James I, in a period, as Lucy
acutely remarks, of so-called peace, 'if that quietness may be called
a peace which was rather like the calm and smooth surface of the
sea whose dark womb is already impregnated with a horrid

tempest'.[25] Apsley's prisoners were illustrious, including Sir Walter Raleigh and Patrick Ruthven, with whom her mother learned chemistry, supplying materials, in order to 'gain the knowledge of their experiments and the medicines to help such poor people as were not able to seek physicians', acquiring 'a great deal of skill, which was very profitable to many all her life' (p13). During the Civil War Lucy would herself act as surgeon, dressing wounds at Nottingham Castle.

Lucy was the eldest and longed-for daughter of the family, from before her birth a special child. 'My mother, while she was with child of me, dreamed that she was walking in the garden with my father and that a star came down into her hand' (p14). This dream was to have far-reaching consequences. We might say that it generated the *Memoirs*, for:

> my father told her, her dream signified she should have a
> daughter of some extraordinary eminency, which thing, like
> such vain prophecies, wrought as far as it could its own
> accomplishment: for my father and mother fancying me
> then beautiful, and more than ordinarily apprehensive
> [intelligent], applied all their cares, and spared no cost to
> improve me in my education, which procured me the
> admiration of those that flattered my parents. By the time I
> was four years old I read English perfectly, and having a
> great memory, I was carried to sermons; and while I was
> very young could remember and repeat them exactly, and
> being caressed, the love of praise tickled me and made me
> attend more heedfully. (p14)

The technique of reader-manipulation evolved here (to quote and then deflate people's grand opinions of her) is Lucy's standard mode of communicating high self-esteem, whilst skirting the charge of unfeminine pride.

But the total picture is of a girl-prodigy, with strength to flout much of her conditioning. Eight specialist tutors plied her with language, music, dancing, writing and needlework, in none of which Lucy pretended the slightest interest; for 'my genius was quite averse from all but my book'. Such passionate bookishness worried Lucy's mother, who tried to restrain it. But when books became forbidden fruit, they carried the sauce of trespass, and 'this rather animated me than kept me back'. Determination and defiance were to characterise Lucy in adult life, speaking out of turn and treading the path of political resistance without reluctance. Sneaking off from 'healthy' play, the child would filch other people's books when her own were locked up. During her free hour after dinner and supper, she 'would steal into some hole or other to read'. With glee, the older Lucy boasts that her father 'would have me learn Latin' (an exclusively male prerogative), and 'I was so apt that I outstripped my brothers who were at school' (pp14–15). Now the piqued brothers, beaten by a mere female, launched themselves after the racing girl, which tickled their father but disturbed her mother, to whom the little meteorite was beginning to seem a questionable blessing. As the older Lucy transcribes her memories, she picks up the authentic tones of the strong-willed child:

> As for music and dancing, I profited very little in them, and would never practise my lute or harpsichords but when my masters were with me, and for my needle I absolutely hated it. (p15)

This cry of loathing expressed mutinous gender heresy. Needlework was essential to femininity; a woman's indoor world being identified with the distaff. Lucy, benefiting by an anachronistically late version of the classical education given to a handful of high-ranking Tudor women like Margaret Roper and Queen Elizabeth, emerges as a child of indestructible will-power who absolutely will not be gainsaid. The accomplishments her mother wished her to learn were the gentlewoman's mode of attaching a high-ranking husband. Unsocialised, Lucy was also unsociable with her fellow girls. 'Play among other children I despised ...'. Already Lucy was a consummate despiser. She appalled her peers by tearing their dolls limb from limb and arrogantly confabulating with the adults on matters beyond juvenile comprehension.

But Lucy's mother was wrong: it *was* possible to attract an eligible young man through assiduous Latinity, as the *Memoirs* in a *jeu d'esprit* of heady recollection recount.

*

Visiting Richmond one summer in the late 1630s, the youthful John Hutchinson enters into the sophisticated musical ambience around the court. Opulent-fleshed, husband-hunting young women billow around him; galaxies of feminine pulchritude, wit, wealth and vanity. John sees through them all, impervious to their 'fine snares'. Banteringly he advises them to back off, unconsciously awaiting the call of soul to soul. One day, he makes the acquaintance of Lucy's vivacious younger sister, Barbara. Accompanying the chattery girl back to her mother's house, he is admitted to the absent Lucy's room. Skimming the titles on a bookshelf, he comes upon a handful of Latin books. Whose are these? My sister's. John is intrigued; hankers after information about this prodigy, sorry to have missed her. Lucy begins to haunt him to the point that he can't hear her name enough. Reclusive and contemplative, she keeps her own company, he is told. The more John contemplates the hidden Lucy's intellectuality, the more 'inflamed' he becomes with 'desire of seeing her' (pp46–8).

At a party, a song is followed by the recitation of a rather striking sonnet composed as an 'answer to it', believed to have been composed by 'a woman in the neighbourhood … it was presently enquired, who?' (p47). John, sharing the conventional comtempt for women's intelligence, 'fancying something of rationality in the sonnet beyond the reach of a she-wit', cannot credit that a woman could have composed such a work. The gentleman, also an admirer of the superwomanly sonneteer, effuses about her good sense, perfections and deep reserve. She does not like to be on display in male company. This is a further magnet to John, in whom 'a strange sympathy in nature' already tingles. But now yet another gentleman joins in the chorus of praise of this wonder.

I must see her, John pants.

You cannot, the infatuates chorus: 'she will not be acquainted with any of mankind' and besides, she is so modest that she hates her perfections to be known.

'"Well," said Mr Hutchinson, "but I will be acquainted with her"'(p48).

The older Lucy relives on the page the joy of their courtship, through the eyes of John's desire. The prose is politic and artful: young Lucy is a shining paragon bathed in the light of universal admiration – but the older Lucy gracefully qualifies her self-advertisements by disclaimers. Uniquely, feminine vanities are froth to the young Lucy, whom the older Lucy re-creates as a charming melancholic: 'She was not ugly; in a careless riding-habit, she had a melancholy negligence both of herself and others, as if she neither affected to please others, nor took notice of anything before her' (p49). The distrait, forbidding young woman, under intense parental pressure to marry, had retired into bookishness to avoid the marriage market; easy prey for detractors, who disparage Lucy to John by pointing out her casual dressing and lack of all 'womanish ornaments' (p51).

Nothing deterred by her possible disfigurement by smallpox, John marries Lucy upon her recovery. Having covertly praised herself to the skies, the older Lucy adjusts the lens by explaining that she merely gravitated to her immeasurable superior: 'The greatest excellency she had was the power of apprehending and the virtue of loving his' (p51). Lucy gives a tactical twist to the patriarchal ideal of Puritan marriage: 'He for God only, she for God in him', by raising herself to an empyrean above the whole race of women, whom her story disparages, the noble partner to an eagle. Lucy presents herself as the model of a republican wife, invincibly co-rebellious.

Women should never rule, states Lucy with a masculine air of authority. She lambasts Charles I's uxorious prostration to his wife as effeminate and fatal to the kingdom, 'which never is in any place happy where the hands that are made only for distaffs affect the management of sceptres' (p70). Superciliously she calls Queen Elizabeth I the mere puppet of her male counsellors. Her own appearances in the story are, however, strong-minded and pugilistic. The pieties about female subordination were in reality irrelevant to a world of civil war, which inevitably involved civilians both as victims and actors. When cavaliers fired Nottingham, 'women were forced to walk by fifty in a night to prevent the burning' (p130). During a siege, a providential cannon bullet 'took off the head of an old woman' collaborating with the enemy, while in another house, a lonely little girl rocking a baby in a cradle was 'struck dead and killed with the wind of the bullet', the baby surviving unscathed (p125). Women acted as spies and couriers on both sides and were sometimes coerced into this role: during Sir Charles Lucas' attack on Nottingham, the mayor's wife was forced to act as messenger between town and castle, 'but just as she went out of the house from them, she heard an outcry among them that "the Roundheads were sallying forth," whereupon she flung down the letter and ran away', and so did the entire thousand cavaliers (p146).

A girl who lost a hand at the defence of Lyme was supposed to have said, ' "Truly I am glad with all my heart that I had a hand to lose for Jesus Christ, for whose cause I am as willing and ready to lose not only my other hand but my life also" '.[26] The speech was heroic; the reality for tens of thousands of women must have been bruisingly otherwise. The worst dream was coming true: fratricidal slaughter and pillage on a mass scale over a period of years; bloodshed and despair of bread. Lucy saw little to glamorise in the butchers' work of a martial age.

*

Though representing herself as her husband's duteous shadow, Lucy was often a prime mover. A less obedient and more high-handed shadow would be hard to find. She got her brother-in-law arrested by pretending he was her husband, when an enemy goaded her with her husband's absence (p90), a prank which dangerously misfired. The pregnant Lucy was instrumental in bringing John Hutchinson out against infant baptism, 'whereupon that infant was not baptised', a radical shift to the left which confirmed their reputation as 'fanatic and Anabaptists' (p211). It was Lucy who detected a minister as a Scottish traitor in their midst, and alerted her husband to the coded meanings of his sermons, telling John 'that she could not bear with nor join in his prayers' (p222). In the chaotic final months of the Commonwealth Lucy dismantled a plot against her husband entirely on her own initiative and behind her husband's back, conducted negotiations with the perfidious Fleetwood over army disorder (p271); and, acting as effectual governor of Nottingham in John's absence, pacified the warring factions (p276).

In the wake of the Restoration, she took her husband's destiny determinedly into her own hands, 'resolved to disobey him' in saving him from the execution suffered by those who had signed

Charles I's death warrant. She wrote to the Speaker, forging her husband's signature. Lucy's astute calculations helped shield John from the fate of hanging, drawing and quartering that met most of his fellow regicides (see pp285–6).

Through emphasising her interference, Lucy can represent John Hutchinson as a man wishing to die for the Good Old Cause but prevented from embracing this fate beside his fellows by an officious wife and family: Providence did it, she claims (p286) – but in this case, Providence looks remarkably like a woman armed with a pen.

*

11 October 1663: John Hutchinson is arrested at Owthorpe and his house ransacked; he is incarcerated in the Tower, on suspicion of implication in the Northern Plot. Lucy and their eldest daughter Barbara accompany him, and all the way he cheers and encourages them. Discourtesy; foul food; diarrhoea and the privy locked at night; spies (or 'trepanners' as they are vividly known, from their endeavour to slice off the top of your head and scoop out the contents) clustering with their bought smiles. Lucy, born in the Tower in the heyday of her family's power, is now forbidden to take lodgings there. She is also forbidden by her husband to intercede for him and this time abstains from defying him.

Sudden removal to Sandown Castle in Kent: a derelict ruin, lashed by winds and rain, manned by a mangy company of 'pitiful weak fellows, half starved and eaten up with vermin' (p319), mostly drunk. There are no beds. Why have we no beds? Where can we procure beds? It turns out that an innkeeper will hire them at a grossly inflated rate. John is lodged in a through-room with five doors, one opening on a platform which leads, in a revelatory manner, nowhere. It hangs above the sea which rushes round the foot of the castle with each incoming tide, and dampens the air in the prison so that the Colonel's hatcase and trunks, and all his leather-goods, are perpetually skinned with mould. However often you wipe off the mould, it slimes back again. The walls are twelve feet thick, built to withstand armies: but pregnable to rain, which seeps in through cracks. The Colonel examines the walls and discovers that they sweat saltpetre so that 'one might sweep off a peck of saltpetre' every day (p320).

The Colonel is a gentleman and, notwithstanding the rudeness of his habitation, displays a gentleman's insouciance at his surroundings. His delicate stomach nauseated by the vile food and galled by a companion of base extraction and tastes, John fortifies himself with Bible reading (he will have no other book). He rides above the world by making wings of sacred words. His Bible is his reality, his transcendence. And, too, there is the inner relaxation from guilt. Throughout, his aching conscience has rued his immunity from penalties; now there is a simplification. He can feel that in suffering for his cause, he has not ignobly slid into craven hiding while others have mounted the gibbet into the glory of disgrace. This inner freedom exalts and enfranchises him, and he flies free of the burdened, conflicted toil in which his wife labours. Be cheerful, he tells his tear-stained family: I have never been more contented in my life.

Lucy, with his daughter, toils daily on foot to and fro from lodgings in Deal. As they cross the beach, they notice the gleam of seashells at high-tide mark. Would he like some of those, do you think? They glean a treasure trove of cockle-shells, which they pour into his hands.

The Colonel sorts the shells into beautiful patterns, which delight his deprived eye. Lucy and Barbara bring more. He lays them out 'with as much delight as he used to take in the richest agates and onyxes he could compass with the most artificial engravings' (p321). John experiences, at altitude, the most refined gratifications art has to offer. People coming in marvel at the cockle-shell paradise.

It is a paradise his wife cannot share. Lucy breaks down. She knows the constitutional frailty of his health. ' "You will die in prison," ' she sobs to him (p321). She is terrified of his being deported to Tangier. ' "God is the same God at Tangier as at Owthorpe," ' he assures her. To Lucy this seems cold comfort. 'Hutchinson,' his keeper calls him, omitting the 'Mr'. Lucy's blood boils at this disrespect but, with suave bearing, John laughs it off.

The Colonel is accorded the special privilege of being allowed to walk out beside the sea with a keeper. But, while Lucy is away fetching their other children from Owthorpe, her husband takes ill and dies, in September 1664.

His message to his wife is as follows: '"Let her ... as she is above other women, show herself, in this occasion, a good Christian, and above the pitch of ordinary women"' (p330).

The Hutchinson aspiration to *superiority* places them in a God-sanctioned elite in a godforsaken world. Nobility, rectitude, faith, principle, rationality are the marks of this elite. It is the paradox of Puritan marriage that these qualities, which were all coded 'masculine', must be mutual and familial. Not exemplary but exceptional, Lucy Hutchinson looks out of her pages with a complex expression of heroic disdain, grief, steely idealism and proud self-abnegation. Her testament ends in a refusal to believe that her husband could have died or that she could have survived. It determines in a cloven word: 'happy are you whom God gives time and ope ...'

10

GEORGE FOX, MARGARET FELL &
A COMMONWEALTH OF DAUGHTERS

June 1652: Judge Thomas Fell was away from his home at Swarthmoor, Ulverston, pursuing his duties as Judge of Assize for the North Wales circuit. His wife Margaret, soul of upright rectitude, was also out when the strange figure turned up on the doorstep. Household retainers and the seven Fell youngsters eyed George Fox as he was ushered in to wait with the local Puritan pastor, William Lampitt. They were soon overheard in heated argument.

Fox was dressed for hill-walking and stream-fording, for foul weather and sleeping under hedges, in the leather doublet and breeches of an intinerant labourer. His rig-out was topped by a white cap, which he kept on when civility required its removal in customary 'hat-honour' to a superior – a clergyman, for instance.

Lampitt glared reproof at Fox's rude hat. Hats would form a running theme in Quaker history: a millinery drama of epic proportions. But the white hat held a special message for a household which had heard Margaret's prophetic dream of a visitant 'in a white hat that should come and confound the priests'.[1] The candid hat topped the crowning glory of Fox's hair, worn uncut in emulation of Samson and the Nazarites, set apart by God. It straggled down his back 'like rat's tails'. His linen, though vindicated by one Judge conducting a bodysearch ('He is not a vagrant by his linen'),[2] was consonant with George's plain-speaking attire, which included collar bands pure of ornamental tassels, and buttons of base metal.

It was thus that an apostle appeared on Judge Fell's doorstep, in the person of a weaver's burly son.

Fox was a subversive, whose mission was to turn the world upside down, inside out. With the scathing wit and repartee of a mirthless comedian, he was citizen of another world where they did and said all things differently. Though still only twenty-seven, he had been gleaning souls for at least five years: within a decade a community of 30,000 to 40,000 people would be gathered as 'Friends'. George's extraordinary eyes were immediately noticed, making people jittery or exalted. His charisma, magnetising many, appalled more. These eyes would make Oliver Cromwell gentle and listening; would cause mobs to lynch Fox or accuse him of witchcraft. 'Don't pierce me so with thy eyes, keep thy eyes off me,' a Baptist was to panic at Carlyle.[3] His voice was capable of almighty decibels, annihilating a fiddler set to drown his singing in gaol 'and made the fiddler sigh and give over his fiddling; and so he passed away with shame'.[4]

'Full of filth', George found Margaret Fell's Independent pastor, Lampitt, whom he lambasted. But then so (to George) were all clergy who lived off the trade of selling God's word. Before Margaret ever reached home, George had begun to slash at her bond with her minister; to cut her loose into a boundless freedom. Several hours passed in dispute, in which George threshed and sifted the priest, vaunting the mother-wit of a natural dialectician, at once mockingly aggressive and subtle as Socrates. The leather breeches and the rat's tails sent the black coat and the shorn head home, trounced and nettled.

*

Margaret arrived back at Swarthmoor in the last hour of her old life. At thirty-eight, she was the high-ranking, haughty and sternly Puritan daughter of a Westmorland family, the Askews, claiming kin with the dynasty of Anne Askew, sixteenth-century Protestant martyr. A managing woman of acute business acumen, Margaret was by no means George's easiest convert. Too many ties of social and religious affiliation bound her to the Puritan establishment. Her guest deigned no outward sign of courtesy, neither bowing, kissing her hand, nor offering any of the verbal tokens of deference civility demanded. Addressing her with the egalitarian 'thou' rather than the respectful and required 'you', the homespun visitor kept his hat clamped on his head. She was given to understand that the stranger had deliberately outraged her minister: 'it struck something at her', recalls George in his *Journal*, 'because she was in a profession with him, though he hid his dirty actions from them' (p114). Many hosts would have had their retainers boot Fox straight out of the house.

Shocked, Margaret was also magnetised. Fox told the household of the Inner Light, available to all; man, woman and child. He vividly explained that Christ had already come into every believer's heart; they might know Truth not by asking priests, smeared with lucre, the claptrap of university-learning, nor even by Bible reading, but by quiet attention to the Light within the self. The young man's words spellbound and agitated Margaret, that law-upholding wife and mother, with authority in the district, conscious of rank, rich of dress, her dark silks stormily rustling.

George stayed overnight. He and Lampitt sparred in front of Mrs Fell. Lampitt may have intimated the Judge's probable reaction to her harbouring of a footloose trouble-maker, when he returned from his labours in Wales. Perhaps he was sentencing similar vagabonds even now: Wales was said to have a total of eight hundred travelling ministers carrying subversive doctrines over hill and vale – though how Walter Cradock managed a headcount must remain for ever a mystery.[5] As George kneaded Margaret, she showed signs of yielding but held back, for, as

George pithily put it in his *Journal*, 'she was not wholly come off' (p114).

On Thursday, 1 July, George refused Margaret's invitation to attend Lampitt's 'lecture day' at Ulverston parish church, in favour of wandering the fields, until a directive from God headed him to the 'steeple-house', where the flock was singing prior to the sermon.

'When they had done singing,' recalls Margaret in her *Testimony* nearly forty years later, 'he stood up upon a seat or form and desired that he might have liberty to speak'.[6] Now the low attacked the high; Fox shook the pulpit with the stertorous voice that awed magistrates and ministers in county after county ('thou hast good lungs', a judge was to exclaim at the trial of Margaret and George in 1664).[7] Margaret, kindled, involuntarily rose to her feet.

'Are you a child of light and have walked in the light?' she heard Fox demand. 'What you speak, is it inwardly from God?'

Margaret, reeling where she stood, realised that her beliefs had only ever been secondhand. Her entire life to date had been meaningless:

> This opened me so, that it cut me to the heart. Then I saw clearly, we were all wrong. So I sat me down in my pew again, and cried bitterly. I cried in my spirit to the Lord, 'We are all thieves, we are all thieves. We have taken the scriptures in words, and know nothing of them in ourselves.' (pp116–17)

The seven young Fells gazed wide-eyed from their pew as the drama unfolded: Margaret, Bridget, Isabel, George, Sarah, Mary, Susannah, descending from a nineteen-year-old to a toddler. They stared at their wildly weeping mother; at orating George; at Mr Lampitt agitating aloft – and now an irate Justice of the Peace, John Sawrey, who commanded the churchwarden to 'Take him away'.

Their mother peremptorily rapped out a counter-command to the bewildered official: '"Let him alone, why may not he speak as well as any other"; and Lampitt said for deceit, "Let him speak"'.[8] The churchwarden, having lunged and grabbed, backed off. Whom to obey? The church was clamorous with contradictory authorities.

Through it all flowed the mighty torrent of George's speech, until God had enjoyed full use of his lungs.

Margaret Fell asserted herself as a high-ranking Puritan with the autocratic tendencies of her class. But her heart lurched at the thought of Judge Fell's return to his sabotaged house. At Swarthmoor that night George won over the Judge's retainers: William Caton, Thomas Salthouse, Mary Askew, Ann Cleaton and others. The house resembled a swelling seedpod, tense with seeds, which would be discharged, when the pod burst, to the corners of the known earth. All were charged with exalted energy. William Caton, a teenager, would carry the Quaker message to Scotland and Holland; Thomas Salthouse to the Midlands and the West Country; Mary Askew would accompany Margaret in strenuous London visits; Ann Cleaton, after imprisonments in Lancaster Castle in 1654 and 1655, was to bear the Friends' message to Barbados, Boston and Rhode Island.

But Margaret at first felt 'stricken into such a sadness, I knew not what to do, my husband being from home. I saw it was the truth. I could not deny it.' Wrenched from the moorings of her allegiance, she wrestled inwardly while Fox roved the area gathering souls for the Light. Two weeks after she first met his eyes, 'The power of the Lord entered upon me. About three weeks end, my husband came home' (p117).

*

Judge Fell and his party negotiated Morecambe Sands from Lancaster to the Cartmel peninsula. The horses picked a wary path across dangerous acres of silt, beneath wheeling gulls, through salt-laden air and the glitter of sheets of esturial water. Crossing the Leven River, he was almost home, a patriarch in middle age, of statesman-like bearing, ex-MP, ex-Parliamentary soldier, a stern believer in liberty of conscience, not above enriching his estates with Royalist lands.

George meanwhile had been coming and going from Swarth-moor, converting, settling meetings, outraging the clergy and magistracy. Two further prophets, James Nayler and Richard Farnsworth, had tracked him to Swarthmoor. Margaret entertained them as the saddlesore Judge was waylaid by the sour cream of the local gentry, with the news that his household had been taken over and his wife taken in by a rogue with rat's tails, probably a witch, and that, should the Judge fail to eject this riffraff, the whole region would be infected. His wife had scandalously got up in church to defend the wicked one. Avid faces were smeared with relish at the shame – perhaps the cuckold's horns – of a proud and dignified man.

'So my husband came home greatly offended,' Margaret writes, in what was probably an understatement. She sent urgently for Fox at Sedburgh.

Having heard out the visiting prophets, the Judge conveyed his thunderous silence into the great hall, there to chew his dinner with bitter herbs. Margaret sat down beside him.

What happened next? Quaker historians fail to gloss her description: 'While I was sitting, the power of the Lord seized upon me. He was stricken with amazement, and knew not what to think, but was quiet and still' (p118). The chewing Judge sat dumbstruck while his virtuous and sane wife exhibited unheard-of symptoms. I doubt whether Margaret was simply sitting in a pious glow.

When early Quakers spoke of seizure by 'the power of the Lord', they commonly referred to raving ecstasies, embarrassing to a sober later generation. Braithwaite's classic history of early Quakerism queasily describes a Friend in church at Malpas in 1653, being visited by 'the ecstatic state known as "the power"', drowning out the priest with his uproar, and causing the congregation to evict him. Promptly returning, the Friend exploded again and was beaten out, 'for he had the power very fiercely as ever I saw any'. Thomas Holme reported that under the influence of 'the power', '[I] scarcely know whether I was in the body, yea or no, and there appeared light in the prison': he quaked, dazzled.[9]

Fork suspended in mid-air, Judge Fell gapes as 'the power' seizes his wife.

Not surprisingly, the chatterbox youngsters turn to statues, uncannily 'quiet and still, grown sober', unable to 'play on their music, that they were learning'. Their father retires to his study, to think things over.

May George Fox come in?

In strides George, hat on, banish the thought of politeness, and speaks out. Children, servants, visiting prophets and Margaret cram into the room. George speaks, Margaret feels, 'very excellently, as ever I heard him ... that if all England had been there, I thought, they could not have denied the truth of those things' (p118). In yearning anxiety, she steals sidelong glances at her husband's face. Experienced at character assessment, he sifts the leather-clad man with the charismatic eyes for signs of taint, querying whether the outlander has gained some sexual hold over his wife. Hearing Fox out, Fell seems favourably impressed but retires to bed without comment.

Next morning, Lampitt prises the Judge out of the house. Framed in a mullioned window, the two men can be seen criss-crossed by diamond lead panes walking tête-à-tête in the garden, out of earshot.

When Lampitt comes indoors, George goes for him with snarling questions as to the veracity of his calling. The priest retreats.

*

Friends multiplied in the area. The Fell household began corporately to glow with the new light kindled within it. Outsiders, awed by the love generated amongst them, included Anthony Pearson, persecutor of Friends, who was converted by the very Friends he was trying in court (Nayler and Howgill). Visiting Swarthmoor he envied the ecstasy into which the household (save its master) had entered: 'I was so confounded, all my knowledge and wisdom became folly.'[10] It must have resembled a visit to another planet.

William Caton, Margaret's foster-son, recalled how this living witness beaconed other Friends to Swarthmoor, which became the focal point for five or six counties around. To her husband's later grumble that there was hardly room in the stables for his own horses and the estate would be eaten out of hay, Margaret seraphically promised hay to spare at the end of the season. There was. God's accounting-system which provides for the sparrows and the lilies was buttressed by Margaret's canny reckoning of fodder.

Judge Fell must sometimes have wondered, who is the father in this house?

Fox inspired intense passion in the Judge's wife, children and servants. An extraordinary letter, apparently written soon after Fox's arrival at Swarthmoor but before Fell's return, survives in which the whole family, adults and children, under the direction of Margaret, rhapsodically plead and pray, in near-blasphemous language, for George's Messianic return:

> Our souls do thirst and languish after you ... you bread of life, without which bread our souls will starve ... Take pity on us, whom you have nursed up with the breasts of consolation ... Oh, our dear nursing father ... Oh, our life ... Oh you fountain of eternal life, our souls thirst after you, for in you alone is our life and peace ... O you father of eternal felicity.

Beseeching postscripts from the younger daughters follow the impassioned main body of the letter:

> O my dear father, when wilt thou come – Susan Fell
> Dear father, pray for us. – Sarah Fell
> Oh my dear heart; shall we not see thee once again – Isabell Fell
> Thou art the fountain of life. – Mary Fell.

Beneath the household signatures stands a personal message from Margaret, which implies that Fox left in anger at some unnamed male's hostility: 'My own dear heart ... you know that we have received you into our hearts'.

She had known Fox perhaps a fortnight.[11]

Later Quaker commentators either cringed at Margaret's 'over-emotionalism'; explained away the 'hysteria' as wise mother's therapeutic taking-at-dictation of the ravings of her bereft children; or erected a blind of scholarship to show that Messianic language was then not accounted blasphemous.[12] But why be ashamed of human complexity? Panic-stricken at losing Fox, but adroit in gaining her ends, Margaret seems to have mobilised the entire clan to fetch his 'kingly power' back. She was at once a passionate and sublimely manipulative woman. Since God had come to Margaret in George, she experienced initial difficulty in distinguishing the two.

The magnetism Fox exerted over Margaret Fell surely had an unacknowledged sexual component, all the more smiting since it was exercised on her fierce spirit, by a young man walking 'separately' from the world, in unattainable asceticism. Eleven years his elder, she was roused to the pitch of her dynamic energies to stand as George's spiritual partner. Until their marriage, eleven years after Judge Fell's death in 1658, they were encompassed in sexual scandal.

Meanwhile the Judge kept his own counsel. He stood apart from the communal excitement; yet did not disown it. At a gathering in his house, he overheard them puzzling where to hold meetings: nowhere was big enough for so many.

'You may meet here, if you will,' said Thomas Fell.

It is one of the most beautiful and moving moments in a story uniquely rich in such episodes, the more so because Thomas was not personally 'convinced'. He said, not '*We* will meet here' but 'You may meet here': and in that 'you' was included his wife, who now belonged at the hub of a movement to which he could not commit himself. He ceded but never shed her: Fell mantled the young movement with his protection.

In the oak-panelled 'Great Hall', Quaker meetings were held from 1652 till 1690. That first Sunday, only Thomas Fell, with clerk and groom, rode to church at Ulverston. Conceding to Margaret the space she could not (as a married woman) claim, he showed a magnanimity only equalled by his resolute shielding of Friends from persecution and imprisonment in the next six years. Fell grew to love and trust Fox. For some time before his death in 1658, he gave up attending church and, sitting in the study, had the double-doors left open between his room and the Great Hall where the Friends met for worship. Their words and silences reached him in the brown-panelled study where he called his soul his own. When he died in 1658, Westmorland Friends lost their legal protection. With hindsight, Fox was sure that 'he knew it was the Truth that I declared'. Judge Fell might have put it more ambiguously.

For consider the explosive household in which he reposed. Seven daughters (and a son) had been born by 1653. One of the Fell cherubs, Mary, aged eight, upon awakening in bed one morning, found herself the recipient of a message from God to arch-enemy Lampitt. A scrap of paper still exists recording the little girl's effusion. It reads:

> Lampitt,
>   The plaiges of God shall fall upon thee and the seven violls shall be powered upon thee and the milstone shall fall upon thee and crush thee as dust under the Lords feete how can thou escape the damnation of hell.
>
>   This did the lord give mee as
>   I lay in bed.
>
>   Mary Fell[13]

Mother, sisters, retainers and George were all superlatively proud of Mary's apocalyptic curse, which Fox recorded in his *Journal*. Ferocity dammed up in good little girls was licensed in first generation Quaker children, who could blast enemies to hell and still be admired – as good little girls.

Father's reaction to this missive is not recorded.

Swarthmoor had begun its movement from patriarchy into matriarchy. Signs of embattled strain in the surface accord of the Fell marriage survive. A letter of February 1653 from Margaret to Thomas in London took a tone of high-handed recommendation. She instructed her husband, 'Dear heart, mind the Lord above all to stand firm and close to the Lord and be not afraid of man ... keep thee pure'. Loading him with commissions, she urges him not to procrastinate, aware that the tasks she sets him mean less to him than to her: 'so hoping that thou will be faithful to me and to the Lord, farewell'. A postscript adds, 'I pray thee sweetheart do not slight these things for they are of great concernment'.[14]

Margaret's speech-patterns rather resemble those of a Puritan husband than a wife. The Judge is treated as his wife's executive, and spiritual inferior.

Whilst exploiting his usefulness to the full, she manoeuvred to evade Thomas' censorship. Sending one of her own books to London for publication, she warned, 'let it come forth speedily and be sent abroad, before my husband come up to London, lest he light of it and prevent the service of it'.[15] This determined out-manoeuvring reflects Margaret's will-power, reinforced by the

Quaker imperative of the Inner Light. Thomas must often have acted to veto actions of Margaret's. Later, in dispute with fellow Quaker Thomas Rawlinson, over his alleged mismanagement of the family iron-smelting business, Margaret's methods were ruthless, as she manipulated the local Meeting against him. 'You are such a great woman,' he snarled, smarting, in 1669, 'that loves to be great in the earth and among friends: to sit as judges and to reign ... even as a queen upon the people'.[16]

*

What was the nature of Fox's magnetic power?

Years before he met Margaret, the wanderer had inspired both men and women with devotion. This was not because of a Ranterish agenda of sexual domination. Fox (though his power-drive can hardly be denied) was a chain-breaker. His secret lay in teaching the poor to value their own inner riches; women to esteem themselves; servants to free themselves inwardly – and all to bond to one another. His mother, Mary Lago, was 'an upright woman', the *Journal* tells us, 'of the stock of the martyrs'. His respect for women as equal spiritual beings sloughed off centuries of tradition in a mind that made itself up in 'the orchard or the fields, with my Bible by myself' (p7). He was a child of his time. But in taking radical Seeking ideas to their logical conclusions, and living those ideas, he uniquely smashed people's mind-forged manacles.

In a later tract, *The Woman Learning in Silence*, Fox was to write:

> So be ashamed for ever, and let all your mouths be stopped forever, that despise the spirit of prophecy in the daughters, and do cast them into prison, and do hinder the women-labourers in the gospel; and saith the apostle, Christ in the male and in the female; and if Christ be in the female as well as in the male, is he not the same? And may not the spirit of Christ speak in the female as well as the male ... For the light is the same, in the male and in the female ... and who is it that dare stop Christ's mouth?[17]

It is easy to see why seventeenth-century women, muted, blinkered, hobbled, and sometimes demonised, were magnetised by this message.

Early in Fox's pilgrimage, he met a group of (presumably) Ranters, who argued that 'women have no souls, adding in a light manner, no more than a goose. But I reproved them and told them that was not right'. In response to their blokish hoots of incredulity, George quoted Mary's Magnificat in the Gospel: 'My soul doth magnify the Lord . . .' (pp8–9), a passage that would later be used by Margaret Fell to devastating effect in her retort to the 'despisers' of women, in *Womens Speaking Justified*: 'Are you not here beholding to the woman for your sermon, to use her words to put into your [*Book of*] *Common Prayer*? Yet you forbid women's speaking'.[18] The Anglican liturgy, whilst denying women's right to speak, traded on a woman's words.

Fox was a liberator of the voices of the oppressed, not ventriloquising through them, but listening to them and bringing them forth. Fox's magnet transferred its power.

In 1647, he reached Nottinghamshire, where he made his first convert and comrade, Elizabeth Hooton (p9). Imprisoned for disturbing the peace in Derby, York and Lincoln, Elizabeth became a magnificent protester: she protested to Cromwell about the corruption of the legal system; the state of the prisons; the hanging of the poor for minor offences (ie for being poor) while the rich could buy immunity; the scandalous state of prisons: 'They lie [in gaol] worse than dogs for want of straw'.[19] In Barbados, she espoused black rights. In New England she was imprisoned, whipped, ejected into the wilderness, returned, was whipped to the point of flaying. George Bishop in his account of the persecutions, *New-England Judged* (1661), tells of the elderly woman's ordeals, 'tied to the whipping post and lashed with ten cruel stripes' ... 'ten more with rods of willows' ... 'in a cold frosty morning, they laid on her aged limbs ten lashes more' ... 'whipped' ... 'whipped in Roxbury ... Dedham ... Madfield ... whipped at cart's tail ... whipped from town to town ...', until the narrator, nauseated as we are by the remorseless pounding of the words 'whip' and 'flog' and 'wilderness', abbreviates his account of 'these tedious and howling wildernesses and cruelties and sufferings'[20] And all the while, the audacious Elizabeth talked back. She harangued. She cried woe. She needled. Back she came to England in 1662 and badgered King

Charles II in person. She died en route for the West Indies in 1672, in her early seventies.

Imagine if George Fox had happened to bypass Skegby in 1647. Elizabeth would perhaps have lived a waspish life amongst the local Baptists to whom she may already have been preaching when George met her, a bit of a battle-axe perhaps. More comfort certainly, as a property owner; no crossing and recrossing the Atlantic, incarceration, trekking the forests of America or seeing off the infamous Governor Endicott, who called her and her elderly companion, Joan Brooksop, witches, and demanded 'What came you for?'

'To do the will of him that sent me.'

'What is that?'

'To warn thee of shedding any more innocent blood.'

'I will hang more.'

'Thou art in the hand of the Lord, who can take thee away first.' And, says Bishop, with retributive relish, the Lord did. Endicott lived to hang no more.[21]

Quaker women's stories are of inner power liberated. Through Fox in those early days, each found a self and a voice which expected to be heard; contempt for merely human laws and customs; assurance of God's love and one another's fellowship. From some, like Elizabeth, he liberated a global voice; a journey, more full of active meaning than a seventeenth-century woman could have dreamed.

Paradoxically, this voice derived from a radical understanding of silence. Listening attentively to the quiet within focused a centre inside the self, which Friends identified not as egoism but 'that of God in you', your 'measure' of God. From this quiet stirred the 'still, small voice' of the Spirit, unable to speak otherwise than truthfully.

Silence, therefore, always previously a sign of women's suppression and inferiority, became their means of liberation and transcendence: in Sarah Blackborow's words, her retirement 'into the silence out of all babbling talk' gave access to 'that witness' in herself which led her out into a public witness. She emphasises 'one heart, and one soul, one body, one head, one power in all over all'. God has power, she writes in another pamphlet, to 'turn the mind in', making nothing of the outward and visible. Friends, Mary

Smith was to write from Middlewich House of Correction in 1667, enjoy 'living refreshment', 'living bread', 'hidden Manna' in their empowering silence. Everyone, writes Elizabeth Bathurst, has 'a Divine Teacher in them' but not everyone is listening. Once you hear the voice, you need to pass along the message, whose origin is not the desire for self-expression but is the Holy Spirit which is 'one in the male and in the female, one spirit, one light, one power'.[22] Women therefore gained access to the depths of their being, with a sense of focus and uncoupling from the bonds of law, kin, custom; illegitimate though socially sanctioned demands.

Fox caused a riot at Leicester when a minister taking questions refused to answer a woman, as being a non-person. 'For the woman asking a question, he should have answered it ... I told him the Church was ... living stones ... a spiritual household', not 'an old house made up of lime, stones, and wood' (p24).

In the ensuing rumpus, the priest came down, and the congregation bayed at George in what he liked to call 'jangling'; after which tumult, 'the woman that asked the question aforesaid was convinced, *and all her family*' [my italics]. Where women first responded, there was often a rippling-out of 'Truth' along a network of relationships.

Constantly he was subject to 'bruising, beating, blooding, stoning, and throwing me down'. Friends did not ask to suffer; but they *could* suffer. Quakers hit back by not hitting back. Militant and aggressive rather than passive and masochistic,[23] their resistance rested on Christ's meeting of blows with assertive patience. Battered to the ground at Ulverston with willow rods, hedge stakes, clubs and staves, George's defiance took the form not of blows but the taunt, ' "Strike again, here is my arms and my head and my cheeks" ' (p127). And they did. '[With] a carnal weapon I do not fight,' George wrote in a powerful letter to Cromwell from prison in 1654, 'but am from those things dead; from him who is not of the world, called of the world by the name George Fox' (p198).

Not of the world: Cromwell was being addressed by a spirit, by The Spirit. Soldiers who became Quakers refused to defer to superiors or submit to military discipline, and they didn't intend to kill people. The peace-soldiers had to be ignominiously discharged.

Such passive resistance had a feminine quality, seen in terms of the gendering of behaviour in the period. Quiescence that was not acquiescence but self-affirmation was a moral posture which abdicated behaviour thought proper and natural to masculinity.

The movement set itself visibly apart from worldly, male and caste norms. Following Christ's command to turn the other cheek, Fox's anomalous reactions asked the thoughtless to pause and ponder. Non-violence either incensed or shamed attackers. Arrested at Swarthmoor after the Restoration by raging horsemen, George answered coolly, '"Here is my back, here is my cheek, strike on." At which words their heat assuaged' (p376). They stuck the hefty George on 'a poor little horse' behind the saddle, 'and I lighted off him and told them they should not abuse the creature'. Loving one's neighbour involved a compact with all sentient life.

After the abortive Fifth Monarchist rebellion of 1661, massive persecution of Friends began. Thousands were arrested, Quaker communities decimated. You could not go shopping for a soldiery that 'dragged men and women out of their houses, and some out of their sick beds by the legs' (p397). Margaret Fell delivered the first public statement of the Quaker peace testimony to the king's hands in June 1660, *A Declaration and an Information from Us, The People Called Quakers*: 'We are a people that follow after those things that make for peace, love and unity ... Our weapons are not carnal, but spiritual, who have given our backs, our cheeks and our hair to be smitten'.[24] This preceded George's more famous pacifist *Declaration* of January 1661. The conscientious objectors of the First World War were born from these magnificent parents, in repudiation of the masculine warrior ethic which, equating power with physical force, calls into question the whole meaning of 'civilisation'. Quaker quietism witnessed to a power culturally associated with women: power to endure rather than to strike. Milton, himself forced into a quietist position after the loss of his republican dreams, expresses it movingly in *Paradise Regained*: 'Who best/Can suffer best can do' (III 194–5). Seventeenth-century women responded intensely to that revolutionary equation of power with suffering; and underwent as equal partners a common travail.

*

Bathed in 'a sea of polymorphous spiritual nurture and eroticism',[25] early Friends recapitulated in a blissful experience of oneness the 'oceanic' feeling of primal belonging. Gender dissolved; adults became babes in arms; egalitarian ecstasy floated them in solution with one another. They transcended the harshness of their pilgrimage by turning to Fox as 'nursing father' and Fell at Swarthmoor as 'nursing mother'. Ann Audland wrote from Banbury Prison: 'my dear and near and eternal mother, by thee I am nourished ... I even feed with thee and lie down with thee in the life for evermore'; 'thou art my natural mother, by thee I have been nourished and refreshed'. Her husband John Audland wrote, 'I read thee daily thou art bound up in me sealed closed and enjoyed forevermore ... breathe to me more and more and I shall feel thee ... most glorious is thy dwelling place'.[26] If these endearments later took on a formulaic character, at first they were vital and spontaneous: the tender style testifies to the way Quakerism uniquely fed the emotional need in its early, ardent exponents, from which could spring heroic action.

But the nursing mother was also an administrative genius. As the movement extended, and persecution gathered, Margaret established Swarthmoor as a centre of communications and postal sorting office for Quaker itinerant prophets, managing legal suits and campaigns against priests and tithes. She initiated a funding system for national and global missions and relief of prisoners' families beggared by tithe-refusal. She defined her activities with fine simplicity: 'Friends brought things to me, and I answered them.'

Margaret became for the first generation of Friends the still centre of their travels, trials and vicissitudes. The journeying ministers had to be shod and cloaked for the winter roads. Item: for Thomas Holme, breeches and shoes; for Edward Burrough, travelling cutlery; for Elizabeth Fletcher, one hat; for Jane Waugh, one pair of shoes; for Elizabeth Coward, one petticoat and one waistcoat.[27] To all she sent fellowship and solidarity, in that strong-minded handwriting, filling the sheet from edge to edge.

Swarthmoor was a matriarchy. Imagine all those daughters ... each one a different kind of prodigy. The one son was seen as a bad nut, with whom she was to enter into bitter conflict. Margaret could domineer and intimidate. Acting head of household during Judge Fell's lifetime, she was actual head for over four decades after his death. When she and Fox married in 1669, Fox waived his patriarchal right to his wife's property (as did Presbyterian Richard Baxter with his higher-ranking wife),[28] so that she retained control of her own estates and affairs until her death at the age of eighty-eight.

The rift of iron in Margaret's temperament was matched by a certain worldliness and materialism. She wore black silk and was known as a woman of magnificent bearing, in contradiction of the 'plain dress' ethos of Quakerism. In Thurloe's *State Papers* there is a hostile description of Margaret as she appeared in 1658: 'one that is past the cloud, and hath liberty to wear satins and silver and gold lace, and is a great gallant'.[29] Fox sent her lace from Ireland in 1669, and ordered 'Spanish black cloth' for a gown, 'and', he added wryly, 'it did cost us a pretty deal of money'.[30]

Sarah Fell, who acted as bailiff and steward of the Swarthmoor estate from 1664 until her marriage in 1681, inherited her mother's managerial skills. Her fastidious ledger for 1673 to 1678 survives, allowing us to picture the economic world of a northern gentry family, employing about fifty-five servants and day-labourers on the farm. Sarah administered and minuted every farthing, acted as unofficial local banker making loans (with or without interest according to means), managed an investment in a Bristol shipping venture and ran Force Forge, a smelting works. When the forge lost money, Margaret pursued the manager, fellow Friend Thomas Rawlinson, with accusations of fraud, in an acrimonious dispute in which she manipulated the local Quaker meeting and resorted to litigation (against the principles of Friends). To Rawlinson, Margaret and her family were 'all so proud and haughty and full of oppression scorning high-minded', and Margaret herself was 'a great, rich woman'.[31]

The great rich woman employed labour at the going rate. Peggy Dodgeson was a farmhand brawny enough to do men's work. Accordingly she was set to humping manure, harrowing, hay-making, peat-stacking, washing, hemp-pulling ... not for a man's wage but for a penny a day, the standard woman's rate of pay and half that of a man.

How can we reconcile Margaret Fell's otherworldliness with her tight-fistedness; her manipulation of rank with her egalitarian principles; her tenderness and her punitive punch? We can't – any more than we can resolve our own contradictions. Caste and pugnacity gave her a unique effectiveness as co-ordinator of a national movement. A controversialist of formidable calibre, she went for the government with the focused ferocity she unleashed on Rawlinson, in head-on confrontation. She outfaced and down-talked judges; braved gaol; lobbied a king for months on end. Margaret's written works number about fifty, toward 19 per cent of all the writings by Quaker women in the century, addressing public issues of theology and politics as spokesperson for the movement. Most of these works were composed before 1668, when, despite Quaker emphasis on the inner nature of Christ's Second Coming, Friends could not help but harbour an expectation of the imminence of the World's End. Her interventions in history (including five millennarian epistles to the Jews) were urgent in tone.

Margaret's style – or rather, non-style – is trenchant and commanding, tough and rugged, with massive sentences clambering vigorously over a rough-hewn grammar; probably a genuine voice-print, since she dictated most of them. She trounces the priesthood in *A True Testimony from the People of God* (1660) as bearing secondhand messages; challenges readers of every estate to think for ourselves. 'Let all people search and read ... whether these are the true prophets or the false?', 'Let any honest, reasonable heart judge'. 'Now let the people seriously consider':

> Here is the chief difference between them and us: they have the words and declaration of Christ and the apostles, declared from the Spirit of life; we have the Spirit which these words were declared from.[32]

She lambasts Ranters in *Some Ranters Principles Answered* (1656): 'You dark blind sot ... Here, you serpent, are spewing forth your poison and blasphemy ... You blasphemous beast ...'.[33] She addresses the newly restored king in 1660 in the magnificent manifesto, *A Declaration and an Information*:

We are the people of God called Quakers, who are hated and despised and everywhere spoken against as people not fit to live, as they were that went before us ...

We are a people that follow after those things that make for peace, love and unity.

... And now I am here to answer what can be objected against us on the behalf of many thousands ... who was moved of the Lord to leave my house and family, and to come two hundred miles to lay these things before you, who to the will of the Lord am committed.

Margaret Fell.[34]

As head of a gentry family, Margaret had privileged access to the royal family. Yet she identified herself proudly with the 'hated and despised', riffraff such as her lawyer-husband had often gaoled. And she spoke, in what is now her most famous work, *Womens Speaking Justified* (1667) for women's spiritual equality: 'God has said that his daughters should prophesy as well as his sons ... Does the church only consist of men?'[35]

Writing was another form of direct action, and, like her public speaking, an encroachment on a male domain. Margaret despatched peremptory letters to Cromwell, to the Council of Officers, to Members of Parliament. She arrogantly harried the local authorities. Issued epistolary attacks on priests. Blasted bribe-taking Justice Sawrey as 'a caterpillar, which shall be swept out of the way'. She swept full sail up the aisle of Lampitt's church.

'Good Mistress Fell, go into your own pew, or else go your way,' was the oil he poured, and, taking her arm, attempted to manoeuvre her out of the way.

'Hold thy hands off me.'

Wrenching free, she delivered a tirade to Lampitt, and followed up by lecturing Justice Sawrey on justice, and the oppression of the poor.

Fuming, Sawrey wrote to her, care of her husband, urging Judge Fell to keep his cacophonous wife under control.

Sawrey was judged by the Almighty and drowned in Morecambe Bay.[36]

*

Margaret stayed put as co-ordinator and support when, in 1654, the sixty 'First Publishers of Truth' moved south, two by two.

Two women were the first to reach London, Isabel Buttery and a friend.

Anne Blaykling was the first Quaker to reach Norfolk, the first to be imprisoned there.

The first missionaries to America were women: Mary Fisher, Ann Austin, and Elizabeth Harris. Mary and Ann were 'stripped stark naked' by the New England authorities, 'and searched and misused' as witches, a trauma which Ann, 'a married woman, and mother of five children, suffered not the like in the bearing of any of them into the world'.[37]

The methods of both sexes were aggressive and provocative. Church service interruption, buzzing and screeching at the minister and subsequent mayhem, with lynchings, mob-violence and arrest, characterised their campaigns. Quaking, foaming at the mouth, stripping off, standing with a clay pot or dust and ashes on the head, these hullabaloo-creators were in other contexts the soul of austere quietude, presenting to contemporaries an incomprehensible gender paradox. Plain-dressed, plain-speaking Quaker women, pure of ribbons and frippery, hair falling loose or fetched up into plain caps, bawled down the minister ('Come down thou greedy dog, woe unto thee,' as Margaret Fell's servant Ann Cleaton brayed at the rector of Aldingham). When the authorities gaoled them, they expressed amazement that the civil (uncivil) authorities should be provoked by their harmless conduct. A vast pamphlet literature was disseminated like clouds of dandelion seed through prison grilles. Ann Audland, charged with blasphemy, wrote from Banbury Prison in 1655:

> William Allen, Justice of the Peace so called, but little peace
> I find in thee; We came to the town of Banbury ... [and]
> were moved to go to the steeple-house, to speak the word of
> the Lord to Priest and People; and in obedience to the Lord,
> we went, and stayed till the Priest had done, and then my
> friend spoke to the priest, and the rude multitude came and
> harried her forth ... Then I spoke to the Priest, Man, here,
> see the fruits of thy Ministry, and presently the rude people

hurried me forth ...

And know this O man, that the Lord God will be avenged of all unjust Justices ...

O blush, and be ashamed of what you call your Church, who are so suddenly in a tumult! Was there ever such a thing heard of among the Saints, that they would be in a tumult, when one came in peaceably among them, not offering wrong to any?

Therefore, give over, and never call it a Church, who are fighters and strikers, scoffers and scorners, tumulters and false accusers.[38]

No peace in the Justice of the Peace; no grace in the 'Minister (as ye call him)'; a congregation happy to beat you up when you come in as God's apostle to minister to their souls: what could Friends do but cry 'Woe' at the tops of their voices? Ann addresses both minister and JP as 'Man': social blasphemy to 'Sir'. She 'thou's them. She talks back on behalf of God-in-Ann ('And know this O man'), asserting divinely sanctioned superiority over her social and ecclesiastical 'masters'. There is relish in this combative violation of the code of female obedience, common to all this literature, a proud defiance which unites common and Bible English in rising cadences of hectoring scorn. Ann claims kin with Moses and St Paul.

Quaker women's 220 publications may seem a small number when placed beside the 3633 male Quaker works printed before 1700; but eighty-two female authors add up to a not insignificant proportion of the 650 total, in an age of 90 per cent female illiteracy and 100 per cent exclusion from political life. It was an extraordinary corporate breakthrough. We know of 243 women and girls who came to public attention but these were a fraction of the 20,000 Quaker women who witnessed, prophesied, demonstrated.

Sixteen-year-old 'Little' Elizabeth Fletcher was one of the first to reach Ireland; the first (with Elizabeth Leavens) to take the Quaker message to Oxford, whose scholars expressed their gratitude and superior reasoning skills by sousing them in muddy water and dragging them to a pump where they jetted water into their mouths and other parts, completing their argument by dashing Elizabeth violently on to a gravestone. The Oxford magistrates added to this a bloody whipping.

Oxford and Cambridge were a Quakers' bane. Hester Biddle writes, 'I spent many years in Oxford, where the carriages [behaviour] of the scholars did trouble me ... they were so wild'.[39] She delivers twin blasts of the trumpet against the university cities, *Wo To Thee Town of Oxford* and *Wo To Thee Town of Cambridge*.

> Woe to thee town of Cambridge, thy wickedness surmounteth the wickedness of Sodom; therefore repent whilst thou hast time, lest I consume thee with fire ... therefore will I uncover thy nakedness and thy shame will I unfold ... the well-favoured harlot lodgeth in thee, the mother of witchcraft ... horror and terror, and pain shall take hold upon them as upon a woman in travail, and many shall cry, but there shall be none to deliver them; therefore repent while I give you a day ... for I gave Jezebel a day ...
>
> *I came not to bring peace but war*, saith Jesus.
>
> Oh Cambridge, thou art full of filth ... murdering and killing the just in you, and whipping, and stocking them that the Lord hath sent to you ...
>
> Remember you are warned in your lifetime and all left without excuse.
>
> *Hester Biddle*[40]

Few Quaker men and no women held university degrees: neither did Christ. They prided themselves on being a privileged elite, with primary knowledge from the Spirit who condemned all institutionalised teaching. Wrath carried a retaliatory joy as women gave militant voice to God-sanctioned rage. Hester's 'I' is God's 'I'; she speaks for him with a masculine tongue, borrowing a language of insult, curse and invective from Old Testament prophets and Christ himself, who cursed the book-bound intellectuals of his day ('Woe unto you, ye blind guides' – Matthew 23:1–37). She sheds her womanhood as outward show. Indeed, it is not Hester who is the 'woman' but the men inside the city, with their pomp and corruption. The powers-that-be are identified here with 'the well-favoured harlot, the mother of witchcraft', 'a woman in travail' and 'Jezebel'.

What then, to Friends, was a 'woman'? If it seems an odd question to us, their usage appeared to contemporaries a compound of lunacy with blasphemy.

A hostile source reports that:

> Williamson's wife ... said in the hearing of diverse ... that she was the eternal Son of God; and when the men that heard her, told her that she was a woman, and therefore could not be the Son of God: she said, no, you are women, but I am a man.[41]

Quakers confronted the immemorial tradition of misogyny within the Bible and Christianity by denying that they were 'women' at all in its sense as 'lower being', 'subordinate' 'sinful human'. Rulers were the 'women' who should keep quiet. Anyone with the Light in her soul, restored to original perfection, was either a perfected woman or had a 'man' within her, Jesus Christ. Such a person, who happened to be gendered female (as this world goes), not only may but must speak.

Hence, Margaret Fell in her riposte to Justice Sawrey's accusation that 'I was puffed up with malice and pride and that the people saw it so', sneered that he and his people had no eyes in their heads. For who was the 'man'? – Margaret. Who was the 'woman'? – blind Sawrey: 'thou art the woman that goes abroad and dost not abide in thine own house'.[42]

Priscilla Cotton and Mary Cole were committed to Exeter Gaol in 1654, as being 'silly women' speaking out of turn. The nettling phrase 'silly women' reverberates throughout their tract, *To the Priests and People of England* (1655). Silly women know far more than mad men. Mary and Susannah in the Bible '(silly women, as you would be ready to call them, if they were here now)' knew more of the Messiah than all the learned rabbis of their day. It's a pity the ministers of Exeter can't be silly women.

> it's weakness that is the woman by the Scriptures forbidden ...
> Indeed, you yourselves are the women, that are forbidden to speak in the Church, that are become women,

for two of your Priests came to speak with us, and when
they could not bear sound reproof and wholesome doctrine
... they railed on us with filthy speeches.[43]

A 'woman' is a weak person. The ministers are weak. Therefore, the
ministers are women.

In a world whose norms are recognised as madness, such
arguments turn the world upside down, ie, the right way up.

Who are these salesmen that peddle religion for commercial
gain to cry down women speaking from the heart? demanded
Quakers. Fox and Fell were adamant on the principle, even when the
issue split the movement. Margaret's famous *Womens Speaking Justified* was written in prison at Lancaster Castle and published in 1666:

All this opposing, and gainsaying, of women's speaking has
risen out of the bottomless pit and spirit of darkness that
have spoken for these many hundred years together in this
night of apostasy ... That spirit has limited and bound all up
within its bond and compass.[44]

She distinguishes two kinds of women: the 'true woman' who,
knowing the Light, has power to forbid the false 'woman', 'tattlers
and busy-bodies' of both sexes, and especially the Pope and his
rabble ('both he and the false church are called "woman", in Rev.
17'). But the priests are thieves who raid the Bible for women's
words – Judith, Deborah, Anna, Mary and Mary Magdalene, the
woman of Samaria – and sell the stolen goods in the marketplace
as their own. Christ is husband to all of us, male and female.

George Keith, in his beautifully written defence of women's
preaching, *The Woman-Preacher of Samaria* (1674), reflects upon
the story of the woman to whom Christ revealed himself: no
university taught her, nor was she ordained by bishop or
presbytery. It was all far simpler than that: 'first of all, she was
taught by Christ, by Christ himself ... being thus taught, she
believed on him, and then she went and preached him. This is an
excellent pattern, and example unto all true ministers'.[45] Faith and
Inner Light, sole qualifications for ministry, carry their own
credibility: but the clergy is a mass gathering of the dimmest male

wits of well-off families. Parents wondering what on earth to do with the 'greatest Dunce or Dolt' of their offspring, incapable of studying for the bar or medicine, destine the runt for the church. That's all he's fit for. It ensures that he's called 'Sir' and, if he makes it to a bishopric, he'll be 'my Lord'.

The woman of Samaria preached without wage. Nowadays, 'no money, no preaching'.

In a postscript, Keith recollects where he's seen and heard women standing up in the Church of England speaking out before the whole congregation, in a 'place not unlike your pulpits, but that it is larger, that it may hold three or four'. Yes indeed, he has seen it filled with women who are asked by the priest to address the congregation: the whore's gallery, where 'penitent' women are coerced into public penance.

Keith has heard one or two veterans who have become so handy at their public confession as to speak 'by way of exhortation, and instruction, that she seemed to speak almost as well, and to as good purpose, as the Priest himself '.[46]

William Mather's attack on the Women's Meetings, *A Novelty: Or, a Government of Women, Distinct from Men*, objects to harebrained females being given any authority outside the home. 'Women Judges' should never be allowed to decide any issue, 'who come into the Seat of Council, rustling in gaudy flowered stuffs, silks, from top to toe, mincing with their feet, etc'.[47] These sartorial disqualifications do not extend to charity work, to which females are fitted; nor is he against 'silently waiting at the Feet of Jesus'. Contemptuous of all 'Female Government', Mather is also uneasily alive to the self-contradiction in a movement founded on spiritual liberty. Perhaps he is less conscious of what hits the reader's eye on his title page. The tract is printed in London by 'Sarah Hawkins'.

*

Throughout the 1650s, oppression grew. 1656 saw the re-enactment of the Elizabethan Law against vagrants and sturdy beggars, explicitly to stem 'the Quakers, who greatly increase, and pester and endanger the Commonwealth', as Dr Clarges, MP told Parliament on 5 December.[48]

But what about travelling minstrels? Shouldn't they be excepted? Mr Robinson opined that they corrupted the common people 'by their lewd and obscene songs'.

> *Sir Thomas Wroth:* Harpers should be included.
>
> *Mr — :* Pipers should be comprehended.
>
> *Alderman Foot:* I hope you intend not to include the *waits* of the City of London, which are a great preservation of men's houses in the night.
>
> *Sir William Strickland:* The general word minstrel will be best; for if you go to enumerate, they will devise new instruments.
>
> *Mr Butler:* Music is a lawful science, and I love it; but, in regard you restrain it to those places, I think the general word will serve well enough.
>
> *Colonel Whetham:* I hope you will not deprive men of their voices.
>
> *Mr Speaker:* Singing is a natural, playing an artificial music.[49]

Having censored popular music in the name of bourgeois godliness, Cromwell's Second Protectorate Parliament passed on to the notorious case of the Quaker, James Nayler, who had ridden into the City of Bristol on an ass. In the pouring rain of late October 1656, soaked to the skin, Nayler was led by a drenched crew of women carrying branches, singing 'Holy holy holy, Lord God of Israel', casting clothes upon the mud before his horse. They welcomed him in as Christ the King riding into Jerusalem. This 'blasphemy' was a dark turning-point, at which the whole movement threatened to founder.

Many MPs bayed for the death penalty but eventually prolonged debate decided for 'mercy':

> *Colonel White* proposed that his tongue might be bored through.
>
> *Colonel Barclay,* that his hair might be cut off.
>
> *Major-General Haines,* that his tongue might be slit or bored through, and that he might be stigmatised with the letter B.
>
> *Colonel Coker,* that his hair might be cut off.

> *Sir Thomas Wroth.* Slit his tongue, or bore it, and brand him with the letter B.
>
> *Major-General Whalley.* Do not cut off his hair; that will make the people believe that the Parliament of England are of opinion that our Saviour Christ wore his hair so, and this will make all people in love with the fashion.
>
> *Sir Gilbert Pickering.* His hard labour and imprisonment will be sufficient. I have, within these two days, talked with a very sober man of that sect, who tells me Nayler is ... bewitched, really bewitched; and keeping him from company, especially from that party that bewitched him, your imprisonment will do.

Later Sir Gilbert again insisted that 'it is a woman that has done all the mischief'.[50]

Leading Friends also saw Nayler as literally bewitched by women, Richard Hubberthorne writing to Margaret Fell, 'That power of darkness in the women rules over him'.[51] Martha Simmonds and Hannah Stranger were held to have set up Nayler over Fox as head. Talking down all other voices, they worshipped Nayler as Messiah, playing upon his tenderness of heart, falling at his feet. Quaker history sees Nayler as the gentle victim of Eve-like temptresses who mastered him through tears, sexual power and flattery.[52] In the bitter struggle for control of the movement, Martha and Hannah, along with Dorcas Erbury (whom Nayler 'raised from the dead' in Exeter Gaol), Judy Crouch and a person called Mildred, have been demonised as renegade females who ruined a tender-hearted man. When Nayler was taken into custody at Bristol, a letter from Martha's husband, found in his pocket, informed him in a postscript, 'Thy name shall be no more James Nayler, but Jesus'.[53]

Nayler was brought in to answer for himself at the bar of the House of Commons.

'"I was never guilty of lewdness; or so reputed,"' he asserted. '"I abhor filthiness."'

'"It is likely the women kneeled as much to others,"' he went on when pressed on why he accepted their prostration. '"It is not true. They gave no worship to me, I abhor it, as I am a creature.'' When he had been dismissed, many were in accord with Mr Butler's glib, '"This fellow has not only committed blasphemy himself; but, I fear me, he caused many others to commit blasphemy"'. Others were less sure. Lord Strickland, having listened with deep care to Nayler's answers, found:

> This fellow is one made up of contradictions. The Quakers teach humility, but he exalts himself ... I do not believe (by what I have heard,) that he did say he was Jesus or Christ, though I think the women do believe him to be Christ.[54]

Day after day, the status of the Inner Light in Nayler and his disciples was debated, as though there were no other business in England.

Finally Parliament resolved by ninety-six votes to eighty-two to spare Nayler's life. He was whipped by the hangman through the streets from the pillory at Westminster to the Old Exchange, sustaining 310 lashes; then pilloried again. His tongue was bored through and his forehead branded with the letter 'B' for 'Blasphemer'; he was ridden face backwards into Bristol; whipped again; imprisoned in Bridewell for hard labour. When the Quaker Rebecca Travers bathed his wounds, she found no skin left on the whole of his blood-coated back and arms, which were ingrained with filth.

Nayler's tragedy was the climax of the power struggle between himself and Fox, in which the adulation which seems to have turned Nayler's head raised a dark mirror to the spellbound awe in which Fox was held. When Nayler at a critical moment, rueing the split, had offered a kiss of reconciliation, George insulted him by offering his foot to kiss.

Martha Simmonds was credited by Quakers and MPs alike with sexual control of Nayler. It is equally possible that Nayler exercised an unconscious sexual power over the vulnerable women who clustered around him, not despite, but because of the fact that he was a genuinely beautiful character. It was so much easier to blame Martha, since appeal to a misogynist archetype distracted attention from the contradictions she exposed in the movement.[55]

George's unforgiving bitterness is easy to comprehend. As the tragedy spiralled toward its catastrophe, he was in Doomsdale Prison at Launceston, a stinking cesspit, where witches and murderers were kept before execution. You did not expect to come out alive:

> the prisoners' excrements had not been carried out for scores of years ... It was all like mire, and in some places at the top of the shoes in water and piss.

When the prisoners burned straw to smother the retching stink, the smoke bothered the gaoler above, who retaliated by pouring 'the excrements of the prisoners' down a hole in the ceiling, so that Fox and the Friends were covered from head to foot in faeces.[56]

When Susanna Kemp brought in food, the gaoler arrested her for breaking and entering.

Anne Downer made the two-hundred-mile journey south to Cornwall from London, a shorthand-expert who could act as secretary to the prisoners and prepare them food.

But Nayler's Martha, 'which is called thy mother' as Fox spat in contempt, came waltzing in to Fox's cell, singing at him, and demanding he yield place as head of the movement to Nayler.

To glimpse the horror of Doomsdale is to gauge the wound Nayler dealt Fox. Sustaining his faith and the movement in an ordurous prison, Fox felt powerless against the odium cast by his beloved enemy's infidelity, and his vagrant flock, not only upon himself but on the meaning of his life's journey.

Heartbroken after his mutilation and disgrace, Nayler's contrition was only matched by his patience and dignity under reproach. Fox shut the door on him in the heat of his wrath. Just in time, Fox thawed and forgave. Nayler died at King's Repton in 1660, praising the spirit of gentle endurance: 'I found it alone, being forsaken. I have fellowship therein with them who lived in dens and desolate places in the earth, who through death obtained this resurrection and eternal life.'[57]

Margaret Fell had written a letter of remonstration to Nayler,[58] begging him to 'mind what thou art doing', lest he lead astray the gullible. She states her love toward him: 'And I could lie down at thy feet that thou might trample upon me for thy good', offering a human shield against his disastrous course, and so, she says, would Fox, against whom Nayler has rebelled. Her grammar, wrestling with contrary tensions, becomes convoluted as she seeks to heal the breach – a breach not only between Fox and Nayler, but surely within herself, within Fox. For wasn't the charismatic Fox all-but-worshipped? Wasn't she? The letter in any case never reached Nayler, who had reeled out of Exeter Castle, giddy with fasting and Martha.

*

Martha Simmonds' head-on clash with the male Quaker leadership aroused its disgust. It reminded some Friends of women's reputation for dangerous wildness, Delilah to Nayler's Samson. Sister of the left-wing printer, Giles Calvert, and wife of Quaker printer Thomas Simmonds, Martha portrays herself in her writings as having been a desperate seeker after truth, before finding the Friends. In *A Lamentation for the Lost Sheep* (1656) she writes that 'for seven years together I wandered up and down the streets', with a sense of spiritual death in her heart, enquiring after a true faith, till, leaving off her search, she spent 'seven years more ... living wild and wanton, not knowing a cross to my will' until her eyes were opened to 'a measure of [God] in me', a light she longed to share.[59] There is nothing controversial here. But Martha's belligerent commitment to her dissident light represented a lawlessness always latent in the 'Inner Light' principle. In 1655 she had walked through Colchester 'in sackcloth and barefoot with her hair spread and ashes upon her head, in the town, in the frosty weather, to the astonishment of many'.[60] Martha developed a chant to drown out male voices in Meetings: an excoriating buzzing-singing, in which she repeated one word for, say, an hour.

The demonic rantings of Mildred and Judy, the drive for dominance of Martha, reminded the male leadership of its worst fears. The release of the Spirit, intended to bring loving union, might instead release the power-urge women had immemorially suppressed, in parodic bawlings, filibustering, ego-outbursts. Some women must have felt overwhelmed by the lifting of constraint upon their sphere and powers of action.

Elizabeth Morgan ranted her way through Chester 'and by

her unwise and exalted spirit led George Bishop astray for a time', and into Gloucester, where she ecstatically declared her message: 'Ephraim is a heifer unaccustomed to the yoke.' Heifers who had thrown off the yoke ran amok in Worcester, where Susanna Pearson, in pity for a suicide's mother, exhumed a corpse which, in emulation of Elisha, she attempted to raise from the dead, laying 'her face upon his face, and her hands upon his hands'. Without success. Ann Gargill was unruly in Amsterdam. Another female menace was Jane Stokes, 'a bad spirit'. Elizabeth Barnes shredded the Bible.[61]

When schism in the Quaker movement opened in the 1660s and 1670s, it would centre upon the role and behaviour of women.

*

With the Restoration in 1660, Margaret Fell, widowed for two years and now forty-six, abdicated her homebound role, leaving Bridget in charge of the children and household. She spent fifteen months in London, lobbying King Charles II for tolerance of Quaker principles on oaths and an end to persecution. Her imperious instructions to Bridget to hold the fort, run the estate, cope with persecution, mind the children and 'not desire my return till the Lord that brought me hither give me back again'[62] are militant statements of higher duty than to the merely human family, and perhaps of the excitement of a public role at the centre of power. It was the first of ten visits to London.

The Fifth Monarchy Rising was followed by punitive legislation which kept the gaols full of Quakers: the Act of Uniformity and the Quaker Act (1662), the Conventicle Acts (1664 and 1670), which issued in orgies of persecution. Prison and prison-visiting became a Quaker way of life. Pepys watched the thuggish behaviour of Monck's troops, breaking up a Quaker meeting, in February 1660: 'the soldiers did use them very roughly and were to blame'.[63] County records show the relentless assault on Friends' Meetings, often held in widows' houses, involving them in harsh and repeated fines, as these in the north:

17 July, 1670: there was a numerous meeting or conventicle ... at the house of Ann Marsland of Hanford in the parish of Cheadle and County of Cheshire, widow ... 27 August,

> 1670 ... And do further adjudge that the said Ann Marsland
> hath forfeited £20 according to the said Act.[64]

Margaret's pen was fiercely active in these years with epistles and
polemics. Two spells in London preceded a one-thousand-mile
journey visiting Friends' Meetings, and her own trial in 1664, with
Fox, at Lancaster Assizes.

*

Margaret appears flanked by daughters, Isabel, Sarah, Susannah
and eleven-year-old Rachel, a sight calculated to stir gentry
sympathies in Judge Twisden, who 'set a stool and a cushion for her
to sit upon' and had the Fell girls 'plucked ... up' from behind the
bar to sit in proximity to his benignly paternalistic self.

Margaret's tactics, after the daughter-flaunting entrance,
involve a parade of rank and patronage. She asserts that she has
been promised immunity by the king himself, 'from his own
mouth, that he would not hinder me of my religion'. Quoting
verbatim, she seeks to daunt the court by the fact of her intimacy
with majesty. '"God forbid" (said he) "that I should hinder you of
your religion, you may keep it in your own house"'.[65] When this
fails, she dominates by demanding to address the jury. Forbidden,
she speaks anyway:

> Judge: The jury is here to hear nothing, but me to tender
>   you the oath, and you to refuse it or take it.
> Margaret Fell: You will let me have the liberty that other
>   prisoners have, and she turned to the jury and said
>   ... Friends I am here today on account of my
>   conscience and not for any evil or wrong done to
>   any man ... Christ commands me not to swear at
>   all. (p6)

Twisden deplores Mrs Fell's everlasting tongue. 'Will you take the
oath or no?'

Margaret refuses to say 'no', and she is certainly not going to
say 'yes'. She talks over the judge, explaining to the jury that she is
only there because of her conscience. She nimbly treads the path of
honest prevarication, sidestepping thus:

'Will you take the Oath of Allegiance?'

'I have already said that I owe allegiance and obedience to the king.'

'This is no answer; will you take the oath or will you not take it?'

'I say I owe allegiance and obedience unto Christ Jesus, who commands me not to swear.'

'I say unto you that's no answer, will you take it or will you not take it?'

'If you should ask me never so often ...'

'... will you take the Oath? We must not spend time.'

Margaret gives a pithy resumé of her history of oath-taking up to the present moment. 'I never gave an oath in my life, I have spent my days thus far, and I never took an oath ...'

The clerk's arm wilts as he stands there tendering the Bible and asking her to oblige by removing her gloves. Margaret's impeccably gloved hands disdain the invitation to break half a century's custom.

'I never laid my hand on the book to swear in all my life, and I never was at this Assize before ...'

This being her history to date, she does not care, she confides, if she never hears an oath read in her life, since they grieve the Lord (pp6–7).

Margaret is removed from the court. In clumps George and refuses to take off his hat. Discussion of hats commences.

Twisden has Margaret appear again, and attempts to ease her out of her catastrophic situation by legal advice: 'I would do you all the favour I can'; but Margaret stands rootfast.

Fox and Fell remain in Lancaster Castle until the next Assizes in August: Judge Turner, Baron of the Exchequer, is confronted by Margaret with two of her commonwealth of daughters, Susannah and Rachel, presented by the mother as living emblems of her integrity: 'I am clear and innocent of wronging any man upon the earth, as my little child that stands by me here.'

Turner, unimpressed by this display of family values, engages with Mrs Fell's notorious tongue, which objects to the interventions of her old enemy, Colonel Kirkby and the sheriff in the trial, scolding them as she might her own children, 'Let us have no whispering.' She also takes the opportunity to put in a strong protest against the atrocious prison conditions at the Castle.

When the savage sentence of 'praemunire'[66] is passed against her, confiscating Margaret's entire property and imprisoning her for life as an outlaw, an official non-person, Margaret's riposte is predictably impressive: '"Although I am out of the King's Protection, yet I am not out of the protection of the Almighty God."'

Rain, wind and snow lashed into the dungeons at Lancaster Castle, so that 'in the winter time it is not fit for neither beasts nor dogs to lie in'.[67] Smoke choked her lungs. Hardy and spartan, she was proud to be 'worthy to suffer'. The praemunire was waived, and she remained in prison for four years on this occasion.

Eleven years after Judge Fell's death, the 55-year-old widow married George Fox at Bristol. For nearly two decades Fox and Fell had stood together as 'nursing father' and 'nursing mother' of a movement now numbering tens of thousands. Disparity in age and rank fuelled the sexual scandal that had haunted their association, and now climaxed in the suggestion that Margaret bore Fox's stillborn baby at this period. If Margaret's age seems to rule this out, it is not impossible that the partners may have nourished a belief in the mystical conception of a baby that never came. Shrewd and astute as they were, they lived with a sense of miraculous vocation, in a world shimmering with apocalyptic possibilities. Figures of biblical stature, they would not have deemed God incapable of creating in Margaret a new Sarah, the 'mother of nations' who bore Isaac when Abraham was a hundred years old and she herself well beyond the menopause (Genesis 17–21). Francis Bugg, venomous scandal-monger, recorded the rumour of a false pregnancy, for which the deluded aged couple prepared 'baby-clouts' and called in a midwife, 'but there came nothing forth, all proved wind'.[68]

Fox explained the marriage as a symbol of the church's restoration to perfection. He flinched from the suggestion that it had anything to do with sex or procreation, which he fastidiously proclaimed to be 'below me'. Sexuality may have been a painful problem area for the austere Fox.

Certainly the marriage was not distinguished by its intimacy. No sooner were they married, than they separated. 'Then, within

ten days after, I came homewards,' Margaret tells us. Fox carried on
turning the world upside down. They were to spend far more time
apart than together, as anomalous in marriage as in single life:

> And though the Lord had provided an outward habitation
> for him, yet he was not willing to stay at it, because it was
> so remote and far from London, where his service most lay.
> And my concern for God, and his holy eternal truth, was
> then in the North ... so that we were very willing, both of
> us, to live apart for some years upon God's account ... And
> if any took occasion, or judged hard of us because of that,
> the Lord will judge them; for we were innocent.

Margaret Fox had her own calling and work. It differed not at all
from that of Margaret Fell.

Margaret's fortitude and stamina never lessened. Her
penultimate journey to London was made at the age of seventy-six
in 1690, the last time she ever saw her husband, 'for he lived but
about half a year after I left him'.[69] She rode on horseback across
the treacherous sands of the Leven and Morecambe, where once
her enemies met her first husband with news of Fox's takeover of
the Judge's household. At Lancaster she hired a coach to London:
an immense journey for an elderly woman. Fox had lived to see the
Toleration Act passed in 1689, giving limited religious freedom
and emancipating Quakers from the worst of their nobly borne
sufferings. She survived him by twelve years, making a final
journey to London at the age of eighty-three, to die at Swarthmoor
in 1702 aged eighty-eight.

Into her eighties, Margaret remained a militant controversialist. She bridled at the Quaker uniform that was coming in as
the movement began to retrench and segregate itself from worldly
vanity. She saw the grey costume, and the taboo on the wearing of
coloured, floral or striped fabric, or silk, as in itself a form of
ostentation. The octogenarian spoke up roundly for 'Gospel
freedom' of dress and was shocked at the holier-than-thou, police-
our-sister spirit springing up amongst second generation woman
Friends, who censured extravagant tying of handkerchiefs at the
breast, hoods with long tabs, powdering of hair and skirts shorter
than was holy.

With her old salt and bite, she mimicked this deadening spirit of reproach: 'But we must be all in one dress, and one colour. This is a silly poor Gospel. It is more fit for us to be covered with God's eternal Spirit, and clothed with his eternal Light,'[70] a unisex garment everyone could proudly wear.

Margaret Fox is buried at Sunbreck burial ground, on the edge of Birkrigg Common, between rough stone walls, above the fell that sweeps down to the dazzle of Morecambe Bay. Beautifully the Early Friends lie together, unmarked by headstones, at one with each another beneath the simple grass.

11

ANNA'S TRUMPET BLASTS THE QUAKERS
ANNA TRAPNEL IN THE LATE 1650S

What did Anna Trapnel, the vessel of the Voice, make of the Quakers? What did Friends make of Anna?

For Anna sang on throughout the 1650s. The Lord's vociferous handmaiden was brave enough, after the trauma of Bridewell, to persevere with her agenda of Fifth Monarchist defiance; nor, with time, did Anna's energies run low. Quite the contrary. She was canvassing in Wales in 1656, and was said to be meditating an excursion to the Continent. Perhaps the baptism by total immersion which she seems to have undergone on leaving prison refreshed her inner being. Perhaps the rival claim of the now swarming Quakers to intimacy with the Spirit fuelled her campaign.

Anna is known to have sung for a week in February; for three days and nights in October, 1657; four in December, continuing straight through into January 1658. A five-day opus in March. In full voice through the second half of June, and off again in the first week of August.[1] Her shorthand-taker scribbled down all he could make out. Droves crammed in to catch the newest news from the Almighty, including gaggles of Quakers, curious but on the riled side of sceptical. The public tendency to equate them with Fifth Monarchists because of their personal and sometimes ecstatic acquaintance with the Spirit, as well as contempt for merely human law, aroused their bale.

Ironically, a folio book of nearly one thousand pages in the Bodleian used to be labelled *Quaker Poems*. Anna and Friends would have been equally livid. For the everlasting doggerel which burbles down these leaves is excruciatingly recognisable as Anna's: the handmaiden who had been tuning up now for nearly a decade and a half, as she advertised in one verse:

> O Spirit, poor Instrument hath found
> Thee a very constant friend ...
> Poor Instrument hath found thee, Lord,
> For fourteen years together.[2]

Stressing seniority, Anna was driving home to the callow Quakers that she came before them, was preferred to them, and expected to be the songster of the New Jerusalem.

As Anna's amanuensis records, the Quakers kept trying to interrupt, but without success, 'for with more power and swiftness the Voice went on'. Bear in mind that these Quakers were seasoned interrupters, with heckling skills second to none, and you get some sense of the power of Anna's song to swell and hurtle – timely accelerations that brought the secretary new problems, which the Voice gently chided:

> O brother dear, then learn now
> To be more nimble in your Pen
> To take this matter, and how,
> In what manner it doth come down.

She wondered in her trance, 'Why are you brethren so dull/In taking the Spirit's matter?', marvelling at their inability to keep up with the speeding quills of the 'weaker sex'.

Quaker visitors were unimpressed with Anna's performance.

They came in batches, and listened with patience to the prophetess's utterances. On one occasion, three men sat down and listened for two hours, at the end of which stint they:

> spake against the truth at the Name of Christ, and election; then the Voice answered their several objections, which were in the psalm: they said, 'We were told she could neither hear nor see, and yet she answers our words, and knows we are in the room, and names me one in the room'.

The Quaker men seem to have done Anna the courtesy of attending seriously, and led off by taking theological issue with the notion of the elect. But when the prophetess, allegedly dead to the world, entered into debate, they labelled her a cheap fraud and, the scribe went on, began to slander the Fifth Monarchy. God was not having this and imparted to Anna 'a louder voice, that did drown this; and so swift, that the writer could not take [down] all'. This bellowing eruption was too much for the tympanums of the Quakers, who were 'not able to tarry in the room' but departed 'raging' and routed. On she went. And on. She pounded Cromwell. Army. Crowns. She praised baptism by total immersion. Violently attacked her fellow Fifth Monarchist Venner for his violence; lavished praise on fellow revolutionaries Tillinghast and the late John Pendarves. Trounced libraries:

> Thou shalt not run to Antichrist's libraries,
> To fetch from thence any skill
> To read the Revelation of Christ,
> But be with knowledge filled.[3]

There is only one known copy of this last surviving odyssey of chant before her tremendous tongue lost its echo: 'Antichrist's Library' has tenderly preserved it for us.

12

QUAKER WOMEN ON THE ROAD
BARBARA BLAUGDONE, KATHARINE EVANS & SARAH CHEVERS, MARY FISHER, MARY DYER, JOAN DANT

Passers-by catching sight of the woman dossing in the disused pig-trough near Bridgwater, Somerset, probably gave her little thought. Female vagrants may often have found that trough a Godsend as they traipsed from parish to parish. They would have identified her as one of the mass of pregnant girls abandoned; wives tracking absconded mates; 'vagrant whore'; Irish refugee or out-of-work labourer.

In time of housing crisis and a crashing economy, paupers inhabited vaults, holes and caves in Coventry. John Evelyn, the diarist, records seeing cave-dwellers in Nottingham. Some vagrants, glad of sheep pens to shelter in, huddled to the fleecy warmth of their fellow creatures, and were ejected by magistrates.[1]

In fact the pig-trough dosser was a respected Bristol schoolteacher – or rather, had been respected until she embraced the call to take up residence with the poor and despised in barns, ditches and lock-ups. Barbara Blaugdone was amongst the golden harvest gathered at Bristol in September 1654 by Quaker missionaries, northerners John Camm and John Audland, at emotional mass-meetings where, shedding silk, ribbons and silver, hundreds opted out of a consumerist culture. When the ex-linen-draper Audland, twenty-four years old, a bonny, pink-complexioned man, went into ecstasies 'like a woman in travail', declaring spiritual war on the modern world, Bristol Seekers wept and quaked. Numbers at meetings were staggering: 500, 2000, 3000. Broadmead Baptist Church lost a quarter of its members, including Dennis Hollister, who donated his orchard as a meeting-place.[2] A vast spiritual awakening shook Bristol; followed by riots and conflict.

Into that orchard stepped genteel Barbara Blaugdone. One of the great pioneers of her day, she was to be on the move for nearly half a century. She tells her story in a little book entitled *An Account of the Travels, Sufferings and Persecutions of Barbara Blaugdone*, unequalled for the bold brevity of its telling. The auto-biography was published in 1691. By this time, Quaker men had chillingly erected an apparatus for censoring preaching and writing, to depoliticise and sober the visionary element in the movement. Women especially were muzzled. In 1689 the all-male Second Day Morning Meeting disallowed two of Blaugdone's works but let through this incendiary travelogue, told in the no-nonsense, brusquely matter-of-fact style of one who has gone out for a walk ... but never come back.

Barbara was an independent, self-supporting woman, whose assertion of faith swiftly deprived her of job and livelihood. In her new plain clothes she flaunted contempt for her employers' gentility and 'thou'd them as equals. She:

> willingly took up the Cross, and yielded obedience unto it, in plainness of speech and in my habit: & the people were so offended with it, when I went into their public places and steeple-houses to speak, that they took away their children from me, so that I lost almost all my employment, and they kept me in prison a quarter of a year at a time: and great was my sufferings in that day.[3]

Conditioned in feminine timidity, Barbara backed away from the inner imperative to speak her own truth and be corporately howled down, pitched out, locked up: 'his Spirit strove much with me, before I could open my mouth ... for I was neither hasty nor forward' (p9). Slowly but surely, 'the Lord gave me dominion': overcoming her shyness, Barbara trained herself in public speaking, 'till I could go into other places, and say what I had to say, and come forth again quietly.'

Barbara's story shows how Quaker women's radical action was felt to threaten public order. It involved vagrant, 'whorish' behaviour. Barbara's rebellion took her into the realm of hunger, outlawry and disrepute. She became a vegetarian and gave up wine and beer, drinking only water for a whole year – in an age when wine and beer were staple drinks from childhood. If prolonged fasting tempered and exalted the spirit, rejection of superfluous foods also aligned her with the mass of the poor. The staple diet of husbandmen was dark bread (adulterated with peas, beans, oats or acorns), cheese, cider or beer and milk. They got little bacon and could not afford beef. West Country people, man, woman and child, drank a quart of beer or cider a day. Fasting, often seen as a Quaker fetish, actually set them beside the mass of have-nots, whose acquaintance Friends made in the gaols of England, and whose cause they were to plead through the centuries.

There was an enraged grassroots backlash in Bristol. A mob of apprentice lads stood ever ready to manhandle and pelt with stones and dirt such church-disturbers as Barbara's fellow Bristolean, Elizabeth Marshall. Alderman Camm sanctioned and exploited yob-violence by encouraging rioters to thrash her with 'staves and cudgels'.[4] The same popular aggression against women that gained outlet in scold-ducking, skimmington-riding and watching loose women flogged, was unleashed against the Quaker women who 'ran naked (or semi-naked, in sackcloth) for a sign'. Quaker men and women did this in emulation of the Old Testament prophets, witnessing against pride and apostasy: but the 'sign' was read as a lewd sexual gesture when performed by women, and provoked violent reaction. In Bristol, Sara Goldsmith was moved by God to:

> put on a coat of sackcloth of hair next her, to uncover her head, and to put earth thereon, with her hair hanging down about her, and without any other clothes upon her, except shoes on her feet; and in that manner to go to every gate, and through every street within the walls of the city, and afterwards to stand at the High Cross ... as a sign against the Pride of Bristol ... very cross to her own will.

Well-nigh lynched, she was hauled before the authorities, outraged at her immodest and 'mad' get-up. A debate about what constituted outrageous clothes ensued. '"If I had appeared in gay clothing, then you would not have been troubled,"' she pointed out.[5] Bishop adds that 'Had Sarah Goldsmith appeared in the fantastic dress of this vain & wanton age, or in a spirit of lightness and haughtiness', she would have been thought highly acceptable. Quaker women were sinners not only against female modesty but conspicuous consumption.

The 'Inner Light' licensed in austere Quaker women an aggressive exhibitionism which seemed indistinguishable from the rare but spectacular cases of 'unruly women' of uproariously bawdy character: Mary Combe, for instance, an innkeeper's wife, who'd fish for men's genitals in their breeches and, lying down on the highway between Axbridge and Crosse, halloo passers-by 'by spreading her legs abroad saying: "Come play with my cunt and make my husband a cuckold"'. Mary organised a drinking-orgy in 1653 to which only cuckolds and cuckold-makers were invited, and made it her custom to pull up her skirts and bestride a man of choice; wander round the roads naked and make obscene suggestions to affront the godly.[6] Such women obviously had enormous popular appeal, defying feminine norms in the name of carnival sensuality. Quaker streakers (who often hated doing it) defied sexual norms with an anti-patriarchal agenda incomprehensible to the public.

Public reaction to Quaker women's anomalies often took a murderous character. Barbara Blaugdone and Mary Prince, coming arm-in-arm from a meeting at George Bishop's house, were assailed by a man who came roaring at them; struck off Mary's hat; thrust a knife 'into the side of my belly, which if it had gone but a little farther, it might have killed me' (p10). Thick wadding of smock and petticoat-layers saved Barbara from serious abdominal injury. The two shocked women measured up to the bloodiness of the hatred their pacific militancy had unleashed. Arm-in-arm they moved away, to part company, Mary for America, Barbara to Devon.

Prison sentence followed prison sentence – in Marlborough, Molton, Barnstaple and Bideford. The Earl of Bath's household, with whom Barbara had been on visiting terms and whose souls she now engaged to reach, showed less than hospitality. The servants set a 'wolf-dog' on Barbara, who must by this time have been looking and smelling very like a tramp, but, 'God's power' (perhaps through the medium of Barbara's magisterial voice), 'smote the dog, so that he whined, and ran in crying and very lame'. Unfazed by the canine welcome, God's gritty and ragged minister addressed the soul of the Countess of Bath who heard her out but pointedly refrained from inviting her in, 'although I had eat[en] and drank at her table many a time' (p13). The detail testifies to the headlong leap Barbara had voluntarily taken down the ladder of social respectability, from dinner-companion to down-and-out, to be queasily turned away at the gates.

At Exeter, Barbara was imprisoned with gypsies. Romanies, distinguished by swarthy complexions and earrings, an alternative society with their own language, were treated as vagrants and suspected as thieves.[7] The eye-opening nature of the experience is evident: Barbara and her fellow middle-class travellers mingled with castes of persons dismissed as subhuman by the elite. She seems to have recoiled at the realisation of how she was now perceived, before coming to terms with her chosen status.

But Barbara was worse than a gypsy. She was read as a gender threat. At Exeter, in a private room the following day, the sheriff and beadle:

whipped me till blood ran down my back, and I never started at a blow ... and sang aloud; and the Beadle said, *Do ye sing; I shall make ye cry by and by*; and with that he laid

more stripes, and laid them on very hard ... Ann Speed was
an eye witness of it. and she stood and looked in at the
window and wept bitterly. (pp15–16)

The whipping was an act of quivering power-lust; a lust Barbara
was proud to disappoint. The Beadle's imploring rod drooped,
balked of conquest. Exaltation surged in Barbara: she would not
have been dismayed, she says, to have been whipped to death. Total
resistance rang along her nerves and sang off her tongue, and a
sense of glory filled her as she turned her back on the whip. Cynics
classed the Quaker rhapsody of physical pain with sexual
perversity: Samuel Butler's 'A Quaker ... delights in persecution, as
some old extravagant fornicators find a lechery in being whipped.'[8]
To Barbara the hieroglyphic wounds on her back wrote her into a
proud tradition of female Protestant witness reaching back to the
resistance of Anne Askew on the rack and pyre, the 'heretic'
showing the weakness of the impotent State.[9]

The penalties Friends incurred, foreign to the gentry, were all
too familiar to the vagrant underclass: pedlars, tinkers, ex-soldiers
and mariners, entertainers, unlicensed healers and fortune-tellers,
the drifting unemployed. Flogging, courted and construed by
Friends as heroism, was endured by the poor as a brutal norm. It is
chastening to reflect that Nayler's whipping, boring through the
tongue, and branding were judged extreme, like the ear-chopping
of Burton, Bastwick and Prynne, because such punishments were
almost exclusive to the lower orders. As Major Audley laconically
reminded Parliament: 'It is an ordinary punishment for swearing, I
have known twenty bored through the tongue.'[10]

*

Ann Speed washed and dressed Barbara's bloody back. Both
women were harried out of Exeter, trailed by the Beadle for two
miles. As soon as he had abandoned pursuit, Barbara and Ann
doubled back and re-entered Exeter to visit their fellow prisoners.

Barbara's night in the pig-trough was followed by
imprisonment in Bideford, where her integrity so haunted the
mayor that he set her free and accompanied her some distance. At
their parting, after three or four miles, he was visibly moved when
she knelt at the roadside to pray for him. Let out of Marlborough

prison, she went back and convinced her judge, Isaac Burgess. Barbara's dogged pertinacity forced her back and back, retracing her steps to have another go. She would not and could not admit defeat.

The formidable, never-admit-defeat woman secured the release of two Quakers at Basingstoke, 'and thus the Lord made my journey prosperous' (p21).

Barbara's Devon journey, described decades after the events, seems to have been remembered haphazardly and not (like Fox's) from careful notes, to judge by the tipsily zigzag route she charts. In early 1656, she looked further west. She took ship from Bristol for Cork, a 250-mile journey, from which storms threw the ship a further 200 miles northwards to Dublin.

Before her lay Jonah-like seascapes, with storms, wrecks and deliverances. As the boat crashed through mountainous waves, the seamen knew who to blame: the solitary Quaker woman was a deviant who might well be a witch, hexing the voyage, 'and they conspired to fling me overboard' (p21). Ashamed to cower in the Master's cabin, she ventured on deck to pray aloud for the sailors' safety, which quietened them and roused favourable comparison with their priest huddled belowdecks.

Barbara disembarked at Dublin on the February day in 1656 on which Quaker pioneers Howgill and Burrough were banished from Ireland. She was entering and they were leaving a country of absolute and complex suffering, of which Quakers, like most other English people, had no understanding. Only seven years ago Cromwell had heinously avenged the 1641 rising by the bloodbaths of Drogheda and Wexford. Waves of land-grabbing English Protestant colonists had been eating Ireland alive for generations. Cromwell carried on the brutal 'transplantation' policy. Between 1652 and 1657, most Catholic landholders were uprooted and driven westward, their lands seized to fund the war and pay English soldiers. The remaining Catholic Irish, a pauperised peasantry, lived in squalid hovels beyond the Dublin enclave in a wolf-infested wilderness. Howgill classed them as 'robbers and murderers that lives in holes and bogs where none can pass'.[11] These bog-people were demonised by the English as whiskey-drinking, crucifix-wearing lay-abouts: non-persons.[12]

It was into this violent arena of complex, antagonistic agendas that Barbara Blaugdone disembarked in 1656. Howgill, Burrough and Elizabeth Fletcher had settled Meetings from Dublin to Cork and created mayhem in the English Army. Henry Cromwell, Commander-in-Chief of the Army in Ireland, saw Quaker agitators as a menace to military control of Ireland. As he wrote to Thurloe in the month of Barbara's arrival, 'their principles and practices are not very consistent with civil government, much less with the discipline of an army'.[13] Friends were arrested and sent packing.

Barbara Blaugdone went straight to Henry Cromwell amongst his princely retinue at his headquarters. When he joined her in the withdrawing room and sat down on a couch, she upbraided him for persecuting Quakers, suggesting a wait-and-see policy as not only pious but politic. '[If] it was of God, it would stand, but if of man it would fall.' Barbara, by now a seasoned disputant, spoke so trenchantly that Henry Cromwell repeatedly turned to his Independent minister, standing alongside, and 'would say, *There's for you Mr Harrison*' (p22). After Barbara had harangued him and gone, he was said to be listless and brooding, unable to bring himself to 'go to bowls nor to any other pastime'.[14] It must however be noted that the apathetic mood soon wore off.

Barbara pressed on to Cork, her militancy provoking violence and imprisonment:

> And I was in jeopardy of my life several times, but the Lord prevented it. And I was made to speak in a market-place, and there was a butcher swore he would cleave my head in twain, and had his cleaver up to do it, but there came a woman behind him and caught back his arms, and stayed them till the soldiers came and rescued me.(p27)

All Barbara's life that enraged butcher would be frozen in tableau, rearing over her with his blade suspended; restrained by her fellow woman. In Cork, Barbara had kin. Or rather, once had kin. Appalled at her way of addressing them, 'in so solemn and awful a manner that her speech caused them to tremble', they rejected her as a witch, running away when they saw her coming or having their servants drag her out of their houses along the stones.

A communal sigh of relief was exhaled when Barbara took ship back to Bristol.

When she returned (because Barbara always did return), the ship broke up.

In a powerful scene, Barbara was 'ordered by God' to stay aboard until everyone else had left. She stayed in the cabin, where 'the waves beat in upon me in abundance, almost ready to stifle me' (p29), then clambered up on deck and, taking a flying leap, became entangled in ropes. At this moment, the ship lurched back. Barbara escaped being crushed, and was saved providentially, of course. But her God was a no-nonsense God. The account is sparing, matter-of-fact. Barbara got on with the job.

In Dublin Gaol, the straw on the ground where she slept was saturated with overflowed faeces when it rained. The putrid water ran in under her back. Barbara coped.

Limerick could only be reached by boat. Piracy flourished round the exposed southern coast, where captured travellers sometimes found themselves sold into slavery. English women were especially prized, as realising high prices in the Mediterranean slave markets.[15] Barbara's boat was duly boarded by pirates, 'and I began to consider, whether there was any service for me to do among those rude people, but I found little to them' (p37). The pirates' Inner Light seemed to dictate that they relieve Barbara of the coat on her back. Cold but unfazed, Barbara escaped.

She would like us to take note that she always paid her way in her travels. An independent, self-supporting, straight-talking woman is answerable to none in this world. And Barbara refrains from going into harrowing detail, abridging her account of her sufferings, 'which I forbear to mention, being not willing to be over-tedious'.

*

It is difficult to assess what, beyond heroic witness, Barbara Blaugdone achieved in Ireland. Quakers did not come to Ireland, any more than did the Cromwellian administration, with a view to comprehending the spiritual and political condition of the nation: they came to change it. When George Fox visited Ireland in 1669, no sooner had he landed than his nose literally twitched at the unEnglish smell of the '"corruption of the nation ... the blood and the massacres and the foulness"'.[16] By now there were about thirty groups in Leinster, Ulster and Munster, which Fox helped the apostle of Irish Quakerism, William Edmondson, formally to settle. Edmondson had named one of his daughters Hindrance and his youngest son Trial. Hindrances and trials were turned to profit by patience and industry. Friends prospered in Ireland, becoming (so to speak) the soul of the mercantile community, especially in the textile trade, because of their principled fair dealing. Ironically, second generation Friends escaped serious persecution, as members of the Protestant Ascendency, weathering the turbulence leading up to the 'Glorious Revolution' and the Battle of the Boyne.

Prosperity brought its own uneasy problems. Friends had acquired property and influence through the colonial theft of Ireland from the Irish. Now they saw their thrift, integrity and prudent hard work blessed by riches. To check conspicuous consumption, Irish Friends evolved strict rules and discipline for members, who policed one another for signs of being 'guzzling drinkers', smokers of unholy tobacco, or gadding girls accompanying travelling women ministers for a lark. They denounced one another's hairstyles, ruling that males with hair of their own cease to shear it and adorn their pates with 'great ruffling periwigs'.[17]

It was not precisely the vision that had animated Barbara Blaugdone in her pig-trough.

*

To Quaker travellers, friendship mattered more than any relationship save their bond to God. Two-by-two, they hiked, rode or sailed from continent to continent, gaol to gaol. Katharine Evans and Sarah Chevers were the epitome of the friendship ideal, heroic in their tender solidarity in the jaws of the Papal Inquisition. Subjected to comparable pressure, other Friends might suffer nervous breakdowns, as did John Perrot, held by the Inquisition at Rome. Katharine and Sarah remained obdurately sane during their three-year incarceration on the island of Malta. When Friends came to deliver them, they were found to be knitting.

Whatever they did and experienced was done and experienced together.

To Katharine, writing to her husband and children, whom

she abandoned for her pilgrimage, Sarah is 'My dear and faithful Yoke-Fellow, Sister and Friend'. *Yoke-fellow?* – the term has reverberations at once biblical and marital. The primary human bond is now with female friend, not husband. 'O my dear Husband!' exclaims Katharine, 'praise the Lord that ever thou hadst a wife that was found worthy to suffer for the name of the Lord.'[18] The love bonding the two women breathes throughout their joint account of their experiences in Malta, *A Short Relation of some of the Cruel Sufferings*, written in prison and published in 1662, the year before their release. It is a unique testament of resistance by two tough women, of immense corporate will-power and mutual trust, each of whom felt that she did not wish to survive without the other.

They had proved themselves as itinerant preachers in Scotland, the Isle of Man, Ireland and England. In 1655 or 1656, Katharine was deported from the Isle of Man, being hustled out of bed and onto a ship by a soldier before she was well awake. She had been stripped and flogged in Salisbury marketplace. Thus tempered, the two women felt called to sail the same route as the Apostle Paul around the Mediterranean. It is amusing to read William Braithwaite's staid account of the women's expedition, which he describes in *The Beginnings of Quakerism*. He identifies them as 'Katharine Evans, wife of John Evans, of English Batch, near Bath, and Sarah Chevers, wife of Henry Chevers, of Slaughterford, in Wiltshire'.[19] We do not ask who a woman is but rather to whom she belongs, runs the adage. Braithwaite repeats the assumptions of the Inquisitorial friars who detained the two women in that Malta hellhole, demanding their husbands' and parents' names, only to be informed that 'We were servants of the living God, and were moved to come and call them to repentance' (p7). Katharine and Sarah were married in the deepest sense to one another, in the Light. When the women eventually did return home to the bosom of their families, off they sped again, to spread their message in Scotland, Wales and Ireland.

These female Pauls were determined to make Alexandria. Leaving Plymouth, they underwent a stormy journey to Leghorn, and thence (as a stopping-off post for Cyprus) to Malta, where the Consul and his wife betrayed them to the Papal Inquisition, operating in the island through the Knights Hospitallers, a military-religious order of the Roman Catholic Church. In this classic encounter, Counter-Reformation is arrayed against Reformation; southern European against northern; male against female. The friars have not a clue what the women mean by what they say. To them, the women seem mad. To the women, the friars seem mad.

How do you know your inspiration comes from God? the friars ask Sarah. She experiences his Living Presence, she replies.

Is your 'GF' a sort of rival Pope? they wonder. They have heard of 'GF' as a Quaker-in-Chief, and can only conceive of religious leadership as a pontificate.

'"No; The Lord did move us to come."' The idea of personal authority speaking conclusively within the self, without deference to human master, is at once incomprehensible and anathema to the interrogators.

Katharine weeps when she realises the Consul's wife has sold them out. People do not come out of these places alive.

The party of Inquisitors is a motley crew by the two women's English standards. On the second day, a magistrate, two friars, a man bearing a black rod, a scribe and a keeper all pile solemnly in to examine them separately.

We are born of the spirit, they tell the friars, who stare bemused. Our blood will be on your hands, they warn. The six men pile out again, pointing out that 'It was impossible we could live long in that hot room' (p16).

The furnace-heat is indeed literally killing. Katharine's mind seems to boil in her skull, as her body sickens: 'I was in a very great agony, so that sweat was as drops of blood' (p17). From the fever flame visions of death and resurrection.

The returning Inquisitor thinks she's beginning to break. '"Nay,"' says Katharine, '"my body is weak because I eat no meat".' He will give her meat, he oozes; but she cannot eat. One sweating night, God gets the women out of bed: '"Arise, put on your clothes"'. They are to stand at the door. Here the 'power' comes upon them; quaking and dazzled, they scarcely know whether they are in or out of the body. The night fills with sinister sounds: gaolers clinking keys, rushings up and down in the pitch black.

Katharine lies for twelve days and nights ill and fasting, her bed drenched in sweat.

Sarah is suddenly not there. Instead, Katharine's bed is surrounded by menacing forms. Katharine maintains silence, not deigning to acknowledge their presence, midway perhaps between sick faint and spiritual trance. This is intolerable to the visitors. A friar jerks at Katharine's hand, saying, '"Is the Devil so great in you that you cannot speak?"' (p19).

'Depart from me thou worker of iniquity, I know thee not. The power of the Lord is upon me, and thou call'st him Devil.'
He took his crucifix to strike me in the mouth and I said, 'Look here!' (p19)

She denounces his crucifix; affirms her own authority. The friar commands her obedience and again raises his crucifix as a weapon. Katharine caustically points out that, to her knowledge, the Apostles did not go around assaulting folk with crucifixes.

She ought to be grateful, he pouts, that he has brought along a doctor to see to her health. I have my own personal doctor, God, she ripostes, and I don't need yours. 'He said I should be whipped and quartered and burned that night in Malta, and my mate, too.'

She advises him not to bother trying to scare her. God will judge him.

The friar smartingly sulks to Sarah, telling her Katharine has called him 'worker of iniquity'.

'"Did she?"' replies Sarah blandly. '"Art thou without sin."'
'"I am."'
'"Then she hath wronged thee,"' replies Sarah with irony lost on the smug friar. Then, within tongue-in-cheek brackets, Katharine slips to us this wry comment: '(But I say the wise reader may judge)' (p20).

Drumbeats. Incomprehensible proclamation at the prison gates. Four in the morning: a drum and a gun and a party approaching their door.

God breathes the message into Sarah: '"Arise out of thy grave-clothes"': she stumbles up, expecting to be killed. The women stand together and wait.

The noises withdraw.

Katharine is so ill 'that my dear fellow-labourer in the work of God, did look every hour when I should depart the body ... [and] when we should be brought to the stake' (p21). For weeks they live in hourly expectation of death.

You will never come out of this room alive, taunt the friars who seek to frighten Sarah with the thought that 'thousands of devils ... would fetch my soul to hell'. Sarah, master of the laconic retort, assures them she has no such fears. Her sharp answers cause the friar to fall down on his knees and 'howl' in frustration, to the women's jubilation. The physician is also out of temper with Sarah at her refusal to bow to him as her superior.

Inklings of hunger creep into Katharine's stomach. She tries to keep up her fast, but, to her relief, her physician (the God Within) advises a little nourishment.

Visions come: apocalyptic, earth-shaking, the entire Book of Revelation brought to life in that fetid cell. Katharine tells of the darkening of the sun, the moon turning to blood and the stars falling down the heavens as if the cosmos were contained in those four walls. The woman clothed with the sun and with the moon at her feet appears. The Beast of the Apocalypse. The Last Trumpet blasts into the two women's mindspace, the War of Heaven plays itself out, and Pharaoh's armies are drowned in the Red Sea. If we imagine it as some epic film projected on to the walls of the prison, perhaps we can spy into the lurid and dynamic colour of that vision, born of sensory deprivation, the effects of hunger and transcendent faith. The two women feed on these God-sent visions, interpreting their present incarceration, superficially an abject loss of freedom and face, as central to a historical process in which they play epic parts.

Katharine is keenly aware of Sarah's sympathetic pains, for 'my dear sister in Christ was in as great affliction as I ... to see my strong travail night and day ... [she] would willingly have given me up to death, that I might have been at rest' (p25). Katharine hates to think what would be Sarah's predicament, left alone without her support amongst these tormentors.

They can't for the life of them conceive why, whenever the friars visit, they have a doctor in tow: '"Do you keep us in this hot room to kill us, and bring us a physician to make us alive?"'

The heat is more than they can bear. At night they crawl to a chink at the door, the only ventilation. They long for day but when day comes, they await darkness. Parched and weeping, they dream of death. 'And with the fire within, and the heat without, our skin was like sheep's leather and the hair did fall off our heads' (p26).

They write a protest to the Inquisitor. He replies by having their inkwells confiscated.

Their Bibles have already been taken.

Why?

The women's property and lives now belong to the Inquisition.

Why?

Because you brought out books and papers to Malta.

But if there was anything untrue in the papers disseminated, you could write against it.

We scorn to write to fools and asses that do not know true Latin.

Nothing more clearly exemplifies the gulf between Reformation and Roman minds. The friars assume the fixity and centralisation of Truth, which it is blasphemy to question. Books are proscribed and the Bible may not be read by individuals in their native language. The women belong to a culture of free dispute, whereby Truth is proved by open debate, Milton's 'Let [Truth] and Falsehood grapple; who ever knew Truth put to the worse, in a free and open encounter?'.[20] Nearly two decades after Milton's defence of freedom of speech and press, Katharine and Sarah have the naïveté and nerve to introduce the Papal Inquisition to the democracy of pen and ink. The riposte with which the friars attempt to squelch them (the women's ignorance of the Latin of international dispute) reminds us not only of Quaker contempt for learning but English Protestantism's insistence on the dignity of English. *A Short Relation* was popular in England not only among Friends: it spoke to a larger Protestant constituency, going into several editions of the expanded version in the early eighteenth century. It should be recognised as a classic Reformation English text – ironically written at a period when the ideal of free expression had been smashed in England. Anti-Catholic propaganda, however, never went out of fashion.

*

The friars hatched new ideas for controlling the women. Since Katharine was so ill, and Sarah in reasonable health, it made sense, they felt, for Katharine to be isolated in a cooler room.

> I took her by the arm and said, 'The Lord hath joined us together, and woe be to them that should part us.' I said I rather choose to die there with my friend than to part from her. He was smitten and went away and came no more in five weeks and the door was not opened in that time. Then they came again to part us, but I was sick and broken out from head to foot. They sent for a doctor and he said we must have air or else we must die ... [The Inquisitor] gave order for the door to be set open six hours in a day. They did not part us till ten weeks after ... Death itself had been better than to have parted in that place. (p27)

Katharine's statement of allegiance to Sarah follows Christ's language when he spoke to the Pharisees against divorce:

> For this cause shall a man leave father and mother, and shall cleave to his wife: and they twain shall be one flesh ... What therefore God hath joined together, let not man put asunder. (Matthew 19:3–4)

Katharine and Sarah, arm in arm, claimed to be bound under the marriage vow in a union both sacramental and infrangible. But each had left a human husband behind in England for a life of mutual dedication. Katharine cites but reinterprets Scripture according to the priority of spirit over letter. In their devotion they seem to stand on the rim of the grave of separation: 'Death itself had been better ...' It is misleading to gloss this as 'perhaps, a lesbian relationship',[21] which is irrelevant to same-sex friendship among first generation apostolic Friends. The love they expressed and lived was biblical in compass and quality: theirs was the union of David with Jonathan, Ruth with Naomi, an intense form of that oneness in Christ experienced by all Friends. When Howgill left Burrough in Dublin in 1655, Burrough wrote to Margaret Fell that his eyes are 'full of tears, for I am separated outwardly from my dear beloved brother ... my right-hand man'.[22] The difference for women couples lay in their subversion of the gender code that subordinated wives to husbands.

Parting indeed proved challenging but, because their union was in the spirit, physical distance could not sunder them. Katharine boasts that 'they found we were more stronger afterwards than we were before' (p27).

Other expedients suggested themselves to the friars' minds. Would the women care for some of these flagellants' hemp scourges? Their offer was spurned.

*

The worst came about: the two women were parted: '"You will never see one another's faces again."' Weeks of hunger in solitary confinement passed. Katharine's famishing face met the visiting friar, who asked what she wanted. '"One to wash my linen, and something hot to eat; I am weak"' (p31). Sarah agreed to do her friend's washing, and by fiddling the laundry arrangements, Katharine and Sarah kept the lifeline between them open, amusedly proud to rival the Jesuits for cunning.

Friars flitted between the women, urging conversion. Sarah cracked her fingers in their faces. Pull her joint from joint, she taunted them, she would not break under torture.

'Two very good hens' were the next bait (pp35–6). Katharine devoured the tempting chickens with starving eyes, but refused to accept them, since it was the Friends' principle to be independent of alms. The friar considered it ungracious of her to reject the Inquisitorial hens. His everlasting crucifix was being poked at her again. Accept it. Katharine enquired as to whether Daniel in the Lion's Den needed a crucifix, or Jonah in the whale's belly.

> He stood up and opened his mouth; and *I* stood up to him, and denied him ... and said, he had no power over me. And away he went to Sarah with the hens, and told her, that I was sick, and I would be glad to eat a piece of one if Sarah would dress one of them presently, and the other tomorrow. (Mark this Deceiver, this Liar!) (p36)

Sarah repudiated the hens, with equal vehemence, and probably in the same words. The chickens landed in other stomachs.

The friars came two at a time to each woman, oscillating between threats and unction, to be told, "'The more you persecute us ... the more stronger we grow'". During a year's separation, Katharine had neither fire nor candle for more than two hours. Bait in the form of linen, wool, stockings, shoes and money was offered to the threadbare women.

Suddenly, to her astonishment, an Englishman's face appeared at Sarah's window, high above the street. He had been captured by the Turks, then captured from them by the Turks' enemy, the Maltese, and converted. Hauled down and imprisoned, he would (the friars gloated) be hanged.

Sarah worked out how to send Katharine secret messages. There was a special pleasure in hoodwinking the fools and asses, and aspersing them on paper. Katharine, touched by the Englishman's reaching-out to them, asked Sarah in her reply to try to supply him with daily food. To cheer her friend's spirits, she wrote of her joy in Christ and her absence of fear, prophesying safe return to England, and recounting a discussion she had had within her spirit with George Fox 'to my great refreshment' (p42).

When the friar broke their system and intercepted the letter, he was filled with bile; translated it into Italian and marched in with the Inquisitor's Lieutenant. The precious ink was removed.

However, the interception of the letter had done some good by vindicating the poor Englishman, who was released the following morning. Sarah was threatened with a halter. Her bed would be removed, her trunk, half her money ... even the friar's companions regretted his bilious pathology.

The friars were sometimes dumbstruck, to find the women deafeningly obeying God's instruction to '"LIFT UP YOUR VOICE LIKE A THE NOISE OF A TRUMPET"'.

*

After a year and seven months, money had run out. The Inquisitor's Chamberlain offered to buy their hats to raise funds. 'We said we came not there to sell our clothes, nor anything we had' (pp45–6). The two went on hunger-strike. 'We were weak, so that Sarah did dress her head as she would lie in her grave, poor lamb' (p47). There, in a semi-shroud, prepared for her end, Sarah lay, with her mate beside her, until starvation brought light-headed stillness, and it was unclear to the friars whether the women were alive at all. When they did eat, they retched.

'"You are foolish women,"' the friars said.

'"We are the Lord's fools, and the Lord's fools are right dear, and precious in his sight, and woe to them that do offend them."'

The friars were taken aback, since the tradition of the 'wise fool'[23] was an honourable one in their own church.

'"We are the Lord's fools too,"' flashed back the friar, not to be outdone, 'and showed us their deceitful gowns, and their shorn Crowns', saying, '"We do wear it for God's sake, to be laughed at by the world."'

This scene of farce is one of many easy laughs which Katharine's and Sarah's narrative milks from an English Protestant readership accustomed to ridiculing the bald pates of monks, 'ducking to one another with their shaven reverences', which, like the weird fashion of the Church of England prelates ('shrouds and tackle, with a geometrical rhomboid on their head'), caused onlookers to 'burst our midriffs rather than laugh', according to Milton.[24] Few English people had actually seen a monk or friar. Sarah and Katharine endorse a long tradition of satire through their first-hand mockery.

Katharine was to be sent to Rome. A chill went through her.

No, both were to be sent. The friar applied to go on ahead to the Holy See and be quit of visiting a witch like Katharine.

The hypocritical Consul, with his hand held out, offered a dollar.

'I said, "Thou art a condemned person and standest guilty before God; yet nevertheless repent ... "'

The Consul slipped the scribe a knowing grin, but Katharine noted quivering in his lip and belly; he seemed to be having trouble keeping upright. She had as good as cursed him. He couldn't help any of it, he bleated – could he? The ill-wishing he read in her face was consummated to her satisfaction when, having failed to honour even his trifling promise to supply them with pen and paper, he was 'consumed as a snail in the shell'. The next time they heard of him, he was dead (p53).

Five doors with locks separated Katharine and Sarah. Sarah experimented and, finding herself an adept lock-picker, picked her way through to a place where they could see one another, though not talk. The Lord moved Sarah to exercise her gifts yet further, so that she glided through to Katharine's very door. Caught and locked up, out she came again.

When an English boat was in the harbour, they intuited its presence. Captain Francis Steward of London and an Irish friar docked in Malta and petitioned for their release. The Captain met them with the Consul at the court-chamber, 'with tears in his eyes', saying that the Inquisition refused to release them because they would not promise to stop preaching when they came out. They were welcome to free passage with him. When he had gone, conditions worsened. The Inquisitor himself unnervingly climbed into a tower 'and looked down upon us as if he would have eaten us'. Weeks of privation ensued. Suddenly he was up there again, staring. Sarah called up, to have the doors opened: they needed to wash their clothes. Once a week this was allowed, and then every day.

'"Quake! Quake!"' bellowed mimicking mockers beneath the window. Katharine endured that.

Not so easy to bear was the statement by the 'enemy' 'that they had pressed my dear yoke-fellow with stones, which was a great trouble to me, because I did not suffer with her'. Katharine came to believe Sarah had indeed been killed, a lie that was replaced by another, that 'my (dear and faithful) yoke-fellow should be sent to Rome, and I should tarry at Malta' (p76). Now indeed Katharine's faith was shaken. Either God was harsh and unjust, or in some way she, Katharine, had failed to match her friend's integrity and was unworthy to accompany her mate to Rome. She refused sleep, this time not in resistance to the friars but to God himself, searching, demanding some answer.

She discovered that Sarah was alive, and still there.

Sarah now takes over the pen and the telling. After recalling the deportation threat, she describes Inquisitorial bafflement when the women, separated, replied to the same questions in identical words. 'They would go from me to Katharine, and they would bid her speak as Sarah did, and she did, to their condemnation. Praises to the Lord, Amen' (pp77–8). This identical twinning of voices and scripts stemmed not only from Katharine's and Sarah's human atunement, but also from Friends' agreed answers to given questions. In a real sense, these two bonded women were one woman – spirit of one Spirit. The story on the page before us, told by two voices in harmonious recitative, was also the story of a unified consciousness.

At last the friar conceived a genuine brainwave, suggesting they work for a living by knitting clothes for their fellow prisoners, and mending their tattered garments. In accepting, they pointed out however that they did so *not* at the friar's bidding but at the behest of the Inner Light. Permission to knit derived from the same source as the joint and single letters the book anthologises, to Inquisitor, friar, husbands, children, and to God himself, in their victorious hymns and verses composed in gaol. The total effect is of focus and energy, in seemingly unlimited supply.

Katharine and Sarah had left England in 1659. By 1662, prison must have come to seem a way of life. Returning from Smyrna in Turkey, their fellow Quaker, Daniel Baker, interceded for them with the Lord Inquisitor, offering (in the way of Friends) to be imprisoned in their place, 'then he offered to lay down his own dear precious life for our liberty. Greater love can no man have than to lay down his life for his friend,' Katharine wrote to her husband. The offer was refused, the Inquisitor promising that the women would die in prison unless a bond for 4000 dollars were given and a guarantee of non-return.

Ironically, it was through Roman Catholic intervention that Katharine and Sarah obtained their liberty. The Catholic Queen Mother, Henrietta Maria, had a priest in orders, Lord d'Aubigny, who obliged George Fox by exercising his influence on the Maltese authorities. The women reached home in an English frigate, late in 1662, after three and a half years in a time-warp. To their thanks, Lord d'Aubigny gently replied by hoping that 'when you pray to God you will remember me in your prayers'.[25]

*

Malta and Venice formed the boundaries of the 'civilised' world for English people of the seventeenth century. Beyond lay the Turkish Ottoman Empire posing a threat to the west both legendary and actual. In the popular mind, Turks were subhuman ('barbarians') and demonic (Islamic 'infidels'). The sultan was seen as the epitome of a bloodthirsty tyrant, who (as the traveller Fynes Moryson reported in his *Itinerary*), 'begin their tyrannical government with the cruel strangling of all their brothers'.[26] In 1658, the reigning sultan was the seventeen-year-old Mohammed IV, whose viziers had revived the military threat to Europe. It was to the sultan that Mary Fisher, an unmarried ex-serving maid in her mid-thirties, directed her path, a menial addressing an oriental potentate, along with his court in full panoply.

How did a Selby servant come to arrive in the tent of Christendom's enemy, near the point where European maps petered out into the sketchy contours of hypothesis?

Mary was convinced with her employers, Richard and Elizabeth Tomlinson, in 1652: all dashed straight out to prophesy, and Mary, admonishing the minister in a church, had the immense good fortune to be flung into the same prison as Elizabeth Hooton and Jane Holmes, lately ducked as a scold in Malton.[27] This prison sentence was as good as a university education in Quakerism: Mary signed her name to her five fellow prisoners' anti-tithe pamphlet, *False Prophets and False Teachers described*, denouncing university-trained ministers, their be-ringed wives, their blindness to poverty and oppression.[28] Mary's name comes last in the list, attached to Jane's: indicating perhaps not only her newborn status as Quaker but also her newness to the art of writing. Before graduating to prison, Mary had been illiterate. Evidently she proved a quick learner. She was soon writing to the judge rebuking the death sentence he had passed on three horse-thieves: 'Lay it to heart and let the oppressed go free.'[29] Horse-theft however counted as grand larceny, without benefit of clergy, with a 60 per cent hanging rate for those convicted. On this occasion two of the men were brought back from the gallows.

Come her release a year later, Mary was fizzing with aggressive energy. She and Elizabeth Williams explained to the students of Sidney-Sussex College, Cambridge, that they were 'Antichrists' and their college 'a cage of unclean birds, and the synagogue of Satan'. The scholars replied with stones and insults. When the mayor demanded their names and husbands' names, the women could only reply that their names were 'written in the Book of Life' and their husband was Jesus Christ. This answer provoked a flogging, stripped to the waist, as whores, throughout which ordeal they sang 'The Lord be blessed, the Lord be praised' with determined blitheness.[30] Further imprisonments followed, and in 1655 Mary sailed for Barbados and New England, with Ann Austin. They docked at Boston Harbour in the *Swallow* on 11 July 1656, the first Quaker missionaries to reach the Massachusetts Bay Colony. George Bishop tells their story in *New-England Judged*.[31]

The deputy governor, Richard Bellingham, welcomed Mary and Ann by rifling them for books and papers on shipboard, confiscating a hundred tracts, which were burned in Boston marketplace by the hangman. Imprisoned without pen, paper or candle, they were treated with cruelty bordering on the pathological, as if, Bishop suggests with distaste, instead of 'two poor women arriving in your harbour', the colony had been invaded by 'a formidable army' (p7). Here Bishop captures the fear and sense of threat motivating the extreme reactions of the New England theocracy to the Quakers. The colony's rigidly patriarchal Calvinistic elitism was hostile to nonconformity, and especially in dissident Eves offering the apple of independent thought to its upright Adams. It remembered Anne Hutchinson, who, preaching a covenant of grace, had been tried for antinomianism in 1638 and banished.

Governor Endicott menacingly warned against breaking the laws of the colony, 'for then ye are sure to stretch by a halter'.

But what were these laws? Might they have a copy?

No, they may not.

Obscenely strip-searched for signs of witchcraft, Mary (a single woman) and Ann (mother of five) underwent what felt like the equivalent of licensed rape.

Bishop has to wonder about New England hospitality: 'Is this your entertaining of strangers, your civility, your manhood to those who travelled so many miles to visit you in the movings of the Lord ...?' (p13). He contrasts the barbarity of New England Puritans with the natural civility of the Indians, in feeding, warming and sheltering Friends in wigwams, drying their clothes round the fire and guiding exiles through the forest. Compared with New Englanders, Bishop comments, so-called 'barbarous' cultures are models of civilisation: as witness Mary Fisher's pilgrimage to Turkey in 1657.

Mary set out in a group of three men and three women Friends for the Near East. Charting her journey on a modern map, one is struck by how little our world is theirs, even to place-names, in the wake of defunct empires. After rounding Spain into the Mediterranean, they landed at Leghorn (modern Livorno) on the north-west coast of Italy on 29 July, leaving after three weeks for Zante (the Greek island of Zakynthos). Here John Perrot and John Buckley headed for Greece, while the others (John Luffe, Mary Prince, Beatrice Beckley and Mary Fisher) continued on to Smyrna, the port on the Turkish coast now known as Izmir. The English Consul, judging as crackpot their notion of turning the sultan into a Quaker, shooed them kindly but firmly back the way they had come. They therefore determined on sailing round Greece and landing at Venice, in order to approach the Turk by a back-door route. Off they sailed but storms ran them into Zakynthos again. Mary Fisher, Beatrice Beckley and John Buckley at once landed and made for Adrianapolis (the modern Edirne), where the sultan was encamped with 20,000 men, pursuing the Ottoman Empire's war with Venice. The route here blurs. Either Mary Fisher, now separated from all her companions, walked five or six hundred miles across Greece and round the Aegean coast or took ship across the Aegean, hiking the rest of the way. Nobody threatened her, Bishop reminds the barbarian New Englanders. She passed peacefully through an alien land. Mary must have arrived in spring 1658.

What did Mary expect to say to the sultan? She did not know – yet.

The scourge of Christendom sat encamped with his army, a ruler terrifying to his own people, none of whom was willing to guide Mary to his encampment, 'fearing his displeasure' (p22). She found her way alone, and got someone to pass the message to the grand vizier in his tent 'that there was an English women with something to declare from the Great God, to the Great Turk'. But what would she say? Mary took along with her no conscious agenda, but rather her listening quiet, knowing 'it would be given her in that hour, what she should speak'. Word came back that the sultan would hear her next morning.

The court was ranked in gorgeous panoply around the sultan, according to the custom in which the Turks honoured ambassadors, probably in a crescent form, their imperial symbol. Three interpreters were provided. England had supported Venice against Ottoman aggression, and, in the year of Mary's visit, was urging the English agent in Russia to encourage the Russians to attack 'the great Turk, the common foe of Christendom'.[32] Mary had come to the centre of a European nightmare, to find that the 'infidel' was human after all. Something of the vividness of that strange and exotic encounter is caught in the snatches of dialogue that survive. Sultan Mohammed first asks, 'Is it so as I have heard, that you have something to say to me from the Lord?'

'Yea.'

'Speak on.'

But Mary is silent. Everyone waits. Mohammed misinterprets muteness for bashfulness and graciously 'supposing that she might be fearful to utter her mind before them all', enquires whether she would prefer a smaller audience.

'Nay.' For Mary is not in the least shy. Her silence is full of confident attention to the prompting of her inner voice. At once recklessly audacious and austerely restrained, she takes time to find the right words. When one realises that traditionally Turkish courtiers danced attendance on every flicker of the sultan's facial expression, but that there was a prohibition on eye contact, something of the simplicity of Mary's culturally gate-crashing courage is understood. One can't help feeling that she was lucky in her amiable sultan, who had refused to have his younger brothers murdered at the beginning of his reign.

'Speak the Word of the Lord to us; and do not fear,' the teenage monarch requests. 'We have good hearts, and can hear it.'

The sultan is told of the Inner Light, of his especial need for it, and the difference it would make to himself, his nation and the entire world if he became a Friend. He and his court listen gravely until she has finished speaking. And we may be sure that Mary did not limit herself according to a merely human clock.

'Have you more to say?' he asks, when she is quiet.

'Do you understand what I have said?'

'Yes, every word. It is the Truth.'

Evidently Mary took questions after her talk, for the sultan wished to know her opinion of the Prophet Mohammed.

She does not know Mohammed, she admits, only Christ, the Light of the World. As for Mohammed, he must be judged according to the fruitfulness of his prophecies, for if they don't come to pass, 'the Lord never sent him', a pragmatic quotation from Deuteronomy 18:22.

'It is the truth,' he can concede to this common sense.

The sultan wonders if Mary will consider staying on in Turkey, after so long a journey. When she declines, he offers an escort to Constantinople, to be assured that the Arm of the Lord, which brought her here, will bring her home unscathed.

Mary reached Constantinople (the modern Istanbul) safely, 'without the least hurt or scoff', which (for George Bishop is still blasting this tale as propaganda at the 'Christians' of Massachusetts Bay) spoke highly for the army and the Great Turk, 'and your everlasting shame and contempt' (p24). Since the name 'Turk' was an insult in the English language and 'to turn Turk' signified treachery, Mary's experience of Turkish courtesy, tolerance and human care was an indictment of the rabid prejudices of New England.

Mary remembered the sultan fondly as having been 'very noble unto me. He received the words of truth without contradiction', for the Turkish people (unlike the Britons in Italy and Turkey) were God-fearing.[33] Sir Thomas Bendish, English ambassador at Constantinople, wrote to the Protectorate that the English in Turkey were being made a laughing-stock by lunatic Quakers. Marching in and denouncing services, they showed 'several notorious contempts of me and my authority'. Sir Thomas had ordered them home.[34]

Mary reached England by the following year, in time to sign the Quaker Women's petition against tithes. At the age of thirty-nine, she married William Bayley, a Quaker shipmaster of Dorset, and had three late children. Her husband died in 1675. Three years later, aged fifty-two, she married John Cross of London, and the family emigrated to South Carolina, where she lived until old age. People pointed her out as 'one whose name you have heard of, Mary Fisher, she that spoke to the Grand Turk'.

*

'She did hang as a flag for others to take example by,' quipped a
member of the General Council of Boston which executed Mary
Dyer in 1660. Never a truer word.

For today a statue of Mary rests in the grounds of Boston
State House as a symbol of liberty of conscience.[35] She sits in
monumental calm, hands loosely joined on her lap, over the
inscription:

MARY DYER

QUAKER

WITNESS FOR RELIGIOUS FREEDOM

HANGED ON BOSTON COMMON 1660

Mary, a former member of the colony, had allied herself with the
rebel Anne Hutchinson, at whose expulsion in 1638 she and her
prosperous milliner husband had moved to tolerant Rhode Island.
She was, New Englanders believed, marked with the Beast, as
proved by the fact that she had given birth to a 'monster' ('a
woman, a fish, a bird, & beast all woven together', as the sapient
Reverend John Eliot recalled in 1660). Anne Hutchinson, midwife
and preacher, was supposed to have given birth to thirty such
monsters, spawn of her 'mishapen opinions' according to the
misogynistic governor, John Winthrop. Anne had helped Mary
bury the stillborn baby girl in the forest. Five months later
Winthrop and fraternity, exhuming the pathetic remains, had
paraded them as testimony of Mary's evil. Here was 'scientific'
'proof' of female depravity.[36]

Anne was later killed in a raid by Native Americans. Mary, her
husband and surviving child returned to England, where she
became a Quaker and travelled for five years as a minister, before
coming to Boston in 1657. Here she was imprisoned and banished.
The following year, the Massachusetts General Council passed the
act banishing 'the cursed Quakers' on pain of death. In 1659, a
party of English Friends and Salem Quakers came to Boston to
challenge the Act. One of the Salem women, Alice Cowland,
brought linen to shroud the corpses of those who expected to lose
their lives. William Robinson and Marmaduke Stephenson were
imprisoned, and Mary Dyer, hearing this, came to share their

witness. All three were banished under threat of death.

Within a month they were back. Death sentences followed, Mary's reaction to hers being the characteristic 'Yea, joyfully shall I go'.[37] Her letter to the Council denies forcing her own neck into the noose, through insisting on coming back – and back, and back, knowing the penalty of such conduct. She has returned, she says, to lay down her life for her persecuted Friends, 'with whom my life is bound up'. 'Woe is me for you! Of whom take you counsel?' (p288).

Drums pounded as the three Friends walked to their execution, 'hand in hand all three of them, as to a wedding-day' (p125). Prurient Marshall Michaelson, shocked at such brazenness, rapped out at Mary, '"Are you not ashamed to walk hand in hand between two young men?"'

'"It is an hour of the greatest joy I can enjoy in the world."' She turned to him brimming, rapturous eyes.

William, Marmaduke and Mary took leave of one another, but only for the moment. They expected to meet within ten minutes in another world. The woman, scheduled to die last, watched her friends mount the ladder, fall, twitch and, probably after several minutes' horrific struggle (hanging is not an easy death), go still. The dead bodies were cut down and fell to the ground, smashing one of the skulls, 'and when down, their shirts were ripped off with a knife, and their naked bodies cast into a hole of the earth' (p125).

Up the ladder, Mary's arms and legs were tied, the halter slipped over her head, and her face covered with a handkerchief. She waited, hushed, to follow her friends.

A reprieve, gained by her son without her knowledge, was brought at the last minute and read out. Off came the halter. Light mocked her eye. She was told to come down, but, shocked and silent, stayed where she was, until eventually grappled down.

Mary was imprisoned, then banished. She wrote, still shaking with shock, to the Council the day after her friends had got away, 'When I heard your last Order read [the reprieve], it was a disturbance to me, that was freely offering up my life to him that gave it me, and sent me hither so to do'. Having reached the peace of journey's end, she found herself incomprehensibly condemned to survival. 'I was so far disturbed, that I could not retain any more the words thereof, than that I should return to prison, and there remain forty and eight hours' (p312). The phrase 'forty and eight hours' tolling in her mind, she falteringly accepted her sentence of life. 'I came at his command and I go at his command.'

The Council congratulated itself on a publicity coup. Who could now accuse the colony of failing in Christian clemency?

Mary returned, of course, to be sentenced to death. Her distraught husband, to whom Mary was an eternal enigma, but evidently a very dear one, and who had not seen her for six months, wrote a letter of paroxysmic distress to Governor Endicott: 'I ... cannot tell how, in the frame of her spirit, she was moved to run so great a hazard to herself ... by her inconsiderate madness; Oh! do not deprive me of her, but I pray give her me once again ... Pity me!'[38] In May 1660, she was executed. As she was led to the gallows, people taunted and reviled her. 'Yes,' she answered to some impertinence, 'I have been in paradise several days'.[39] She could, as Bishop taunts her murderers, 'look Death in the face'.

After one further execution, the tide turned. Public opinion in England revolted against the atrocities revealed in Bishop's book. Charles II stopped the murders by sending a mandamus to the livid New England authorities, with typically urbane wit, by hand. The hand was that of an exiled New England Quaker, Samuel Shattuck, and, to compound the wit, he arrived by Quaker-owned ship.

What was the point of Mary Dyer's death? Was it the suicidal gesture of a religious hysteric?

Looking forwards in American history, we are struck by the fact that four out of five of the women who initiated the world's first Women's Rights Convention in 1848 were Quakers. Though by this date Quakers consituted only a tiny percentage of Americans, their influence on abolitionism, reform of prisons, education, treatment of the mentally ill, child labour, immigrant welfare and Native American rights was out of all proportion to their numbers. Lucretia Mott was a Quaker; Susan B Anthony; Alice Paul. It has been strongly argued that American feminism,[40] with its emphasis on non-violence, race and class rights, consensus discussion and ties with the peace movement, shows its Quaker heritage. Trained in the committee work of Women's Meetings, these women carried the fire of the apostolic first generation.

Susan B Anthony, abolitionist and women's rights pioneer, belonged to a long line of Rhode Island Quakers: the first of these is said to have been converted by Mary Dyer.

*

To end on this heroic upbeat is tempting but delusory. Our travelling companions have been otherworldly women of global aspirations, in whose wakes we trail with awe. Other women mapped out a path with comparable resource but more prosaic destinies – and perhaps with more to teach us about the realities of women's history.

Pedlars, tinkers, badgers and hawkers incessantly moved between hamlets, villages and towns all over England, mostly grubbing for a living at the bottom of the social heap. Many were women. They dealt in small wares and haberdashery, travelling the rutted paths which passed for roads, loaded with backpacks, under attack by shopkeepers for undercutting sales.

Even in such a world, however, the frugal, within a supportive community, might thrive. Joan Dant was a weaver's widow of New Paternoster Row, Spital Fields, who became a pedlar. As a respected Quaker, with the use of the Quaker network, her probity drew trade and wealth. Joan's story typifies the irony by which Friends, pauperised by conscience, in the long term prospered by conscientiousness, to become the soul of Cadbury's chocolate, Rowntree's sweet empire, Clarks shoes. Joan Dant began by carrying stockings, gloves and handkerchiefs house-to-house, trudging with a backpack. Gradually she amassed capital, enabling her to engage in wholesale trade and exports. Debts due from Paris and Brussels appear in her executor's accounts. She lived with austerity, and died in 1715, aged eighty-four and worth £9000. 'I got it by the rich,' she wrote, 'and I mean to leave it to the poor.' She echoes the Puritan work ethic which regarded worldly prosperity as a sign of divine approval when she writes to her executors, 'It is the Lord that creates true industry in his people, and that blesseth their endeavours', alluding to the parable of the talents, but with the saving reflection that the garnerings of such industry should be ploughed back in to the common stock, 'to do something for the poor, – the fatherless and the widows in the Church of Christ, according to the utmost of my ability'.[41] Joan's great journey was to constitute a redistribution of wealth – from the affluent, both Quaker and non-Quaker, to unprovided Friends.

For such travelling, toiling, accounting women, it may properly be said that piety paid.

CONCLUSION – BUT NEVER THE END
THE RESTORATION

In 1642, the Wars of Religion were fought out in St Katherine's Creechurch at Leadenhall Street one May Sabbath during Mr Wells' sermon. He boomingly urged his flock 'not to sleep but to stir themselves up'.

Mrs Clark and Mrs Atkinson, ancient enemies, were occupying the same pew; and at the minister's admonition, Mrs Clark, who had been shooting baleful looks at her peacefully snoozing neighbour, administered what she was later to describe as a gentle jog to Mrs Atkinson's knee, to awaken her. This was her plain duty as a congregant and a Christian.

Mrs Atkinson, rudely roused from Sabbath calm, took sharp offence. She manifested her ingratitude for Mrs Clark's spiritual concern by calling her an 'envious housewife and drunken sow'; she went on to hiss, 'Oh, you bold drunken slut, do you kick me?'

But then, the godly gossipers who discussed these ruderies

agreed, Mrs Atkinson was always 'a deboist [debauched] woman'.

Mrs Clark held her peace. With swelling breast, she remained in her pew, putting space between her person and her odious neighbour, rushing home after service to inform her husband that she would never again share a pew with the slothful swearer.

Never.

The battle now passed to the menfolk. Mr Clark stalked into church and reported the abomination to Mr Wells and his churchwarden, who summoned Mrs Atkinson's husband to the vestry.

Mr Atkinson expressed spousal outrage at such slander. Mrs Clark had kicked his wife, out of the blue, in God's house, while Mrs Atkinson was concentrating on the sermon. Tempers became heated in the vestry. Atkinson called Clark 'a blockhead and a Roundhead', together with other abuse not minuted.

Now Mrs Atkinson was fetched to give her point of view. She stormed in, 'in a great heat and full of bitterness', and swore, with indignation, that if Mrs Clark had not kicked her, 'she wished she might never go home else alive and that she might never speak more.'

It was a vow she would live just long enough to rue.

Stomping through the churchyard, she 'sank down dead' and never spoke another word, except to find just time enough to pack in 'just as she was dying', a curse on Mrs Clark: 'A pox take you: you are one of the holy sisters.'[1] No sooner had she uttered this malediction than her tongue turned black.

The godly nudger was thus clearly vindicated by divine Providence, which decided the quarrel in favour of 'Roundhead' husband and 'holy sister' wife. Widower Atkinson no doubt conveyed the story to his circle as a typical instance of Puritan trouble-makers hounding an innocent woman to her death. The story evokes the unpopularity of the much-sneered-at 'holy sisters' of the Revolution, with their veneer of smarm over invincible egotism: the Pharisee who unctuously thanked God that he was not as other men.

For Nehemiah Wallington, recorder of this incident, God's arm was around Mrs Clark, who fulfilled to the letter her duty to correct her neighbour and suffered the martyr's mortification of being slurred as a drunken sow in public. The English Civil War has been called the 'last of the religious wars' rather than the first of the European Revolutions;[2] and the temper of mind of its participants seems foreign to moderns. But beneath the holy row of Mrs Clark and Mrs Atkinson the ghost of unacknowledged social conflicts stirs. The two occupy the same pew, which groups them in the same social class: bourgeois, and probably, like Wallington, moderately well-off artisans – the top of the the lower ranks but not the bottom of the higher. Never, vows Mrs Clark, will she share the same pew again. Perhaps each suspected the one of having funds or social aspirations mortifying to the other; maybe there was business competition between the two husbands, a simmering grudge either personal or economic? When Mrs Atkinson is kicked awake, she pours out a torrent of bad language exceedingly shocking to the holy ears of Mrs Clark, a shock foreknown and intended. For as a Puritan, Mrs Clark is expressing in clothes, gestures, speech-patterns and attitudes her *superiority* to her neighbour: an intolerable elitism.

The English Revolution was not a war waged by plebs and 'middling sorts' against the gentry. But it did involve an upheaval which challenged the social order, in which birth, affluence and even gender came under fierce stress. The last might be first and the first be last; the poor might inherit the earth while the rich were trampled in the mire – next week perhaps.

Wallington had heard of a Baptist woman in Dover, married to a non-Baptist husband who insisted their child be baptised – a profanation this unnamed zealot took care to avoid by cutting off the baby's head, and 'did then present the dismal spectacle to her husband and bid him baptise him then if he would'.[3]

The smoky smell of the apocryphal lingers about the more sensational anecdotes, fumes to scare the propertied into defence of assets and order. Hostile testimony, tenth-hand rumour, faulty memory, pure invention, propaganda and false witness blur the evidence. But that there was a breakout is undeniable. Imagine yourself a woman recruited by one of the London sects in 1641 or 1642. The very fact of 'separation' from the mass organisation that has immemorially controlled ordinary people's lives brings a shift in self-awareness. Encouraged to examine your soul, form judgements and make account of yourself to God and congregation, you are on your own with that duty, and yet simultaneously amongst friends, searching out meaning together. You are defined by God-sanctioned resistance to authority, amongst outsiders who are closely bonded insiders in an autonomous spiritual community. Most of all, you are taught, for the first time in your life, that you matter: your life has meaning beyond its function as someone's maidservant or mother. An inner drama of cosmic dimensions takes place within you. You can alter the path of history.

Prayer was political action. Wallington called 1641 'a praying year'. Robert Baillie told of how the London 'godly' in great numbers met in private houses, to hold 'fasts and prayers, and hear sermons, for whole days, sundry times in the week'. Joseph Lister recalled how his mother opened her house to meetings of the devout, 'weeping, praying, and wrestling' day and night; and how they seemed to be on perpetual fast, at which the bored boy's stomach growled furiously.[4] They were praying for the reform of Parliament: never mind the vote, if you can combine with the Absolute to steer English history. As a woman, you would have felt that you had a share in political power for the first time in your life.

The godly exercised muscle through direct action. Imagine being one of the throng of men and women who, in Halstead, Essex, tumbled the prayer book from the hand of the curate attempting to baptise a child, and kicked it round the church, calling it 'a popish book'. You then tore the surplice and hood out of the clerk's hands and shared the satisfaction of hearing it rip from end to end. When the constable arrested the ringleaders, you helped release them. Or you were one of the hundred 'rude rascals' at St Olave's Church, Old Jewry, who, as the bishop entered the pulpit, roared in the ears of the mayor and MPs 'A Pope, a Pope, a Pope!' When thrust out, you stoned the church windows.[5] Direct action politicised women and men; it gave them a taste of and for legitimate antagonism.

As a woman, you glimpsed a world where you had a say. You might see one of your fellow women preach on a tub or at a private meeting. That very sight extended your sense of the limits of the possible.

The words of cobbler or woman might be much to your taste, closer to your experience than the rhetoric of ordained priests. The smell of shoe-leather or baking that so offended gentry nostrils might strike you as more wholesome than the odour of unearned lucre wafting off the polysyllabic paid ministers. Many men and women voted with their feet and came to listen, and not just to view a freak-show. It was a novelty for women to find that they could choose their own minister, and go to hear the charismatic person of their choice. Thomas Edwards met a girl buying a gold ring from a goldsmith in the Strand. Was she going to be married? No, she was buying it for the 'minister of the church into which she was to be admitted a member'.[6]

Through Edwards' smears, a fragment of untarnished reality glints. Maidservants nowadays had opinions and affiliations. Congregations might help them learn to read and write. Menial girls had a value, beyond their ability to scrub, cook and obey – to themselves and others. That in itself was revolutionary.

*

With the Restoration of King Charles II in 1660, the old order was restored; the women and tinkers suppressed. That momentous year, the lads had been bawling 'Kiss my Parliament' instead of 'Kiss my arse', and a picture of a shitting Rump was set up in the Exchange. Pepys recorded the disintegration of the Revolution in a jubilee of bonfires and bell-ringing: standing at the Strand Bridge he counted thirty-one fires on the night of 11 February:

> and all along burning and roasting and drinking for rumps – there being rumps tied upon sticks and carried up and down. The butchers at the Maypole in the Strand rang a peal with their knives when they were going to sacrifice their rump. On Ludgate-hill there was one turning of a spit, that had a rump tied upon it, and another basting of it. Indeed, it was past imagination, both the greatness and the suddenness of it. At one end of the street, you would think there was a whole lane of fire, and so hot that we were fain to keep still on the further side merely for heat. (p52)

Rumps everywhere, rumps basted, lathered, spiked. Barebones' windows smashed (twice) by roistering louts. Monk's soldiers roughing up Quakers. The King's arms set up in the revolutionaries' sanctum at Allhallows in Thames Street, 'John Simpson's church,' gloats Pepys, 'which, being privately done, was a great eyesore to his people when they came to church and saw it'.[7]

This was not only John Simpson's church but, we remember, Anna Trapnel's. What did Anna feel about the return of the king, maypoles going up, theatres about to reopen, Harrison eviscerated, Powell imprisoned, fun and games licensed, her own soul-drama spurned? The last we hear of her in print is that final fanfare in 1658, though she must have been still active in 1660, for she was attacked in print. Possibly our Anna may be the Anna Trapnel who was married in Woodbridge, Suffolk, in 1660. Ursula Adman, who had heroically shared Anna's imprisonment and braved the rats, was arrested in 1669, for holding Fifth Monarchist meetings in her house in Middlesex. Katharine Chidley was dead by 1665; silent long before. Elizabeth Lilburne was still being paid her £2 pension in 1660, having struggled to retrieve her property, to support her fatherless children. By 1688, only one of the ten, Lilburne's youngest daughter, Bethia, survived. Of Mary Cary there is no word. These folk were now 'the Fanatiques', a nightmare past for the ruling classes, which seemed to rear in panics and plots like Overton's Rebellion in 1660, Venner's Fifth Monarchist Rising in 1661, after which savage repression set in. One of Venner's fifty rebels was said to be a woman in full armour.[8]

Pepys was with the fleet that brought the triumphant king back to his kingdom. So too was Lady Ann Fanshawe, who described the exultant serenity of the crossing in her *Memoirs*:

> who can sufficiently express the joy and gallantry of that voyage? To see so many great ships, the best in the world; to hear the trumpets and all other music; to see near an hundred brave ships sail before the wind with their waist cloths and streamers ... above all, the glorious majesties of the King and his two brothers, – was so beyond man's expectation and expression. The sea was calm; the moon shone at full; and the sun suffered not a cloud ... by whose light and the merciful bounty of God he was set safely on shore at Dover in Kent upon the 25th of May, 1660.

So great were the acclamations and numbers of people that it reached like one street from Dover to Whitehall.[9]

The voyage home was like a crossing to a worldly New Jerusalem, the Channel strangely calm and luminous as a mythical seascape seen in a dream or masque.

*

In October, Pepys matter-of-factly records the end of Harrison, the Fifth Monarchist. The procedure was that the traitor be lashed to a sledge and pulled by horses to (in this case) Charing Cross. He was hanged but cut down before dead, roused to consciousness and his genital organs sliced off and stuffed in his mouth. Still alive, he was eviscerated and his bowels cast into the fire. The executioner reached up and wrenched out his heart. His head was chopped off, boiled and covered with pitch, and his body hacked into quarters. A week later, Pepys viewed Harrison's head (with Cook's) from the turret of a colleague's house, stuck up 'on the other side of Westminster Hall. Here I could see them plainly'. It was all most interesting, but scarcely more so than a dish of anchovies or a chine of beef. Sight-seeing Pepys viewed Harrison's head and turned away, chatting. Harrison had died with cheerful courage. 'Where is your good old cause now?' sneered the hostile London crowd, as the Fifth Monarchist was dragged to his end. He placed his hand on his heart: 'In my breast, and I shall seal it with my blood.' Pepys records the gossip 'that his wife doth expect his coming again'.[10] While, in some, trauma shook all faith in God, others elect faith in holy absurdity outstared utter defeat.[11]

Church services and architecture were reasserting hierarchy. Communion tables gave way to railed altars again. On the south side of the nave of St Olave's, Hart Street, Sir William Batten and Sir William Penn, with their hangers-on, built a gallery for the pick of naval gentry and their retainers, approached via a covered staircase, sequestering quality from non-quality. In November it was almost ready and, having eaten 'some hog's pudding', Pepys, the two Sir Williams, and two Mr Davieses strutted along in some excitement to try it:

> There being no women this day, we sat in the foremost pew and behind us our servants; but I hope it will not be always

so, it not being handsome for our servants to sit so equal
with us.[12]

The base-born breathing down their betters' necks spoiled the
relish of the gentry's lofty perch.

Pepys basked, plumply replete with *nouveau* caste. The
church had again become a solid haven for worldly elitism,
upholding rank and privilege, a shopfront for sexual merchandise,
in a new heyday of sexual freedom under a king of many mistresses.
The diarist attended a church in Clerkenwell solely to ogle the two
Boteler beauties, who crammed in beside him in his pew. 'But the
pew by their coming being too full, I went out into the next and
there sat and had my full view of them.'[13]

The enemies of 'steeple-houses' were still legion; and even
moderate Puritans struck back in spasms of the old spirit. Adam
Martindale, disgraced Presbyterian Cheshire minister, was proud of
his wife's direct action against the yob-erected, magistrate-
sanctioned maypole in the vicinity of the church: she and three
women friends 'whipt it down in the night with a framing-saw'.[14]
In the August after the king's Restoration, Manchester minister
Henry Newcome was shocked at the irruption of a female 'in
sackcloth and ashes', who 'stood with hair about her ears, before
the pulpit all sermon time. They said it was Judge Fell's wife'. The
Presbyterian Newcome, sandwiched between Quaker wildcats and
idolatrous maypoles, expressed amazement that 'these wild beasts
[Quakers] ... have not before this time over-run us.'[15] Beneath its
sabbath calm, Restoration England spasmed with nervous tics. The
energies that had powered the Revolution, far from being spent,
erupted in the very households of the elite, in pale young faces that
denied and defied their parents' worldly values.

Mary Penington's spiritual autobiography tells of how, after
conversion to Quakerism, she and her husband Isaac endured
scalding mockery and abuse from 'those of our own rank, and
those below us, nay, even our own servants'.[16] Mary, by her first
marriage, was the mother of Gulielma Maria Springett, born in
1644. Gulielma married William Penn in 1672. Penn was the
renegade son of Pepys' colleague and drinking companion, Sir
William Penn, the wealthy admiral who built that high gallery at

St Olave's, to tower above the *hoi polloi*.

Sir William, squiffy at the Dolphin with his jolly pew-sharers, had an embarrassing white sheep as heir. The son, to the father's horror, ran to the good. Penn became a Quaker, endured many imprisonments and founded the Quaker colony of Pennsylvania.

His colony was to be a home of religious toleration, inner light and inner law. Sober, devout women there would have spiritual parity with men; enjoy Meetings and ministry of their own. But utopia proved, as ever, elusive. Penn's Heaven was a patriarchy, whose two elective assemblies rested on male property qualifications. Women, along with children and idiots, would be viewed as politically covered. And 'scolding', as it turned out, would remain a punishable offence in Pennsylvania: gags and cucking stools would be required for loudmouthed women in that peace-loving land.[17]

*

In *An Essay to Revive the Antient Education of Gentlewomen* (1673), the intellectual, Bathsua Makin, demanded for women access to education equivalent to that of men, the 'whole encyclopaedia of learning'. She instanced the achievements of women in 'these late times' of Civil War when women 'defended their houses and did all things as soldiers', appearing 'before committees'. Guilefully, Bathsua claimed that education would make women more rather than less biddable; better wives; more submissive and less prone to thinking aberrantly for themselves on sacred and incontrovertible matters. 'Heresiarchs creep into houses and lead silly women captive; then they lead their husbands ...'.[18] Later, Anglican Mary Astell would propose a collegiate system whereby unmarried gentlewomen could acquire higher education.

While the Restoration saw a retreat into a narrower bargaining-position, a contraction of women's claims, it also witnessed the emergence of professional women authors like playwrights Aphra Behn and Mary Delarivière Manley. Some hard-headed businesswomen throve. Women still practised as unofficial doctors and midwives, long after being driven out by male 'professionals'. Complex forces, economic and political, push-pulled second generation radicals into postures of strategic withdrawal. If Quaker women were quelled and bonneted by a movement that became increasingly obsessed with internal discipline and censorious of ecstatic prophesies; if by the 1670s, they were limited by the prohibition upon marrying out, and their ministry curbed, Women's Meetings remained and gutsy individuals still spoke out. In the latter years of the century, women Dissenters (Presbyterians, Congregationalists, Baptists) still outnumbered men by just under two to one. They played a staunch part in keeping nonconformity alive under persecution.

Though the future of women's liberty lay with Mary Astell and education reform rather than Jane Lead's mystical feminism; with Mary Wollstonecraft and Emmeline Pankhurst rather than Joanna Southcott, the women of the English Revolution had kicked a door wide open which, slammed in their faces, took centuries of communal effort to prise open again.

While I wrote his book, the air rang with echoes. Before me on my desk lie several recent newspaper cuttings.

The Reverend Francis Bown, forty-eight, opponent of women priests in Hull, refuses to take down a church sign overlooking a busy junction:

THE ANGLICAN PARISH HAS NO PART IN THE APOSTASY
OF PRIESTESSES

Frown-marks pit Bown's forehead in the shape of a belligerent cross. His congregation of twelve souls is reported to be fiercely behind this glowering remnant of a late-lost cause.

A second cutting shows a buoyant and boyish Reverend Paul Williamson, forty-seven, vicar of St George's, Hanworth, outside the Appeal Court after losing a fifth case claiming that Queen Elizabeth II broke her coronation oath by allowing women's ordination. The judge rebuked his endless judicial nuisances – but the debonair vicar, basking in flashlights, confides to newsmen this heroic message: 'I shall not take the slightest bit of notice. They can clap me in irons. I am here for Christ, not their silly witterings.' Legal bills for accusing the Archbishop of Canterbury of treason and heresy total more than £60,000:

It's not much money to spend if you care about the truth ... Priestesses are a heresy and they don't belong in the Church – they are a passing vile veneer.

Where have we met these two before? Surely they are hundreds of years old?

As if by Providential coincidence, today's headline runs:

FIRST WOMAN CLAIMS HER PLACE AT CHURCH'S
INNER SANCTUM.[19]

On the spot where Colet preached and Donne thundered (though not in the building, which was rebuilt by Wren after the Great Fire), the Reverend Lucy Winkett has been appointed minor canon to St Paul's Cathedral. The Dean of St Paul's says he just wanted the best person; the Chancellor of St Paul's says, 'I don't believe her to be a priest'; and that mysterious soughing and seething one catches like a fading nightmare must be centuries of deans and canons turning in their eminent graves.

NOTES

The following abbreviations have been used for works frequently cited:

Braithwaite (1): William C Braithwaite, revised by HJ Cadbury, *The Beginnings of Quakerism,* William Sessions & Joseph Rowntree Trust, York, 1981 edn.

Braithwaite (2): William C Braithwaite, revised by HJ Cadbury, *The Second Period of Quakerism,* William Sessions Ltd, with Joseph Rowntree Trust, York, 1979.

CPW: Complete Prose Works of John Milton, Don M Wolfe, ed, 8 vols, Yale University Press, New Haven, 1953–82.

Fraser: Antonia Fraser in *The Weaker Vessel: Women's Lot in Seventeenth-Century England,* Weidenfeld & Nicolson, 1984.

Higgins: Patricia Higgins, 'The Reactions of Women, with special reference to women petitioners', in *Politics, Religion and the English Civil War,* Brian Manning, ed, Edward Arnold, London, 1973.

Kunze: Bonnelyn Young Kunze, *Margaret Fell and the Rise of Quakerism,* Macmillan, Basingstoke and London, 1994.

Ludlow: Dorothy Paula Ludlow, 'Arise and Be Doing': English 'Preaching' Women, 1640–1660, unpublished PhD thesis, 1978.

Mack: Phyllis Mack, *Visionary Women: Ecstatic Prophecy in Seventeenth Century England,* University of California Press, Berkeley, 1992.

SCL: A Sincere and Constant Love: An Introduction to the Work of Margaret Fell (a selection of MF's works), Friends United Press, Richmond, Indiana, 1992.

Ross: Isabel Ross, *Margaret Fell: Mother of Quakerism,* Ebor Press, York, 1984 edn.

Somers: A Collection of Scarce and Valuable Tracts, Collected by Lord Somers, Sir Walter Scott, ed, vols IV, V & VI, London, 1811.

PRELUDE – TRAVELLING ABROAD TO THE PAST

1   'The Anarchy, or the Blessed Reformation since 1640', lines 6–10, in W Walter Wilkins, ed, *Political Ballads of the Seventeenth and Eighteenth Centuries,* vol I, Longman, London, 1860.

2   1 Timothy 2: 11–12; Martin Luther, *Table Talk,* in *Luther's Works,*

vol 54, 8, no. 55, TG Tappert, ed, Fortress Press, Philadelphia, 1967. See CJ Blaisdell, 'The Matrix of Reform: Women in the Lutheran and Calvinist Movements', in RI Greaves, ed, *Triumph over Silence: Women in Protestant History*, Greenwood Press, Westport and London, 1985, pp13–44, for the Calvinist and Lutheran inheritance.

3   John Perrot to Quakers from Lyons, c. 1661, quoted in *Braithwaite*, (2), pp231–2.

4   Quoted in JC Davis, *Fear, Myth and History: The Ranters and the Historians*, Cambridge University Press, 1986, p102.

5   The pamphlet is reprinted in JC Davis, op. cit., p159.

6   Elizabeth Avery, *Scripture-Prophecies Opened ... in Several Letters Written to Friends*, Giles Calvert, London, 1647, np.

7   John Dryden, 'MacFlecknoe', line 101, in James Kinsley, *Poems and Fables*, Oxford University Press, 1970.

8   Mary Cary, A Word in Season to the Kingdom of England ... 'To the Reader', Giles Calvert, London, 1647, np.

9   See Christopher Hill, *The World Turned Upside Down*, first published 1972, Penguin, Harmondsworth, 1975 edn, pp67, 306–23; *The English Bible and the Seventeenth-Century Revolution*, Allen Lane, Penguin, London, 1993, p308; *The Experience of Defeat. Milton and Some Contemporaries*, Penguin, Harmondsworth, 1985 edn, p21.

Chapter 1: WOMEN OF SPIRIT

1   See William Harrison, *Description of England*, Philip Stubbes, *Anatomie of Abuses*, and Stephen Gosson, *The Confutation of Plays*, in WC Hazlitt, *The English Drama and Stage: Documents Relating to Theatres*, London, 1869.

2   Though Frenchwomen wore 'les caleçons', Englishwomen did not wear knickers until the late eighteenth century. See C Willett and Phillis Cunnington's fascinating *The History of Underclothes*, Michael Joseph, London, 1951, pp53–67.

3   Letter of John Chamberlain to Sir D Carleton, 25 January 1620, quoted in MB Rose, *The Expense of Spirit: Love and Sexuality in English Renaissance Drama*, Cornell University Press, Ithaca, 1988, pp69–70.

4   For 'flyting', see Harold Stein, 'Six Tracts About Women: A Volume in the British Museum', *The Library*, 4th series, vol XV, 1935, pp38–48. See also Alcuin Blamires *et al*, *Woman Defamed*

and *Woman Defended: An Anthology of Medieval Texts*, Clarendon Press, Oxford, 1992; S Anderson and JP Zinsser, *A History of their Own: Women in Europe from Prehistory to the Present*, vol 1, Penguin, Harmondsworth, 1988.

5 Rachel Speght, *A Mouzell for Melastomus, The Cynical Bayter of, and foul mouthed Barker against EVAHS SEX ...*, London, 1617, printed in Simon Shepherd, ed, *The Women Sharp Revenge: Five Women's Pamphlets from the Renaissance*, Fourth Estate, London, 1985.

6 Geoffrey, Chaucer, 'The Prologue' to *The Monk's Tale, Canterbury Tales*, lines 1904–7, in *Complete Works*, FN Robinson, ed, Oxford University Press, 1948.

7 See DE Underdown, 'The Taming of the Scold: The Enforcement of Patriarchal Authority in Early Modern England', in *Order and Disorder in Early Modern England*, A Fletcher and J Stevenson, ed, Cambridge University Press, 1985; JA Sharpe, *Crime in Seventeenth Century England: A County Study*, Cambridge University Press, 1983, pp156–8.

8 See Underdown, op. cit., pp123, 134; and his *Revel, Riot, and Rebellion: Popular Politics and Culture: England 1603–1660*, Clarendon Press, Oxford, 1985, for details of cucking machinery in towns and wood pasture areas, and analysis of the link with the contemporary sense of escalating disorder.

9 Quoted in *Fraser*, p114.

10 For the significance of skimmingtons, see JA Sharpe, *Early Modern England: A Social History, 1550–1760*, Edward Arnold, London, 1987, pp94–8; GR Quaife, *Wanton Wenches and Wayward Wives. Peasants and Illicit Sex in Early Seventeenth Century England*, Croom Helm, London, 1979, p200.

11 Quoted by Dorothy M Owen, 'Lincolnshire Women in History', in *The Lincolnshire Historian*, vol 2, no 6 (1959), p34.

12 For judicious treatment of women's rioting, see chapter 12 of Olwen Hufton's magisterial *The Prospect Before Her: A History of Women in Western Europe*, vol I, 1500–1800, HarperCollins, London, 1995.

13 *Ludlow*, pp48f.

14 See DP Thomson, *Women of the Scottish Church*, Munro & Scott, Perth, 1975, p60.

15 Ibid., p65.

16 Arthur Lake, Bishop of Bath and Wells, 'A Sermon Preached at St Cuthbert's in Welles when certain Persons did Penance for being at Conventicles where a Woman Preached', no 7, part IV of *Sermons with Some Religious and Divine Meditations,* W Stansby for Nathaniel Butter, London, 1629, p68.

17 *Ludlow,* p9.

18 CV Wedgwood, *The King's Peace: The Great Rebellion, 1637–1641,* Collins, London, 1955, pp69–70, 238.

19 'T.E.', *The Lawes Resolution of Womens Rights,* printed by assignes of John More, 1632, pp124–6. On women's rights within marriage in seventeenth-century law, see Anne Laurence, *Women in England: 1500–1760: A Social History,* Weidenfeld & Nicolson, London, 1994, chapter 15; Lawrence Stone, *The Family, Sex and Marriage: England 1500–1800,* Penguin, Harmondsworth, edn 1990, pp136ff.

20 John Milton, *Eikonoklastes, CPW,* vol III, pp421–2.

21 Ibid., p530.

22 Anon, *The True Portraiture of the Kings of England* ... in *Somers Collection of Scarce and Valuable Tracts,* Sir W Scott, ed, London, 1811, vol VI, p83.

23 Sir Robert Filmer, *Patriarcha or, the Natural power of Kings,* in John Locke, *Two Treatises of Government Preceded by Sir Robert Filmer's 'Patriarcha',* London, 1884, p36.

24 Anon, *The Parliaments Kalendar of Black Saints, Or a New Discovery of Plots and Treasons,* 1644, G Bishop, London, p4.

25 The scene is vividly described in Pauline Gregg, *Free-born John: A Biography of John Lilburne,* Harrap, London, 1961, pp50–1.

26 SR Gardiner, *The Fall of the Monarchy of Charles I,* London, 1882, p391.

27 *The Journal of Sir Simonds d'Ewes* ... , W Havelock Coates, ed, Yale University Press and Oxford University Press, New Haven, London, 1942, p37.

28 Antonia Fraser, *King Charles II,* Weidenfeld & Nicolson, London, 1979, p198.

29 Samuel Butler, *Hudibras: Written in the Time of the Late Wars,* AR Waller ed, 1678 edn, Cambridge University Press, 1905, Part II, Canto 2.

30 William Lithgow, 'The Present Surveigh of London and England's State', London, 1643, in *Somers,* vol IV, pp534–45; Valerie Pearl,

London and the Outbreak of the Puritan Revolution, Oxford, 1961, pp262ff; Brian Manning, *The English People and the English Revolution,* pp196ff.

31 See *Fraser,* pp185–201.

32 JT Gilbert, *The History of the Irish Confederation and the War in Ireland 1641–49,* np, Dublin, 1882–91, vol I, pxlv; Charles Carlton, *Going to the Wars,* p166.

33 James Strong, *Joanereidos* (1645); Richard Baxter, *The Breviate of the Life of Margaret Baxter* (1681), JT Wilkinson, ed, as *Richard Baxter and Margaret Charlton. A Puritan Love-Story,* Allen & Unwin, 1928, p134.

34 Letter quoted by GN Godwin in *The Civil War in Hampshire (1642–45) and the Story of Basing House,* Southampton, 1904, pp121–2.

35 Richard Lovelace, 'Going to the Wars', in *Lucasta* (1649); William Shakespeare, *Henry IV, Part I,* V. i. 133–41.

36 WW Wilkins, Political Ballads, lines 23–30, 59, 62.

37 Katharine Chidley, *The Justification of the Independant Churches of Christ,* London, 1641, p5.

38 See John Morrill, *The Nature of the English Revolution,* Longman, London, 1993, p360.

39 These figures are accepted by Phyllis Mack, in *Mack,* p171.

40 See Keith Lindley, 'London and Popular Freedom in the 1640s', in *Freedom and the English Revolution: Essays in History and Literature,* RC Richardson and GM Ridden, Manchester University Press, 1986, pp111–24; Brian Manning, *The English People and the English Revolution, 1640–1649,* Heinemann, London, 1976, pp14–98, for what is still the most vividly actualising account of how it felt to live through the revolution.

41 See Joseph Frank, *The Beginnings of the English Newspaper, 1620–1660,* Harvard University Press, Cambridge, Massachusetts, 1961, pp21, 149.

42 *A Discovery of Six Women Preachers in Middlesex, Kent, Cambridgeshire, and Salisbury ... ,* np, London, 1641; *Lucifers Lacky,* London, 1641.

43 John Rogers, *Ohel Bethshemesh. A Tabernacle for the Sun: or Irenicum Evangelicum,* for RI and G and H Everden, London, 1653, p463, mispaginated as 563.

44 See Claire Cross, ' "He-Goats Before the Flocks": A Note on the

Part Played by Women in the Founding of Some Civil War Churches', in *Popular Belief and Practice, Studies in Church History*, vol 8, GJ Cuming and Derek Baker, eds, Cambridge University Press, 1972, pp195–202. The Bedford list of founding members is given on p200.

45 For women's role in the Fifth Monarchy movement, see BS Capp's *The Fifth Monarchy Men: A Study in Seventeenth-Century English Millennarianism*, Faber & Faber, London, 1972, pp174ff.

46 Peter Hausted, *A Satyre against Separatists, or the Conviction of Chamber-Preachers*, np, London, 1642, p3.

47 Daniel Rogers, *Matrimonial Honour: or A Treatise on Marriage*, London, 1650 edn, pp284–5.

48 For Mary Bilbrowe, see *Ludlow*, p16.

49 Gerrard Winstanley, *The New Law of Righteousness* (1649), in GH Sabine, ed, *Works of Gerrard Winstanley, with an Appendix of Documents Relating to the Digger Movement*, np, New York, 1965, pp62, 191.

50 Olwen Hufton, *The Prospect Before Her*, p465.

51 Thomas Edwards, *The Second part of Gangraena: Or A Fresh and further Discovery of Errors, Heresies, Blasphemies ...* , by TR and EM for Ralph Smith, London, 1646, pA1ᵛ.

52 Jacob Bauthumley, *The Light and Dark Sides of God* (1650), reprinted in Norman Cohn, *The Pursuit of the Millennium*, np, London, 1957, p336.

53 Cotton Mather, *Magnalia Christi Americana: Or, The Ecclesiastical History of New-England ...* (1702), Silas Andrus, Roberts, & Burr edn, Hartford, 1820, vol II, p446.

54 *Records of the Churches of Christ Gathered at Fenstanton, Warboys and Hexham, 1647–1720*, Hanserd Knollys Society, 1854, pp330–1. See Christopher Hill, *The World Turned Upside Down*, 'Seekers and Ranters', chapter 9, for a vividly entertaining account.

55 Quoted in CV Wedgwood, *The Trial of Charles I*, Collins, London, 1964, p175.

56 See David Cressy, *Bonfires and Bells. National Memory and the Protestant Calendar in Elizabethan and Stuart England*, Weidenfeld & Nicolson, London, 1989, pp22–3, 45, 86.

57 Alice Clark, *Working Life of Women*, p86.

58 For female literacy, see David Cressy, *Literacy and the Social Order: Reading and Writing in Tudor and Stuart England*, Cambridge

University Press, 1980, p145.

59 *Wonderful News from Bristol*, broadsheet written by publisher, Benjamin Harris, 1676.

60 Richard Gough, *The History of Myddle* (1701–6), Caliban Books, Firle, Sussex, p81.

61 Reprinted in *Her Own Life: Autobiographical Writings by Seventeenth-Century English Women*, Elspeth Graham *et al*, eds, Routledge, London, 1989, p152.

62 Quoted by Anne Laurence, *Women in England, 1500–1760*, p78.

63 Margaret Cavendish, Marchioness (later first Duchess) of Newcastle, *A True Relation of my Birth, Breeding and Life*, printed for J Martin and J Allestrye, London, 1656, pp383–4.

64 Margaret Cavendish, *Poems and Fancies*, TR for J Martin and J Allestrye, London, 1653, sig. A2ʳ; *The Letters of Dorothy Osborne to William Temple*, GC Moore Smith, ed, Clarendon Press, Oxford, 1928, Letters 17 and 20, pp37 and 41.

65 Susanna Parr, *Susanna's Apology Against the Elders. Or, A Vindication of Susanna Parr*, np, London, 1659.

66 John Rogers, *Ohel or Beth-shemesh*.

67 Sarah Wight, *A Wonderful Pleasant Profitable Letter ... To a Friend ...*, London, 1656.

68 Underdown, *Revel, Riot and Rebellion*, pp286–7.

69 For the joke, see Shakespeare's *The Taming of the Shrew*; for the lived reality, see Lynda E Boose's 'Scolding Brides and Bridling Scolds: Taming of the Woman's Unruly Member', *Shakespeare Quarterly*, vol 42 (1991), pp179–224.

70 The Stockport bridle is described by JP Earwacker in *East Cheshire: past and present; or A history of the hundred of Macclesfield in the County Palatine of Chester* (1877), vol I, p420.

71 *A Relation concerning Dorothy Waughs Cruel Usage by the Mayor of Carlisle* in *The Lambs Defence Against Lyes. And a True Testimony given concerning the Sufferings and Death of James Parnell*, London, 1656, p29.

72 TN Brushfield in *Journal of the Architectural, Archaeological and Historical Society for Chester*, ii (1855–62). See also JW Spargo, *Juridical Folklore in England Illustrated by the Cucking-Stool*, Durham, North Carolina, 1944.

73 Quoted in *Mack*, p49.

74 King James I and VI, *Demonologie*, Edinburgh, 1597.

75 Robin Briggs, *Witches & Neighbours. The Social and Cultural Context of European Witchcraft*, HarperCollins, London, 1996, p260. Alan Macfarlane's *Witchcraft in Tudor and Stuart England: A Regional and Comparative Study*, Routledge, London, 1970 remains classic.

76 Reginald Scot, *Discoverie of Witchcraft* (1584), quoted *Fraser*, p106.

77 John Webster, 'Practitioner in Physic', *The Displaying of supposed Witchcraft* ... , London, 1677, p82. See also Peter Elmer's invaluable *The Library of Dr John Webster: The Making of a Seventeenth Century Radical*, Wellcome Institute for the History of Medicine, London, 1986, for the relationship between Webster's radical mysticism and his rational scepticism.

78 J Taylor, *The Witchcraft Delusion in Colonial Connecticut, 1647–1699*, Grafton Press, New York, 1908, p43. See also the documentation of the Lancashire witches, 'The Voluntary Confession and examination of Elizabeth Southerns, alias Demdike', 'a very old woman, about the age of 4 score years ... a general agent for the Devil in these parts', and *The Wonderful Discoverie of the Witchcrafts of Margaret and Phillip[a] Flower* (1619), reprinted in *Witchcraft*, Barbara Rosen, ed, Edward Arnold, London, 1969, pp358, 369–81.

79 See Patricia Crawford, *Women and Religion in England, 1500–1720*, Routledge, London, 1993, pp129ff, for this double standard.

80 *Mack*, p120.

81 Frances Hill, *A Delusion of Satan: The Full Story of the Salem Witch Trials*, Doubleday, New York, 1995, *passim*, but especially pp24–52, for her exemplary treatment of the repressed girl-accusers' attention- and power-seeking hysteria.

82 Keith Thomas, *Religion and the Decline of Magic*, Penguin edn, Harmondsworth, 1991, p546.

83 George Fox, *Journal of George Fox*, John L Nickalls, ed, Religious Society of Friends, London, 1975 edn, pp15, 155–6.

84 Thomas, *Religion and the Decline of Magic*, p632.

85 *The Copy of a Letter Written by Mr Thomas Parker, Pastor of the Church of Newbury in New England to His Sister, Mrs. Elizabeth Avery* ... , London, 1650.

86 Anne Docwra, *An Epistle of Love and Good Advice to my Old Friends and Fellow-Sufferers* ... , London, 1683, pp1–4.

87 Francis Bugg, *Jezebel Withstood, and her Daughter Anne Docwra, Publickly Reproved, for Her Lies and Lightness* ... , London, 1699, p58, 60, 61.

88 Anne Docwra, *An Apostate-Conscience Exposed, and the Miserable Consequences Thereof Disclosed For Information and Caution*, T Sowle, London, 1699, pp18, 23–5; Francis Bugg, *Jezebel Withstood*, p64.

89 Anne Docwra, *The Second Part of An Apostate-Conscience Exposed...*, T Sowle, London, 1700, Preface.

90 Francis Bugg, *The Christian Ministry of the Church of England Vindicated and Distinguished from the Antichristian Ministry of the Quakers*, London, 1699, p6.

91 Anne Docwra, *A Treatise Concerning Enthusiasm*, London, 1699, p39.

92 John Dryden, *Absalom and Achitophel*, I, lines 529–30.

Chapter 2: THE WRITING ON THE WALL

1 Quoted in Esther S Cope, *Handmaid of the Holy Spirit: Dame Eleanor Davies, Never Soe Mad a Ladie*, Michigan University Press, Ann Arbor, 1992, p24.

2 Noted in a number of Lady Eleanor's pamphlets, including *The Lady Eleanor, Her Appeale*, London, 1641, p10.

3 See Norman Cohn, *The Pursuit of the Millennium*, Oxford University Press, 1970, still the classic introduction.

4 *The Lady Eleanor, Her Appeale*, 1646 edn, p15.

5 Ibid., pp21–2.

6 This tale is told by Peter Heylyn in *Cyprianus Anglicus*, London, 1688, part II, p266.

7 See Cope, *Handmaid of the Holy Spirit*, p79.

8 Lady Eleanor Davies, *The Restitution of Prophecy*, London, 1651, pp35–6.

9 Theodore Cianfrani, *A Short History of Obstetrics and Gynecology*, Thomas, Springfield, Illinois, 1960, p138. See also Isidore of Seville's pronouncement that contact with menstrual blood ensures 'fruits fail to germinate, grape-must goes sour ... Any dogs which consume it contract rabies', *Etymologies*, printed in Alcuin Blamires, *Woman Defamed and Woman Defended*, p44.

10 *The Problemes of Aristotle, with Other Philosophers and Physitians ...* R Waldegrave, Edinburgh, 1595, pE4.

11 *The Works of William Laud*, Parker Society, 1840–60, vol V, p346.

12 Quoted in Cope, *Handmaid of the Holy Spirit*, p94.

13 Lady Eleanor Davies, *For the Most Honourable States*, London, 1649, p6.

14 Cope, *Handmaid of the Holy Spirit*, p125.

15 Ibid., p155. See P Hardacre 'Gerrard Winstanley in 1650', *Huntingdon Library Quarterly*, 22 (1959), pp345–9.

16 Quoted in *The Complete Poems of Sir John Davies*, AB Grosart, ed, Chatto & Windus, London, 1876, vol I, pplv–lvi. The monument was destroyed in the rebuilding of St Martin-in-the-Fields.

Chapter 3: PEACE WOMEN & SEA-GREEN LEVELLERS

1 Quoted in Patricia Higgins' seminal essay, 'The Reactions of Women, with special reference to women petitioners', in *Politics, Religion and the English Civil War*, Brian Manning, ed, Edward Arnold, London, 1973, pp185–6. The petition was *To the Right Honourable the house of peers now assembled in the Parliament. The humble petition of many poore distressed women in & about London*.

2 See CV Wedgwood, *The King's War: 1641–1646: The Great Rebellion*, Collins, London, 1958, p63.

3 *Journals of the House of Commons*, II, 1 February 1641 (2).

4 See *Higgins*, pp187–8.

5 *Certaine Informations*, no 30 (August 7–14), 1643, p231.

6 Quoted *Higgins*, p190.

7 Ibid., p192.

8 Jonathan Priestley, 'Some Memoirs Concerning the Family of the Priestleys', in *Yorkshire Diaries and Autobiographies in the Seventeenth and Eighteenth Centuries*, Surtees Society, vol LXXVII (1883), p26–7.

9 J Rushworth, *Historical Collections* (1708), vol V, p143.

10 *Higgins*, p195.

11 Letter of 9 August 1643, in *The Knyvett Letters: 1620–1644*, Bertram Schofield, ed, Constable, London, 1949, p126.

12 Ibid., p127.

13 Quoted ibid., p126.

14 Samuel Butler, *Hudibras, Part II*.

15 Christopher Hill, *The World Turned Upside Down*, p24; Ivan Root, *The Great Rebellion, 1642–1660*, Batsford, London, 1966, p59.

16 John Lilburne, *The Juglers Discovered,* London, 1647, p2.

17 Bulstrode Whitelock, *Memorials of the English Affairs,* London, 1682, p193.

18 *Higgins,* pp202–3.

19 Ibid., p205.

20 Women's petition of 24 April 1649. *To the Supreme Authority of this Nation, the Commons assembled in Parliament: The humble Petition of divers well-affected Women* ... , London, 1649, p9.

21 Ralph Josselin, *Diary,* p104.

22 *The Mournful Cries,* printed in Don M Wolfe, ed, *Leveller Manifestoes of the Puritan Revolution,* Humanities Press, New York, 1967, pp275–8.

23 *To the Supreme Authority of England the Commons assembled in Parliament. The humble Petition of divers well-affected Women,* London, 5 May 1649.

24 Gregg, *Free-born John,* p65.

25 John Lilburne, *Englands Birth-right Justified,* London, 10 October 1645, Preamble.

26 Quoted by Gregg in *Free-born John,* p53.

27 Ibid., pp314, 321, 339.

28 [Richard Overton], *To the right Honourable, the Knights, Citizens, Burgesses, the Parliament of England, assembled at Westminster, The Humble Appeal and Petition of Mary Overton, prisoner, Bridewell,* London, 1647, p8.

29 Richard Overton, *The Commoner's Complaint: Or, A Dreadful Warning from Newgate, to the Commons of England,* np, 1646, pp7–8.

30 John Lilburne, *Thomas Prince and Richard Overton, The Picture of the Council of State,* np, London, 1646, Lilburne's testimony, p14.

31 Thomas Prince's *Narrative of the Proceedings,* in *The Picture of the Council of State,* p49.

32 Quoted *Higgins,* p218. Thomas May, *The History of the Parliament of England* (Oxford, 1854 edn), recalled that the Parliamentary army, funded by widows' mites, had been called 'the thimble and bodkin army', p219.

33 Daniel Rogers, *Matrimonial Honour,* pp60–1.

34 *To the Supreme Authority of England the Commons Assembled in Parliament. The humble Petition of divers well-affected Women ... Affecters and Approvers of the Petition of September 11, 1648,* 5 May 1649.

35 *The Women's Petition to the Right Honourable, his Excellency, the most Noble and Victorious Lord General Cromwell ...* , London, 27 October 1651.

36 *To the Parliament and Commonwealth of England, The humble Petition of divers afflicted Women, in behalf of Mr. J. Lilburn Prisoner in Newgate*, London, 25 July 1655.

37 See *Higgins*, pp212–13.

38 'Advertisement from London. 29 July 1653', *Bodleian MSS*, Clarendon 46, fol. 131^v.

39 *Higgins*, p203.

40 *The Parliament of Ladies. Or Divers remarkable passages of Ladies in Spring-Garden; in Parliament Assembled* (np, 1647), pp12, 15, 13; *News from the New Exchange, Or the Commonwealth of Ladies, Drawn to the Life, in their several characters and concernments*, London, 1650, pp3, 7–8, 10.

41 *The Ladies, A Second Time Assembled*, London, 1647, p7.

42 *The Knyvett Letters*, 23 May 1644, p151.

43 For Milton's radical links, see Christopher Hill, *Milton and the English Revolution*, Faber edn, London, 1979.

44 John Milton, *History of Britain, CPW*, vol V, pp79–80.

45 See, for instance, ASP Woodhouse, ed, *Puritanism and Liberty: Being the Army Debates (1647–9)*, from the Clarke Manuscripts with Supplementary Documents, Dent, London, 1938, pp367–9: 'It is improbable that this petition was actually composed by the women. Its principles are none the less interesting.'

46 'Advertisement from London. 29 July 1653', *Bodleian MSS*, Clarendon 46, fol. 131^v.

47 See *Ludlow*, p124.

48 See Capp, *The Fifth Monarchy Men*, p67 for these figures and the groups' instability as compared with the modern party system.

49 Ibid., pp62–3.

50 See Cromwell's speech of 4 July 1653 printed in Ivan Roots, ed, *Speeches of Oliver Cromwell*, Dent, London, 1989, pp9, 21, 25.

51 Capp, *The Fifth Monarchy Men*, p73.

52 *Unto every individual Member of Parliament: The humble Representation of divers afflicted women-Petitioners to the Parliament on the behalf of Mr John Lilburne*, 29 July 1653, broadsheet.

53 Citation of exemplary biblical and classical women, a stock method of debate, is here transferred to a modern political arena.

54 The Fifth Monarchist model of government was a theocracy, ruled by a parliament of church-nominated saints. The 'ungodly' would not vote. See *Certain Quaeres Presented by many Christian People*, London, 1649.

55 *A Petition of Women, Affecters and Approvers of the Petition of September 11th, 1648*, 5 May 1649.

56 *The Putney Debates*, printed in Woodhouse, *op. cit.*, p53.

57 John Lilburne, *The Freeman's Freedome Vindicated*.

58 See Alice Clark, *Working Life of Women in the Seventeenth Century*, pp150–3.

59 See WS Holdsworth, *A History of English Law*, Little, Brown, Boston, 1922–38, vol III, pp520–33, for an account of the traditional privileges lost by women in the Early Modern period at common law.

60 Sir Simonds d'Ewes, quoted *Fraser*, pp258–9.

61 See Holdsworth, *A History of English Law*, vols V, pp310–15; VI, pp644–8. See also Ferdinand Lundberg and Marynia F Farnham, *Modern Woman: The Lost Sex*, Harper & Row, New York, 1947, appendix VII, 'The Destruction of Women's Legal Rights'.

Chapter 4: A NOTE ON 7000 INCENDIARY HANDMAIDS

1 *These several Papers was sent to the Parliament ... being above seven thousand of the Names of the HANDMAIDS AND DAUGHTERS OF THE LORD; And such as feels the oppression of Tithes ...* , Mary Forster, ed, for Mary Westwood, London, 1659.

2 See Brian Manning in *The English People and the English Revolution*, p292, on tithe abolition as a potential attack on all property rights.

3 In many parishes, tithes had been impropriated by wealthy laymen, who raked off immense profits.

Chapter 5: MASTER EDWARDS' GANGRENE

1 Whereas Hill (*passim*) and Morton in *The World of the Ranters. Religious Radicalism in the English Revolution*, Lawrence & Wishart, London, 1970, found Edwards at once quotable and (within reason) reliable, revisionists harshly dismiss them as Marxist ideologues and dupes: 'Relying on Thomas Edwards for evidence ... is like relying on Horatio Bottomley or Joseph Macarthy for sound, objective depictions' (JC Davis, *Fear, Myth*

and History, p126). This revisionism has in turn come under fierce attack as 'anti-history ... whose objective is to destroy the findings of scholarship and leave in their place nothing but a knowing sneer' (EP Thompson, 'On the Rant', quoted in James Holstun's review of *Reviving the English Revolution: Reflections and Elaborations on the Work of Christopher Hill*, Geoffrey Eley and William Hunt, eds, Verso, London, 1988, in *Seventeenth Century News*, vol XLIX (No. 51–2, pp2–3). My attitude to Edwards involves, as the reader will gather, a judicious swallowing of the spicy gist, savouring it with large pinches of salt.

2   *The First and Second Parts of Gangraena*, 3rd edn, London, 1646, p30. The following references are to this edition, save where otherwise stated.

3   Anon, *A Discovery of 29. Sects here in London, all of which except the First, are most Devilish and Damnable*, London, 1641, pp4, 7–8.

4   Robert Baillie, *Anabaptism, The True Fountaine of Independency, Anitnomy, Brownism, Familisme*, Samuel Gellibrand, London, 1647.

5   Daniel Featley, *The Dippers Dipt. Or The Anabaptists Ducked and Plunged Over Head and Ears, at a Disputation at Southwark*, London, 1645, pB2ᵛ.

6   Ephraim Pagitt, *Heresiography: Or, A Description of the Heretics and Sectaries of these Latter Times*, 2nd edn, London, 1645, p59.

7   John Goodwin, CRETENSIS: *Or A Brief Answer to an Ulcerous Treatise, lately published by Mr Thomas Edwards, intituled GANGRAENA*, printed by MS for Henry Overton, London, 1646, pp9, 47.

8   Daniel Featley, *The Dippers Dipt*, pC2ᵛ.

9   Ibid., pC3ʳ.

10 John Vicars, *The Schismatic Sifted. Or, The Picture of the Independents, Freshly and Fairly Washt-over again*, Nathaniel Webb & William Gramham, London, 1646, p34.

11 'A report of the Trial of Mrs Anne Hutchinson before the Church in Boston', in *The Antinomian Controversy, 1636–1638: A Documentary History*, David D Hall, ed, Wesleyan University Press, Middletown, Connecticut, 1968, pp349–88.

12 See Christopher Hill, *Society and Puritanism in Pre-Revolutionary England*, Secker & Warburg, London, 1964, chapter 13, 'The

Spiritualisation of the Household' for the Puritan patriarchal 'little church' of the household unit, ruled by 'a father, and so a master', p431.

13 John Saltmarsh, *Groanes for Liberty ... with a Beam of Light, discovering a way to peace, Also Quaeres For the better understanding of Mr Edwards Last Book called Gangraena*, Giles Calvert, London, March 1646, p26.

14 Jeremiah Burroughes, *A Vindication of Mr Burroughes, Against Mr EDWARDS his foul Aspersions ...* , for H Overton, London, 1646, pp3–4.

15 Thomas Edwards, *The Second Part of Gangraena: Or A Fresh and further Discovery of the Errors, Heresies, Blasphemies ... A Reply to ... Mr Saltmarsh, Mr Walwyn, and Cretensis against Mr Edwards late Book ...* , by TR and EM for Ralph Smith, London, 1646, pp10–11.

16 John Milton, *The Doctrine and Discipline of Divorce. Restored to the good of both sexes ...* (1643), in *CPW*, vol II, Ernest Sirluck, ed, p326.

17 John Milton, *Tetrachordon, Expositions upon the four chief places in Scripture which treat of Mariage, or nullities in Mariage* (1644), ibid., p591.

18 Appendix to the 3rd edn of parts I and II of *Gangraena*, pp113ff.

19 John Lanseter, *Lanseters Lance, FOR Edwards'es Gangrene*, np, London, 1646, ppA3–4ʳ. Parts of this tract are reproduced in AL Morton's *The World of the Ranters*, pp26–35.

20 Peter Studley, *The Looking-Glass of Schism ...* , RB for Thomas Alchorne, London, 1633, pp214–15, 175. The 1626 visitation report at Lichfield Joint Record Office shows that 'Daniel Chidlowe et uxor' ('and wife') were presented for absenteeism; Katharine was one of seven refusing to be churched.

21 Katharine Chidley, *A New-Yeares-Gift, OR, A BRIEF EXHORTATION to Mr Thomas Edwards; That he may break off his old sins, in the old year ...* , London, 1645. Thomason dates it 1644.

22 On Joan Whitup, see *Ludlow*, p60. On Dorothy Hazzard's anti-churching initiative, see *The Records of a Church of Christ at Bristol, 1640–1687*, Roger Hayden, ed, Bristol, 1974, p88.

23 Thomas Edwards, *Antapologia: Or, A Full Answer to the Apologeticall Narration ...* , by GM for Ralph Smith, London, 1644.

24 Samuel Chidley, *Thunder from the Throne of God against the Temples of Idols*, London, MP, 1653. See *Ludlow*, p119.

25 Samuel Chidley, *To His Highness the Lord Protector &c. AND To the Parliament of England*, np, nd.

26 Katharine Chidley, *A New-Yeares-Gift*, p11.

27 By Pauline Gregg in *Free-born John*, p355.

28 See JA Sharpe, *Crime in Seventeenth-Century England*, London, 1983, pp91–114; 141–52. Philanthropic programmes grew from the revolutionary years onwards, eg Peter Chamberlain, *The Poor Mans Advocate*, Giles Calvert, London, 1649; Thomas Firmin, *Some Proposals for the imploying of the Poor, especially in and about the City of London*, London, 1678.

29 J Maddocks and Henry Pinnell, *Gangraenachrestum, or A Plaister to Allay the tumor and prevent the spread of a pernitious Ulcer*, London, September 1646, p8.

30 Thomas Edwards, *Gangraena*, part III, pp170–71.

31 The signatures of Katharine and Samuel Chidley may be seen witnessing the founding covenant of Lanseter's Bury church in 1646, reproduced in 'The Bury St Edmunds Church Covenants' in *Transactions of the Congregational Historical Society*, vol 2 (1905–6), TG Crippen, ed, p334. The renewed covenant of 1648 shows only three of the fourteen original members, including Lanseter, and is all-male, three of whom are illiterate.

Chapter 6: THE SPIRIT OF THERAPY IN AN EMPTY NOTHING CREATURE

1 Henry Jessey, *The Exceeding Riches of Grace Advanced By the Spirit of Grace, In an Empty Nothing Creature, (viz.) M[ris] SARAH WIGHT Lately Hopeless and Restless*, JM, for Henry Cripps, Lodowick Lloyd, & Livewell Chapman, London, 1652 edn, pp44–5. John Stachniewski, in *The Persecutory Imagination: English Puritanism and the Literature of Religious Despair*, Clarendon Press, Oxford, 1991, delightfully called this exchange 'ultimate one-downmanship', p41.

2 Jessey lists seventy visiting VIPs, analysed by BR Dailey in 'The Visitation of Sarah Wight: Holy Carnival and the Revolution of the Saints in Civil War London', in *Church History*, vol 55, 1986, pp452–4.

3 See Murray Tolmie, *The Triumph of the Saints: The Separatist*

Churches of London, 1616–1649, Cambridge University Press, 1977, pp109–110 for Cradock.

4 For the Holy Maid tradition, see Alan Neame's *The Holy Maid of Kent. The Life of Elizabeth Barton, 1506–1534*, Hodder & Stoughton, London, 1971, pp36–51, 80–3, 174, 336.

5 See Murray Tolmie, *The Triumph of the Saints*, pp19–21.

6 Dailey ('The Visitation of Sarah Wight') is surely right to note that the black girl is the only sufferer with whom Sarah does not try for intimacy.

7 Sarah Wight, *A Wonderful Pleasant and Profitable Letter ... To a Friend ... Published for the Use of the Afflicted*, James Cottrel, London, 1656.

8 Henry Jessey, *A Looking-Glass for Children. Being a Narrative of Gods gracious dealings with some little Children*, JL for Philemon Stephens, London, 1649; *The Lord's Loud Call to England. Being a True Relation of some late Various and Wonderful Judgments ... As also of the Odious Sin of Drinking Healths ...* , London, 1660, Samuel Pepys, *Diary*, vol I, 2 May 1660, p122; James Fisher, *The Wise Virgin. Or, A Wonderful Narration of the hand of God ... in afflicting a Childe of 11 years of age ...* , for John Rothwell, London, 1653.

9 *The Wonderful Works of God. Declared by the strange Prophecie of a Maid*, London, 1641. See Bernard Capp's account of prodigy-stories in 'The Fifth Monarchists and Popular Millennarianism', in *Radical Religion in the English Revolution*, JF McGregor and B Reay, eds, Oxford University Press, 1984, p179.

10 John and Anna Furly, *A Testimony to the True Light, also A True Relation how the Lord made manifest Strength in Weakness*, London, 1670, pp24, 27.

11 Quoted *Mack*, p34.

Chapter 7: WOMEN COUNSELLORS FOR MEN OF BLOOD

1 *Eikonoklastes* (1649), in *CPW*, vol III, p595. The tract answers *Eikon Basilike* ('The Image of the King'), a book of meditations and prayers supposed to have been composed by Charles I in captivity. See Stevie Davies, *Images of Kingship in 'Paradise Lost': Milton's Politics and Christian Liberty*, Missouri University Press, 1983, pp17, 44–9.

2 See Judge David Jenkins, *A Plea, Delivered in to the Earl of Manchester and the Speaker of the House of Commons ...* , London,

1647: The king 'is a father; the child (in law) is called *pars patris* [part of the father]'; 'The king is God's vicar on earth', *Somers*, vol V, pp93, 97. It was commonplace to speak of Charles I as 'crucified' and 'the Royal Martyr'. See JN Figgis, *The Divine Right of Kings*, Cambridge University Press, 1992, chapter VII.

3   See *Ludlow*, p198.

4   Elizabeth Pool, *A Vision, wherein is manifested the disease and cure of the KINGDOME ... TOGETHER WITH a true copy of what was delivered to the General Council of the Army [5 Jan 1649]*, London, 1649, p1.

5   CV Wedgwood, *The Trial of Charles I*, p93.

6   Elizabeth Pool, *An(other) Alarum of War, Given to the Army ...* , London, 1649.

7   Set out in Judge David Jenkins, *Lex Terrae; or, Laws of the Land:* 'The law saith the king can do no wrong; that he is physician of the realm, father of the nation, husband of the realm ... espoused to his realm at his coronation' (*Somers*, vol V, p108). Elaine Hobby in *Virtue of Necessity: English Women's Writing 1649–88*, Virago, London, 1988, p29, calls it 'popular metaphor', but it was understood to be neither metaphor nor analogy.

8   Elizabeth Pool, *A Vision*, p5.

9   Elizabeth Pool, *An(other) Alarum*, p10.

10 Andrew Marvell, 'An Horatian ode upon Cromwell's Return from Ireland', lines 55–60, 63–4, in ES Donno, ed, *The Complete Poems*, Penguin, Harmondsworth, 1972.

11 *Diaries and Letters of Philip Henry, 1631–96*, Matthew Henry Lee, ed, London, 1882, p2.

12 Mary Pope, *A Treatise of Magistracy, shewing the Magistrate hath been and for ever is to be the Chief Officer in the Church ...* , London, 1647.

13 Mary Pope, *Heare, heare, heare, A WORD OR MESSAGE from Heaven. To All Covenant Breakers*, London, 1649.

14 Ibid., pp23, 25.

15 Mary Pope, *Behold, here is a Word or, An Answer to the Late Remonstrance of the Army*, Mrs Edwards, London, 1649, pp4, 5. Thomason dates this 24 January, 1649.

16 Mary Pope, Ibid, pp15, 8.

17 See Elizabeth Warren, The Old and Good Way Vindicated ... , for Henry Shepherd and William Ley, London, 1645; *Spiritual*

Thrift, by CL for Henry Shepherd, London, 1647; *A Warning-Piece from Heaven, against the Sins of the Times*, by Richard Constable for Henry Shepherd, London, 1649.

18 Mary Cary, *The Little Horns Doom & Downfall: A Scripture-Prophesie of King James, and King Charles, and of this Present Parliament, unfolded.* 'By M. Cary a servant of Jesus Christ', 'Printed for the author', London, 1651, ppa1–a2. The original was written 'above 7 years since' ('To The Reader').

19 Mary Cary, *A New and More Exact Mappe or Description of New Jerusalems Glory when Jesus Christ and his Saints with him shall reign a thousand years*, WH, London, 1651, pp208, 209.

20 See H McLachlan, *Sir Isaac Newton's Theological Manuscripts*, Liverpool, 1950, pp119–21.

21 See Christopher Hill's delightful account of 'End of the World' schemes in *Puritanism and Revolution*, Secker & Warburg, London, 1958, chapter 12 (see p317 for Beverley); and his *The English Bible and the Seventeenth Century Revolution* for a latter-day account of Mary Cary within the tradition (pp308–9).

22 Mary Cary, *The Little Horns Doom*, pp45, 47.

23 Mary Cary, *A New and More Exact Mappe*, pp244, 284.

24 Mary Cary (signed 'M.R.'), *Twelve New Proposals to the Supreme Governors of the Three Nations now assembled at Westminster ...* , Henry Hills, for RC, London, 1653.

25 Mary Cary, *The Little Horns Doom*, 'To the Reader', np.

Chapter 8: ANNA TRAPNEL'S JOURNEY TO CORNWALL

1 Anna Trapnel. *The Cry of a Stone, or a RELATION of Something Spoken in Whitehall ... Relating to the Governors, Army, Churches, Ministry, Universities: and the whole Nation ...* , London, 1654, p42.

2 *Anna Trapnel's Report and Plea, or, A NARRATIVE OF her Journey from London into Cornwall ...* , for Thomas Brewster, London, 1654, 'To the Reader', np.

3 *The Complaining Testimony of Some (though weak, and of the least) of Sions Children ...* , for Livewell Chapman, London, 1656, p2.

4 See Capp, *The Fifth Monarchy Men*, pp102–3.

5 Thurloe, *State Papers*, vol V, pp756–7. See PG Rogers, *The Fifth Monarchy Men*, Oxford University Press, pp64f.

6 Ibid., p65.

7 Anna Trapnel, *A Legacy for Saints; Being Several Experiences of the dealings of God with Anna Trapnel, in, and after her Conversion* ... , T Brewster, London, 1654, p2.

8 Dailey in 'The Visitation of Sarah Wight' assumes that Sarah precedes Anna: careful reading of Anna's *Legacy for Saints* shows that this is unlikely. Anna's visions began '7 years ago', ie, around 1646–7, and the next significant political event is the Army's entry into London, via Southwark, in 1647. 'Some years later' came Dunbar. Hence Nigel Smith's vague equation of the Blackheath visions with 'the end of the Barebones Parliament' is six years out (*Perfection Proclaimed. Language and Literature in English Radical Religion, 1640–60*, Clarendon Press, Oxford, 1989, p49). Anna may seem to witter, but this was in part precautionary: her calendar and symbolism bear detailed scrutiny.

9 Described by Antonia Fraser, in *Cromwell: Our Chief of Men*, Weidenfeld & Nicolson, London, 1973, p205.

10 Ibid., quoted p363.

11 Bulstrode Whitelock, *Memorials of the English Affairs from the beginning of the Reign of King Charles I to the Happy Restoration of King Charles the Second*, London, 1853, vol III, p239.

12 The whole letter (dated 21°-10-54, from London), is in the Rawlinson MSS. A21, p325; reprinted in full by Champlin Burrage, 'Anna Trapnel's Prophecies', in *English Historical Review*, vol XXVI, 1911, pp531–2.

13 Antonia Fraser in *Cromwell: Our Chief of Men*, catalogues the Protectoral family's acquisitions.

14 Arise (Rees) Evans, *An Echo to the Voice from Heaven* (bound with *A Voice from Heaven to the Common-wealth of England*), self-printed, London, 1652, p8.

15 Elinor Channel, *A Message from God (by a Dumb Woman) to his Highness the Lord Protector ... Published according to her Desire by Arise Evans*, London, 1653–4, p7.

16 See Patricia Crawford, *Women and Religion in England, 1500–1720*, Routledge, London, 1993, pp15–17, 163f.

17 Speech of Dr Clarges (5 December 1656) in *Diary of Thomas Burton, Esq. Memoirs of the Parliaments of Oliver and Richard Cromwell*, John Towill Rutt, ed, London, 1828, p22.

18 Ursula Adman is taken by Capp (*Fifth Monarchy Men*, p239) to

be Anna Trapnel's sister, but Anna may have meant 'sister' here as elsewhere metaphorically.

Chapter 9: THREE PURITAN MARRIAGES

1 *The Diary of Ralph Josselin, 1616–1683*, Alan Macfarlane, ed, Records of Social and Economic History, New Series III, Oxford University Press for British Academy, London, 1976.

2 See Alan Macfarlane's illuminating account of the diary as record of Puritan 'investment' and spiritual-economic accounting, in *The Family Life of Ralph Josselin, A Seventeenth Century Clergyman. An Essay in Historical Anthropology*, Cambridge University Press, 1970, pp5, 27–71. See also Paul Delany, *British Autobiography in the Seventeenth Century*, Routledge & Kegan Paul, London, 1969, p52.

3 On major epidemic diseases see JA Sharpe, *Early Modern England*, pp49–53; Carl Bridenbaugh, *Vexed and Troubled Englishmen, 1590–1642. The Beginnings of the American People*, Clarendon Press, Oxford, 1968, pp25ff.

4 Daniel Rogers, *Matrimonial Honour: Or A Treatise of Marriage*, London, 1650 edn.

5 See Stevie Davies, *Henry Vaughan* (Seren, Bridgend, 1995), chapter 6, for a symmetrically opposite Royalist experience of the 'terrible hope' of Judgement.

6 See 15th Book of *The Practice of Physic* in *The Rational Physician's Library* by Abdiah Cole and Nicholas Culpeper, London, 1661: 'Of Women's Diseases'. Hair-raising procedures like brimstone baths are always inferior to 'Copulation, if it may be legally done', for 'Green-sickness', p403.

7 Jane Sharp, *The Midwives Book, or, The whole Art of Midwifery*, Simon Miller, London, 1671, fought with asperity male interference with midwifery and women's exclusion from anatomy dissections. Elizabeth Cellier called for maternity and training hospitals, collecting data for twenty years. See also Culpeper's self-help book, *A Directory of Midwives; or, a Guide for Women, in their Conception, Bearing and Suckling their Children*, London, 1651. Hilda Smith's 'Gynecology and Ideology' in *Liberating Women's History. Theoretical and Critical Essays*, Illinois University Press, Urbana, 1976, offers a fascinating treatment of this subject, pp97–114.

8   'Womb-fury' is discussed in Cole and Culpeper's *The Practice of Physic*, pp417–20.

9   Anon, *Aristotles Master-Piece, Or The Secrets of Generation Display'd In All Parts Thereof. Very Necessary for all Midwives, Nurses and Young Married Women*, R How, London, 1690, p124; edn 12, p23. Roy Porter and Lesley Hall comment on the similarity with Jane Sharp's equation of clitoris with penis in *The Compleat Midwife's Companion*, chapter 12, *The Facts of Life: The Creation of Sexual Knowledge in Britain, 1650–1950*, Yale University Press, New Haven, 1995, p303, n124.

10 'Wherefore did [God] create passions within us, pleasures round about us, but that these, rightly tempered, are the very ingredients of virtue?' (Milton, *Areopagitica* [1644], in *CPW*, vol II, p555).

11 I have treated this more fully in *John Milton*, Harvester Wheatsheaf, New York, 1991, p70f.

12 Milton, *An Apology for Smectymnuus, CPW*, vol I, pp891, 892.

13 William Gouge, *Of Domesticall Duties*, London, 1622. See JA Sharpe, *Early Modern England*, pp66–7.

14 All references to the writings of Wallington are to Paul S Seaver's *Wallington's World. A Puritan Artisan in Seventeenth-Century London*, Methuen, London, 1985.

15 See tasselled strings and gilded laces of Sir Henry Gage, c. 1645; John Hutchinson's luxuriant curls are only a couple of inches shorter than the ringlets of James, Duke of York, 1661, reproduced in Valerie Cumming, *A Visual History of Costume. The Seventeenth Century*, Batsford, London, 1984, pp79, 93.

16 Lucy Hutchinson, *Memoirs of the Life of Colonel Hutchinson*, NH Keeble, ed, Dent, London, 1995 edn, p14. Walker's portrait of John Hutchinson is reproduced on the cover.

17 Milton, *Paradise Lost*, IV. 303.

18 See Valerie Cumming, *A Visual History of Costume*, pp86–98; Iris Brooke, *English Costume of the Seventeenth Century*, Adam & Charles Black, London, 1934, pp40ff.

19 See Milton's bitter treatment of Dalila who 'treacherously/ Had shorn the fatal harvest of thy head' (Chorus, *Samson Agonistes*, lines 1023–5), 'a thorn/Intestine' who leads the Chorus to conclude, 'Therefore God's universal law/Gave to the man despotic power/Over his female in due awe' (lines 1053–5).

20 John Aubrey, *Minutes of the Life of Mr John Milton*, reprinted in

The Early Lives of Milton, Helen Darbishire, ed, Constable, London, 1932, p3.

21 Garden design in the seventeenth century was conceived as a noble art rather than a dilettante hobby. See Roy Strong, *The Renaissance Garden in England*, Thames & Hudson, London, 1979, for the dynastic and cosmological conception of the garden.

22 But see Alfred Wood, *Nottinghamshire in the Civil War*, London, 1937, for Lucy's inaccuracies.

23 This duality is explored by NH Keeble in '"The Colonel's Shadow": Lucy Hutchinson, Women's Writing and the Civil War', in Thomas Healy and Jonathan Sawday, eds, *Literature and the English Commonwealth*, Cambridge University Press, 1990, pp227–47.

24 John Donne, 'A Nocturnall upon S. Lucies day, Being the Shortest day', lines 17–18, in HJC Grierson, ed, *Poetical Works*, Oxford, 1971 edn.

25 *The Life of Mrs Lucy Hutchinson. Written by Herself: A Fragment*, printed in NH Keeble, ed, *Memoirs*, p4.

26 John Vicars, *God's Ark Topping the Worlds Waves, or the Third Part of the Parliamentary Chronicle*, London, 1646, p259.

Chapter 10: GEORGE FOX, MARGARET FELL & A COMMONWEALTH OF DAUGHTERS

1 Recorded by Fox in his *Journal*, p119.

2 Quoted in *Ross*, p9.

3 See *Braithwaite (1)*, p475. Ocular 'fascination' was believed to bewitch victims, by malign emanations.

4 George Fox, *Journal*, p164.

5 Walter Cradock, *Glad Tidings*, London, 1648, p50.

6 *The Testimony of Margaret Fell Concerning Her Late Husband George Fox ...* , printed in *SCL*, p116.

7 See George Fox's account of the trial in the *Journal*, p467.

8 George Fox, *Journal*, p115; Margaret Fell, *Testimony*, in *SCL*, pp116–17.

9 *Braithwaite (1)*, pp124, 125. See Thomas Holmes' letter to Margaret Fell, c. 5 April 1654, Swarthmoor Collections, I, p190.

10 Letter of 9 May 1653, by Anthony Pearson, reprinted with omissions in *Ross*, pp20–21.

11 This letter is reprinted in *SCL*, pp103–4.

12 See *Ross* pp36–8; *SCL*, pp97–100. Braithwaite points out that Fox

crossed out analagous passages in other hero-worshipping letters, and aptly compares the tenor with that of the Nayler cult (*Braithwaite (1)*, pp105–6).

13 Swarthmoor MSS, VII, 24.

14 Letter by Margaret Fell to Thomas Fell of February 1653, printed in full in *Ross*, pp119–21.

15 Letter by Margaret Fell of 21 October 1657, Spence MSS, III, 49.

16 Thomas Rawlinson, letter to Margaret Fell, Rawlinson Manuscript; see *Mack*, p303.

17 George Fox, *The Woman Learning in Silence, or The Mystery of the Womans Subjection to her Husband*, London, 1656, reprinted as a pamphlet, Paul Thompson, Annscroft, 1995, p3.

18 Margaret Fell, *Womens Speaking Justified, Proved and Allowed of by the Scriptures, SCL*, p74.

19 Elizabeth Hooton to Oliver Cromwell, 1653, Portfolio Manuscripts 3/3, 10, FHL, quoted in Emily Manners, *Elizabeth Hooton: First Quaker Woman Preacher (1600–1672)*, Headley Brothers, London, 1914, p10.

20 George Bishop, *New-England Judged, By The Spirit of the Lord*, London, 1703 edn, pp20, 415–20.

21 Ibid., pp405–6.

22 Sarah Blackborow, *The Just and Equal Balance Discovered*, London, 1660, pp7, 8; *A Visit to the Spirit in Prison*, London, 1658 (this tract is mispaginated, 1, 4, 5, 9, 7, 8, 7 in FHL copy; Mary Smith, *These Few Lines are to All ...* , London, 1667, p1; Elizabeth Bathurst, *Truths Vindication, or, A Gentle Stroke to wipe off the Foul Aspersions*, London, 1679, p51; Sarah Backborow, *The Just and Equal Balance Discovered*, pp13–14.

23 Barry Reay, *The English Quakers and the English Revolution*, MT Smith, New York, 1985, p9; Patricia Crawford, *Women and Religion in England, 1500–1720*, chapter 8.

24 Margaret Fell, *A Declaration and an Information from Us, The People Called Quakers, to the Present Governors ...* , *SCL*, p54.

25 *Mack*, p57. I am indebted to Mack's memorable analysis of the egalitarian ecstasy which bonded the early movement.

26 Quoted, with many analogous examples, by *Mack*, p153ff.

27 See *Ross*, pp64–5, for samples from the accounts.

28 See Baxter's moving testament to his deceased wife, *The Breviate of Margaret Baxter* (London, 1681), for his marriage condition,

'That I would have nothing that before her marriage was hers, that I ... might not seem to marry her for covetousness' (p109).

29 *State Papers of John Thurloe*, VIII (4), *Journal of the Friends Historical Society*, October, 1911, p165.

30 See *Journal of the Friends Historical Society*, XI, p157, letter 18 of Abraham MSS.

31 See *Kunze*, pp102ff for the account of the dismaying Rawlinson affair.

32 Margaret Fell, *A True Testimony from the People of God (Who by the World are Called Quakers)*, np, London, 1660, in *SCL*, pp22, 25.

33 Margaret Fell, *Some Ranters Principles Answered*, appended to *A Testimony of the Touchstone and A Trial by the Scriptures* ... , *SCL*, pp87, 90, 94.

34 Margaret Fell, *A Declaration and Information from Us, The People called Quakers* (delivered by hand to Charles II, 1660), in *SCL*, pp49–55.

35 Margaret Fell, *Womens Speaking Justified*, *SCL*, pp73, 77.

36 Spence MSS, III, 144, 146, 147.

37 George Bishop, *New-England Judged*, p12.

38 Ann Audland, *A True Declaration of the Suffering of the Innocent ... Wherein is discovered the zeal of the Magistrates and People of BANBURY* ... , Giles Calvert, London, 1655, pp1–4.

39 Hester (or Esther) Biddle, *The Trumpet of the Lord Sounded forth unto these Three Nations* ... , 'By one who is a sufferer for the Testimony of Jesus, in Newgate, Esther Biddle', London, 1662, p13.

40 Hester Biddle, *Wo to Thee Town of Cambridge*, London, 1655, broadsheet.

41 Francis Higginson, *A Brief Relation of the Irreligion of the Northern Quakers*, London, 1653, pp3–4.

42 Margaret Fell to Justice Sawrey, 1653, Spence MSS, 3/146.

43 Priscilla Cotton and Mary Cole, *To the Priests and People of England, we discharge our consciences* ... , London, 1655, p6.

44 Margaret Fell, *Womens Speaking Justified*, *SCL*, p70.

45 George Keith, *The Woman-Preacher of Samaria; a Better Preacher ... than any of the Men-Preachers of the Man-made Ministry in these THREE NATIONS*, np, London, 1674, pp2, 8. The story of the woman of Samaria is in the Gospel of John, 4:28–30.

46 Ibid., p20.

47 William Mather, *A Novelty: Or, a Government of Women, Distinct from Men, Erected Amongst Some People Called Quakers*, Sarah Hawkins, London, nd, p5.

48 *Diary of Thomas Burton*, p22.

49 Ibid., p23.

50 Ibid., pp153, 155.

51 Quoted in Mabel Richmond Brailsford, *A Quaker from Cromwell's Army: James Nayler*, Swarthmore Press, London, 1927, p131.

52 Brailsford, ibid., is a classic exponent of the demonisation of Martha Simmonds as 'the villain of this piece', a 'half-crazy woman', the 'fountain and origin of evil' (pp97, 106, 157). This punitive, misogynist attitude, also found in Braithwaite and Ross, implies the rawness of the wound to Quaker self-esteem *300 years* after the events.

53 See Brailsford, ibid., p114.

54 Diary of *Thomas Burton*, pp46–7, 51, 56.

55 Patricia Crawford in *Women and Religion*, pp166–80, attacks the myth of Martha Simmonds as destructive madwoman, substituting a view of Martha as 'challenger for Quaker leadership' in a male hierarchy. I am not convinced that, in that group dynamic, Martha knew quite what she was doing. See also Christine Trevett, 'The Women around James Nayler, Quaker: a matter of emphasis', in *Religion*, 20, 1990, pp249–73.

56 George Fox, *Journal*, pp252–3.

57 Recorded as Nayler's dying words in his *Collected Works*, p696. Quoted *Braithwaite (1)*, p275.

58 Complete letter printed in Appendix 9 of *Ross*, pp396–8.

59 Martha Simmonds, *A Lamentation for the Lost Sheep of the House of Israel* ... , Giles Calvert, London, 1656, pp4–5.

60 HJ Cadbury, ed, *Letters to William Dewsbury and Others*, 1948, p41.

61 *Braithwaite (1)*, pp388, 409, 426.

62 Letter from Margaret Fell to Bridget Fell, 1660, Spence MSS. III, 71.

63 Samuel Pepys, *Diary*, 1660, vol I, p44.

64 *Records of Quarter Sessions*, printed in B Nightingale, *Early Stages of the Quaker Movement in Lancashire*, Congregational Union of England and Wales Inc, London, 1921, pp129, 132, 154, 155.

65 My account of Margaret Fell's trial is taken from Margaret Fell's

and George Fox's *The Examination and Tryall of Margaret Fell and George Fox (at the several Assizes held at Lancaster ...*), np, London, 1664.

66 'Praemunire' is explained by a contemporary source as deriving from the 'process of summons against immigrant Papists', 'to be imprisoned during life, to forfeit lands and goods, and to be put out of the protection of the Law' (Sergeant Thorpe, *Judge of Assize Court for the Northern Circuit ... to Grand Jury at York Assizes...* , Matthew Walbancke & Richard Best, London, 1649, pp12–13), Margaret Fell was being outlawed as an enemy to the Crown.

67 Margaret Fell to Assize Judges, August 1664, Spence MSS, III, p132.

68 Quoted *Kunze*, p56. Kunze's suggestion that 'prior marital sexual activity may have occurred' seems to me on balance unlikely (p57), in view of Fox's deep sublimation of eroticism, but her treatment of the relationship is fascinating.

69 Margaret Fell, *Testimony*, in *SCL*, p123.

70 Margaret Fell, Epistle to Friends, of April 1700, quoted in *Ross*, p380.

Chapter 11: ANNA'S TRUMPET BLASTS THE QUAKERS

1 For dates see Champlin Burrage, 'Anna Trapnel's Prophecies', in *English Historical Review*, vol XXVI, 1911, p527.

2 Anna Trapnel, untitled volume of verse in Bodleian Library, 1658, p366. See also Anna's last known publication, *A Voice for the King of Saints*, 1658.

3 Op. cit., p842.

Chapter 12: QUAKER WOMEN ON THE ROAD

1 See AL Beier, *Masterless Men: The Vagrancy Problem in England 1560–1640*, Methuen, London, 1985, pp84–5.

2 *Braithwaite (I)*, pp165–70.

3 Barbara Blaugdone, *An Account of the Travels, Sufferings and Persecutions of BABARA BLAUGDONE*, London, 1691, p9.

4 George Bishop *et al*, *The Cry of Blood. And Herod, Pontius Pilate, and the Jews Reconciled*, Giles Calvert, London, 1656, pp16–20.

5 Ibid., pp98–9, 100.

6 GR Quaife, *Wanton Wenches and Wayward Wives ...* , pp156–8.

7 AL Beier, *Masterless Men*, p58.

8 Samuel Butler, *Characters*, CW Davies, ed, Case Western Reserve University Press, 1970, p199.

9 Anne Askew's account of her racking was in *The latter examination*, published by John Bale after her burning as heretic in 1645: 'I lay still and did not cry, my lord Chancellor and master Rich, took pains to rack me [with] their own hands, till I was nigh dead' (pp44r–47r). See Elaine V Beilin, 'Anne Askew's Self-Portrait in the Examinations', in *Silent But for the Word. Tudor Women as Patrons, Translators, and Writers of Religious Works*, MP Hannay, ed, Kent State University Press, Ohio, 1985, pp77–91.

10 *Diary of Thomas Burton*, p154.

11 Letter of Francis Howgill to Kendal Friends, Boswell Middleton Collection, p92.

12 See Liam de Paor, *The Peoples of Ireland. From Prehistory to Modern Times*, Hutchinson, London, 1986, pp156–7; Antonia Fraser, *Cromwell: Our Chief of Men*, pp533–57, on Henry and Oliver Cromwell and Irish policy.

13 Quoted *Braithwaite (1)*, p215.

14 Ibid., p218.

15 See Carl Bridenbaugh, *Vexed and Troubled Englishmen*, pp234–6.

16 Letter of George Fox, 1669, quoted in *Braithwaite (2)*, p260.

17 See *Braithwaite (2)*, p509.

18 Instead of referring to *A Short Relation of some of the Cruel Sufferings of ... Katharine Evans and Sarah Chevers*, I refer throughout to the augmented *A True Account of the Great Tryals and Cruel Sufferings undergone by those Two Servants of God, KATHARINE EVANS AND SARAH CHEVERS ... added A Short Relation from George Robinson ...* , for R Wilson, London, 1663.

19 *Braithwaite (1)*, p428.

20 John Milton, *Areopagitica*, CPW, vol II, p561.

21 *Her Own Life: Autobiographical Writings by Seventeenth-Century Englishwomen*, Elspeth Graham *et al*, eds, Routledge, London, 1989, p130.

22 Quoted in *Braithwaite (1)*, p214.

23 The classic (though anti-clerical) text is Erasmus' *Praise of Folly*. From St Paul's 'I speak as a fool', he moves to 'folly' as Christlike and unworldly innocence (see Desiderius Erasmus, *Praise of Folly*, tr. B Radice, AHT Levi, ed, Penguin, Harmondsworth, 1971, pp191–203).

24 John Milton, *Areopagitica, CPW*, vol II, p504; *Of Reformation in England, CPW*, vol I, pp611–12.

25 This is memorably told in *Braithwaite (1)*, p432.

26 Fynes Moryson, *Itinerary*, in *Shakespeare's Europe: The Fourth Part of Fynes Moryson's Itinerary*, introd, Charles Hughes, Manchester University Press, Manchester, 1902, pp 3, 13. See also SC Chew, *The Crescent and the Rose: Islam and England during the Renaissance*, Oxford University Press, 1937.

27 See *Mack*, p168.

28 Thomas Aldam *et al, False Prophets and False Teachers described* (1652), signed by six Friends, 'Prisoners of the Lord at York Castle, 1652', p8.

29 Letter of Mary Fisher to the Judge in York, nd, AR Barclay MSS, vol 324, no 173, FHL. See Sharpe, *Crime in Seventeenth-Century England*, for horse-theft as felony.

30 Joseph Besse, *A Collection of the Sufferings of the People Called Quakers*, London, 1753, vol I, p85.

31 George Bishop, *New-England Judged*, pp1–25.

32 John Milton, *State Papers*, 1656, in *CPW*, vol V, part II, p778.

33 Letter of Mary Fisher to T Killam, T Aldam and J Killam and wives in London, 13 March 1658. William Caton MSS, vol 320, I/165, FHL.

34 Letter of Sir Thomas Bendish, 24 July 1658, in Thurloe, *State Papers*, vol VII, p287.

35 There is a photograph of the statue in Margaret Hope Bacon's *Mothers of Feminism. The Story of Quaker Women in America*, Harper & Row, San Francisco, 1986.

36 Letter of Rev. John Eliot to Thomas Brooks, London, 19 May 1660, as printed by Johan Winsser in 'Mary Dyer and the "Monster" Story', *Quaker History*, 79, 1990, pp30–31. See John Winthrop, *A Short History of the Rise, Reign, and Ruine of the Antinomians and Libertines*, quoted in *The Antinomian Controversy, 1636–1638*, DD Hall, ed, Wesleyan University Press, Middletown, Connecticut, 1968, p214, for Anne Hutchinson's 'monsters'; Amy Schrager Lang, *Prophetic Woman: Anne Hutchinson and the Problem of Dissent in the Literature of New England*, California University Press, Berkeley, 1987, pp52–71.

37 George Bishop, *New-England Judged*, p22.

38 Letter of William Dyer to Governor Endicott, 1660, quoted by

James Bowdon in *The History of the Society of Friends in America*, Charles Gilpin, London, 1850, vol I, pp199–200.

39 Quoted in *Braithwaite (1)*, p515.

40 By, eg, Mary Hope Bacon in *Mothers of Feminism, passim*.

41 Alice Clark, *Working Life of Women*, p32.

CONCLUSION – BUT NEVER THE END

1 Nehemiah Wallington recorded this story in his notebook. See PS Seaver, *Wallington's World*, pp62–3.

2 See John Morrill, *The Nature of the English Revolution*, pp34–6.

3 PS Seaver, *Wallington's World*, p61.

4 *The Letters and Journals of Robert Baillie*, David Laing, ed, Edinburgh, 1841, vol I, p291; *The Autobiography of Joseph Lister*, T Wright, ed, London, 1842, pp5–6.

5 For an exciting account of these events, see Brian Manning, *The English People and the English Revolution*, pp32–3.

6 Thomas Edwards, *The First and Second Parts of Gangraena*, pp16–17.

7 Samuel Pepys, *Diary*, 1660, vol I, pp52, 54, 113.

8 Capp, *The Fifth Monarchy Men*, p174.

9 *The Memoirs of Ann Lady Fanshawe*, HC Fanshawe, ed, John Lane, Bodley Head, London and New York, 1907, pp94–5.

10 Samuel Pepys, *Diary*, 1660, vol I, pp265–6, 270.

11 See Christopher Hill, *The Experience of Defeat*, p72.

12 Samuel Pepys, *Diary*, 1660, vol I, p289.

13 Ibid., p152.

14 *The Life of Adam Martindale, Written by Himself*, Richard Parkinson, ed, Chetham Society Publication, Manchester, 1845, pp151–7.

15 *The Autobiography of Henry Newcome*, R Parkinson, ed, Chetham Society Publication, Manchester, 1862, vol I, pp121–6.

16 Mary Penington, *Experiences in the Life of Mary Penington* … , Norman Penney, ed, The Biddle Press, Philadelphia; Headley Brothers, London, 1990 edn, p52.

17 See *Mack*, p301.

18 Bathsua Makin, *An Essay to Revive the Antient Education of Gentlewomen*, London, 1673, partially reprinted in *The Female Spectator: English Women Writers before 1800*, Mary R Mahl and Helene Koon, eds, Indiana University Press, Bloomington, The

Feminist Press, New York, 1977, pp126–135.

19 'Priest defends "sexist" sign', *Guardian*, 15 July 1996; 'Judges give ultimatum to rebel vicar', *Guardian*, 7 September 1996; 'Diehard foe of women priests', *Guardian*, 6 November 1996; 'First woman claims her place', *Guardian*, 13 February 1997.

1 Primary sources: printed pamphlets, books, petitions, broadsheets by women

Adams, Mary, *A Warning to the Inhabitants of England, and London In Particular*, np, 1676.

Astell, Mary, *Reflections upon Marriage*, (3rd edn, with 'a Preface, in Answer to some Objections'), London, 1706

Audland, Ann (and Jane Waugh), *A True Declaration of the Sufferings of the Innocent, Wherein is discovered the zeal of the Magistrates and People of Banbury*, Giles Calvert, London, 1655

Avery, Elizabeth, *Scripture-Prophecies Opened ... In Several Letters Written to Christian Friends*, Giles Calvert, London, 1647

Barwick, Grace, *To all Present Rulers ... whether Parliament or whomsoever of England*, for Mary Westwood, London, 1659

Bathurst, Elizabeth (and Anne Bathurst), *An Expostulatory Appeal to the Professors of Christianity*, London, 1679?

——*Truth's Vindication, or, A Gentle Stroke to wipe off the Foul Aspersions*, London, 1679

Biddle, Hester, *Wo to thee Town of Cambridge*, London, 1655

——*Wo to thee City of Oxford*, London, 1655

——*The Trumpet of the Lord Sounded forth unto these three nations*, London, 1662

Blackborow, Sarah, *A Visit to the Spirit in Prison; and An Invitation to all people to come to Christ ...* , for Thomas Simmonds, London, 1658

——*The Just and Equal Balance Discovered: with A true measure ...* , for MW, London, 1660

Blaugdone, Barbara, *An Account of the Travels, Sufferings and Persecutions of BARBARA BLAUGDONE*, London, 1691 (1704)

Boulbie, Judith, *A Testimony for Truth*, London, 1665

Cary, Mary, *A New and More Exact Mappe. OR, Description of New Jerusalems Glory when Jesus Christ and his Saints with him shall reign a thousand years ...* , printed for the author, London, 1651

——*The Little Horns Doom & Downfall: A Scripture-Prophecie of King James and King Charles, and of this Present Parliament, unfolded*, 1647, published with *A New and More Exact Mappe*, 1651

——*The Restitution of the Witnesses, and Englands Fall from (the*

Mystical Babylon) Rome ... 2nd edn, 'corrected, and much enlarged, and all objections answered by the Author.' H Hills for RC, London, 1653

——*Twelve New Proposals To The Supreme Governours of the three Nations now assembled at Westminster*, Henry Hills, for RC, London, 1653

——*A Word In Season To The Kingdom of England. Or, A Precious Cordial for a distempered Kingdom* ... , Giles Calvert, London, 1647

Cavendish, Margaret, Marchioness of Newcastle, *Poems and Fancies*, London, 1653

Channel, Elinor, *A Message from God (by a Dumb Woman) To His Highness the Lord Protector. Together with A Word of Advice to the Commons of England and Wales ... Published ... by Arise Evans*, London, 1653/4.

Chidley, Katharine, *Good Counsell, the Petitioners for Presbyterian Government* ... , (broadsheet), London, 1645

——*The Justification of the Independant Churches of Christ*, London, 1641

——*A New-Yeares-Gift, OR, A BRIEF EXHORTATION to Mr Thomas Edwards; That he may break off his old sins, in the old year* ... , London, 1645

Cotton, Priscilla and Mary Cole, *To the Priests and People of England, we discharge our consciences and give them warning*, London, 1655

Cotton, Priscilla, *As I Was In The Prison-house* ... , London, 1656

Davies, Lady Eleanor, *The Gatehouse Salutation From the Lady Eleanor* ... , London, 1646

——*Given to the Elector Prince Charles of the Rhine* ... , London, 1648

——*The Lady Eleanor her Appeal* ... , London, 1646

——*To the most Honourable States* ... , London, 1649

——*Samsons Legacie*, London, 1643

Docwra, Anne, *An Apostate Conscience Exposed, and the Miserable Consequences Thereof Disclosed*, T Sowle, London, 1699

——*An Epistle of Love and Good Advice to my Old Friends and Fellow Sufferers ... The Old Royalists* ... , London, 1683

——*The Second Part of an Apostate-Conscience Exposed: Being an Answer to a Scurrilous Pamphlet*, T Sowle, London, 1700

——*A Treatise Concerning Enthusiasm*, T Sowle, London, 1700

Dyer, Mary, [Letter] *To the General Court now in Boston*, and *Last*

Letter, 1659, in George Bishop, *New-England Judged, By the Spirit of the Lord*, in two parts, London, 1703 edn, pp288–91, 311–12

Evans, Katharine and Sarah Chevers, *A True Account of the Great Tryals and Cruel Sufferings undergone by these two faithful servants of God, Katharine Evans and Sarah Chevers*, printed for Robert Wilson, London, 1663

Everard, Margaret, *An Epistle of Margaret Everard to The People Called Quakers and the Ministry among them*, 1699

Fell, Lydia, *A Testimony and Warning ... [to] the Governor, Magistrates and People inhabiting the Island of Barbados*, London, 1676

Fell, Margaret (and George Fox), *The Examination and Tryall of Margaret Fell and George Fox ... 1663/4. And ... 1664*, np, 1664

Fletcher, Elizabeth, *A Few Words in Season To all the Inhabitants of the Earth ...*, Robert Wilson, London, 1660

Forster, Mary, *A Declaration of the Bountiful Loving-Kindness of the Lord, Manifested to this Hand-maid, Mary Harris ...* , London, 1669

——*Some Seasonable Considerations to the Young Men and Women ...* , London, 1684

——(ed), *These several papers was sent to the Parliament .... Being above 7 thousand of the Names of the HAND MAIDS AND DAUGHTERS OF THE LORD ...* , for Mary Westwood, London 1659

Furly, Ann and John, *A Testimony to the True Light*, also *A True Relation how the Lord made manifest Strength in Weakness*, London, 1670

Hendericks, Elizabeth, *An Epistle to Friends in England*, np, 1672

Hooton (or Hooten), Elizabeth, *et al, False Prophets or False Teachers described*, London, 1652

Howgill, Mary, *The Vision of the Lord of Hosts*, 'By a Handmaid of the Lord, M.H.', London, 1662

Lead, Jane, *Divine Revelations and Prophecies* (first published 1700), Nottingham, 1830 edn.

Leveller Women's Petitions:

——*To the Supreme Authority of this Nation ... The humble Petition of divers well-affected Women ...* , London, 24 April, 1649

——*To the Supreme Authority of England the Common ... The humble Petition of divers well-affected Women ... Affecters and approvers of the Petition of Sept. 11, 1648*, London, 5 May 1649

——*The Womens Petition To the right Honourable, his Excellency, the most Noble and Victorious Lord General Cromwell* ... , London, 27 October 1651

——*To the Parliament of the Common-Wealth of England, The humble Petition of divers afflicted Women, in behalf of Mr. John Lilburne* ... , London, 29 July 1653

——*Unto every individual Member of Parliament: The humble Representation of divers afflicted women-Petitioners* ... *in the behalf of Mr. John Lilburne*, London, 29 July 1653

Lynam, Margaret, *A Warning From the Lord unto all Informers* ... (broadsheet), 1680?

Makin, Bathsua, *An Essay To Revive the Antient Education* ... , London, 1673

Markham, Jane, *An Account of the Life and Death of our Faithful Friend and Fellow-Labourer in the Gospel, Thomas Markham*, T Sowle, London, 1695

Parr, Susanna, *Susannas Apology Against the Elders. Or, A Vindication of Susanna Parr*, np, London, 1659

Pool (or Poole), Elizabeth, *An Alarum of War, given to the Army, and to their High Court of Justice (so called)* ... , London, 1649 (reprint, with additions, of *A Vision*)

——*An(other) Alarum of War, given to the Army* ... , London, 1649

——*A Vision, wherein is manifested the disease and cure of the* KINGDOME ... *together with a true copy of what was delivered* ... *to the said General Council* ... , London, 1648

Pope, Mary, *Behold, here is a Word or, An Answer to the Late Remonstrance of the Army*, Mrs Edwards, London, 1649, bound with:

——*Heare, heare, heare, heare, A WORD OR MESSAGE from Heaven, To All Covenant Breakers*, London, 1649

——*A Treatise of Magistracy* ... , London, 1647

Redford, Elizabeth, *A Word of Councel and Advice, from the* LORD (broadsheet), London, 1701

Sandilands, Mary, *A Tender Salutation of Endeared Love*, J Bradford, London, 1696

Sharp, Jane, *The Midwives Book. Or the whole art of Midwifery discovered* ... , London, 1671

Simmonds, Martha, *A Lamentation for the Lost Sheep of the House of Israel* ... , 'written by one of the children of the Lord, who is known to the world by the name of Martha Simmonds', Giles

Calvert, London, 1656

Smith, Mary, *These Few Lines Are To All* ... , London, 1667

Stirredge, Elizabeth and Dorcas Dole, *A Salutation of my Endeared Love ... once more unto you of Bristol*, London, 1683

Trapnel, Anna, *Anna Trapnel's Report and Plea, or, A Narrative of her Journey from London into Cornwall*, for Thomas Brewster, London, 1654

——*The Cry of a Stone, or a RELATION of Something Spoken in Whitehall by Anna Trapnel, being in the Visions of God*, London, 1654

——*A Legacy for Saints; Being Several Experiences of the dealings of God with Anna Trapnel, In, and after her Conversion* ... , T Brewster, London, 1654

——*Strange and Wonderful News from White-Hall* ..., London, 1654

——*Untitled volume of verse in Bodleian Library* (shelf mark S.I. 42 Th.), 1658

——*Voice for the King of Saints and Nations; or a Testimony of the Spirit of the true crucified Jesus* ... , London, 1658

Wails, Isabel, *A Warning To The People of Leeds* ..., np, 1685

Waite, Mary, *A Warning to all Friends*, London, 1679

Warren, Elizabeth, *The Old and Good Way Vindicated* ... , for Henry Shepherd and William Ley, London, 1645

——*Spiritual Thrift* ... , by RL for Henry Shepherd, London, 1647

——*A Warning-Peece from Heaven* ... , by Richard Constable for Henry Shepherd, London, 1649

Waugh, Dorothy, *A Relation Concerning Dorothy Waughs cruel usage by the Mayor of Carlile*, in *The Lambs Defence against Lyes. And a True Testimony given concerning the Sufferings and Death of James Parnell*, London, 1656

White, Elizabeth, *The Experiences of Gods Gracious Dealing with Mrs Elizabeth White*, London, 1673

Whitrow, Joan, *et al*, *The Work of God in a Dying Maid, being A Short Account of the Dealings of the Lord with One Susanna Whitrow about the age of fifteen Years*, London, 1677

Wight, Sarah, *A Wonderful Pleasant Profitable Letter ... to a Friend* ... , James Cottrel, London, 1656

2 Primary Sources: printed pamphlets, books, broadsheets by men

Anon, *An Advertisement of Two Incomparable Medicines. Mr*

STRINGER'S Elixir ... and his SALT OF LEMON (broadsheet)

—— *The Complaining Testimony of Some (though weak, and of the least) of Sion's Children*, for Livewell Chapman, London, 1656

—— *A Discovery of 29. Sects here in London ...* , London, 1641

—— *A Discovery of Six Women Preachers in Middlesex, Kent, Cambridgeshire, and Salisbury ...* , np, London, 1641

—— *The Doleful Lamentation of Cheap-side Cross: Or old England sick of the staggers ...* , for FC and TB, London, 1641

—— *The Ladies Companion: or, Modest Secrets and Curiosities, never before made public*, Ann Baldwin, London, c.1690s

—— *Lucifers Lacky*, London, 1641

—— *The Parliaments Kalender of Black Saints: Or a New Discovery of Plots and Treasons*, G Bishop, London, 1644

—— *The Phanatiques Creed, or A Door of Safety*, Henry Broome, London, 1661

—— *The Way of Trying Prophets ...* (broadsheet), London, 1707

—— *Wonderful News from Bristol*, Benjamin Harris, 1676

—— *The Wonderful Works of God. Declared by a strange Prophecie of a Maid, that lately lived neere Worksop in Nottinghamhire ...* , for John Thomas, London, 1641

Baillie, Robert, *Anabaptism, The True Fountaine of Independency ...* , Samuel Gellibrand, 1647

Besse, J (ed), *An Abstract ... of the Sufferings of the People called Quakers ...* , J Sowle, London, 1733

Bishop, George, *et al, The Cry of Blood. And Herod, Pontius Pilate, and the Jews Reconciled ...* , Giles Calvert, London, 1656

—— *New-England Judged. By The Spirit of the Lord*, in 2 Parts, London, 1703 edn

Brinsley, John, *The Arraignment of the Present Schism of New Separation in Old England*, London, 1646

Bugg, Francis, *The Christian Ministry of the Church of England Vindicated ...* , London, 1699

—— *Jezebel Withstood, and her Daughter Anne Docwra, Publickly Reproved, for Her Lies and Lightness ...*, London, 1699

Burroughes, Jeremiah, *A Vindication of Mr. Burroughes, Against Mr. EDWARDS. his foule Aspersions, in his spreading Gangraena, and his angry Apologia ...* , H Overton, London, 1646

Calamy, Edmund, *England's Looking-Glasse, Presented in a Sermon ...* , December 22, 1641, London, 1642

Chamberlen, Peter, *The Poor Man's Advocate, or England's Samaritan* ... , Giles Calvert, London, 1649

Chidley, Samuel, *Bells Founder Confounded* ... , London, 1653?

——*A Cry against a Crying Sin* .... *killing Men merely for Theft*, Samuel Chidley, London, 1656 edn

——*To His Highness the Lord Protector &c AND To the Parliament of England*, np, London, 1653 or after

——*Thunder from the Throne of God Against the Temples of Idols*, MP, London, 1653

Cole, Abdiah and Nicholas Culpepper, *The Rational Physician's Library*, London, 1661

Edwards, Thomas, *The Casting Down of the last and Strongest hold of Satan* ... , George Calvert for TR and EM, London, 1647

——*The First and Second Part of Gangraena*, 3rd edn, London, 1646

——*The Second Part of Gangraena: Or A Fresh and further Discovery of the Errors, Heresies, Blasphemies* ... , TR and EM for Ralph Smith, London, 1646

——*The Third Part of Gangraena* ... , London, 1646

Evans, Rhys (Arise), *A Voice From Heaven to the Commonwealth of England*, 1652, bound with *An Echo to the Voice from Heaven*, printed 'from own house in Long-Alley, Blackfriars', 19 December 1652

Farnsworth, Richard, *Witchcraft Cast Out From the Religious Seed and Israel of God* ... , Giles Calvert, London, 1655

——*A Woman Forbidden to Speak in the Church*, Giles Calvert, London, 1654

Featley, Daniel, *The Dippers Dipt. Or The Anabaptists Ducked and Plunged Over Head and Ears* ... , London, 1645

Fox, George, *et al, For the King, and Both Houses of Parliament* ... , Robert Wilson, London, 1661

Goodwin, John, CRETENSIS: *Or A Brief Answer to an Ulcerous Treatise, lately published by Mr Thomas Edwards, Intituled* GANGRAENA, for Henry Overton, London, 1646

Hausted, Peter, *A Satyre against Separatists, or the Conviction of Chamber-Preachers*, for AC, London, 1642

Hetherington, John, *The Anabaptists Ground-work for Reformation*, London, 1644

Higginson, Francis, *A Brief Relation of the Irreligion of the Northern Quakers*, London, 1653

Hubberthorne, Richard, *The Horn of The He-Goats Broken ...* , Giles Calvert, London, 1656

Jessey, Henry, *A Looking-glass for Children ...* , for Robert Boulter, London, 1673 edn

——*The Exceeding Riches of Grace Advanced By the Spirit of Grace, In an Empty Nothing Creature, (viz) M^ris SARAH WIGHT Lately Hopeless and Restless,* JM for Henry Cripps, Lodowick Lloyd, and Livewell Chapman, London, 1652

Keith, George, *The Woman-Preacher of Samaria; A Better Preacher than any of the Men-Preachers of the Man-Made Ministry in these THREE NATIONS,* London, 1674

Lanseter, John, *Lanseters Lance for Edwardses Gangrene,* np, London, 1646

Lilburne, John, *The Oppressed Mans Oppression Declared ... As also, there are thrown unto Thomas Edwards ... a bone or two to pick,* London, 1647

Lilburne, John, Thomas Prince, Richard Overton, *The Picture of the Council of State,* np, London, 1649

Lovelace, Richard, *Lucasta,* 1649

Mather, William, *A Novelty: Or, a Government of Women, Distinct from Men, Erected Amongst some People, called Quakers,* Sarah Hawkins, London, nd

Muggleton, Lodowick, *A True Interpretation of the Witch of Endor,* 2nd edn, London, 1724

Nayler, James, *Deceit Brought to Daylight: In Answer to Thomas Collier,* Giles Calvert, London, 1656

——*Milk for Babes and Meat for Strong Men,* Robert Wilson, London, 1661

Neville, Henry, *The Parliament of Ladies. Or Divers remarkable Passages of Ladies in Spring-Gardens ...* , np, London, 1647

——*The Ladies, A Second Time Assembled in Parliament,* np, London, 1647

——*News from the New Exchange. Or The Common-wealth of Ladies ...* , London, 'Printed in the year, of Women without Grace, 1650'

[Overton, Richard], *To The Right Honourable, the Knights, Citizens, and Burgesses, the Parliament of England ... The Humble Appeal and Petition of Mary Overton, Prisoner in Bridewell,* London, 1647

Overton, Richard, *The Commoner's Complaint: Or, A Dreadful*

Warning from Newgate, to the Commons of England, np, London, 1646

Pagitt, Ephraim, *Heresiography: Or, A Description of the Heretics and Sectaries of these Latter Times*, 2nd edn, London, 1645

Parker, Alexander, *A Testimony of God, and his way, and worship against all the false ways and worships of the world*, Giles Calvert, London, 1656

Parker, Thomas, *The Copy of a Letter Written ... To His Sister Mrs. Elizabeth Avery ...* , John Field for Edmund Paxton, London, 1650

Pordage, John, *Innocence Appearing, Through the Dark Mists of Pretended Guilt*, Giles Calvert, London, 1655

——*Theologia Mystica, or, The Mystical Divinity of the Eternal Invisibles*, London, 1683

Ricraft, Josiah, *A nosegay of Rank-Smelling Flowers, such as grow in Mr. John Goodwin's Garden ...* , Nathaniel Webb and William Grantham, London, 1646

Rogers, Daniel, *Matrimonial Honour: Or A Treatise of Marriage*, London, 1650 edn

Rogers, John, *Ohel or Beth-shemesh. A Tabernacle for the Sun: or Irenicum Evangelicum*, for RI and G and H Everden, London, 1653

Saltmarsh, John, *Groanes for Liberty ... with A Beam of Light ... Also some Quaeres for the better understanding of Mr. Edwards Last Book called Gangraena ...* , Giles Calvert, London, 1646

——*Reasons for Unity, Peace, and Love. With an Answer... to ... Mr Gataker ...[and] Master Edwards his second Part, called Gangraena ...* , Giles Calvert, London, 1646

Scandrett, Stephen, *An Antidote Against Quakerism*, London, 1671

Smith, Semnel (Ordinary of Newgate), *A True Account of the Behaviour, Confessions and Last Dying Speeches of the Criminals that were executed at TYBURN (1690)*, Langley Curtis, London, 1690

Stillingfleet, J, *Seasonable Advice Concerning Quakerism*, London, 1702

Strong, James, *Joanereidos: or, Feminine Valour: eminently discovered in Westerne Women ...* , London, 1645

Stucley, Lewis, *Manifest Truth: or an Inversion of Truths Manifest ...* , EM for M Keinton, London, 1658

Studley, Peter, *The Looking-Glasse of Schisme ...* , RB for Thomas Alchorne, London, 1633

Swetnam, Joseph, *The Arraignment of Lewd, idle, Froward, and unconstant women* ... , G Purstqwe for Thomas Archer, London, 1615

Taylor, John, *Ranters of both Sexes, Male and Female* ... , London, 1651

'T.E.' *The Lawes Resolution of Womens Rights*, printed by asignes of John More, London, 1632

Thorpe, Sergeant, *Judge of the Assize Court for the Northern Circuit, His charge ... 20th of March 1648/9*, Matthew Walbanke and Richard Best, London, 1649

Vicars, John, *Coleman-Street Conclave Visited*, for Nathaniel Webb and William Grantham, London, 1648

——*God's Arke Overtopping the Worlds Waves, or the Third Part of the Parliamentary Chronicle* ... , London, 1646

——*The Schismatic Sifted. Or, The Picture of the Independents, Freshly and Fairly Washt-over again*, Nathaniel Webb and William Grantham, London, 1646

Walker, Henry, *Spiritual Experiences, Of sundry Beleevers* ... , for Nathaniel Webb and William Grantham, London, 1646

Walwyn, William, *The Fountain of Slander Discovered*, H Hills, to be sold by Mr Larnar, London, 1649

Webster, John, *The Displaying of Supposed Witchcraft* ... , London, 1677

Wood, Hugh, *A Brief Treatise of Religious Womens Meetings, Services and Testimonies*, A Sowle, London, 1684

3 Primary Sources in Modern Editions

Baillie, Robert, *The Letters and Journals of Robert Baillie*, David Laing ed, Robert Ofle, Edinburgh, 1842

Barbour, Hugh (ed), *Margaret Fell Speaking*, Pendle Hill Pamphlet Lebanon, Pennsylvania, 1976

Baxter, Richard, *A Breviate of the Life of Margaret, the Daughter of Francis Charlton and Late Wife of Richard Baxter* ... , John T Wilkinson, ed, as *Richard Baxter and Margaret Charlton, A Puritan Love-Story*, Allen & Unwin, London, 1928

Birch, Thomas (ed), *A Collection of the State Papers of John Thurloe, Esq* ... , 7 vols, London, 1742

Blamires, Alcuin, with Karen Pratt and CW Marx (eds), *Woman Defamed and Woman Defended: An Anthology of Medieval Texts*, Clarendon Press, Oxford, 1992

Bund, JM Willis (ed), *Worcester County Records. The Quarter Sessions Rolls Part I*, Kalendar of the Sessions Rolls, 1591–1621, Worcester County Council, Worcester, 1899

Bunyan, John, *Complete Works*, Richard L Greaves, ed, 13 vols, Clarendon Press, Oxford, 1979 –

Burton, Thomas, *Diary of Thomas Burton, Esq, Member in the Parliaments of Oliver and Richard Cromwell*, 4 vols, John Towill Rutt, ed, London, 1828

'The Bury St Edmunds Church Covenants' in *Transactions of the Congregational Historical Society*, vol 2, 1905–6, TG Crippen, ed, Thacker, London, 1906

Butler, Samuel, *Characters*, CW Davies, ed, Case Western Reserve University Press, 1970

——*Hudibras: Written in the Time of the Late Wars*, AR Waller, ed, Cambridge University Press, 1905

Charles I (King of England), *Eikon Basilike: The Portraiture of His Majesty Charles I*, CM Phillimore, ed, Oxford and London, 1879 edn

Clegg, James, *Diary of James Clegg of Chapel en le Frith, 1708–1755*, Vanessa S Doe, ed, Derbyshire Record Society, vol II, 1978

Cromwell, Oliver, *Speeches of Oliver Cromwell*, Ivan Root, ed, Dent, London, 1989

Darbishire, Helen, *The Early Lives of Milton*, Constable, London, 1932

d'Ewes, Sir Simonds, *The Journal of Sir Simonds d'Ewes, from the First Recess of the Long Parliament to the Withdrawal of King Charles from London*, W Havelock Coates, ed, Yale University Press, New Haven, 1942

Donne, John, *Poetical Works*, HJC Grierson, ed, Oxford University Press, 1971 edn

Dryden, John, *Poems and Fables*, James Kinsley, ed, Oxford University Press, 1970

Evelyn, John, *Diary and Correspondence*, 4 vols, William Bray, ed, Henry Colburn and Co, London, 1857

Fanshawe, Ann, *The Memoirs of Ann Lady Fanshawe*, HC Fanshawe, ed, Bodley Head, London, 1907

Fell, Margaret, *A Sincere and Constant Love*, Terry S Wallace, ed, Friends United Press, Richmond, Indiana, 1992

Fincham, Kenneth (ed), V*isitation Articles and Injunctions of the Early*

Stuart Church, vol I, Boydell Press, Church of England Record Society, 1994

Firth, CH (ed), *The Clarke Papers. Selections from the papers of William Clarke, Secretary to the council of the Army, 1647–1649 ...* , Camden Society, 1894

Fox, George, *Journal of George Fox*, John L Nickalls, ed, introduced by Geoffrey F Nuttall, Religious Society of Friends, London, 1975

——*The Woman Learning in Silence* (reprinted as pamphlet) Paul Thompson, Annscroft, 1995

Foxe, John, *The Actes and Monuments*, George Townsend, ed, 8 vols, AMS Press, New York, 1965

Gough, Richard, *The History of Myddle*, Peter Razzell, ed, Caliban Press, Firle, Sussex, 1979

Haller, William (ed), *Tracts on Liberty in the Puritan Revolution 1638–47*, Columbia University Press, Gloucester, Massachusetts, 1933

Haller, William, and Godfrey Davies (eds), *The Leveller Tracts, 1646–1653*, Columbia University Press with Huntingdon Library, New York, 1944

Hayden, Roger (ed), *The Records of a Church of Christ in Bristol, 1640–1687*, for the Bristol Record Society, Bristol, 1974

Hazlitt, WC, *The English Drama and Stage: Documents Relating to Theatres*, London, 1869

Hutchinson, Lucy, *Memoirs of the Life of Colonel Hutchinson*, NH Keeble, ed, Dent, London, 1995 edn

Josselin, Ralph, *The Diary of Ralph Josselin, 1641–1683*, Alan Macfarlane, ed, Records of Social and Economic History, New Series III, Oxford University Press for British Academy, London, 1976

Kenyon, Lloyd (ed), *Orders of the Shropshire Quarter Sessions*, vol I, printed for Shropshire County, Salop, 1926

Knyvett, Thomas, *The Knyvett Letters: 1620–1644*, Bertram Schofield, ed, Constable, London, 1949

Lister, Joseph, *The Autobiography of Joseph Lister*, T Wright, ed, London, 1842

Luther, Martin, *Table Talk*, in *Works*, vol 54, TG Tappert, ed, Fortress Press, Philadelphia, 1967

Marvell, Andrew, *The Complete Poems*, ES Donno, ed, Penguin, Harmondsworth, 1972

Mather, Cotton, *Magnalia Christi Americana: Or, The Ecclesiastical History of New-England* (1702), Silas Andrus, Roberts & Burr edn, Hartford, 1820, vol II

May, Thomas, *The History of the Parliament of England, which began November 3, 1640,* Oxford University Press, 1854

Milton, John, *Complete Prose Works,* Don M Wolfe, ed, 8 vols, Yale University Press, New Haven, 1953–82

——*The Poems,* John Carey and Alastair Fowler, eds, Longman, London, 1968

Moryson, Fynes, *Itinerary,* in *Shakespeare's Europe: The Fourth Part of Fynes Moryson's Itinerary,* introduced by Charles Hughes, Manchester University Press, 1902

Osborne, Dorothy, *Letters of Dorothy Osborne to William Temple,* GC Moore, ed, Clarendon Press, Oxford, 1928

Parliament of Great Britain, Public Record Office, *Calendar of State Papers, Domestic Series. The Commonwealth,* 13 vols, HMSO, London, Kraus Reprints, Vaduz

Penington, Mary, *Experiences in the Life of Mary Penington (Written by Herself),* Friends Historical Society, London, 1992 edn

Penn, William, *The Papers of William Penn,* Mary Maples Dunn and S Richard Dunn, eds, University of Pennsylvania, Philadelphia, 1981

Pepys, Samuel, *The Diary of Samuel Pepys,* Robert Latham and William Matthews, eds, 11 volumes, HarperCollins, London, 1995 reprint

Peters, Hugh, *Good Work for a Good Magistrate,* 1651, introduced by Brendan Clifford, Athol Books, Belfast, 1992

Priestley, Jonathan, (ed), 'Some Memoirs Concerning the Family of the Priestleys', in *Yorkshire Diaries and Autobiographies in the Seventeenth and Eighteenth Centuries,* Surtees Society, vol LXXVII, 1883

Roberts, Daniel (ed), *Memoirs of the Life of John Roberts, 1623–83,* 1746, Friends Home Service Committee, London, 1973 reprint of 1859 edn

Rollins, Hyder E, (ed), *Cavalier and Puritan: Ballads and Broadsides Illustrating the Period of the Great Rebellion,* New York University Press, 1923

Schofield, B (ed), *The Knyvett Letters 1620–44,* Norfolk Record Society, vol XX, Constable, London, 1949

Scott, Sir Walter (ed), *A Collection of Scarce and Valuable Tracts,*

Collected by Lord Somers, vols IV, V & VI, London, 1811

Shepherd, Simon (ed), *The Women's Sharp Revenge: Five Women's Pamphlets from the Renaissance*, Fourth Estate, London, 1985

Shropshire Parish Register, Diocese of Lichfield, vol XV, St Chad's, Shrewsbury, vol I. Privately printed for Shropshire Parish Register Society, 1913

Trapnel, Anna, Letter of 21 December, 1654 concerning AT, printed in full from Rawlinson manuscript, in Champlin Burrage, 'Anna Trapnel's Prophecies', in *English Historical Review*, vol XXVI (1911), pp526–35

Underhill, EB (ed), *Records of the Church of Christ gathered at Fenstanton, Warboys and Hexham 1644–1720*, Hanserd Knollys Society, Haddon Brothers, London, 1854

Whitelock, Bulstrode, *The Diary of Bulstrode Whitelock 1605–1675*, Ruth Spalding, ed, Records of Social and Economic History New Series, XIII, Oxford University Press for British Academy, London, 1990

Wilkins W Walker (ed), *Political Ballads of the Seventeenth and Eighteenth Centuries*, vol I, Longman, Green, Longman & Roberts, London, 1860

Winstanley, Gerrard, *The Works of Gerrard Winstanley, with an Appendix of Documents Relating to the Digger Movement*, GH Sabine, ed, np, New York, 1965

Wolfe, Don M (ed), *Leveller Manifestoes of the Puritan Revolution*, Humanities Press, New York, 1967

Woodhouse, ASP (ed), *Puritanism and Liberty, Being The Army Debates (1647–9) ... with Supplementary Documents*, Dent, London, 1938

4 Secondary Sources

Anderson, Bonnie S, and Judith P Zinsser, *A History of their Own: Women in Europe from Prehistory to the Present*, 2 vols, Penguin, Harmondsworth, 1988

Ashton, Robert, *Reformation and Revolution, 1558–1660*, HarperCollins, London, 1985

Bacon, Margaret Hope, *Mothers of Feminism. The Story of Quaker Women, in America*, Harper & Row, San Francisco, 1986

Beier, AL, *Masterless Men: The Vagrancy Problem in Britain 1560–1640*, Methuen, London, 1985

Berg, Christina, and Philippa Berry, 'Spiritual Whoredom: An Essay on Female Prophets in the Seventeenth Century', in *1642: Literature and Power in the Seventeenth Century*, Francis Barker *et al*, Essex University Press, Colchester, 1981

Boose, Lynda E, 'Scolding Brides and Bridling Scolds: Taming of the Woman's Unruly Member', *Shakespeare Quarterly*, vol 42, 1991, pp132–50

Bowdon, James, *The History of the Society of Friends in America*, Charles Gilpin, London, 1850

Brailsford, Mabel Richmond, *A Quaker from Cromwell's Army: James Nayler*, Swarthmore Press, London, 1927

——*Quaker Women 1650–1690*, Duckworth & Co, London, 1915

Braithwaite, William, revised by HJ Cadbury, *The Beginnings of Quakerism*, William Sessions & Joseph Rowntree Trust, York, 1981 edn

——revised by HJ Cadbury, *The Second Period of Quakerism*, William Sessions & Joseph Rowntree Trust, York, 1979 edn

Bridenbaugh, Carl, *Vexed and Troubled Englishmen, 1590–1642: The Beginnings of the American People*, Clarendon Press, Oxford, 1968

Briggs, Robin. *Witches & Neighbours. The Social and Cultural Context of European Witchcraft*, HarperCollins, London, 1996

Brooke, Iris, *English Costume of the Seventeenth Century*, Adam & Charles Black, London, 1934

Capp, BS, *The Fifth Monarchy Men: A Study in Seventeenth-century English Millennarianism*, Faber & Faber, London, 1972

Carlton, Charles, *Going To The Wars. The Experience of the British Civil Wars, 1638–1651*, Routledge, London, 1992

Carroll, Berenice A (ed), *Liberating Women's History: Theoretical and Critical Essays*, Illinois University Press, Urbana, 1976

Carroll, KL, 'Early Quakers and "Going Naked As a Sign"', *Quaker History*, 67 (1978), pp69–87

Cianfrani, Theodore, *A Short History of Obstetrics and Gynecology*, Thomas, Springfield, Illinois, 1960

Clark, Alice, *Working Life of Women in the Seventeenth Century*, Routledge & Kegan Paul, London, 1919 (1982 edn)

Cope, Esther S, *Handmaid of the Holy Spirit. Dame Eleanor Davies, Never Soe Mad a Ladie*, Michigan University Press, Ann Arbor, 1992

Crawford, Patricia, *Women and Religion in England, 1500–1720*, Routledge, London, 1993

Cresly, David, *Bonfires and Bells: National Memory and the Protestant Calendar in Stuart England*, Weidenfeld & Nicolson, London, 1989

——*Literacy and the Social Order. Reading and Writing in Tudor and Stuart England*, Cambridge University Press, 1980

Cross, Claire, '"He-goats Before the Flocks": A Note on the Part Played by Women in the Founding of some Civil War Churches', vol 8, *Popular Belief and Practice, Studies in Church History*, GJ Cumming and Derek Baker, eds, Cambridge University Press, 1972

Cumming, Valerie, *A Visual History of Costume of the Seventeenth Century*, Batsford & Drama Book Publishers, London, 1984

Cunnington, C Willett and Phillis, *The History of Underclothes*, Michael Joseph, London, 1951

Dailey, Barbara Ritter, 'The Visitation of Sarah Wight: Holy Carnival and the Revolution of the Saints in Civil War London', in *Church History*, JC Brauer *et al*, eds, vol 55, 1986

Davies, Stevie, *Henry Vaughan*, BorderLines Series, Seren, Bridgend, 1995

——*The Idea of Woman in Renaissance Literature: The Feminine Reclaimed*, Harvester, Brighton, 1986

——*Images of Kingship in 'Paradise Lost': Milton's Politics and Christian Liberty*, Missouri University Press, Columbia, Missouri, 1983

——*John Milton*, Harvester Wheatsheaf, Hemel Hempstead, 1991

Davis, JC, *Fear, Myth and History: The Ranters and the Historians*, Cambridge University Press, 1986

Delany, Paul, *British Autobiography in the Seventeenth Century*, Routledge & Kegan Paul, London, 1969

Edwards, Ruth Dudley, *An Atlas of Irish History*, Routledge, London, 1989

Elmer, Peter, *The Library of Dr John Webster. The Making of a Seventeenth Century Radical*, Wellcome Institute for the History of Medicine, London, 1986

Ezell, Margaret JM, *The Patriarch's Wife: Literary Evidence and the History of the Family*, North Carolina University Press, Chapel

Hill, 1987

Figgis, JN, *The Divine Right of Kings*, Cambridge University Press, 1896

Fletcher, Anthony and John Stevenson, *Order and Disorder in Early Modern England*, Cambridge University Press, 1985

Frank, Joseph, *The Beginnings of the English Newspaper, 1620–1660*, Harvard University Press, Cambridge, Massachusetts, 1961

Fraser, Antonia, *Cromwell: Our Chief of Men*, Weidenfeld & Nicolson, London, 1973

——*King Charles II*, Weidenfeld & Nicolson, London, 1979

——*The Weaker Vessel. Woman's Lot in Seventeenth-Century England*, Weidenfeld & Nicolson, London, 1984

Gardiner, SR, *The Fall of the Monarchy of Charles I*, London, 1882

Gilbert, JT, *The History of the Irish Confederation and the War in Ireland 1641–49*, vol I, np, Dublin, 1882–91

Godwin, N, *The Civil War in Hampshire (1642–45) and the Story of Basing House*, Southampton, 1904

Graham, Elspeth, Hilary Hinds, Elaine Hobby and Helen Wilcox (eds), *Her Own Life: Autobiographical Writings by Seventeenth-Century Englishwomen*, Routledge, London, 1989

Greaves, Richard L, *Deliver Us from Evil: The Radical Underground in Britain, 1660–1663*, Oxford University Press, 1986

——*Triumph over Silence: Women in Protestant History*, Greenwood Press, Westport, Connecticut, 1985

Gregg, Pauline, *Free-born John: A Biography of John Lilburne*, Harrap & Co, London, 1961

Hall, David D, *The Antinomian Controversy, 1636–1638*, Wesleyan University Press, Middletown, Connecticut, 1968

Hamilton, Elizabeth, *Henrietta Maria*, Hamish Hamilton, London, 1976

Hannay, Margaret Patterson, *Silent But For The Word: Tudor Women as Patrons, Translators, and Writers of Religious Works*, Kent State University Press, Ohio, 1985

Haythorne, Philip J, *The English Civil War, 1642–1651. An Illustrated Military History*, Blandford Press, Poole, Dorset, 1983

Hey, David G, *An English Rural Community: Myddle Under the Tudors and Stuarts*, Leicester University Press, 1974

Higgins, Patricia, 'The Reactions of Women, with special reference to women petitioners', see Brian Manning (1975), pp178–222

Hill, Christopher, *The English Bible and the Seventeenth Century Revolution*, Allen Lane, The Penguin Press, London, 1993

——*The World Turned Upside Down. Radical Ideas During The English Revolution*, Penguin, Harmondsworth, 1972 edn

——*The Experience of Defeat. Milton and Some Contemporaries*, Penguin, Harmondsworth, 1985 edn

Hobby, Elaine, *Virtue of Necessity. English Women's Writing 1649–88*, Virago, London, 1988

Hogrefe, Pearl, *Tudor Women: Commoners and Queens*, Ames, Iowa, 1975

——*Women of Action in Tudor England: Nine Biographical Sketches*, Ames, Iowa, 1977

Holdsworth, WS, *A History of English Law*, vols III–VI, Little, Brown, Boston, 1922–38

Huehns, Gertrude, *Antinomianism in English History, With Special Reference to the Period 1640–1660*, Cresset Press, London, 1951

Hufton, Olwen, *The Prospect Before Her. A History of Women in Western Europe*, vol I, 1500–1800, HarperCollins, London, 1995

Ingrams, Martin, 'Ridings, Rough Music, and Mocking Rhymes in Early Modern England', in *Popular Culture in Seventeenth-Century England*, Barry Reay, ed, Croom Helm, London, 1985

Keeble, NH, '"The Colonel's Shadow": Lucy Hutchinson, Women's Writing and the Civil War', in *Literature and the English Commonwealth*, Thomas Healy and Jonathan Sawday, eds, Cambridge University Press, 1990, pp227–47

Kitttredge, George Lyman, *Witchcraft in Old and New England*, Russell and Russell, New York, 1958 edn

Koehler, Lyle, *A Search for Power: The 'Weaker Sex' in Seventeenth-Century New England*, Illinois University Press, Urbana, 1980

Kunze, Bonnelyn Young, *Margaret Fell and the Rise of Quakerism*, Macmillan, London, 1994

Lang, Amy Schrager, *Prophetic Woman: Anne Hutchinson and the Problem of Dissent in the Literature of New England*, California University Press, Berkeley, 1987

Laurence, Anne, 'A Priesthood of She-Believers: Women and Congregations in Mid-Seventeenth Century England', in *Women in the Church*, WJ Sheils and Diana Wood, eds, *Studies in Church*

History, vol 27, Basil Blackwood, Oxford, 1990

——*Women in England 1500–1700: A Social History*, Weidenfeld & Nicolson, London, 1994

Lindley, Keith, *Fenland Riots and the English Revolution*, Heinemann, London, 1982

Ludlow, Dorothy Paula, *'Arise and be Doing': English 'Preaching' Women, 1640–1660*, Indiana University unpublished PhD thesis, 1978, Ann Arbor University Microfilms Ltd, Michigan, 1980

Macfarlane, Alan, *The Family Life of Ralph Josselin, A Seventeenth Century Clergyman. An Essay in Historical Anthropology*, Cambridge University Press, 1970

McGregor, JF and Barry Reay, *Radical Religion in the English Revolution*, Oxford University Press, 1984

Mack, Phyllis, *Visionary Women. Ecstatic Prophecy in Seventeenth-Century England*, California University Press, Berkeley, 1992

Manners, Emily, *Elizabeth Hooton: First Quaker Woman Preacher 1600–1672*, Headley Brothers, London, 1914

Manning, Brian (ed), *The English People and The English Revolution 1640–1649*, Heinemann, London, 1976

——*Politics, Religion and the English Civil War*, Edward Arnold, London, 1975

Menefee, Samuel Pyeatt, *Wives For Sale. An Ethnographic Study of British Popular Divorce*, Blackwell, Oxford, 1981

Morrill, John, *The Nature of the English Revolution*, Longman, London, 1993

Morton, AL, *The World of the Ranters: Religious Radicalism in the English Revolution*, Lawrence & Wishart, London, 1970

Neame, Alan, *The Holy Maid of Kent: The Life of Elizabeth Barton, 1506–1534*, Hodder & Stoughton, London, 1971

Nightingale, B, *Early Stages of the Quaker Movement in Lancashire*, Congregational Union of England and Wales, 1921

Owen, DM, 'Lincolnshire Women in History', *The Lincolnshire Historian*, vol 2, no 6 (1959)

de Paor, Liam, *The Peoples of Ireland. From Prehistory to Modern Times*, Hutchinson, London, 1986

Pearl, Valerie, *London and the Outbreak of the Puritan Revolution*, Oxford University Press, 1961

Porter, Roy, and Lesley Hall, *The Facts of Life, The Creation of Sexual*

Knowledge in Britain, 1650–1950, Yale University Press, New Haven, 1995

Poulson, Charles, *The English Rebels*, Journeyman, London, 1984

Quaife, GR, *Wanton Wenches and Wayward Wives: Peasants and Illicit Sex in Early Seventeenth Century England*, Croom Helm, London, 1979

Richardson, RC, and GM Ridden (eds), *Freedom and the English Revolution: Essays in History and Literature*, Manchester University Press, 1986

Rogers, PG, *The Fifth Monarchy Men*, Oxford University Press, 1966

Roots, Ivan, *The Great Rebellion, 1642–1660*, rev edn, Alan Sutton, London, 1995

Rose, MB, *The Expense of Spirit: Love and Sexuality in English Renaissance Drama*, Cornell University Press, Ithaca, 1988

Rosen, Barbara (ed), *Witchcraft*, Edward Arnold, London, 1969

Ross, Isabel, *Margaret Fell: Mother of Quakerism*, Ebor Press, York, 1984 edn

Russell, Conrad, *The Crisis of Parliaments. English History, 1509–1660*, Oxford University Press, 1974 (corrected edn)

Seaver, Paul S, *Wallington's World: A Puritan Artisan in Seventeenth Century London*, Methuen, London, 1985

Sharpe, JA, *Crime in Seventeenth-Century England: A County Study*, Cambridge University Press, London, and Editions de la Maison des Sciences de l'Homme, Paris, 1983

——*Early Modern England. A Social History, 1550–1760*, Edward Arnold, London, 1987

Smith, Nigel, *Perfection Proclaimed: Language and Literature in English Radical Religion, 1640–1660*, Clarendon Press, Oxford, 1989

Stachniewski, John, *The Persecutory Imagination: English Puritanism and the Literature of Religious Despair*, Clarendon Press, Oxford, 1991

Stein, Harold, 'Six Tracts about Women: A Volume in the British Museum', *The Library*, 4th series, vol XV, Oxford University Press, 1935, pp38–48

Stone, Lawrence, *The Family, Sex and Marriage in England, 1500–1800*, Penguin, Harmondsworth, 1979 edn

Strong, Roy, *The Renaissance Garden in England*, Thames & Hudson,

London, 1979

Taylor, JT, *The Witchcraft Delusion in Colonial Connecticut, 1647–1700*, Grafton, New York, 1908

Thomas, Keith, *Religion and the Decline of Magic: Studies in Popular Beliefs in Sixteenth- and Seventeenth-Century England*, Penguin, Harmondsworth, 1991, edn

——'Women and the Civil War Sects', *Past & Present*, 13 (1958), pp42–62

Thompson, EP, *Witness Against the Beast: William Blake and the Moral Law*, Cambridge University Press, 1993

Thomson, DP, *Women of the Scottish Church*, Munro & Scott, Perth, 1975

Tolmie, Murray, *The Triumph of the Saints: The Separate Churches of London, 1616–1649*, Cambridge University Press, 1977

Trevett, Christine, *Women and Quakerism in the Seventeenth Century*, Sessions Book Trust, York, 1992

Underdown, DE, *Revel, Riot and Rebellion. Popular Politics and Culture in England, 1603–1660*, Clarendon Press, Oxford, 1985

——'The Taming of the Scold: The Enforcement of Patriarchal Authority in Early Modern England', in *Order and Disorder in Early Modern England*, A Fletcher and J Stevenson, eds, Cambridge University Press, 1985

Wedgwood, CV, *The King's Peace: The Great Rebellion, 1637–1641*, Collins, London, 1955

——*The King's War, 1641–1647: The Great Rebellion*, Collins, London, 1958

——*The Trial of Charles I*, Collins, London, 1964

Whiting, CE, *Studies in English Puritanism from the Restoration to the Revolution, 1660–1688*, Society for Promoting Christian Knowledge, New York, 1931

Wiesner, Merry E, *Women and Gender in Early Modern Europe (New Approaches to European History)*, Cambridge University Press, 1983

Winsser, Johan, 'Mary Dyer and the "Monster" Story', *Quaker History* 79 (1990), pp20–34

Wright, Lawrence, *Clean and Decent. The Fascinating History of the Bathroom & the Water Closet ...* , Routledge & Kegan Paul, London, 1960

INDEX